# YOUNG TRUDEAU

# YOUNG TRUDEAU

## Son of Quebec, Father of Canada, 1919–1944

### VOLUME ONE

## MAX AND MONIQUE NEMNI

*Translated by William Johnson*

A DOUGLAS GIBSON BOOK

100

McCLELLAND & STEWART

**Library and Archives Canada Cataloguing in Publication**

Nemni, Max
    Young Trudeau : 1919–1944 / written by Max Nemni and Monique Nemni;
translated by William Johnson.

Translation of: Trudeau, fils du Québec, père du Canada.

ISBN 13: 978-0-7710-6749-5
ISBN 10: 0-7710-6749-6

    1. Trudeau, Pierre Elliott, 1919–2000 – Childhood and youth. 2. Trudeau,
Pierre Elliott, 1919–2000 – Political and social views. 3. Québec (Province) –
History – 1930–1945. I. Nemni, Monique, 1936– II. Johnson, William, 1931–
III. Title.

FC626.T7N4413 2006      971.4'03'092      C2006-900758-6

We acknowledge the financial support of the Government of Canada through the
Book Publishing Industry Development Program and that of the Government of
Ontario through the Ontario Media Development Corporation's Ontario Book
Initiative. We further acknowledge the support of the Canada Council for the Arts
and the Ontario Arts Council for our publishing program.

Typeset in Sabon by M&S, Toronto
Printed and bound in Canada

A Douglas Gibson Book

This book is printed on acid-free paper that is 100% recycled,
ancient-forest friendly (100% post-consumer recycled).

McClelland & Stewart Ltd.
75 Sherborne Street
Toronto, Ontario
M5A 2P9
www.mcclelland.com

1  2  3  4  5      10  09  08  07  06

*To the memory of*

Pierre Elliott Trudeau,
a man good and true

and
*to the light of our lives*
our daughters,
Colette and Jacqueline

and our grandchildren,
Julien, Rachel, Nicolas, Zoé, and Mark.

# CONTENTS

# INTRODUCTION

ON A FEBRUARY AFTERNOON IN 1995, we were driving along Highway 20 on our way to Montreal. We had left Quebec City planning to arrive at our destination an hour early. We did not want to take a chance on being late for our meeting with Pierre Trudeau. But, what with the snow-clogged roads, we arrived at the Indian restaurant on Crescent Street barely a few minutes before the appointed time. He, as usual, was punctual. We were quite nervous, and for good reason. We had come to talk about our plan to write his intellectual biography. We had known him, now, for five years. We had told him of our intention, and he had expressed an interest. He wanted to discuss it with us, and that was the reason for our encounter.

As we shared a convivial meal, we explained as best we could what we had in mind. Trudeau listened carefully and asked a few questions. It was not his private life that interested us particularly, we told him, but we wanted to focus on his ideas, his political vision, and on how they evolved from his earliest years. To what extent, when he was actually in power, was he able to apply his ideals? He listened with interest. Finally, with some concern in his voice, he asked: "And what do you expect of me?" "Not much, really," we replied. "We might, as the occasion arises, want to ask you a few questions, have access to unpublished documents that you still keep at home, ask you to help us contact some of the people who were close to you . . ."

He kept nodding in agreement. "No problem," he said. Then, after a silence, he added: "I presume that you will want to maintain your intellectual autonomy. I understand, and I approve. So here is what I suggest:

you will show me each chapter as you go along, I will make my comments, and you do with them whatever you choose."

We were stunned. It was all we could do not to jump up for joy. "That suits us perfectly," we said, as calmly as possible.

The bill arrived. He wanted us to be his guests. We refused and insisted that we should be paying. "Well, then," Trudeau said, "let's do what I do with my pals. We will share the bill." "That's fine," we said. "But that means that we pay two-thirds." "No," Trudeau said, speaking to Max. "We share fifty-fifty. I take half of Monique." And so it happened. Until his death, he took half of Monique.

When we got back home, we were jubilant. We began working out our program and our timetable for the research that we were undertaking – until April.

Anne-Marie Bourdouxhe, the daughter of Trudeau's long-time associate Gérard Pelletier, resigned as the publisher of the periodical *Cité libre*. Though we sat on the editorial board, we expressed not the slightest interest in replacing her, and for a simple reason. We had absolutely no experience in actually publishing a magazine. And besides, we had set out on a project that was much closer to our hearts. Weeks went by. For a variety of reasons, the board of directors was unable to agree on any of the available candidates. Beginning in March, the directors began courting us. They increased the pressure. With a referendum on the secession of Quebec just months away, they asked us how we could live with ourselves if we allowed the only French-language magazine that stood strongly against secession to die. We were unsettled. We did not know which way to turn.

After many sleepless nights, we met Trudeau in a Chinese restaurant one April evening to lay before him our dilemma: if we agreed to take on *Cité libre*, we must drop our projected biography. He was understanding, he shared our anxiety about the political situation in Quebec, and he came up with the suggestion that we agree to publish the magazine for a year, until the referendum was well behind us. And that was the decision that we conveyed, clearly spelled out, to the board of directors of *Cité libre*.

It happened, though, that no one had anticipated the extent of the trauma that the 1995 referendum would trigger, before as well as after the event, among those who voted Yes as well as among those who voted No. With no one in line to take over, we could not bring ourselves to abandon *Cité libre*. On the contrary, we became convinced that it must expand and be read from coast to coast, and in both official languages. That is what we carried out in 1998.

Meanwhile, our relationship with Trudeau had settled into a friendship. We spoke often on the phone, we used the familiar "*tu*" with each other, we met regularly until his death in 2000. During the five years that we published the review that he and Pelletier had founded, he gave us his unfailing moral support amid all the inevitable controversies. He listened sympathetically when, now and then, we expressed our dismay at being unable to work on his intellectual biography. And he would come back with the same answer: "What you are doing at *Cité libre* is very important. No one else can do it. As for the other project, there is no rush." But there is a rush, we would counter. He would only laugh.

Time would tell that there was in fact a rush. Still, we do not regret our decision. But, since he left us, we have often wondered what this book would have been like if we had written it while he was alive. Would we have had access to the wealth of documents that have now been made available to us? And, if so, how would we have reacted to the discoveries that we have now come upon? Would we have had the courage to discuss them with him? And how would he have reacted? We cannot know for sure.

There were moments of such disarray over our discoveries and the sheer scope of our undertaking that we were often tempted to let it drop. But we were always drawn back to what sometimes took on the fascination of a detective story, with its intrigues and its startling twists and turns. We also felt bound by our promise to Trudeau to write his intellectual biography. Did he have any idea of where that would lead us? We think that, in fact, he did, since our discoveries were all buried in the immense cache of papers that he had collected from early childhood and which he eventually turned over to the national archives of Canada. Why, otherwise, would he have refrained from destroying them, knowing full well that we were impatiently awaiting the opportunity to plunge into them?

We set out to follow the footsteps of a man who was larger than life, with an omnivorous appetite for knowledge, for understanding, for experience, through books, through adventures, through intense daily life. We had to locate him carefully in the religious, political, social, and economic context in which he grew up. That forced us to become familiar with everything that influenced him: the Second World War, the Vichy regime in France, the papal encyclicals of Leo XIII and Pius XI, the attitude of the Vatican toward the several European dictatorships of the 1930s and 1940s, the attitude of the Catholic Church in Quebec toward the Depression of the 1930s and the war; the Jesuits with their history, mission, and philosophy of education; the conscription crisis, and so many other issues that were part of his life. These remain controversial subjects still, on which experts disagree. In addition to mastering these historical circumstances, because the young Trudeau was a compulsive reader, we had to become acquainted with his intellectual world of novelists, poets, playwrights, historians, philosophers, economists, political scientists, and theoreticians of revolution.

To understand Trudeau required seeing him in his time and place, and he grew up during a period of crisis and of violent ideological conflicts within Western civilization. To follow his intellectual development also necessarily casts a new light on a period of the history of Quebec and of Canada that has largely remained in the shadows. To understand him is at the same time to acquire a new understanding of the society which fashioned him in his younger years, and which in his maturity he strove so hard to refashion.

So let us set off on a voyage of discovery. We will find the young Pierre Trudeau, who has remained unknown until now.

*Chapter 1*

## THE TRUDEAU ENIGMA

*He haunts us still.*

— STEPHEN CLARKSON AND CHRISTINA McCALL
*Trudeau and Our Times,* 1990

IN 1993, nine years after Pierre Trudeau had left office, the British news-paper *The Independent* divided Canadian prime ministers into two broad categories: "The first comprises those whom the rest of the world has largely forgotten, if it ever knew about them; the second comprises Pierre Trudeau."[1]

The statement conveys the rest of the world's impression of Pierre Trudeau, whose dashing and irreverent style had the pundits of the world wagging their tongues in several languages. Did Quebec's opinion leaders also share this appreciation for one of their own? No one, of course, is a prophet in his own country. But Pierre Trudeau was not only born in Montreal, he grew up there, and there he returned at the close of his brilliant nineteen-year interlude in politics, to spend the remaining sixteen years of his life. So it is enlightening to canvass how Quebec's French-speaking opinion leaders viewed their eminent *compatriote.*

In 1972, four years after Trudeau became prime minister and just in time for the 1972 federal elections, a book was published with the provocative title *L'anti-Trudeau.* It was a 273-page collection of forty-nine texts written on various occasions by different authors, but with a single common denominator: each article attacked Pierre Trudeau. The twenty-nine pamphleteers anthologized included a broad range of Quebec's intelligentsia and its political class. René Lévesque, for instance,

contributed four diatribes. The founder of the separatist Parti Québécois
was then four years away from being elected premier, and another four
from holding his 1980 referendum on secession. Claude Ryan contributed seven pieces and was the most prolific. Ryan was still the
influential editor-publisher of the daily *Le Devoir*. He would leave journalism six years later to confront Premier Lévesque as leader of the
Quebec Liberal Party. Also on the anti-Trudeau roster was Jacques
Parizeau, one of the mandarins of the Quiet Revolution who had converted to separatism in 1969. In 1994, he would be elected premier
himself and, a year later, would hold his own referendum on secession,
coming within a whisker of winning a majority.

That list of anti-Trudeau authors included the poet Gaston Miron,
who, when he died in 1996, would be the first private citizen in Quebec to
receive a state funeral. On the firing squad, too, were Quebec's two most
fashionable sociologists, Fernand Dumont and Marcel Rioux. Quebec's
most eminent English-speaking philosopher, Charles Taylor, a professor at
McGill University, contributed one of the lengthier pieces. The main thrust
of the book was summarized in a foreword by the three editors who had
put together the symposium: "The passages which follow tell us that
Trudeau is formalist, idealist, arrogant and dangerous."[2]

Dangerous? Dangerous for whom? In one of the selected pieces, originally published in 1971, Claude Ryan attacked Trudeau for "treating
today with incomprehensible disdain, from the height of his promontory,
those who rank as the most substantial thinkers that Quebec has produced
and who, say what he will, display none of that narrow isolationism that
he chooses to ascribe to them out of sheer demagogy."[3]

This paradox reveals one dimension of the Trudeau enigma. But the
charge against him goes even further. As stigmatized by his detractors,
Trudeau combined his defining arrogance with an incapacity to understand Quebec. Claude Ryan stated it baldly: "When confronted with
difficult questions, Mr. Trudeau increasingly adopts attitudes that reveal
him as an outsider with respect to the current political debates in
Quebec."[4] That theme of Trudeau the outsider, the rootless individual
who lost touch with the society in which he was born, was to recur constantly in the writings of French-speaking Quebeckers, both before and
after his tenure as prime minister. An example is the biography of
Trudeau published in 1989 by journalist Michel Vastel. Its very title,

*Trudeau: Le Québécois*,[5] was intentionally ironic. For Vastel, Trudeau was definitely not in his heart and soul, in his mind and sensibility, a *Québécois*, even though he could speak French and was from Quebec. "In 1944," Vastel wrote, "Trudeau was essentially a French-speaking person in search of an identity."[6] The title of his book's English translation expressed his intent: *The Outsider: The Life of Pierre Elliott Trudeau*.[7]

Before Trudeau had completed his first mandate as prime minister, Claude Ryan had become convinced that the man would never be re-elected. Surely the rest of Canada would come to realize its mistake in thinking that Trudeau truly represented Quebec. "[Trudeau] is preparing for the day when . . . public opinion in English-speaking Canada will come to realize that he has lost all contact with the dynamic elements of his own society and will brutally invite him to go back where he came from."[8] That prophecy would turn out to be somewhat infelicitous. Trudeau would quit the federal scene only thirteen years later, still solidly supported in Quebec.

Fernand Dumont was a towering figure among Quebec's sociologists. Also writing before the end of Trudeau's first mandate, he went further than Ryan in predicting disastrous consequences from Trudeau's supposed incapacity to understand Quebec: "In the not too distant future, historians will demonstrate that Mr. Trudeau destroyed the Canadian Confederation because he failed to perceive its flaws in time and so failed to propose meaningful reform."[9]

Twenty years after the appearance of *L'anti-Trudeau*, Laval University political scientist Guy Laforest published his 1992 book titled *Trudeau et la fin d'un rêve canadien (Trudeau and the End of a Canadian Dream)*. Laforest bestowed on Trudeau the invidious title of "Lord Durham," after the British commissioner of inquiry who recommended in 1839 that French Canadians become English-speaking, so that French would disappear. Durham also proposed that their government of Lower Canada be absorbed into a united Province of Canada. For Laforest, the Canadian dream had consisted of a Canada as a duality of two equal languages and two equal cultures. Laforest divined in Trudeau's vision of federalism, which granted national status to the French language but no special status to the Quebec government, the determination to "crush the collective identity of the Québécois."[10] Then, in 1993, when Trudeau had long been retired from politics, a pioneer of political science in

Quebec, Léon Dion, himself a federalist, echoed Claude Ryan's sentence on Trudeau by charging him with a "repeatedly flaunted contempt for French Canadians."[11]

The paradox is striking. The Québécois opinion leaders who spoke out publicly about Trudeau generally depicted him as a snob best characterized by his arrogance, his contempt, and his determination to trample on the identity of his own Quebec people. Year after year, in speech after speech, in page after page, the same stereotype was thrown up with steadfast perseverance. It raised an intriguing question: How could a majority of Quebeckers, presumably of sound mind, have voted with such remarkable loyalty for the man who supposedly did not respect them, and whose whole political career was designed to put them in their place? If the constant charges were founded, would one not expect the Québécois to reciprocate and show nothing but hostility for Trudeau?

That conflict between Trudeau and Quebec's aspirations was not put forward exclusively by politicians, journalists, and intellectuals whose first language was French. Take, for example, Kenneth McRoberts, a political scientist who made his reputation as an expert on Quebec. He advanced the view that Trudeau's policies fuelled Quebec separatism. "For many members of the new middle class, the goal of sovereignty had been born simply out of frustration with the way in which the federal government, especially during the Trudeau years in power, had hindered this expansion of the Quebec state."[12] In other words, without Trudeau, there would be no separatism.

With such a convergence of testimonies, one would expect that Trudeau had been kept in power for sixteen years – with only a nine-month interruption – over the opposition of Quebeckers, by what is often called "English Canada." But some commentators posit the same gap of understanding between Trudeau and English-speaking Canadians. In 2003, three years after his death, the respected *Toronto Star* journalist Graham Fraser wrote: "Pierre Trudeau had very little knowledge of, interest in or affection for the rest of Canada."[13] In support of his broad assertion, Fraser offers only this: "In his memoirs, Trudeau's friend and federal colleague, the late Gérard Pelletier, wrote: 'To suppose I have some attachment to the Canadian political entity would be a mistake, because I feel none.'" The underlying assumption seems to be one of ignorance and indifference by association. If Gérard Pelletier announced that he didn't care a fig about Canada, his friend Trudeau must feel the same.

In a study published by the Institute for Research on Public Policy, authors Donald Lenihan, Gordon Robertson, and Roger Tassé concluded that Pierre Trudeau's policies on federalism were based on false premises, were incompatible with true federal principles, and ran counter to the aspirations of the Québécois, of Westerners, and of aboriginals. The authors summarized their argument as follows: "Our study examines how the political philosophy of liberalism – especially as incorporated into 'pan-Canadianism' under former Prime Minister Pierre Trudeau – contrasts and conflicts with the more federalist aspirations of moderate Quebec nationalists, Western regionalists and Aboriginal peoples."[14]

Their charge gained credibility from the credentials of two of the authors. Gordon Robertson was a mandarin and had served as Clerk of the Privy Council – the top federal civil servant – from 1963 until 1975. He had actually served as Trudeau's deputy minister during his first two mandates as prime minister. Ironically, he had also been Pierre Trudeau's boss when, early in his career, the young man had worked for two years in the Privy Council. Roger Tassé was formerly Deputy Minister of Justice and Deputy Attorney General of Canada – the principal legal adviser to the federal government. According to these authors, Pierre Trudeau's policies betrayed the interests of great blocs of Canadian citizens.

Many Canadians believe, on the contrary, that the Canada in which they live was recast for the better by Pierre Trudeau, that he gave the country a new foundation by the Canada Act of 1982, and that we are now, to use political scientist Alan Cairns's term, "Charter Canadians,"[15] proud to celebrate and enjoy the rights granted by the Canadian Charter of Rights and Freedoms. And yet, it is rare to find a favourable judgment passed on Pierre Trudeau in most of the publications produced by French-speaking Quebec intellectuals or even the English-speaking intelligentsia. The attacks, though, are multitudinous. Meanwhile, ordinary Canadians have not forgotten him. In the memorable sentence that begins his 1990 biography by Stephen Clarkson and Christina McCall, "He haunts us still."[16] When he was four days short of his eightieth birthday, a public opinion poll of October 18, 1999, reported that "Trudeau remains a fixation."

What could explain this combination of fascination and abhorrence that he inspired during his lifetime, and that persists even today? *The Independent* had its own explanation. "Although the world may remember Trudeau for the wrong reasons, the trivial reasons – his irreverence, his flamboyance, his feisty young wife – it at least remembers him. He was a fashionable man from an unfashionable country, a bright spark struck from a dull flint."[17]

These characteristics of Trudeau that set him apart from all Canadian prime ministers – his style, his flamboyance, his irreverent pirouettes, his nocturnal dates with stars like Barbra Streisand, and other extravagances of his private life – might possibly explain why he is remembered abroad. They do not begin to account for the massive and loyal support that Quebec voters always rendered him, from the time of his first election after he was chosen as Liberal leader in 1968. That support even increased over time. When he sought his first mandate, he won 54 per cent of Quebec's vote. Twelve years later, when he returned to the voters for the fifth and final time, his Liberals swept Quebec with 74 out of 75 seats and 68 per cent of the vote.[18]

What was the secret of his success? *Toronto Star* journalist Richard Gwyn came up with a theory. In 1976, he noted that Trudeau's support in the opinion polls had fallen below that of any previous Canadian prime minister. It seemed absurd to think that he could be re-elected. And yet . . . "There is a quality in the man that persists," Gwyn averred, though unable to provide a rational definition of that elusive quality. By 1980, he had a better idea: "Now I understand: he is a great magician." And so he titled his book *The Northern Magus*.[19] But Peter McCormick, who teaches political science at Alberta's University of Lethbridge, offered another explanation in 1999. Trudeau fascinated "because he was a giant . . . and since him we've had nothing but pygmies."

Magician, giant, writer, joker, flirt, superb athlete, outstanding intellectual. When he had reached the age of seventy, an opinion poll found Trudeau to be Canada's sexiest man. How could one human being provoke so much admiration and, at the same time, such relentless hatred?

———◦◦———

It might be asked, why, in what is intended as an intellectual biography, should we even draw attention to Trudeau's character traits? Simply because it is impossible to sever his intellectual development from his personality. His vision, his political and social insights, did not spring fully formed from a disembodied intellect. They matured gradually within a nurturing environment that included family, neighbours, friends, schools, and his society. Part of his fascination for us as authors was to reconstruct the boy slowly maturing into a man, and to witness the tension between his early socialization in the Quebec of the 1930s and 1940s and his dawning awareness of wider vistas as he left the certitudes of adolescence to explore the turbulence of a world then in the process of being destroyed by war.

———◈———

Joseph Philippe Pierre Yves Elliott Trudeau, who would later become known as Pierre Elliott Trudeau, was born in Outremont, a middle-class suburb on the Island of Montreal, on October 18, 1919. The First World War had ended, but it left Quebec nationalism exacerbated by the struggle over conscription, which French Quebec had vehemently opposed, while the rest of Canada had imposed it, provoking deadly riots and many desertions. That struggle initially split the Liberal Party of Canada and would eventually destroy the Conservative Party in Quebec for at least a generation as French Quebec clung defensively to the Liberal Party. In the first post-war elections of 1921, the Liberals captured every one of Quebec's sixty-five constituencies. In the five general elections between 1921 and 1940, if the Depression election of 1930 is excluded, Conservatives managed to win a cumulative total of only thirteen seats, and those only in ridings with a substantial English-speaking population.

Pierre was the second of three children. His sister, Suzette, was a year older, his brother, Charles – known as Tip – was three years younger. Unlike most French Canadians, Pierre was born into a family that was then economically secure and would soon be downright rich. In 1933, in the middle of the Depression, when many families had trouble putting food on the table, the entire Trudeau family, including Pierre's maternal grandfather, enjoyed a two-month trip to Europe.

Unquestionably, the family fortune affected Pierre's life, including his intellectual development. He could make choices that were unavailable to most of his contemporaries, such as studying at Harvard University, then in post-war Paris at the Institut d'études politiques (known familiarly as

"Sciences Po"), and at the London School of Economics. Since he was never forced to earn a living, he could go wherever his fancy led him. He travelled the globe, though he usually chose to do so in an austere style. He had the privilege of being able to take off for abroad whenever he felt the urge. And he never had to stick to a job he didn't like.

Some commentators have claimed that the family wealth isolated Pierre from ordinary people. Michel Vastel, for one, wrote of Pierre Trudeau that "being the son of a millionaire in the midst of the Great Depression gave him a privileged status." To illustrate the point, Vastel added: "It was in the father's limousine driven by a chauffeur that the two Trudeau brothers swept up Côte-Sainte-Catherine Road to [their school] Collège Jean-de-Brébeuf. Meanwhile some of their friends, like [the future labour leader] Michel Chartrand, walked several kilometres to save the four cents that a bus ticket would have cost them."[20] The bare facts are slightly different. The Trudeaus did employ a man named Elzéar Grenier as a jack-of-all-trades, who served as chauffeur when needed. Every Monday morning, he drove Suzette Trudeau downtown to the Sacred Heart Convent, where she was a boarder, and he returned on Friday to fetch her home for the weekend. On Mondays, Pierre and Tip would hitch a ride to Brébeuf, which was on the way. As the car had jump seats, it also accommodated some of their young neighbours.[21] But, the rest of the week, the brothers got to school by streetcar, or they walked.

Trudeau was always aware that his parents' fortune made it possible for him to lead a privileged life. But no one, as far as we know, ever heard him boast about it or saw him make a display of conspicuous consumption. Quite the opposite: he was often criticized for being tight with his money. At the same time, even his critics recognize that he was willing to help others with both money and his services when the occasion arose. Jacques Hébert, the controversial publisher and writer, had run afoul of the authorities in the 1960s, when he published a book that claimed a murder trial was a miscarriage of justice. He recalled how Trudeau had rushed to support him with legal expertise at a very difficult time. "When I was having my problems with the law because of my book, *J'accuse les assassins de Coffin*[22], Trudeau was at that time a professor at the Université de Montréal. He took a month's leave of absence without pay to defend me free of charge. . . . And the entire trial was taking place in Quebec City."[23] His case was not unique. In the 1950s, when Trudeau was for a time in private practice on Montreal's Saint-Denis Street, it was known that he would offer his services without charge to anyone who came to him with "an interesting case."[24] Several witnesses acknowledge that Trudeau helped people financially, always with great discretion.

What people were worth in the monetary sense remained always a matter of total indifference to him. From an early age, he treated money with detachment. He could as readily sleep on a bench in a railway station as glide around in a convertible Mercedes, as happily feast on spaghetti as on caviar. In his system of values, money was secondary. "I don't want to be judged according to the size of my bank account,"[25] he insisted. And no one ever heard him appreciate others on the basis of their wealth. For him, money was useful for getting what one wanted, including valuable objects, but only on the condition that you did not become dependent on it. The Trudeau children were able at a young age to practise on a Steinway piano. They had a state-of-the-art gramophone which allowed them to invite friends to listen to classical music at their home every Sunday. Later, Pierre would treat himself to a Harley-Davidson motorcycle. But, at the same time, he was quite able to make do without the expensive things in life. Trudeau raised that non-dependence to the level of a principle: "I can't say that I don't become attached [to objects]. I have to make an effort, I don't want to become a slave to objects."[26] When he was asked what values he would choose to communicate to his children, he replied: "I would want them as much as possible not to be slaves to material goods. To appreciate a good meal, a good book, to enjoy holidays, that's fine. But to become miserable if one is without, I consider that a form of slavery. And I hope that my children . . . will learn, just as my parents taught me, to remain somewhat detached from all that."[27] His parents, as we shall see presently, were not alone in impressing upon him that lesson. And he practised what he professed. Throughout his life, he frequently displayed that detachment, that frugality, which verged on asceticism.

---

Young Pierre's early experiences were unusual in other respects than his family's fortune. Most French Canadians at that time, and even until the Quiet Revolution of the 1960s, had few contacts with "the others" – *les Anglais*, the Protestants, the Jews, the immigrants who did not eak French. The notable exceptions were the Irish, because they shared with French Canadians the Catholic faith and often worshipped in the same church. With them alone, intermarriage was common. But the Trudeaus' social contacts covered a wide spectrum. Pierre's mother, Grace, was *née* Elliott. Her father was an English-speaking Protestant of Scottish descent, her mother a French-speaking Catholic with the maiden name of Sauvé. Grace's parents had chosen to bring up their sons as Protestants, their daughter as a Catholic. Moreover, on Durocher Street where the Trudeaus lived, their immediate neighbours were Jews. "Our houses were semi-detached," Suzette recalled with a laugh, "so we could just climb over the second-floor balcony to our neighbours." From their earliest days, the Trudeau children were exposed to English and French, to Protestants and Jews.

What language did they speak at home? The biographers don't agree. Some claim that Grace was perfectly bilingual, while others maintain that she spoke French with a heavy English accent. In his biography of Trudeau, journalist George Radwanski has them mostly communicating in English. "At home, the Trudeau children usually spoke English to both parents – to their mother because it was her first language, and to their father because he wanted to practise and polish his command of it."[28]

So what do the Trudeaus themselves report? Suzette is categorical. "We were all bilingual. Mother was an Elliott. I was more fluent in English. My father knew that French was a more difficult language than English, so he wanted us to speak French. With my mother, my father often spoke English, but he told us that it was to improve his English. Between themselves they spoke both languages. All of us spoke both languages. Pierre would speak English with me and French with Tip. It's only later that people began to make an issue of it."[29]

Pierre Trudeau agreed with his sister. Asked how language was handled at home, he wrote in his *Memoirs*: "My answer is: it was the most natural thing in the world. I never felt that there *was* any problem. My father spoke to us in French, and my mother spoke in either language, depending on the subject and on how she felt at the time. My Trudeau grandmother, uncles, aunts, and cousins always spoke French; my Elliott grandfather spoke English with my mother, but switched to French to talk with my father."[30] The children, then, used both languages, easily flowing from the one to the other according to

circumstances and the person they addressed. Would such mental gym-
nastics cause difficulties for young Pierre? "Very few and very minor
ones," was his answer. "You might say that, long before it was formally
invented, I benefited from 'total immersion.'"[31]

—— ◦◍◦ ——

Clearly, the Trudeau children's speaking ability was not hampered by
their bilingual environment. But were they affected in their intellectual
development and in their sense of identity? The question arises because
the influential nationalist historian Lionel Groulx maintained in his pedagogical novel, *L'Appel de la race* (*The Call of Race*) that the children of
ethnically mixed marriages suffer from a form of schizophrenia because
they are inhabited by two different souls. Groulx has his hero exclaim: "So
it is really true that the mixing of races produces cerebral disorders!"[32]
Another character in the novel explains: "Such miscegenation . . . always
provokes a degree of degeneration when the races, even if they are superior, are too different from each other."[33] Groulx spoke of "races" in the
sense of what today we would call nationalities or ethnicities. The
"mixing" that is central to the novel occurs when the hero, Lantagnac –
a brilliant French-Canadian lawyer in Ottawa who has taken on English
ways – marries an English-speaking Protestant who converts to
Catholicism. Their children are indeed deeply troubled. But Lantagnac
goes through a spiritual rebirth, rediscovers his French roots, banishes all
English influences from his life, and becomes a prominent defender of
French in Ontario. His wife leaves him, taking two of the children. He
may have lost his family but he has regained his French soul.

One might have expected an outcry when the novel was published in
1922. On the contrary: it met with resounding success. A fifth edition
was published in 1956, with an introduction by the linguist Bruno
Lafleur, who wrote: "This book won for Father Groulx the virtually unanimous acclaim – too enthusiastic at times – of the students of the 1920s."[34]
And what about Pierre Trudeau, whose family situation was almost identical to that condemned in *L'Appel de la race*? Trudeau must have encountered the book when, as an adolescent, he read voraciously just about every
significant work that cast light on the fate of French Canadians. Groulx's
influence was at its height during the 1930s. Surprisingly, amid the volu-
minous notes that the youth kept on his readings, nowhere does one find

Trudeau grappling with the thesis of the novel. It can be safely assumed
that Trudeau could not agree that a mixed marriage enfeebles the minds
of the offspring.

What is surprising is that most of Trudeau's biographers have subscribed to an assumption similar to Groulx's, namely that Trudeau was
psychologically dislocated because his family environment left him with
an identity crisis for life. Some writers even went so far as to interpret his
entire political enterprise as an attempt to solve the personal crisis that
stemmed from the language duality of his childhood. Stephen Clarkson
and Christina McCall, in the celebrated biography that won them the
Governor General's Award,[35] noted that the students at Collège Jean-de-
Brébeuf, where Trudeau studied, were taught that French Canadians
enjoyed a moral superiority. From this premise, the authors deduced
that "The young Trudeau obviously found the pride that this attitude
encouraged a useful disguise for his general unease and his mounting
ambivalence about being a French Canadian." They assert young Pierre's
"general unease" and "mounting ambivalence" as a fact. It's a bold assertion. But the authors present not one document or a single testimony to
support their claim. Was it not at least as credible that he revelled in the
sense of pride instilled by his teachers simply because he identified himself
as a French Canadian?

In a 1997 book, Kenneth McRoberts quoted with approval the
Clarkson–McCall theory and took it even further. Trudeau's major policies, he asserted, were founded on his ambivalence about his identity. His
family made it possible for him to achieve a rare level of bilingualism, but
at the cost of serious identity problems. "The result was profound: he
was unable or unprepared to identify exclusively with either English
Canada or French Canada. Instead he fastened upon the supremacy of
the individual. To a much greater extent than most Canadians, he had a
compelling reason to do so."[36] Aha! If Trudeau championed the primacy
of the individual, he did so not out of a philosophical or ethical conviction, but because he was unable to identify with either of the two language
communities. The Charter of Rights and Freedoms itself was his solution
to his own identity problems, rather than a protection for every
Canadian citizen. Such being the case, the wonder is that so many of his
compatriots now consider themselves "Charter Canadians." How on
earth did the Charter become so popular, and especially in Quebec?

McRoberts also invokes Trudeau's identity problems to explain his aversion to ethnic nationalism. Its true foundation was not a philosophical principle, but rather a psychological deficiency. "Needless to say, such an intense rejection of nationalism and of ethnically or culturally defined collectivities came naturally to someone who himself did not feel a clear membership in any such collectivity."[37] For McRoberts, Trudeau's birth in a bilingual family left him wounded for life. This assumption underlay his thesis, expressed in the title of his book *Misconceiving Canada*.

There is one point on which the biographers agree: Trudeau was an outstanding athlete. He impressed Canadians by his feats on the diving board, his water skiing, his scuba diving, his heli-skiing in the Rockies, his judo, his youthful thousand-mile canoe trip to the far north. Yet in his younger years, he anguished over his size and his slight build. He decided to prove that no one and nothing would ever intimidate him. So he worked at overcoming his fears and proving to himself that he could handle any situation that arose. In his many travels, he sought out adventure. "I wanted to know how I would cope in different countries, with people I could not communicate with in any language I knew. I have to admit, I was looking for adventure. I was always on the lookout for sinister-looking faces, without trying to provoke, but placing myself in situations that could take a bad turn, just to test whether I would have the smarts to extricate myself. And there were times when it nearly ended badly. If you try hard enough to prove you're alive, you just might end up on a slab. But it always worked out."[38]

At the end of his studies at the London School of Economics, Trudeau set out on a twelve-month world tour. He travelled with a backpack, sleeping in youth hostels, in railway stations, and sometimes under the stars. He cast aside all luxuries and often travelled in discomfort and even danger. In the multitude of countries that he visited, he wanted to experience life at first hand, much as the people themselves lived it. "I decided to use the modes of travel of Everyman: on foot with a backpack, in third-class coaches on trains, on buses in China and elsewhere, and aboard cargo boats on rivers and seas." He travelled where he could not understand the language and entered war zones where even foreign correspondents prudently chose not to venture, testing himself to confirm that he could overcome panic.39 Twice he could have been killed. During the 1948 attack by the Arab states against the newly proclaimed independent State of Israel, he was seized by Arab soldiers, charged with spying, and was in danger of being executed. He risked his life again while exploring ruins in Ur, the birthplace of Abraham, when he was attacked by three robbers.

The once-timid lad displayed again his acquired nerve when he attended Montreal's June twenty-fourth Saint-Jean-Baptiste Day parade in 1968. It happened to fall on the eve of the federal elections, the first since he had won the Liberal leadership in April, and so become prime minister. A commando of separatists led by Pierre Bourgault, head of the Rassemblement pour l'Indépendance nationale, began hurling rocks and bottles at the reviewing stand where the guests of honour sat. These included, besides the prime minister, Premier Daniel Johnson Sr. and Montreal mayor Jean Drapeau. While the others fled, Trudeau angrily shook off his RCMP bodyguards and remained, smiling and waving, as police and demonstrators battled below and the parade filed slowly by. The scene of violence and Trudeau's resolve, carried live on television screens across the country, helped him win a majority government the next day. Some cynics decided that he held his ground because he knew it would boost his political fortunes. But anyone who had followed his development would have known that he would never back down under threat. It was a matter of principle.

<hr />

In his youth, Trudeau took great pleasure in startling people, in provoking them. He came across as a show-off. He might, in the middle of a party, suddenly stand on his head. Several of those who knew him well admit that, at first, his behaviour put them off; they were embarrassed and even downright annoyed. Marc Lalonde acknowledges that Trudeau's outlandish behaviour "got on my nerves." He recalls one evening when newspaper publisher Pierre Peladeau was holding a reception at his home. The other guests arrived in business attire but Pierre showed up in a bathing suit and proceeded to do flips and somersaults in their host's swimming pool. "But, after a while, you got used to him. You accepted his antics because that's how it was, that was just Trudeau. You gave up trying to understand."⁴⁰ Still, the mystery remains: how could such a shy man act so whimsically?

In his younger years, his favourite accomplice for such stunts was his friend Roger Rolland, who many years later would become one of his speechwriters and finally an honorary pallbearer at his state funeral. They attended different colleges – Rolland was a student at another Collège – but they met through an acquaintance and remained fast friends for life. They founded what they called the "Club of the Dying." Their trick was to attend a social event where they would suddenly go stiff, keel over, and hit the floor, as if fainting or dead. They were soon joined in their prank by a Jesuit priest, a teacher at Jean-de-Brébeuf whose given name was Rodolphe Dubé, but who was best known as François Hertel, the pen name under which he had become famous for his iconoclastic essays and novels. Though he was never Pierre's teacher, he did become a personal friend. The three jokesters revelled in the consternation their charade provoked.

Another prank carried out by Trudeau and Rolland would become notorious as "the motorcycle incident." It would often be cited as evidence of Trudeau's irresponsible attitude toward the Second World War. The story has as many variants as there are storytellers, each embroidering freely on the known facts. According to Roger Rolland's account, Pierre and he decided to pay a surprise visit on their motorcycles to friends who were spending that summer in the Laurentians, at Morin Heights. They were members of the professional acting troupe, the Compagnons de Saint-Laurent. As a joke, the two visitors decided to go in costume. They rummaged through the attic where Rolland's parents had stored their souvenirs brought back from Europe. Roger donned an old spiked Prussian helmet, Trudeau an old French helmet. They each pinned a row of medals to their trench coats, put on army boots and goggles, and strapped an old sabre around his waist. They never thought for a moment that their outlandish disguise could be taken seriously.

As they set out for the mountains, Rolland took the lead. At one point Trudeau roared up to him and shouted, "Hey, pal, a woman flagged me down and told me, 'The German went that way!' " That was when it dawned on them that some people could be taken in. After a good laugh, they decided to keep up the pretense. Rolland recounts what happened next. "We stopped for lunch at a small restaurant outside

Sainte-Agathe. When we got the bill, I pulled out some Napoleon-era coins my father had brought back and I handed them to the waitress. She took them to the kitchen and soon we heard her father saying loudly, 'Call the police!' The daughter pleaded, 'But Dad, they seem very nice. I'm sure they're going to pay.' – 'Call the police, I tell you!' In fact, they didn't call the police. We did pay."

When they reached the cottage where their friends were staying, they decided to fool them by climbing in through an upstairs window. They found a ladder and crept up through the bushes. As it turned out, all the actors were away, with only a young caretaker left behind. When he spotted their helmets and their sabres, the poor lad was frightened out of his wits. They immediately wound up their practical joke. But, Roger Rolland later commented, he was utterly shocked that their prank could have been interpreted afterward as thumbing their nose at the war effort. They had picked these costumes simply because they were there, not to convey some political message.[41]

What does this incident suggest? Perhaps Rolland was being candid when he claimed that they were just having fun, but one wonders how two educated young men in their early twenties, in the midst of a world war, could find such a prank appropriate. Let us recall, however, that in 1942 – at about that same time – while the Allies, including Canada, were desperately on the defensive against the assaults of the Nazis and other Axis powers, a University of Montreal medical student named Jean-Louis Roux thought it funny to sport a swastika on the sleeve of his lab coat. When his joke became known decades later, in 1996, the prominent actor-director and noted civil libertarian was forced to resign his position as Quebec's lieutenant-governor. But it was very different at the time of the prank, as Roux was to write: "None of my professors, none of my fellow students was shocked. Some found it funny, some were even startled, but that was it. And yet it could have turned out quite differently if some informer had brought it to the attention of the Royal Canadian Mounted Police, who didn't take such matters lightly. At no time did the university authorities demand that I remove that symbol of a totalitarian regime."[42] It was a sign of the times, of the atmosphere and attitudes prevalent in Quebec, that young men like Trudeau and Roux could indulge in pranks that they considered merely amusing, while a later generation would find them shocking.

All his life, Trudeau would display this playfulness and fondness for pranks. Even once installed as prime minister, he always found time and opportunity to tease his friends and to play tricks on his children. The news media and the Canadian public alike were entertained by his out-breaks of irreverence. Who could forget his sliding down a banister, somersaulting off a diving board, or his memorable pirouette in the shadow of Her Majesty Queen Elizabeth? His portfolio of incongruities grew impressive. His critics interpreted his pranks as just Trudeau showing off before the media. Perhaps. But another reading is plausible. Some of his turns were certainly planned; think of his sweeping into a Grey Cup match in 1970, decked out in a cape and a wide-brimmed floppy hat. But there were numerous turns that came spontaneously, inspired by the circumstances. Recall the solemnities of an official visit to the Soviet Union when the Canadian prime minister broke away to chat with an officer waiting to escort the foreign dignitary at the head of his motorcade. Trudeau hopped on the officer's motorcycle and took off for a spin around the yard of the Kremlin. The bemused Soviet officials in attendance were not used to such a breach of protocol.[43] But the news media lapped it up.

Despite these eye-popping incidents, people who were close to Trudeau insist that he was shy. He himself wrote that, in his early years, he was shy and hypersensitive. He would cry on the slightest provocation. "I was one of those delicate children, puny and hypersensitive."[44] So he resolved that he would "correct these weaknesses."[45] Perhaps, in the event, he overcompensated: "As it turns out in such circumstances, you develop a protective shell, an armour. I really made mine a tough one."[46]

———◆———

Trudeau was often described as arrogant. He seemed to take pleasure in crushing an opponent with forceful repartee. He readily resorted to irony, even to insults. In 1950, referring to Quebeckers, he wrote in *Cité libre*: "We depend on our power of blackmail in order to face the future. . . . We are getting to be a sleazy bunch of blackmailers." Another time, with feigned innocence, he called out in a meeting at the University of Montreal: "Is there an intellectual in the hall?" He was a master of rebut-tal and quick with a pithy riposte that would silence an adversary. Some of his put-downs have been memorable.

At a federal-provincial meeting in 1968, Premier Daniel Johnson Sr. referred contemptuously to then Justice Minister Trudeau as "Lord Elliott," insinuating that he was an outsider, not a true Québécois. Without a pause, Trudeau replied: "To call me Lord Elliott when your name is Johnson is to venture on a slippery slope."[47] Years later, he was informed that President Richard Nixon was caught on tape calling Trudeau an "asshole." Again, without missing a beat, Trudeau replied: "I've been called worse names by better people." On another occasion, on a speaking tour, a protester called out: "What happened to your 'just society'?" Trudeau called back: "Ask Jesus Christ! He promised it first."[48]

The charge of being arrogant followed him all his life. And yet, a closer look makes clear that he was rarely the first to attack, and his most biting retorts were made in reply to provocations. His close friends claim that they rarely heard him utter a bad word about anybody, even his worst enemies. He believed in the dignity of each individual human being. Roger Rolland remembers that one day he was working on a speech for Trudeau when he made a nasty comment about John Diefenbaker, ridiculing the former prime minister, now sitting on the opposition benches. Trudeau interrupted him to say, "He is a tough adversary, but he is a good man."[49]

Justin Trudeau has his own story. One day, when he was eight, he was having lunch with his father in the Parliamentary Restaurant when he spotted Joe Clark, then leader of the Opposition, eating at another table. Thinking that he would please his father, he made a disparaging crack about Clark. Trudeau lectured him, "Justin, you must never attack the individual. It's possible to disagree completely with someone without making personal attacks." Thereupon Trudeau rose and led his son to the table where Joe Clark was lunching with his daughter Catherine, and proceeded to introduce the boy to the Clarks.[50]

While Trudeau always had great respect for each individual, he certainly did not have the same respect for every idea. He never wore kid gloves to attack a point of view, regardless of its author, if he thought it false or fallacious. When, in 1991, he gave the Convocation Speech at the official opening of the University of Toronto's Bora Laskin Law Library, Trudeau gave an address analyzing the Supreme Court of Canada's 1981 judgment on the conditions required for Canada's

Constitution to be patriated legitimately. He was very critical of the majority opinion of the court, which held that a constitutional convention required a substantial measure of provincial consent. Among the judges who advanced that judgment was Mr. Justice Brian Dickson, who was present in the audience for the Trudeau speech, and had recently retired as Chief Justice of the Supreme Court. Later that evening, at a celebratory dinner with his friends, Trudeau was asked whether his attack on the decision meant that he had a poor opinion of Mr. Justice Dickson. "Not at all," Trudeau replied with perfect equanimity. "I admire Dickson. After all, I was the one who appointed him to the Supreme Court. But I can't agree with his decision."[51]

Most people meeting Trudeau for the first time were surprised to find him simple and sincere. Alain Stanké, the well-known publisher and television personality, was given for three days the run of the prime minister's residence at 24 Sussex Drive, accompanied by a large television crew. He wrote afterward: "It's something that can be confirmed by the 24 technicians of *Télé-Métropole* – and they run the complete spectrum of political preferences – Pierre Elliott Trudeau is a man who radiates warmth and has a peculiar power of seduction. He is courteous, charming and diplomatic, he is able to fascinate. . . . For the first time in the history of television in this country, all doors were thrown open to us without a single restriction. With good grace and complete simplicity, Pierre Elliott Trudeau and his family welcomed us into their intimacy."[52]

Trudeau was always reserved. Those who knew him best confirmed that he kept wanting to get closer to his friends, but always found it difficult to do so. When he was at Harvard University, now in his mid-twenties, he wrote a letter to Roger Rolland in which he regretted the superficiality of their relations. "I only mean to say that you and I are surely not yet true friends. I doubt that we ever spoke together on any but pretty superficial terms. You'd think, if you stopped to consider our past exchanges, that we were both convinced that we had nothing of substance to learn from each other. And so we did what seemed wisest under the circumstances: we joked, we chatted about literature and the theatre, about nationalism and gossip. . . . We seemed to be saying that we really had nothing to give each other."[53]

In a subsequent letter, he attempted once again to dissect what he called "the strange inadequacy of our relationship as friends." Then, two months later, he came back to the subject: "I haven't the slightest hesitation in saying that the greatest benefit of my coming to Harvard has been the letters I received from my friends. I know you so much better now, and I value you so much more. As for myself, I've been compelled to become a little more human, a little less of a machine, and a little more open to the qualities of the heart."[54] Some time later, he would add: "I would always prefer to be writing to my friends than to be doing anything else."[55] The Trudeau who expressed himself in these personal letters emerges as quite different from the common stereotype of a cold man who could never pour his heart out to his friends.

Another image that attached itself to Trudeau at different times was that of playboy. In 1969, within a year of his becoming prime minister, one of his political opponents predicted: "He's an amateur, a dilettante, a carefree bachelor who is happiest when he travels the world. He will soon tire of his new responsibilities."[56] The truth is that Trudeau was an extremely hard worker who demonstrated an inflexible will. He was also gifted with a remarkable memory. He excelled in debate, where he displayed an apparently effortless eloquence. In fact, though, words did not come to him easily. "Pierre never was a smooth talker," his friend Gérard Pelletier confirmed. He also left the impression of writing with ease, when in fact he had to slave long and hard to produce his bright prose. The evidence is all there in his manuscripts. Whether he was composing the short pieces written when he was young or the major works of his maturity, he would phrase and rephrase his sentences over and over again, searching for the right words to express his ideas. The end result would be impressive, but it was achieved only by assiduous effort. And Trudeau knew it. "Shit, oh shit!" he wrote in French in the margin of a letter to Roger Rolland. "My writing is so laborious!"[57] Later, in the 1950s and 1960s, the editors of the magazine *Cité libre* became all too familiar with the sight of Trudeau showing up at the very last minute, still wanting to make changes to the article he had submitted.

The purist pronunciation of his spoken French also came as the result of a systematic effort. In his early years, he spoke the same loose French with a regional accent that most Québécois did. But, at Brébeuf, a diction teacher made an appearance in class once a week to train the students in articulating precise vowel sounds and clipped consonants. The teacher tried to inculcate an "international" standard of French pronunciation. While almost all the students found the exercises pretentious and ridiculously pompous, Pierre was one of the few who deliberately abandoned the Québécois accent to adopt for life the more elevated international accent. He later explained his conversion in this way: "When I was about fourteen or fifteen, I had begun to read Racine, Corneille, Molière. God knows that the words I was used to speaking were not the same as those I was reading. So I decided, 'Either I change the authors I'm reading or I start speaking somewhat properly.'"[58] One can only imagine how much determination it took to speak French differently than did all those in his environment, and to resist the taunts of schoolmates who found that he was "putting on airs."

He regularly ranked among the top students. "He would inevitably end up first in his class," recalls Pierre Vadeboncœur, who accompanied him through most of his schooling, beginning in Grade 4, and would later be among his most severe critics. The young Trudeau was recognized as a very serious student, one who scrupulously read all the books on the program, but whose reading also ranged far beyond. He would take careful notes on what he read, transcribing passages that impressed him and also jotting down his own appreciation. He worked systematically at broadening his knowledge of literature and developing his taste. Jacques Hébert remembers going with him to a performance of Claude Debussy's opera, *Pelléas et Mélisande*. As they emerged from the theatre, Pierre recited for him entire excerpts from the opera.[59]

———◦———

Much has been written about Trudeau the playboy, the man who flirted with so many women but did not marry until he was fifty. Some of his biographers were quick to diagnose a psychological problem. The co-authors Stephen Clarkson and Christina McCall,[60] as well as Michel Vastel,[61] interpreted his occasional sarcastic utterances about women as the key to understanding his long avoidance of marriage. On the other hand, after dancing with him at the Governor's Ball, playwright and actress Linda Griffith[62] portrayed him as the perfect lover. Why did he marry so late? Whenever he was asked, he would parry the question with a joke. But a letter he wrote in November 1945 to Roger Rolland offers some insight. Trudeau wrote confidingly about his recent breakup with a young woman that they both knew. "Though I could see that I might easily have fallen in love with her, I made sure that she would not fall in love with me, both for her sake and because of my excessive caution. You remember our conversations . . . in which we spoke so solemnly about our love lives. I told you that I was not in a position to fall in love, that I would not be ready to for several more years, until I had fully matured. I can understand my behaviour, but something still remains inexplicable. . . . For instance, why did I so deliberately kill love before it could be born? I had my reasons, of course. But was it reasonable? I was unwilling to rec-ognize something that will be present in every human undertaking: imperfection. I would not love if it meant running a risk. . . . The fact is that I wasn't sure of myself, I was not, as I just said, mature, I was not (I am not) yet myself.

"That all stems from my temperament that you know only too well: calculating, precise, methodical even to the point of pettiness. I do take many risks, but only calculated risks, never risky risks. If it were to do over again, I can't say that I would do the same thing all over again. The risk of love probably was worth taking: at best, we might have enjoyed infinite happiness and, at worst, we would have lived happy and limited days, even if it ended in a breakup because the risk had proved a mistake. A breakup! That's what I was unwilling to risk." Trudeau revealed himself in this letter as he would rarely ever do: as a perfectionist who could not accept less than the ideal love affair, and as an emotionally fearful man who could not countenance the anguish of the end of a rela-tionship. Unfortunately for him, when he finally did make the leap and run the risk of love, he would experience precisely the breakup that he had so dreaded. The dignity that he displayed throughout the ordeal when his marriage foundered would earn him the sympathy of millions of Canadians.

Religion was a dimension of Trudeau's life of which he spoke little. Yet he always remained a committed and practising Catholic. "I believe in eternal life and so I believe in God," he told Stanké in 1977.[63] He attended Sunday mass regularly. He had a thorough grasp of the Bible, which he would sometimes read in the evening with his children. He was known to correct people who had quoted the Bible inaccurately. And, throughout his life, he prayed regularly. It was only after his death that Canadians became aware of the depth of his faith. A recent book, *The Hidden Pierre Elliott Trudeau: The Faith Behind the Politics*,[64] presents the first collection of essays on his faith and its relation with his politics. Yet his religious convictions did not prevent him from going against long-established strictures of the Catholic Church when, as minister of justice, he liberalized the laws dealing with abortion, divorce, and homosexual acts carried out in private between consenting adults.

———◈———

This, then, is the man who began to make his presence felt and his views known on the Quebec scene when he committed himself to the workers' side in the notorious asbestos strike of 1949. Beginning in 1950, he became more prominent with the launch of the intellectual magazine *Cité libre*, where he regularly appeared and propounded ideas that were diametrically opposed to those defended at the time by the consensus of Quebec's French-speaking intellectuals. Fifteen years later, in 1965, he chose the path of federal politics – but only reluctantly, according to a received opinion.

Three years later, in 1968, he would become prime minister of Canada. His admirers, along with those who deprecate his legacy, agree on this: before leaving office in 1984, he had transformed the very foundations of the country. Today's Canada, the Canada of the Canadian Charter of Rights and Freedoms, of two official languages, of no official culture but of official respect for all cultures, this Canada, for better and for worse, is largely owing to him. Eventually, after his work was done, he took his lonely walk in the snow and, rather like a cowboy in a western, disappeared into the setting sun.

Where did he come from? How did a man brought up in the very heart of a Quebec that was ultra-conservative, defensive, Catholic, nationalistic, and turned inward toward its past, eventually defend with such passion and success a vision of Canada that was liberal, open, nonsectarian, cosmopolitan, and turned to the future? The child, it is said, is father to the man. But was it so for Trudeau? The man that he became would eventually become known to the whole world. But what was he like as a child and a youth? What influence did his family, his community, his schooling, his church, have in forming him in the Quebec of the 1930s and 1940s?

Searching for answers, we interviewed Thérèse Gouin, who had been a friend of Trudeau since the 1940s. Though they never became officially engaged, they had intended to marry. While Trudeau was a student in Paris, and she a psychology student in Montreal, Thérèse Gouin ended that relationship to marry Vianney Décarie, who would later be a professor at the Université de Montréal. She and Trudeau remained friends, however, and she declined to tell us why she changed her mind. When we asked her to name the great thinkers who had influenced the young Pierre Trudeau, she answered with a laugh that he was the one who influenced others, that he was never influenced by anyone else. And she added: "It's as though he emerged fully formed, like Athena from the forehead of Zeus."[65]

Unable to subscribe to the theory of spontaneous generation, we strove to understand how this son of Quebec became the father of Canada. As his early portrait slowly emerged, we ourselves could scarcely believe what we discovered.

*Chapter 2*

OBEDIENCE: THE JESUITS'

FIRST PRINCIPLE

*Those who follow God can be recognized by the purity of their
obedience and the renouncement of their own judgment.*

— IGNATIUS OF LOYOLA

PIERRE TRUDEAU, the born contrarian? Pierre Trudeau, the eternal non-conformist, the rebel, the man who, from early childhood, would march to no drumbeat but his own? Such is the image that has remained, projected by both biographers and the man himself. But was it true to its subject?

"I was never able to submit easily to authority or to arguments from authority,"[1] Trudeau confided in 1977 when he was interviewed on camera for "an intimate portrait" by Alain Stanké. The following year, interviewed by his first biographer, journalist George Radwanski, the prime minister gave a similar description of himself as a youth: "I went out of my way in a regular fashion to disobey the imposed discipline. I was one of those troublesome children who was expelled many times from class, but a few times from school, which is very serious to a teen-ager."[2]

Trudeau, speaking in his own *Memoirs* of his childhood, described a boy who was a born skeptic. "Opposing conventional wisdoms and challenging prevailing opinions, with my friends as much as with my teachers, became a habit that has remained with me all my life."[3] He gave an example when he was interviewed by the *Toronto Star*[4] for a profile published just two days after Trudeau won the Liberal leadership in 1968. At school, he said he reacted to the pervasive French-Canadian nationalism by parading before his classmates as an anti-nationalist. "Since they were nearly all nationalists, I would say I wasn't. And when, during history class, they used to applaud the victories of the French armies, I, on the contrary, would applaud the victories of the English armies. I was always taking the opposite stand from people, from my teachers, and this used to get them quite annoyed."

Even signing his name Pierre *Elliott* Trudeau was a bit of anti-nationalist bravado. In elementary school, he was known simply as Pierre. Then, by the time he started high school, he had added *Elliott* as his middle name. True, it was one of the five surnames given him at baptism. It was also his mother's maiden name. But why choose Elliott rather than Joseph, Philippe, or Yves? Obviously it was to proclaim his non-*pure laine* partially Scottish ancestry and to annoy the Quebec nationalists.5

In 1996, Trudeau's long-time friend Gérard Pelletier put together a collection of the former prime minister's writings going back to his student days in 1939. The title was chosen to bring out the common denominator in fifty-seven years of commentary on a wide range of subjects: *Against the Current*.6 But, long before, Trudeau himself had already defined non-conformism as the defining characteristic of his mind. He had written in a foreword to his 1968 collection of essays, *Federalism and the French Canadians*: "The only constant factor to be found in my thinking over the years has been opposition to accepted opinions. . . . In high school, when the only politics I was taught was history, I had already made up my mind to row against the current. But what was then an ill-defined reflex against intellectual regimentation became a conscious choice as soon as I went to university." The wonder is that such a student, rebellious and anti-nationalist, was also "regularly at the top of his class," as his fellow classmate Pierre Vadeboncœur testified: he walked away with most of the prizes.7 How could the rigid and authoritarian school system of the day consent to bestow honours on such a misfit?

Rowing against the current. As we began our research for Trudeau's intellectual biography, we took this much-touted contrarian mindset as a given and we determined to discover the factors in his family and social environment that could explain such an unusual characteristic of his early life. But the further we advanced into our research, the more we were assailed by doubts. Could it be that the constant picture of a non-conformist youth had in fact been projected backward from the man that he notoriously became? Little by little, as our evidence accumulated and new revelations emerged, we were forced to revise our assumptions. We discovered a Trudeau who was remarkably different from what we and everyone else had assumed. And we now invite our readers to accompany us on that voyage of discovery.

———◦———

In today's secularized and ultra-permissive Quebec, it takes a powerful effort of the imagination to return to the 1920s and 1930s and rediscover that almost unrecognizable world of French-Catholic Quebec. From baptism through schooling, marriage, and hospital care to final burial, the Church was everywhere. It was a cause of scandal for someone to miss Sunday mass. Every adult was expected to fast during Lent, avoid meat on Friday, and celebrate the numerous Holy Days of Obligation.

There was no ministry of education. It had been abolished in 1875 to submit to the ultramontane clergy which considered education the domain of the family and the Church, not the state. Schooling was not compulsory in the 1930s: that would only come in the 1940s. French-Catholic education was controlled strictly by the bishops, the religious orders, and religious congregations. Only private secondary schools gave access to French colleges and universities, and they all charged fees. The Church controlled the French universities, and ran the orphanages, hospitals, and shelters for the aged. The Church set up Catholic unions where the chaplain was the real power and strikes were unknown, and workers were told not to join non-sectarian unions. The Church set up publishing houses and owned newspapers. The Church succeeded, following a 1927 fire in Montreal's Laurier Palace Theatre where seventy-eight children died, in having the provincial government ban from movie theatres all children under the age of sixteen. The culture of censorship prevailed.

A Jesuit priest who had taught at Collège Jean-de-Brébeuf in the 1940s, René Latourelle, returned to Quebec after three decades of studying and teaching in Europe. He wrote a book, *Quel avenir pour le Christianisme?*, published in 2000, in which he described what the church was like in Quebec precisely during the years when Pierre Trudeau was a boy: "I know that church well, because I grew up in its bosom. The image

that I retain of it in the years from 1930 to 1950 is that of a religion con-
sisting above all of practices, of commands, of interdictions, rather than
of a doctrine drawn from the single source of the Gospel of Jesus. . . . The
practice of confession verged on delirium. It involved drawing up a list of
one's sins, the number, the seriousness, the circumstances, with the preci-
sion of a grocery list. Woe to the poor mothers caught in a problem with
birth control. Hell was an ever-present threat. There were complaints
about the ecclesiastical power centralizing beyond reason and about the
abusive exercise of that power. The church acted as a true dictatorship
over consciences."[8]

It was in this atmosphere that young Pierre set off on the long process
of his education. "And so I started very early in the 'baby class' – the
nursery school of that era – at École Bonsecours, which was run by nuns.
I have only happy memories of those early days."[9] His earliest schooling
was at the hands of nuns, as was common in Quebec before the 1960s.

After École Bonsecours, young Pierre attended École Querbes, the
Catholic elementary school in Outremont then run by the Saint-Viateur
parish, and named after the priest, Louis-Marie-Joseph Querbes, who
had founded in nineteenth-century France the Institut des Clercs de
Saint-Viateur. And so young Pierre's entire primary school education was
framed by celibates deeply committed to religion. This school had a small
English section as well as the much larger French section. Pierre's parents
placed their son in the English section for the first three grades, then
transferred him into the French section for the remaining grades. From
then until he attended Harvard University as an adult in 1944, all of his
education would be in French.

His new school immediately gave him the opportunity to struggle
against his innate shyness. At Querbes, the English section was rather
like a rural school: the first three grades were held in one room, with the
same teacher. On his first day, little Pierre realized that his pal Gerald
O'Connor, who lived just a few doors away from the Trudeaus on
Durocher Street, was placed with the Grade 2 pupils, while his own desk
was with the First Graders. "It's not fair," he complained to his father.
But instead of going to the school to intervene on behalf of his son, his
father told the little boy that he should go himself and talk to the principal. Pierre, with trepidation, knocked on the door. To his delight, it
worked and he was promoted across the room. "If I remember that

episode to this day, it is no doubt partly because of the outcome. But it is also because I overcame my shyness. Like all children, and maybe more than most, I was shy. I was reluctant to stand out. I had to be pushed into doing so – but then there was no holding me back."[10]

In the English section, Pierre's grades were impressive, even if he didn't always stand first in the class. And his conduct was consistently rated as excellent. His report card for 1928, for instance, gave him an "excellent" for "behaviour, application, politeness and cleanliness." For the remaining years at the school, 1929 to 1932, he came first or second in every subject. No complaints about his behaviour were recorded on his report cards. He gave no sign yet of being an incipient rebel.

———————

In September 1932, just a month short of his thirteenth birthday, Pierre Trudeau entered on the most formative experience of his youth, one that would mark him for life. He began his studies at the educational institution where he would spend the next eight years, from the age of twelve to the age of twenty. Collège Jean-de-Brébeuf – called Brébeuf for short – was no ordinary school, but rather a way of life, now vanished. To convey, today, how it could exert so powerful an influence on the boy requires some explanation. The classical colleges no longer exist, but at the height of their glory, they played an unparalleled role in creating Quebec's French elite, and were the only institutions that gave access to the French-language universities.[11] In 1939, there were 9,000 students registered in the province's classical colleges or one out of every 300 Quebeckers.[12]

Brébeuf, for boys only, was owned, run, and staffed by the Society of Jesus – the Jesuits. They then owned five classical colleges in Quebec, four of them in Montreal, including English-language Loyola College. In 1928, four years before Pierre Trudeau's arrival, Brébeuf had opened its doors, with 580 students. Almost from the start, it was considered the most prestigious college in Quebec. It was located just to the west of Outremont, where the French-speaking bourgeoisie was concentrated. Being conveniently close enabled it to attract students from middle-class families, such as the Trudeaus. It could also draw the bright children of ambitious parents from all over Quebec, the rest of Canada, and even abroad. Over the following decades, Brébeuf would prove to be the prime training ground for Quebec's French-speaking elite. As a Jesuit college, Jean-de-Brébeuf inculcated the spirit of the Society of Jesus's charismatic founder, Ignatius of Loyola.

———— ◦◦◦ ————

Born in 1491, Ignatius of Loyola saw his career as a soldier interrupted when he was struck by a cannonball to the leg and had to endure a long and painful convalescence. Immobilized by his wound, he read a *Life of Christ* and *The Golden Legend*, which related the lives of several saints. Converted, he decided to abandon the military life and the service of an earthly prince to dedicate himself to the service of Christ the King.[13] In 1523, he wrote down the Spiritual Exercises, a course of meditation on the life of Jesus and the ultimate purpose of human beings. In 1534, he founded with seven companions "the Company of Jesus," a name evoking intimacy with Jesus, but also a military formation. Ignatius adopted the motto, *"militare Deo,"* to fight for God, and infused his order with his military cast of mind. The climactic meditation in the Spiritual Exercises evokes a vast plain in which two great armies face each other, one led by Jesus, the other by the Devil, each raising high his standard; Jesus called on all humans to rally to his standard and devote their lives fully to Him. All Jesuits make an annual retreat in which they plunge themselves again in the Spiritual Exercises. The militancy of the Jesuit order, even today, is expressed in the name given familiarly to their superior general: "Father General," and in the strong emphasis on obedience to one's hierarchical superior, to subjecting one's own reason, one's own judgment, to that of the superior. For the Jesuits, "all one's strength must be applied to this virtue of obedience, owed first to the Pope and then to the Superior of the Order. . . . Each one must be convinced that whoever lives in obedience must let himself be guided and directed by Divine Province, through the intermediary of his superiors."[14]

Ignatius wrote that it is "by the purity and the perfection of obedience . . . and the abnegation of [one's own] judgment" that one can recognize "those who, in this Company, follow God . . ."[15] Obedience, for Ignatius, trumped judgment.

Accordingly, the military spirit, with its stress on discipline and obedience, reigned in the Jesuit schools. "Ignatian discipline had priority over all intellectual, social or moral values," Pierre Dansereau recalled bitterly.[16] An alumnus of the Jesuits' Collège Sainte-Marie, Dansereau would become a specialist on ecosystems, with an international reputation. His college, in the rules and regulations communicated to the students, gave this explanation for the capital importance of obedience: "The code of behaviour will form the Christian within the student, because by submitting to it, he is conforming himself to the Will of God. He will consider it as the expression of Divine Will, so as to observe it in the spirit of faith that sanctifies all actions. . . . Discipline is order; order is the principle of perfection: and so it is necessary that order should reign in a house of studies and of education, and order demands above all the respect for authority embodied in the person of the superiors, the professors and the supervisors."[17]

During Trudeau's time at Brébeuf, discipline was considered so important that it was the subject of its own section on the students' monthly report card. And the report went beyond a general comment on a student's behaviour. For each week of the month, in fact, the students were given a grade under each of the following headings:

- Behaviour in the study hall.
- Application in the study hall.
- General behaviour.
- Behaviour in class.
- Application in class.

The grades for behaviour under each of these five headings were given according to the following code, ranging from perfect to very bad. The letter *a* stood for "perfect," the letters *ae* meant "very good," *e* was for "good," *ei* for "mediocre," *i* for "bad," *io* for "very bad."

The report card on the student's behaviour and on his performance in the frequent tests were then dispatched to the parents, accompanied by a monthly letter which the student was required to write to his parents. In his first such letter, dated October 3, 1932, young Pierre explained to his parents why he was writing the letter, and how to interpret the report card. Before the report was actually sent to the parents, it was read out in public before the assembled students, by the top authority of the college, who was called "le Père Recteur." This ceremony was called "Lecture des notes" (the reading aloud of the reports), young Trudeau explained. "At the lecture des notes, the Père Recteur reads out the report of 'optime,' that is, excellent, for those who received only reports of *a* or *ae*. In order to please you and to thank you for all that you do for me, I will always try to bring you that report [of optime]." The letter is stilted and stiff, altogether impersonal for a letter from a son to his parents. But the explanation of the tone came in Trudeau's postscript, written in English: "It may seem funny that I write you this letter although I see you every night but it has to be done once a month to send you our reports. I copied this letter off the blackboard. J.P.E.T." (Note in passing that he was already, in 1932, including the E. for Elliott in his signature.)

To understand how students were educated at Brébeuf, it is essential to grasp the extent to which religion infused every part of their daily life. Ideally, the student was to strive to serve God in all his actions. The Jesuits expressed this succinctly by a four-letter motto that they taught their students: A.M.D.G. The letters stood for *Ad Majorem Dei Gloriam* – for the greater glory of God. Young Trudeau adopted this motto with conviction. To this general orientation, Brébeuf added its own college motto, taken from Psalm 119: *Viam veritatis elegi*, "I have chosen the path of truth." To that standard Trudeau would always prove rigorously true, even though his pursuit of truth would eventually lead him far from many of the truths taught him by his teachers. The figure of Jesus Christ occupied a central place in all aspects of education, as Father Jacques Monet, S.J., confirmed: "The aim of the Spiritual Exercises is, first, to develop in each individual person a close, affectionate – indeed a loving – friendship with the person of Jesus Christ as both the model of human life and the inspiration for one's service to others. Second, it is to integrate into this relationship with Jesus Christ all other relationships and concerns, including the teachings and traditions of the Roman Catholic Church."[18] Trudeau will give great importance to this relationship with Christ.

To seize the importance of religion, consider the routine followed by half-boarders like Trudeau. (Boarders, like the future journalist and writer William Johnson,[19] came even more strongly under the influence of religion.) Every major activity at the school began and ended with a prayer: prayers before and after meals, prayers before and after classes, prayers before and after each session in the study hall. Besides the compulsory attendance at high mass every Sunday, the student's religious obligations included weekly confessions, a three-day annual retreat for the Spiritual Exercises – in one of the senior years it extended to eight days. There were also, according to the liturgical cycle, rosaries, ways of the cross, blessings of the Holy Sacrament, group visits to seven churches on Holy Thursday, the chanted recital of the passion of Jesus in the chapel on Good Friday. Each student was required to have a "spiritual director" who was visited for a talk once a month. In regular religion classes, the students discussed religious themes from passages of the New Testament, argued over ethical issues, and became acquainted with Church documents – such as Pope Pius XI's 1931 encyclical on social justice, *Quadragesimo anno.*

Jesuit education aimed at forming the whole individual, intellectually, physically, and spiritually. But paramount importance was given to religious formation and to Thomistic philosophy. Classical studies included six years of Latin language and literature, five years of ancient Greek. The sciences and mathematics were underemphasized. Sports had an important place, including both team sports such as lacrosse and hockey as well as track and field and competitive skiing. Extracurricular activities included attending concerts of classical music and plays. There were debating clubs and the classical colleges were reputed for turning out fine orators.

Most classical colleges offered an eight-year program. The various grades were not identified by a number, but rather by one or two words descriptive of their academic concentration. Trudeau's years at Brébeuf had him attending the following classes:

- 1932–33: Éléments-Latins
- 1933–34: Syntaxe
- 1934–35: Méthode
- 1935–36: Versification
- 1936–37: Belles-Lettres
- 1937–38: Rhétorique
- 1938–39: Philosophie I
- 1939–40: Philosophie II

Trudeau's school grades, in his first year of 1932–33, were quite respectable. He ranked third in a class of thirty boys. At the end of the

school year he carried off one first prize, two second prizes, and six honourable mentions. In the summer of 1933, in the interval between his first
and second years at Brébeuf, while the Great Depression gripped most
of the Western world, the Trudeau family set off on a two-month tour of
Europe. The party included the parents, the three children, and Grace's
father. They visited Germany, Italy, and France. While in France, they
stopped in Varangeville to visit Grace's brother, Gordon Elliott, who had
settled down there with his British wife, Nancy, after serving as a pilot in
the First World War. He introduced the family to his neighbours, the
painters Georges Braque and Joan Miró. The previous January, Adolph
Hitler had been named Chancellor of Germany; fascism was now in
power there and in Italy. Though Pierre Trudeau was then nearly fourteen, he later averred that he had missed the political meaning of the
demonstrations that he witnessed. "I admit that the gleaming motorcycles of Hitler's soldiers on the highways made a bigger impression on me
than the rearmament they signified."[20]

Back at Brébeuf for his second year, Pierre Trudeau improved his academic performance. He again ranked third, but this time in a class of
forty-six. He carried off three first prizes, three second prizes, and six
honourable mentions. Then, the following year, while he was in the class
called Méthode, an event occurred which would give rise to all kinds of
interpretations about his life and character, that is, the death of his
father in March 1935. As he wrote in his *Memoirs*, "How can I describe
what I felt at that moment? In a split second, I felt the whole world go
empty. . . . My father had long been a presence in my life, a reassuring
force but also a stimulus, a constant challenge. He was the focal point
of my life, and his death created an enormous void. All of a sudden, I
was more or less the head of a family; with him gone, it seemed to me
that I had to take over."[21]

When, more than sixty years later, we interviewed Pierre Trudeau's
sister, Suzette, about the impact of their father's death, she described in
detail the trip which she made with her mother to Florida to recover his
body. She could recall little of importance about her brother Pierre's
reaction to it all, other than the fact that he then showed a greater sense
of responsibility toward her mother and herself, confirming the account

he gave in his memoirs. As for the upheaval in their family life, she noted that they were all, indeed, very saddened, but that "our routine did not change all that much." Fortunately for them, they were left without financial problems. As an example, she pointed out, "We continued anyway to go on trips."

The boy was attached to his father and his death would leave a void. But most of Trudeau's biographers went further, maintaining that the event left the young Pierre devastated. Stephen Clarkson and Christina McCall, in their influential biography, claimed that the trauma of the father's death left the youth "in a state of psychic imbalance"; it was, they said, "a calamity that would significantly disrupt his emotional formation," and "leave him prey to crippling weaknesses."[22] Relying on their analysis, André Burelle, who had been Prime Minister Trudeau's political adviser and speech writer from 1977 to 1984, was to write in 2005: "No doubt the premature death of his father, and his refusal to make a choice between his mother's English-Canadian roots and his father's French-Canadian roots, explain at least in part his visceral rejection of ethnic nationalism."[23]

Clarkson and McCall went even further. Seizing on his supposed outrageous behaviour and the real fact that the adolescent had picked fistfights with strangers, they drew this conclusion: "It was as though he was emulating Charlie Trudeau's exaggerated machismo and at the same time acting out an inner rage at his father for having abandoned him forever by dying, the kind of anger that is often associated with the early stages of grief but that he would never be able to outgrow fully."[24]

The authors defend their startling deduction by giving considerable credence to what Montreal psychoanalyst André Lussier apparently said to American journalist Edith Iglauer, author of a 1969 profile of Trudeau that appeared in *The New Yorker*.[25] Surprisingly, the two authors never interviewed Lussier; instead they relied on his word at second hand – what Iglauer said that Lussier had told her. And Iglauer herself did not quote André Lussier in her very extensive profile of Trudeau, hardly a sign that she found it convincing. The authors, however, relied on her words about Lussier's words, without ever even quoting what she said. On such flimsy evidence, they built a whole theory of Trudeau's personality, which might best be called psychoanalytic mumbo jumbo. Lussier, though younger than Trudeau, had come to know him. He apparently made much of irrational fears and guilt provoked in Trudeau by his father's death. The two authors also made much of the differences between the two parents as a permanent source of tension and division within their older son, applying to Trudeau a psychiatric analysis that had been made of the sociologist Max Weber. Then, in a publication in the year 2004, Clarkson pushed the speculation even further by adding to it an element of violence. He claimed that Trudeau "had long been struggling to assert himself, before a powerful and dominating father who was possibly violent towards his mother."[26]

"Possibly violent"? In evaluating this theory, we looked for evidence of the father's machismo and of his violence toward his wife. Clarkson had offered absolutely none. So, for a picture of their father, we turned to his son Pierre and his daughter, Suzette.

Charles-Émile Trudeau's commonly accepted image is that of the man who loved to drink, celebrate convivially with friends, who spoke a "rough French, the slangy patois of the Québécois,"[27] and who had no interest in the life of the mind. Now, it is true that he was most likely an extrovert, and so quite different from his more reserved wife, Grace. But we were unable to discover the slightest sign of tension or conflict caused by their different temperaments. The thesis that their son Pierre was torn between their two different systems of values is simply a postulate by most biographers, backed by no convincing evidence. In fact, Charles-Émile comes across as a true family man. While his wife and children spent the summer at Mont-Tremblant, he made the long drive up over bad roads every weekend, and often brought along friends. Pierre Trudeau would recall his father's arrivals as festive occasions. In that era, the roles of men and women were clearly differentiated. Charles worked hard at developing his network of service stations; he would return home for dinner in the evening, then go back to the garage for a few more hours. But he showed his concern for his children's education by looking over their homework each evening, and encouraging them to excel. He had his son take boxing lessons, expecting him always to be self-reliant. All told, he was a normal father of the 1930s, with his faults and his good qualities, and the evidence suggests that he was on affectionate terms with his family. He was also an educated man who had obtained a law degree and become a conspicuous success in business, which at that time was unusual for a French Canadian. He even dabbled in politics. In 1929, he had raised money for Maurice Duplessis, then a Conservative member of the Quebec legislature. He also gave money periodically to Montreal's mayor Camillien Houde, who showed his respect by attending his funeral.

Our research revealed an unknown dimension to Charlie Trudeau. He was a reader. He took seriously the great ideological debates taking place in Europe and in Canada during the 1930s. He cared about ideas and about topics that, outside the intelligentsia, were not commonplace in the French-Canadian environment of his time. He took meticulous notes of what he read and often transcribed passages that impressed him – a custom that Pierre Trudeau would also adopt. The father's notes were often a page or more in length. His writing was neat and careful, without words crossed out. We found these notes in Pierre Trudeau's own archives[28]. The son had kept them until his own death. Whether he did so because they were mementoes of his father, or because he found the notes inspiring, we will never know. Nor can we be sure that his archives contain all of his father's transcriptions. What is clear is that the father was anything but a know-nothing. We found no evidence of his purported "exaggerated machismo" or of contempt for the life of the mind.

———◦◦◦———

Is there credible evidence that, after his father's death, Pierre Trudeau's personality and behaviour changed radically? The thesis advanced by several biographers is that young Pierre acquired a double personality: at home, he was an attentive son to his mother. At school, he was an aggressive student, behaving erratically as he went through an identity crisis. Determined to find out the truth, we decided to search through Trudeau's personal archives to see what insight they could provide into whether the father's death affected the son's behaviour at school. Our assumption was that, if the death did indeed have so great an impact on the son's personality, we would surely find signs of it in the detailed monthly report cards on his grades, on his behaviour, and on his application to his studies. His report cards have almost all survived and are now located in the National Archives. What do they tell us?

It would be wrong to assert that young Pierre Trudeau was always the very model of propriety, or that his report cards present an unblemished record. But they most definitely do not support the reputation he gave himself as having been a turbulent pupil. True, his behaviour in the study hall earned him a few unenthusiastic reports of *e* (good), some rare occurrences of *ei* (mediocre), and a single instance of *i* (bad). With few exceptions, though, his report cards rate his conduct as "perfect" or "very good." This is especially true for his conduct and his application in class.

This student, who by his own account could never accept authority, who was supposedly a chronic troublemaker, in fact was to be found month after month with his name on the honour roll. That was true before his father's death, and it would remain true afterward. Was he expelled from class and even from school? There is no evidence of it in the record. No doubt he sometimes acted the clown. But the priests at Brébeuf do not seem to have taken that seriously. On the contrary, they clearly considered him a rising star. His breaches of discipline, through pranks, teasing, and deliberate provocation, were met with indulgence because they were perpetrated without malicious intent. They were even taken as signs of a burgeoning free spirit, and remained within the limits of what was considered tolerable. Trudeau knew and accepted those limits. As he confirms in his *Memoirs*,[29] "It was a joy to constantly test how far I could go without going too far." He came to know the difference between a sally that would throw the teacher off his stride, bringing down his anger, and one that would get the class laughing without provoking the teacher's wrath.

Did his report cards register a substantial change after the father's death? The only possible confirmation that we could find was that his report card of March 1935 – which immediately followed Charles-Émile's death – was torn up into little pieces. But, to our surprise, all the pieces were there and, once reassembled, were fully legible.[30] As before, that report was favourable, both regarding his behaviour and his monthly essay. In April, he stood first out of forty-six students. In May, his reports on his weekly behaviour ranged between *a* (perfect) and *ae* (very good), with a single *e* (good). That month, he stood third in his class.

For the two years that followed the death of his father, Pierre Trudeau's monthly reports reveal nothing out of the ordinary. He continued to perform splendidly as a student. After the summer holidays of 1935, he went into the fourth year, Versification. His reports on his behaviour indicate that his conduct was almost always "perfect" or "very good." And he almost always stood first out of twenty-six students. If the adolescent experienced his father's death as a great emptiness, that did not come out in his behaviour or in his academic results.

In his entire eight years at Brébeuf, there was only one occasion on which he was given a report grade of *i* (bad). That happened nearly two years after his father's death, in the report for February 1937. It was for his behaviour in study hall, and there were special circumstances. His brother, Tip, had caught a contagious disease and was quarantined. As a result, Pierre Trudeau became for the first time and for a few months a boarder at Brébeuf. He seems to have found that extremely regimented life uncongenial. His grades suffered for a short time – he got a grade of 37 out of 60 in translation from the Latin – and he must have acted up at least once in study hall to get that bad report. As for his behaviour in class, it ranged from "perfect" to "good" – somewhat below his usual standard. But, by the end of that year, Trudeau had improved and stood third, receiving an "honourable mention" as "the student who displayed the greatest spirit of order and economy." And his record as a top student would continue through his last three years at Brébeuf. He would accumulate an impressive number of first prizes, second prizes, and honourable mentions.

In addition to his brilliant performance as a student, Pierre Trudeau was active in the life of the college: he won several prizes for athletics, wrote plays that were performed at school assemblies, and was among a group of young people whom Father Rodolphe Dubé – better known as François Hertel – introduced to the world of culture. He also published articles in the student newspaper, the *Brébeuf*, and became its editor-in-chief in 1939. All told, the portrait that emerges is that of a youth who was well adjusted to his surroundings and who was much appreciated by those he dealt with. Let us, therefore, bury forever the fabrication that his father's death had a crippling effect on him and, instead, consider what his life at the college was really like.

———◈———

His brief experience as a boarder at the college during his brother's illness led him to write an unusually long monthly letter to his mother on March 23, 1937. The letter, as usual, was accompanied by the report, which this time contained a rebuke for his misbehaviour in study hall. Trudeau seized the occasion to poke fun at that reproof and at his life as a boarder.

Chère maman,

I am happy to hear that you are in good health and that Tip is improving.

To make my letters more lively, I often [in the past] played at being a boarder; today, I have the pleasure (if pleasure it be!) to be able to write much more naturally: no need to insist on the reason.

Well, yes! I, who have always been rather an even tempered boy, fearing God and respecting my neighbour, when I see myself now, nervous, worried, lost in thought, paler and thinner than ever, I have to wonder whether I will emerge whole from the trial in which fortune has thrust me. A few faithful friends, seeing my tense face, my wrinkled brow, my disheveled hair, have been trying to raise my morale by pointing out the advantages of being a boarder. "You're not forced to travel back and forth morning and evening," "You'll be able to afford a host of small pleasures with the money you save on streetcar tickets." "You'll be able to play pool all day Sunday." "Think of the education that you will be receiving," etc. Unfortunately, I can tell by their faces that they're not convinced themselves.

This month, I've already had a bad report, I won't try to explain it, it is inexplicable. I was just going along living my life as an honest man when, out of nowhere, Bam! A note. What's more, this will surprise you, I have become so blasé that I hardly cried at all when I got the news.

Just think of it, a young girl recently, when she heard that she had a bad report, committed suicide by drinking a quart of ink, and with ink at its current price! So this is no laughing matter: it could be a warning from Providence. It all starts with a bad report and it ends with the rope.

It's not that I'm complaining about being a boarder; I fully understand that it was the only solution, but still it's a shame: so many have turned out badly following similar catastrophes, the like of Peter Blood, John Dillinger, Captain Kidd, and so many other victims of circumstance.

It's a little hard to take, right, Maman? You are perhaps now protesting that it was always understood that I wouldn't be a boarder any longer than the circumstances required.

That's true; perhaps, after all, my pleading was unnecessary. And yet, I wasn't taking any chances in case, when you saw my three "first in composition" grades this month, you might decide to leave me as a boarder until the end of the year, since it was working out so well. After all, maybe these are only misfortunes (!).

So there you are. "Causa dicta est"; [the case has been pleaded] and while I await the verdict (I know it will be in my favour, I always knew it, but I had to write something!), I will mention some of the news of the month:

The sports holiday was a success; Brébeuf defeated Loyola yet again.

Besides the religion classes of Father Lamarche, we had a talk by Father Pouliot on "A Patriot of 1837," and two on career counseling; all were interesting, especially the first.

Today we visited the collection of paintings of Mr. Lallemand; it was quite enlightening.

I could be telling you about some incidents of my life as a new boarder, but for several reasons (including the censorship, the lack of time and of paper) I am obliged to wait till I see you at Easter.

And so. Au Revoir! Till Easter!

Hugs and kisses from your son,

Pierre

As became usual with him in his later years at Brébeuf, Trudeau alternated between writing seriously and writing tongue-in-cheek. This time, the letter, written as always in French, was mostly spoofing. The following year, the editor-in-chief of the *Brébeuf*, Paul Gérin-Lajoie, would describe in the student paper the vice president of the class of Rhétorique, Pierre Trudeau: "The perfect blend of the serious and the playful. Nothing knocks him off balance; he always comes up with the right word, sometimes devastating, but without malice, and all with an ingenuous naïveté that wins him acceptance. He can smile – very subtly – at others and at himself. In addition, first in his class, a true sportsman, a good and devoted friend."[31]

———◆———

Trudeau may have been a combination of the serious and the playful. But there were two subjects that he always took utterly seriously: the Jesuits' system of values and his studies. The Jesuits taught that God would judge human beings according to their actions. In consequence, part of the duty of every good Catholic was to fulfill a social mission. In Quebec, that meant in part that one must struggle for the "survival" of the French-Canadian people. God gave this people a mission that the students explored as an important part of the curriculum. The "knowledge of the providential mission of our race – the mission of a people can be deduced from the capacities and the aptitudes which it received from the Creator," was listed as one of the topics in one of Trudeau's courses in history.

For the people to fulfill its divine mission, it must be led by an elite; and so it was the duty of the students in the classical colleges to prepare themselves to exercise that leadership. They recognized it. This sense of obligation, of *noblesse oblige*, was expressed in the *Brébeuf* by its editor, Paul Gérin-Lajoie, who would later be one of the leading figures of the Quiet Revolution and Quebec's first minister of education since 1875: "The internal and external power of a people depends on the elite. . . . The absence of competence means the degradation of a people. The lamentable and lamented state of the French Canadian race at the present time forces us to acknowledge this fact. . . . It is now that we must work to form this elite, and it is from our ranks that it must emerge, to a great extent, young men of Brébeuf!"[32] Many of the students at Brébeuf were convinced that they had a God-ordained mission to save the people. Certainly Pierre Trudeau accepted that he personally had such a mission. He believed that a good student who was a good Catholic had a duty also to be a nationalist.

Nationalism and religion together constituted the combined fundamental values that infused all the life of the college. Brébeuf even developed a reputation as a bastion of separatism. It was thought that an anti-English attitude was fostered there as well as a revolutionary frame of mind. Gérin-Lajoie felt called upon to defend his college in the student paper against what he considered unfounded charges. The title of his article was already revealing: "French Canadians first and foremost."[33] He meant to rebut the insinuations of ultra-nationalism, but he also succeeded in communicating revealingly how the students felt about the education they received. "I protest vehemently, as editor-in-chief of the official organ of the students of Collège Jean-de-Brébeuf, against this unfounded rumour and those prejudices of suspect origin according to which the authorities and the teaching staff of the college convey to the students ideas of revolting against the Canadian democracy and the sovereignty of the British crown." He went on to concede that individual students might be called "separatists" or "revolutionaries." But that could not in any way describe the attitudes of the authorities or of the student body. He then took up the accusation that the school was "*anti-Anglais.*" Not so, he insisted. But, as a French-Canadian college, Brébeuf was under no obligation to give equal treatment to French and English. He then issued the ringing statement that went far beyond his headline, and that spoke volumes about attitudes then and there: "At Brébeuf, we are French Canadian first and French Canadian only!"

Nevertheless, he insisted, the general atmosphere was broad-minded. The Jesuit teachers fostered freedom of inquiry and a critical sense. The students received an education "calculated to have us acquire precise ideas [about political systems] and to come to our own conclusions." A few paragraphs further on, however, he made clear that this freedom of inquiry and critical sense were to be exercised in the service of a single cause for one and all: "The education that we receive is precisely intended to produce minds that will search for the causes and the explanations, and will thereby be capable of leading opinion, of serving the great causes: *Religion et Patrie.*"[34]

At Brébeuf, it seems, every effort was made in the 1930s to develop free spirits who, remarkably, would then agree to promote the two fundamental values of their Jesuit teachers: Catholicism and French-Canadian nationalism. They remained convinced that they were being taught what they needed to know in order to develop their own unfettered thinking. They saw themselves as free because they had so fully internalized the values of Jesuit education that they could not conceive of not

wanting to defend their people, their religion, and their language. These
students were so convinced that they were independent-minded and free
that they were prepared to rush to the defence of their college, as philosophy student Jean-Paul Bérubé did in a letter to the student paper.

He was writing in response to an article that had appeared in the
student paper of a sister Jesuit college located in Quebec City, Collège
Saint-Charles Garnier. The author, one René Lévesque – the future
separatist premier of Quebec – took aim at the snobbish students of Jean-
de-Brébeuf: "There are some of us here who imagine you as dressed to the
nines, like models in fashion ads, . . . or again as high hats who think they
have everything, '*the best of the world*,' [in English in the French text] and
who, nose in the air, look down on everything that wasn't extracted from
your island. . . . These are illusions and gross misrepresentations, I am
sure, but you will clear up these notions, won't you?"

Bérubé replied:35 "So you want to know what we think of you, here
at Brébeuf? Well, to be perfectly frank, the answer is: not much. Why?
Because we almost never think of you people. This must come as quite
an insult, I imagine, if you think of yourselves as the center of the universe! But it just isn't so."

Bérubé then went on to explain to Lévesque that these petty quarrels
over turf must be set aside "in the interest of the Church and of la
Patrie." What characterized the Brébeuf students, he maintained, and the
reason why outsiders tended to consider them snobs, was that they were
"fundamentally independent, whether taken as a group or individually."
And he added: "When some pedagogues . . . accuse educational institutions of not sufficiently developing the personalities of their students,
they are surely not referring to Collège Jean-de-Brébeuf. No, here we are
not served up pre-digested food. Our teachers point out the way, but they
don't push us into it against our will. Each one of us manages as best he
can, but in his own way." And yet, almost all the students, including
Trudeau, ended up with identical values with respect to Catholicism and
French-Canadian nationalism. And they were convinced that they
reached these values of their own free will.

———— ◆ ————

How did the Jesuits of Brébeuf succeed in putting their distinctive
imprint on students like Pierre Trudeau? An analysis of the course

descriptions in the classical colleges, as well as of their rules and regulations, reveals that the instruction conveyed was kept within a narrow range. The school libraries were notable above all for the important works of literature that, censored by the Church, were missing from the shelves. To bring any book into the college premises required written approval by a college authority, unless the book was on the program. Any book without that approval was confiscated. "The bad book: that was enemy number one," recalled Georges-Émile Lapalme,[36] who in 1961 would become Quebec's first minister of culture. "Those who were on to a new book every week were looked on with suspicion," wrote Albert Tessier, a priest who would become a pioneer of documentary film-making in Quebec.[37] At Collège Sainte-Marie, "reading bad books or immoral newspapers, or bringing them into the college" was considered grounds for expulsion.[38] Why was there such a fear of books?

Gabriel Compayré, the great nineteenth-century French historian of pedagogy, maintained that the Jesuits granted little value to intellectual culture for its own sake. They were rather wary of it and considered it a dangerous weapon that could not be entrusted to just anyone. So they concentrated on forming an intellectual elite, steeped in the faith, that could answer for the ordinary people, who were left in ignorance. Compayré wrote: "For Loyola, everything must be subordinated to faith, and the faith of the common people is best protected by their ignorance."[39] The view that unrestricted reading is dangerous might help to explain the fact that, in 1939, Ontario boasted 460 public libraries while Quebec had only twenty-six, of which all but nine were English. Nine public libraries for all of French-speaking Quebec![40] The church was vigilant over the books available to all French Canadians and not just to students. As recently as the 1960s, many books now considered to be part of a rounded education were on the Index.

In the courses dealing with literature, the emphasis was on control. The French classical period of the 1660s was most esteemed. As a result, noted the young Jesuit François Hertel, students had to read "works that are boring, too serious for their age, too preachy. . . . Why ignore romantic literature even when it is healthy?"[41]

Trudeau testified to the impact that Hertel had on himself and his friends when he wrote that the Jesuit "influenced a whole generation of students, outside as well as within Brébeuf." Trudeau never actually had

Hertel as a teacher, though Hertel taught literature at Brébeuf from 1931 to 1934. He got to know the popular young Jesuit during the two years that they overlapped at Brébeuf. But it was really later, while Hertel was teaching literature in 1936 at Collège Sainte-Marie, that they became close. Hertel felt a kinship with students, and they with him. He made himself available to them outside the classroom and with some – especially the brightest – he maintained true friendships. Roger Rolland, Trudeau's close friend, described Hertel as "an awakener of conscience." Trudeau would appreciate Hertel's "originality, his offhand way of defying social conventions and saying out loud what other people would only think to themselves."[42] He would also appreciate his sense of humour: "We could easily involve him in the weirdest pranks and mischief that we could dream up," like the Club of the Dying that Trudeau, Rolland, and Hertel had invented. But Trudeau's gratitude was for more than just good times. "Hertel was our guide into a number of new fields. In literature, . . . I remember the hours I spent reading, thanks to him, Ibsen and Dostoyevski, Thomas Hardy and Léon Bloy." Trudeau also credited him with introducing him to composers who were not generally known in Quebec, and to French-Canadian contemporary artists such as Alfred Pellan and Paul-Émile Borduas. "He naturally gravitated towards everything that was new or contrary to the tastes of the day."[43]

Hertel's criticism of the narrow range of literary works proposed on the curriculum confirmed his reputation as an innovator. But his advocacy for greater openness had its limits. As intellectual historian Catherine Pomeyrols analyzed it, the syllabus that Hertel had drawn up for his students included many of the authors associated with French nationalism, authors close to France's right-wing *Action française* as well as many Catholic writers. As Hertel stated in his 1938 pedagogical book, *L'enseignement des Belles-Lettres*, he would have his students "study mostly Catholic writers, without forgetting now and then to warn the students against bad masters."[44] So he was in no sense a proponent of unfettered reading. He took the precaution of warning that the readings must always be "healthy." To avoid his students being led astray by their own curiosity, he chose to read aloud in class selected passages from newspapers, magazines, or books that were deemed "dangerous." In this way, he explained, "with the attraction of the unknown being eliminated, most students will no longer be drawn to read the work."45 In this respect, Hertel was following an old Jesuit pedagogical practice. According to Gabriel Compayré, "The Jesuits would most often put in the hands of the youth only excerpts and selected passages. No doubt the main justification put forward for these mutilations was praiseworthy. Out of deference to the purity of childhood, they wanted to suppress in the ancient authors everything that could unsettle modesty, sully the imagination, or provoke precocious thoughts."46

Brébeuf's students were convinced that they had become acquainted with a vast range of authors who gave them a broad education from which to view the world. Trudeau, for example, seems to have been introduced to Italian writers, including Machiavelli; to Spanish writers, including Cervantes and Lope de Vega; to German writers, including Schiller, Goethe, Wagner, and Nietzsche; to Russian writers, including Dostoevsky and Tolstoy; and to a single Norwegian: Ibsen. An impressive list, granted, at first glance, especially given the fact that one of the authors, Machiavelli, was actually on the Index. But some perspective is restored by studying Trudeau's reading notes on these authors. All of them combined take up one half of a notebook.47 By contrast, his notes on the Greek authors, including his notes on the Greek language, cover three full notebooks.

Despite these constraints, the students had the impression that their pursuit of knowledge was unconfined, and Trudeau was no exception. Quite the contrary. He would consider in retrospect that the Jesuits had nourished his mind opulently. In his *Memoirs*, he recalled that his Jesuit teachers had conveyed to him "a passion for knowledge," to the extent that he pursued knowledge even beyond the requirements of his teachers. "I am fascinated by learning about humans and things. For instance, we had this thick textbook on physics and the professor might say: OK, you really don't need to read Chapter 3, because it won't be on the exam. But I just had to read Chapter 3 because I couldn't accept to forego any scintilla of science!"48

Quite obviously, much more than a scintilla of science was kept off-limits to students. And how did Trudeau react to the restrictions on his freedom to read? Why, with the best grace in the world. Even in his personal notes on his reading, which went far beyond what was required by

his teachers, we were unable to find a single indication that he had read
a forbidden book, or ever strayed into "dangerous" passages. What we
did discover was a long list of books that he proposed to read and that
he had submitted for approval to his teacher in his fifth year at Brébeuf,
Father Robert Bernier, as was the practice. Surprisingly, other than
some works by Alphonse Daudet, the list fails to include almost any of
the great French authors of the nineteenth and twentieth centuries.

Is it possible that he did, in fact, taste of forbidden fruit, but sup-
pressed any evidence of his dereliction, even in his private notes while
studying in Montreal, out of fear of discovery? Not at all. Until late in
his twenties, Trudeau never read a forbidden book without first getting
the Church's permission, because he felt conscience-bound by the strictures of Rome's *Index librorum prohibitorum*. He remained submissive
to the Index, not only during his years at Brébeuf, but also while he
studied law at the Université de Montréal, and later while studying at
Harvard University, and even later still when he studied in Paris. And
so, on April 7, 1941, toward the end of his first year at law school, he
wrote to Canon Albert Valois, an official working in the chancellery of
the archdiocese of Montreal, asking for permission to read some presumably dangerous books:[49] "Monsignor," his letter began

> I wish to be dispensed from the law of the Index, with respect to
> the following books:
>
>     – Matière et mémoire – Henri Bergson
>     – L'évolution créatrice – Henri Bergson
>     – Le Prince – Machiavel
>     – Le Contrat social (discours, lettres, etc.) – J-J. Rousseau
>     – L'esprit des lois – Montesquieu
>     – Essais – Montaigne
>     – Le Discours de la Méthode (Méditations, etc.) – Descartes
>     – Le Capital – Karl Marx
>
> I took the precaution of having my request endorsed by my
> former teacher at Jean-de-Brébeuf, the Reverend Father Léon
> Langlois.

Would you please, Monsignor, present to his Excellency, the Archbishop, my humble supplication as well as the expression of my respectful submission, and be assured of my great gratitude.

Your servant,

Pierre Elliott Trudeau

A letter dated two days later informed him that the requested permission was denied. "His Excellency fears too greatly the pernicious effects on you of these readings."[50] But it seems likely that Trudeau made a new representation – perhaps amending the list – because on April 17 the requested permission came through, though with a note of caution: "His Excellency recommends that you use these books only with the greatest prudence, and while remaining on guard." Two of the works, by Bergson and Machiavelli respectively, had been removed from the list. At the time that he submitted his request, he had already read a month earlier another work by Bergson, *Les deux sources de la morale et de la religion*, published in 1932, which was never placed on the Index.

Trudeau did not go to the trouble of seeking ecclesiastical permission for his reading merely because he was then living in a city under powerful clerical influence. No, as the future would confirm, he did so out of conviction. On November 17, 1944, when Trudeau had turned twenty-five and was a student at Harvard, he wrote to the office of the local archbishop, again requesting permission to read books that were on the Index. On November 20, he received his answer from Archbishop's House, Lake Street, Brighton, Mass., authorizing him to "read all the books and documents required for your studies in political science and economics at Harvard University."[51] Trudeau pencilled in, after the word *read*, the words: "and keep . . . even during vacation time." The exchange of letters shows just how seriously the adult Trudeau took the Church's Index of Prohibited Books.

Almost three years later, now studying in Paris, Trudeau again put in a request for a dispensation, so that he could read prohibited books for the sake of his education. On January 29, 1947, the twenty-seven-year-old student received an official document from the archdiocese of Paris that declared: "We grant permission to Mr. Pierre Trudeau, for a period of three years from today, to read books *on the Index* and to keep them in his possession, but while keeping them enclosed so that no one can take them. This permission does not extend to books that treat of immoral subjects or which, *ex professo* [purposely] attack the religion. Mr. Pierre Trudeau must always, before reading a book on the Index, take council from a prudent confessor."[52]

The paradox remains. How is it possible to reconcile Trudeau's submission to these constraints, which today would seem excessive, with his often repeated claim that he could "never accept authority or the argument from authority"? The apparent contradiction is resolved by understanding that Trudeau had fully internalized the teachings of the Church and the values of the Jesuits. During all his days at Brébeuf, and even often while a student at the Université de Montréal, he had the habit of inscribing on all of his notebooks and most of his homework the Jesuit acronym, A.M.D.G., *Ad Majorem Dei Gloriam* – for the greater glory of God.

# Chapter 3

# BRÉBEUF AND THE
# MAKING OF A LEADER

*We were turned into fanatics and happy to be such.*
— JEAN-CHARLES HARVEY
*Le jour,* July 25, 1942

TRUDEAU APPRECIATED ALL OF HIS COURSES, but especially all the classes devoted to religion. In his long letter to his mother of March 23, 1937, which we quoted in Chapter 2, the only classes he mentioned were the religion classes of Father Maurice Lamarche. Two years later, on March 29, 1939, when he was nineteen and in his second-last year at Brébeuf, he jotted down detailed notes to which he gave the title: "Notes inspired by the lectures given by Father Lamarche." He was referring to his professor of philosophy, Maurice Lamarche, S.J. It seems clear in retrospect that the ideas expressed in these notes were to play a notable role in his own moral development and provide him with a model for the kind of man he wanted to become.

> See the truth wherever it is to be found. If one is not strong enough to act accordingly, that is too bad. But one should at least be loyal enough to recognize that what is true is true. . . . One must really be detached from the good things of this earth. . . . A Christian must do everything he does for the love of God: study, eat, live, suffer, enjoy, everything must be done with the *real*[1]

intention of pleasing God. . . . One should not fear to be
uncompromising; mocking smiles make little difference if one
is right. . . . Never back down when faced with difficulties.
Show your colours before God and men. . . . When one has
good ideas . . . of one's own, decide and *put them into execution*
*tion* quickly."

Always look for the truth and recognize it, even if one is not up to acting
accordingly. Act according to one's conscience without worrying about
mocking smiles. Are these not the very principles that Trudeau would
practise all his life? In his notes, Trudeau wrote that Father Robert
Bernier added to what Father Lamarche said: "Be more jovial, more like-
able for everyone. Let the petty politicians talk and smile, but keep back
one's important ideas for one's speeches and writings." To be uncompromising about one's ideas and principles, to recognize the importance
of expressing one's ideas in a structured way, these traits would characterize the future polemicist and, later, the statesman.

Father Bernier, Trudeau's teacher in 1936–37, when he was in the class
of Belles-Lettres, was also the man whom he later remembered as having
most influenced him during his student days: "He not only made you study
the right works but he incited you to read."[2] And Father Bernier agreed
with that assessment when he was interviewed in 1969 by *New Yorker*
journalist Edith Iglauer: "We passed books back and forth. Literature, philosophy, music, painting – all went together."[3] He remembered that period
as ideologically liberal in thought and political philosophy. "I also gave
them a history course. I insisted not only on facts and dates but on
thoughts: the importance of the democratic spirit and the idea of federalism as a way of having political unity and cultural differences in the same
country – a pluralistic society. . . . We could easily enter into the mind of
Locke, de Tocqueville, Acton, Jefferson. Our little life gave the boys
respect for the rational, an instinctive repulsion against the rising
Fascism and Nazism."[4]

Time does dim the memory and sometimes turns wishes into memories. Under Bernier's influence, did Trudeau and his classmates really
penetrate the thinking of John Locke or Lord Acton? If Bernier did
read aloud from their works, it was probably in the spirit of Hertel's

recommendation to disarm curiosity and remove temptation: serve them innocuous samples. Trudeau's notes give no indication of his having read these authors.

Father Bernier's memory also seems to have failed him when he recalled communicating to his students an appreciation for democracy and "an instinctive repulsion [*sic*] against Fascism and Nazism." Trudeau retained a different memory of how fascism was presented at that time. Here is what he told us: "You who read the history books, what do they say today about this period? I know very well what people were saying then. They said that Pétain was a hero and de Gaulle was a traitor. They said that Mussolini, Salazar, and Franco were admirable corporatist leaders. They said that the democratic leaders were sell-outs. That is the atmosphere in which I was brought up. Jean-Louis Roux and Pelletier as well."5 Which of the two is one to believe? Unfortunately for the good priest, Trudeau's retrospective account is faithful to the period.

Father Bernier's claim to have promoted federalism, democracy, and pluralism seems to be based on a memory lapse. In Trudeau's notes from the period, when he was the Jesuits's student, we found no trace of the promotion of federalism, democracy, or a pluralist society. But we did find an interesting clue. In his *Memoirs*, Trudeau recalls that Father Bernier had asked the students to write an essay on how they envisioned their own future. "There must still be a copy of my piece sleeping somewhere in my files. I remember that I expressed extravagant ambitions. I wanted first of all to be a deep sea captain, then an explorer, then an astronaut – a term that had not yet been invented, except to denote a character out of Jules Verne. In short, I wanted to know everything and experience everything, in every realm. Maybe the essay even envisaged that some day, at the end of my life, I might become an important figure such as a governor general or a prime minister. But first, I would have explored the world."6

We were able to discover this essay that was indeed sleeping in his files. The young Trudeau did describe there his little voyage around the world. But an important part of the essay seems to have slipped from his memory. The following passage would seem to suggest that, if Father Bernier sang the virtues of federalism, the lesson seemed to have been lost on his star student.

"If I have the good fortune to get my hands on a war, I will join the air force on the losing side. Then, after first carrying out many hair-raising exploits, I will manage to blow up the enemy's munitions factories and I will win the war for my side. I return to Montreal sometime around the year 1976: the time is ripe to declare Quebec's independence. The Maritime provinces join with us, and so does Manitoba. I take command of the troops and lead the army to victory. I now live in a country that is Catholic and *canadien*."[7]

Preposterous, but true: in 1936, Trudeau saw himself as leading the troops that would make Quebec independent and Catholic in 1976. In fact, in 1976 the Parti Québécois would come to power on a program to hold a referendum on the secession of Quebec. But Trudeau's fantasy of a coup d'état hardly suggests that he was impregnated with the culture of federalism, of democracy, or of pluralism.

Pluralism was not something that pervaded the atmosphere of Brébeuf, at a time when the nationalist leader Lionel Groulx was trumpeting a campaign in favour of "*l'Achat chez nous*" – buy from our own people. "Our people" clearly did not include Jewish merchants or others who failed the ethnic test. Trudeau wrote a play that was performed as part of the celebrations for the tenth anniversary of the college's founding. It was described in the program as "a satirical comedy in one act by Pierre-E. Trudeau." On the title page of his script, he wrote: "A comedy of manners in one act performed for the first time on May 16, 1938, before parents and students with great success." It conveyed the latent xenophobia that was inculcated at that time. The script took up twelve typewritten pages. In a first draft, Trudeau had written down the title he originally intended for the play: "*On est Canadiens français ou on ne l'est pas.*" That was a popular saying, about the equivalent of, "Well, are we or are we not French Canadians?" He then changed the title to *Roulés*, and then to *Dupés*. Both words mean the equivalent of: "We've been had!"

The play had seven characters and was intended to bring out the difference between dishonest and profiteering Jews and honest but too naive French Canadians. Trudeau himself played the role of a young Jew by the name of Ditreau – the name is a pun; with the same sound but spelled differently, it means "talks too much"; the name expressed what the character was meant to convey. Ditreau applies for a job in a French Canadian's tailor shop. The owner of the shop is called Couture – a family name in Quebec which also means "sewing," a humorous touch. Couture was played by Jean de Grandpré, who was later to be chairman of Bell Canada Enterprises and, from 1984 to 1991, chancellor of McGill University.

Before Ditreau is hired, he must prove his ability as a salesman. So he sets about demonstrating how he would sell a cheap suit at a high price, thereby making a fool of the client.

> *Ditreau*: Thanks to my knowledge of psychology, I know how to approach every client according to his character. Now, you see, your store is in a French Canadian neighbourhood. Well, French Canadians prefer to buy from a Jew, in the first place so as not to enrich one of their own, and then because they think they will be able to get a better price. . . .

> *Couture*: (exploding finally) Now it's my turn to teach a lesson: the *Canadien* people is a sleeping lion. It will soon awaken. But I am a light sleeper and I advise you, while it's still time, to take all your things and beat it.

The message was hardly subtle. The moral was that French Canadians must wake up and do what Couture did – throw out all the Ditreaus in their world. That such a play was chosen by Quebec's most elite college to celebrate its tenth anniversary and was "a great success" speaks volumes. It hardly preached pluralism.

The nationalism inculcated at Brébeuf had several dimensions. The play *Dupés* illustrated one dimension, that of anti-Semitism and xenophobia. Other dimensions are evident in a course titled "History of Canada" taught by Father Brossard during Trudeau's school year of 1937–38. We found the typed outline of the course in Trudeau's archives. Each of the following sections refers the students to further readings that we will pass over quickly:

## Introduction: Why study the history of Canada?

A. GENERAL NECESSITY:

1. The formation of a healthy and enlightened patriotism:
Handed over, we have obtained, both by the treaties and by our constitutional struggles, everything which makes it possible to exist « chez nous », as a people, as a distinct nationality. (cf. Groulx, *Naissance d'une race*, Preface: p. 1-13)

2. Knowledge of the providential mission of our race
– The mission of a people can be deduced from the capacities and the aptitudes which it received from the Creator . . .
– As for us, as we are a completely new people, our mission is that of the people from whom we emerged: to propagate Catholic and French ideas in America. . . .

B. PRESENT NECESSITY:

1. To know the French regime . . . for our people are subjected to:
   a)  the impact of world wide materialism: (cf. Daniel-Rops, *Le monde sans âme*, p. 128 and following)
   b)  a decline in faith . . . (cf. Doncœur, Lent 1934 – Sermon: The God crucified, p. 14) . . .

2. To know the English regime: (the source of our legal rights):
   a)  to exploit it in our favour . . .
   b)  to rekindle our patriotism . . .
   c)  so that harmony might reign in Canada . . .
   d)  to prepare our national future (cf. Orientations, Groulx, – conference with the title: nos positions, p. 240-274) . . .

In this enormous enterprise, what will be your assignment, young people? . . . We are leaving you, I know, a very heavy legacy. . . . You have not only the right, you have the duty to recognize our situation with a clear and realistic vision. . . . Young people, I beg of you, stand up and save us. You are caught in the dilemma of dying ignobly or living daringly: choose to live with daring, even if only to demonstrate to this country that needs it so badly, the indomitable strength of your faith, the admirable dignity of Catholicism.

The works of the clerico-nationalist historian Lionel Groulx obviously loom very large in this course outline. The sentences in the quotation are entirely drawn from a speech titled "Nos positions," which Groulx delivered on February 9, 1935, at Quebec's Chateau Frontenac. It was then published that same year in a collection of his writings under the title *Orientations*.[8] As the speech was on the list of compulsory reading, we can be certain that Trudeau read every line. So what vision did Groulx project?

From the beginning Groulx set a tone suggesting a state of crisis. "The little people that we are . . . could come to an end." The Conquest "brought face to face two peoples, two beliefs, two cultures with deep divergences, two *physiques*, if I may say, with terribly unequal power. Which would win out? *To be or not to be*, that would become, in all its tragic simplicity, the formula of our life."[9]

He subscribed to the theory of the two equal founding peoples: "We believe in the legal equality of the two nationalities before the federative constitution."[10] And he proposed a goal that would become the war cry of later nationalists: "To become again masters in our province."[11] He gave examples of how French Canadians were dominated: "What about our cities? I scarcely dare mention Montreal, Montreal which is in the grip of Anglo-Canadian finance, of Anglo-Canadian commerce, of Anglo-Canadian utilities, of American cinema, of suspect and cosmopolitan restaurants, gambling dens, songs, and radio. And then there's Quebec, once the head and heart of New France!"[12] Who were his "interlopes et cosmopolites," which we translated as "suspect and cosmopolitan." They were almost certainly code words referring to Jews. To become again "maîtres dans notre province," he promoted "*l'Achat chez nous*,"[13] a campaign slogan to convince French Canadians that they should make all their purchases from stores belonging to "our own" rather than Jews. This, most likely, was what inspired Trudeau to write his play, *Dupés*.

Groulx, in this speech, best expressed his vision – a fusion of religion and nationality – under the word *mystique*. It must be at once French and Catholic. "What must we do to take hold of ourselves, to reform the line of our destiny? Gentlemen, there is a word that I don't like to turn away from its religious usage, but that I will use for lack of a better and because it is in style: what we need is a mystique. There will be no French state, no French people, without a French mystique. . . . And we need an organic mystique, . . . that is clear, imperious, inebriating, able to raise the genius of a race to a supreme tension – the mystique, the watchword which will go reverberating to the farthest corners of the province: *Un peuple français dans un pays français!*"[14] – a French people in a French country.

It is now obvious that, despite the general assumption to the contrary, Trudeau was entirely familiar with Groulx's thinking, and that Groulx had enormous influence in fashioning the vision of Canadian history propagated by the Jesuits. We can give an example. On September 24, 1937, the students had a choice of two topics for an assignment, one of which began: "You are giving a talk on the reasons for your patriotism and you will comment on this sentence spoken by Lionel Groulx . . ." In the same notebook in which Trudeau had recorded that assignment, he also wrote down what seems to have been talking points for a debate. He proposed that a law should be passed to foster the Catholic religion, the use of French, a high birthrate, and the return to the land where the people would be sheltered from Americanization. These were all ideas expressed in class at Brébeuf, and all were favourite projects of Father Groulx. For example, Father Brossard taught his students that they "must be respectful towards France. It is she that formed us from the beginning and, even today, it is from her that we receive all our intellectual culture." This sentiment was faithful to Groulx. But so was his caution that what they must admire was the Catholic France of the Ancien Régime. "We owe nothing to the blue, white and red flag; it is the first, the fleur de lys flag, that we remember."[15]

———◈———

Inspired by his history classes, on November 20, 1937, Trudeau took part in an oratorical contest and gave a speech that he entitled "The survival of the French Canadian nation."[16] We found the written text in his archives. The topic proposed to the students for development was this: "Do you believe in the historic reality of the French-Canadian nation? Do you believe in its survival?" Trudeau began in Cartesian fashion. First, the reality of the French-Canadian nation had to be established.

But then he quickly added: "I will spend little time on the first point: you all admit the existence of this race of three million people – you are part of it – called the French Canadians: Canadians, because of the country they inhabit and French because, biologically and intellectually, they cannot claim to be anything else. And no one denies that they have the will to live collectively, and have their own proper territory and political organization." Trudeau threw in a play on words. He used the word *propre*, which in French usually means "clean" but can also mean "proper." He went on: "Should I say *propre*?" He paused to let his sarcastic reference to politics sink in, before he added: "But let's go on." Trudeau's speaking style as a student was always to throw in surprises, in the form of puns, ironies, or sly jokes.

He did not waste time demonstrating the existence of *la nation*. The speakers were not asked to prove it, they were asked to affirm their faith in it. Trudeau did so briefly, then turned to what concerned him: *la survivance*. It was an issue of great concern in the 1930s. "It is also a fact that it [la nation] will survive, despite this fatal tendency to continental assimilation." He then proceeded to his demonstration.

His first argument was demographic. He evoked "the famous *canadien* miracle: the rate of survival in the French province of Quebec is double that of Ontario and three times that of British Columbia. The numerical superiority of the Anglo-Saxon element is rapidly diminishing along with the decline in immigration." Trudeau was speaking in the later years of the Depression when Canada had imposed severe restrictions on immigration. In French Quebec, by contrast, thanks to the "revenge of the cradle" preached by priests and politicians alike, families of twelve or more children were not uncommon. So French Canadians could hope some day to constitute the majority in the country. Trudeau agreed with the French-Canadian elite in considering both immigration and emigration as threats: immigration, because it augmented the number of English-speaking Canadians; emigration, because French Canadians moving from Quebec to New England reduced the French-speaking population of Canada. "And so, the more we prevent the emigration of our people by encouraging the return to the land, the swifter will be our ascension."

His speech evoked all the main pieties of the day. "To maintain our French mentality, what we must do is to preserve our language and to

shun American civilization." French Canadians must survive by withdrawing within themselves. There was also the sacred cause of religion,
which was, he said, "of importance beyond all else." He was referring
to the God-appointed mission of the French-Canadian people. "If
Providence permitted the Conquest for our own good, as I have no
doubt, it was because It has a precise role that we are to play: the role of
propagating Catholic and French ideas in the New World." It followed
that French Canadians had an obligation not only to survive, but to
become greater. "And we will only become greater to the extent that we
struggle for our Catholic faith, for our rights as *Canadiens*, and for our
French language."

We do not know what success Trudeau had in the oratorical contest.
But we know for certain that, like a dutiful student, he served up all the
ideas that he had been taught, without a trace of originality. He had
touched on all the great themes outlined in his history class: the revenge
of the cradle, the return to the land, the apostolic mission of the French-
Canadian "race," which is even a biological entity. That day, he was
certainly not rowing against the current.

Nor was it only at Brébeuf that these religio-nationalist convictions
were inculcated in the students. At the other end of the province, by the
sea in the coastal town of Gaspé, another classical college was run by
the Jesuits on behalf of the Catholic diocese there. It was called le
Séminaire de Gaspé, and one of its students would one day engage in
ideological and political warfare with Pierre Trudeau. That student's
name was René Lévesque.

In 1936, the thirteen-year-old René Lévesque had written an article
for the student newspaper – it was called *L'Envol* – in which the boy also
discussed the theme of "*la survivance*" of the French-Canadian nation.
He gave five reasons why "*la survivance*" was justified. We will quote
only two of the five.

> 1. Our religion and our language. "The language is the guardian
> of the faith." That is why I link together these two divisions.
> Surrounded by the Protestants, almost invisible in this immense
> swarming of 137,000,000 Anglo-Saxons who encircle us, we are
> threatened, not by bolts of lightning, but by a slow and sneaky
> penetration. Thus imperiled, we have no other defence than to

struggle, and to struggle for life, that is, for our survival [*la survivance*].

2. The mission of our race. "The French nation," Lacordaire has said, "has a mission to accomplish in the world." In America, it is up to us, the sons of this same France, to fulfill this mission: our duty is precisely to project over materialistic America the light of French culture, of that spiritual culture which, alone, we possess. Now, to do so, as everyone will understand, we must remain "integrally French."[17]

In Montreal, as in the Gaspé, the Jesuits used the same mould to fashion their students' thinking. In both places, the students believed that they were voicing their personal opinions, at which they had arrived freely.

———◦———

This religious indoctrination permeated everything, notably, the teaching of literature. In 1936–37, Trudeau took a survey course called "History and Precepts of Literature," taught by Father Bernier. It covered in principle all periods and all forms of writing. In the class notes that Trudeau took on the various authors studied, based on what Father Bernier said or wrote on the blackboard, there invariably was a reference to the author's faith or morals. About Rabelais, Trudeau wrote: "He believes in God; he renders homage to Jesus Christ as to a great prince, but that's it." And Trudeau scribbled this conclusion: "Hardly a high standard of morality. Inexcusably, he spread filth throughout his writing. . . . There is little pleasure to be had reading him. Notice: vulgar sentiments, French gaiety, style." All the authors were evaluated with respect to their Catholic fervour. The young Trudeau noted that "Their influence stems from their private lives and not merely their writings." And so, the notes dealt in the following terms with Maurice Barrès, an ultra-nationalist writer who had joined the anti-Semitic movement to condemn the innocent Alfred Dreyfus and professed a revanchist patriotism: "He came to the defense of the Catholic religion. However, he was wrong in giving equal treatment to all religions. . . . But he himself lacked the courage to be a Catholic and his works are not sufficiently doctrinal." The Jesuits of Brébeuf faulted the extremist Barrès for an excess of moderation!

Given the centrality of religion at Brébeuf, it will not come as a surprise that Trudeau could have written, in his notes on Plato's *Republic*:
"It is admirable that, before Jesus Christ, one could find in a pagan many
Christian ideas."[18] Like his teachers, Trudeau judged Plato by the standard of Christianity.

————◦————

In one of his notebooks, devoted exclusively to French authors, especially from the nineteenth century, Trudeau would make a note each time
the teacher mentioned a book that was on the Index. Among them was
Charles Baudelaire's *Fleurs du mal*. Surprisingly, though, the teacher
apparently was lenient in his treatment of Baudelaire, except to say that he
was "an unbalanced mind." That observation was redeemed, however, by
this note: "He received the sacraments." On Victor Hugo, Trudeau filled
several pages. The ambivalence of the teacher came through: he did not like
Hugo's pride, but he appreciated that he "sang of nature, country, family."

Authors of the twentieth century were classified, not according to lit-
erary criteria, but under one or the other of two categories: 1) The
Catholic renewal and 2) Authors who were not Catholic. The first cate-
gory included Joris-Karl Huysmans, Maurice Barrès, Paul Bourget, René
Bazin, Léon Bloy, Charles Péguy, François Mauriac, and Henri Petiot,
known as Daniel-Rops. The second category included, for poetry: Paul
Valéry, Émile Verhaeren, Paul Fort; and for prose: Charles Maurras,
André Gide, Marcel Proust, André Maurois, and Georges Duhamel.

In one notebook that dealt with the literary works studied in class,
Trudeau wrote down his own thoughts and often took positions that were
quite at variance with an author's established reputation. Of Molière's
much appreciated play *Le Bourgeois gentilhomme*, he had this to say:
"There's a wealth of bons mots, but otherwise I don't find there any great
quality. The plot is loose and boring, if plot there is."[19] He could even be
critical of Jean Racine, the favourite playwright of the classical colleges. He
read the play *Athalie*[20] twice, with an interval of nine months between
the readings. The first time, he found it "extremely boring"; the second, he
had swung around to describe it as "extremely interesting and beautiful."
Later, he read Racine's *Phèdre* and was moved to enthusiasm: "Decidedly,
the more I read Racine, the better I like him. The play is extremely interesting. . . . We have there an extremely interesting study of guilty passion."

Then, on April 19, 1938, he wrote that the play *Andromaque* was Racine's first masterpiece. The next day he read the comedy *Les Plaideurs* and observed: "Honestly, I just don't recognize Racine. . . . There are several scenes that sparkle with banter and bons mots."

He loved to read, especially the great classics of literature, and was particularly fond of pithy sentences that he encountered in his reading. He copied out entire passages that covered pages in his notebooks. And he recorded his personal reactions, sometimes congratulating himself on having caught the meaning of a work reputed difficult, at other times expressing his pleasure at reading at last a great classic work. After reading Paul Claudel's play *L'annonce faite à Marie*, he wrote: "I had been told that it would be hard to understand, but I'm pleased to say that I really did understand it." In May 1938, after browsing through Charles Péguy's *Prose choisie*, he was moved to emulation: "I didn't get to read much of it, for lack of time. But what I read pleases me enormously. The style is just extraordinary; it is one of the styles that I would most want to have myself. Short sentences, repetitions." Then, after reading Sophocles's *Oedipus Rex*,[21] during the summer holidays of 1938, he was triumphant: "Finally I have read it, the masterpiece of ancient tragedies."

Reading Edmond Rostand's play *Cyrano de Bergerac*[22] filled him with the joy of discovery: "It is probably the play that I have most enjoyed," he noted. "One can't help but be affected by the end of Act V. What sustains the interest of the whole play is the character of Cyrano as painted by Rostand, so that one can't help but admire him." Most of Trudeau's biographers have stressed the admiration that Trudeau felt for Cyrano and they mention the line: "Not to rise so very high, but to do it alone," that Trudeau is said to have quoted during an interview. Stephen Clarkson and Christina McCall again leaped to conclusions about Trudeau's personality: "In identifying with Cyrano, Trudeau was appropriating a mythic model for his life, formulating the dream in which every young adult wraps his goals. . . . His life dream took on a particularly dramatic form: he would perform amazing feats and win special honours. He would yearn – as he openly admitted – to climb alone to the heights."[23]

We consider it an exaggeration to give such importance to Trudeau's admiration for Cyrano. For many francophones, Cyrano stood out among the great heroes of their childhood. That was in no way unique to Trudeau. There is nothing surprising about his quoting a line from Cyrano to express one of his own ideas – especially when you know how much he loved to quote lines. Moreover, what he said to his biographer George Radwanski is illuminating: "I found there an expression of who I was and what I wanted to be: I don't care if I don't make it, providing I don't need anyone else's help, providing what I do make I make alone, you know, without begging for favours."[24]

Trudeau was inspired, not so much by the exploits of Cyrano, as by the fact that Cyrano was willing to fail. Like Cyrano, Trudeau wanted to succeed by himself, owing his success to no one but himself. But if Trudeau did have a model for his own life, it was certainly not Cyrano. The person who inspired him, whom he wanted to imitate, was Christ. He would express this in a speech in defence of eloquence that he wrote out on September 23, 1937: "Eloquence, the real thing, far from being achieved by tricks of speech, rests on sincerity; its goal is truth. Its objective is solely to make men better and happier. . . . The proof stands in the example of just one man, the most eloquent of all, Jesus Christ." He drew the conclusion that true eloquence must be promoted, and that "all false rhetoricians must be driven from the face of the earth."[25] Later, he would publish articles in the *Brébeuf* urging his fellow students to imitate Christ.

While Cyrano was not Trudeau's greatest hero, it is true that he admired the man known for his gigantic nose. But it was for other reasons than those that get mentioned. "He is a good man, sensitive, intelligent, witty and without fear," he wrote. Notice the order he gives to Cyrano's qualities: in first place come goodness and sensibility, to be followed by intelligence and liveliness of mind. Courage came last.

We should point out in passing that here, as in most of his notes on his reading, Trudeau took a great interest in passages that lent themselves to recitation, and in scenes or even entire acts that he could play out. About *Cyrano*, he wrote that the soliloquy in Act II, scene 8 "is beautiful to recite." And he has a note in parentheses that shows that he was not speaking theoretically: "I won the first prize."

One work discussed in Trudeau's notes was John Henry Newman's celebratory sermon "The Second Spring," delivered in 1852 after Pope Pius IX had restored the Catholic hierarchy in the United Kingdom. Newman had been a prominent Anglican at Oxford, part of the "Oxford Movement" that questioned some doctrines of the Church of England. He converted to Catholicism in 1845, and later was named a cardinal, giving a new lustre to the Church in England. In Catholic Quebec, his lustre and his eminence were celebrated as a vindication of Catholicism. The late Claude Ryan, who achieved prominence as publisher of *Le Devoir* and leader of the Liberal Party of Quebec, declared that Newman's words had guided his life.[26] Trudeau also had notes on another Englishman, Charles Forbes, better known as France's Comte de Montalembert. After he moved to France, he became one of the most prominent and ardent defenders of Catholicism, and especially of the freedom of the Catholic Church to establish Catholic schools in the face of republican opposition. Trudeau studied Montalembert's *Trois Discours sur la liberté de l'Église*, dating from 1844, and wrote down Montalembert's famous sentence: "We are the sons of the Crusaders and we will not retreat before the children of Voltaire." No doubt Trudeau had often heard it recited by his teachers.

---

Trudeau's notes also reveal how he reacted to French-Canadian writing. His "first serious book," as he described it, was *Pour nous grandir*, by Victor Barbeau. He found it a little hard-going, but profitable.[27] He wrote down what he took to be the book's leading ideas: "Liberalism leads to excesses: to unemployment, anarchy. The ideal is corporatism, which does not separate people into parties, but unites their interests." There is not in Trudeau's notes the slightest evidence of his disapproval of corporatism. After all, Pope Pius XI had endorsed corporatism in his 1931 encyclical, *Quadragesimo anno*. Almost all of French Catholic Quebec, most notably the Jesuits, were at this time embracing corporatism as the best possible social system.

A novel published in 1937 caused quite a stir in Quebec. It was written by a priest, Félix-Antoine Savard, and was titled *Menaud, maître draveur*. It was considered a masterpiece at the time, and there are some who continue to consider Savard as "the incomparable minstrel of our dispossession."[28] Others find an incoherence and an implausible psychology in the main characters, who become "evanescent and unreal under the sentimental gushing, the patriotic and apologetic obsessions of the author."[29] Others still denounce the book's message of hate toward "*les étrangers*" who are *les Anglais*.[30] Most of Trudeau's contemporaries spoke most enthusiastically about the book. Jean-Louis Roux, the future eminent thespian, while a student at the Université de Montréal, wrote in the student paper, *Le Quartier Latin*, a glowing letter to Savard: "*Menaud, maître draveur* was for me the most beautiful of novels and you were the greatest of poets. . . . I was overcome by emotion before this vibrant poem written to the glory of the peasant."[31] Trudeau, however, had reservations, even as he appreciated it. "There is a multitude of admirable inventions," he wrote. "People go so far as to say that it is the *Canadien* masterpiece. From the first page, the book teaches a lesson of patriotism, of heroism. . . . The conclusion seems to be to love one's country, to defend it against the outsiders [*les étrangers*], while being careful not to become a coureur de bois: one must attach oneself to a piece of land. . . . As for me, I don't find it entirely pleasing as a lesson: it's simply a sad story that is well told. The descriptions are quite beautiful, but some passages seem psychologically weak."

It is notable that Trudeau expressed appreciation for the patriotic appeal to defend one's country – Quebec – against the "*étrangers*," who are, of course, English-speaking Canadians. Menaud, the main character, expresses the utmost hatred for them, as well as for French-Canadian traitors – those who agree to be hired by "*les Anglais*." One might have expected Trudeau to comment on this central lesson of the book, since many of his relatives were among the despised "*étrangers*." But he read the book entirely from the point of view of a French Canadian, contrary to the myth that presented him as riven by conflicting identities. In his environment, resentment against "*les Anglais*" was so commonplace that Brébeuf was accused in some quarters of fomenting xenophobia. André Laurendeau, then publisher of the nationalist publication *L'Action nationale*, felt obliged to come to the defence of the classical colleges in an article with a revealing title: "Do our schools teach hatred for the English?"[32] The editor-in-chief of the *Brébeuf* had provided his own answer to the question: "At Brébeuf, we are French Canadians first and French Canadians only!"[33]

Trudeau read several books by Lionel Groulx, beginning with *Chez nos ancêtres*. It inspired him to write that it "certainly makes me love the country."[34] He was referring to Quebec, not Canada. He devoted his next three and a half pages to copying down passages from Groulx's book. After reading Groulx's *Faites-nous des hommes*, he commented that it was "an interesting pamphlet" and that Groulx "proposes a totalitarian formula: what is needed is a total preparation." Then, on

February 27, 1938, after reading Groulx's *Rapaillages*, he wrote that "the delicate thoughts and the delicious images filled me with nostalgia for the life on the land." Trudeau, born in Outremont, living on the Island of Montreal, where his father had moved from the farm and made a fortune – like *"les Anglais"* – nevertheless found himself pining for a return to the land.

———◦———

In 1939, Trudeau read the first novel of his friend, François Hertel, titled *Le Beau risque*.[35] Though it is mediocre and lacking a coherent plot, its interest lies in Hertel's depiction of adolescent psychology in the Quebec of the 1930s, through the fictional diary of the novel's hero, Pierre Martel. The novel cleaves so close to reality that some scholars, such as Jesuit historian Jacques Monet[36] and political scientist Esther Delisle,[37] concluded that Pierre Martel is a barely disguised alter ego for Pierre Trudeau. There are obvious parallels. Pierre Martel's grandfather lived in the country, as did Trudeau's grandfather. Martel loved nature, poetry, and reading. Trudeau did as well. Martel spent part of his holidays at Old Orchard Beach, Maine; the Trudeau family had a summer residence there. Martel entrusts his diary to his spiritual director, the Jesuit Father Berthier. The name is close to that of Trudeau's favourite teacher, Father Bernier. Martel, as he matures through the novel, comes to reject materialism while discovering his Catholic faith and French-Canadian nationalism. He becomes committed to the campaign of *"l'Achat chez nous"* and for restoring the French face of Montreal. Martel confides that he has come to hate "Old Orchard! An American beach, Jewish and noisy. No fun at all. . . . As far as I'm concerned, I can no longer spend three days there. It makes me ill. And, you know, why should we go traveling abroad when we are so well off at home?"[38]

Two years after reading the novel, Trudeau wrote a letter to Hertel, dated September 5, 1941. His tone evidences the links of friendship that they had established. He tells the priest, among other things, about his recent trip to Old Orchard. "You might be aware of the judgment passed by some celebrated thinker or other," he joked. He then quoted word for word Hertel's passage on Old Orchard in *Le Beau risque*. He even gave the page number. And then he concluded: "My story ends with this beautiful quotation." Hertel had presented Pierre Martel as the model of the "*chef*," the leader, whom French Canadians were impatiently awaiting. He seems to have been inspired by the real-life Pierre Trudeau.

As for Trudeau, if he saw himself as the model for Pierre Martel, he left no record of it in his notes. He wrote, however: "The psychology seems to me right on, and the author caught the state of mind that many young people go through. The ending is touching, when the spiritual director, after he had laid out in theoretical terms what constitutes a true life – intense love of the French Canadian patrie, contempt for the frivolities that keep us far from God, contempt for materialism – then provides an example of the practical active life by sacrificing everything to become a missionary in China." The student was, once again, reflecting the fundamental values of Jesuit education. Father Berthier, for Trudeau, was giving an example of what the real life should be.

In his memoirs, Trudeau did acknowledge that Hertel influenced him, but without ever referring to Hertel's political views. His own biographers, with the exception of Esther Delisle,[39] limited that influence to the realm of culture. Now, Hertel had published writings that were eminently political, and it is inconceivable that Trudeau, such an avid reader, who had devoured the books of Groulx, of Barbeau, and other nationalist authors, could have ignored them. And so we must briefly examine Hertel's views.

In 1936, while he was a teacher at Brébeuf, Hertel published in book form, under the title *Leur inquiétude*,[40] an expanded version of what had previously appeared earlier that year as a series of articles in *L'Action nationale*. Hertel addressed the disquiet of French-Canadian youth, faced with the difficulties of mid-Depression Quebec. He related it to a similar disquiet of young people in the Communist Soviet Union, in Fascist Italy, in Nazi Germany, and in other countries as well. The Anglo-Saxon countries in particular, Hertel maintained, were ruled by the dictatorship of money and of electoral corruption so that youths lost their ideals and their values. French-Canadian youths suffered particularly from anguish because they belonged to a people that was a minority, and so they were deprived of the political instruments needed for the full flowering of their own values.

Echoing Groulx's position, Hertel argued that the fundamental problem stemmed from "a federal government with Protestant inclinations; the supreme domination of a Protestant empire; the radio, which has become a broadcaster of Protestantism; the cinema, a carrier of immorality; our French press itself which, for the most part, is Catholic in name only."[41]

Amid the darkness, Hertel did see a ray of light. Advancing the same perspectives that had been articulated to great effect by Groulx, Hertel saw hope for a solution to the deplorable state of the French-Canadian people in the enthusiasm of young people for nationalist and separatist movements. These young people, he said, as soon as they were summoned by a leader who embodied the true French-Canadian values, would build the future independent and Catholic "Laurentie" – the name given at that time to an independent Quebec. "Un jour la séparation se fera," he predicted. Separation was just a matter of time. The young would discard the Anglo-Saxon system of parties, of liberalism and materialism, to replace them by a social structure founded on Catholicism and nationalism. He expressed no fear that this leader might become a dictator. In fact, expressing ideas that floated in Quebec during that era, he explained that the youths of France, of French Switzerland, and of the Laurentie "only oppose dictatorships that are abusive. They dream, on the other hand, of a liberating dictatorship, one that will come to sweep away the impotent and noisy parliamentary systems."[42]

Could anything be clearer? The priest teaching at Brébeuf who was held up as having had such influence on the young people of the 1930s projected on them his hope that he would see them found the new Laurentie. Other Jesuits communicated a similar vision formulated by Groulx. Officially, however, the nationalism communicated at Brébeuf was not separatist. Paul Gérin-Lajoie, editor-in-chief of the college newspaper, was categorical: "There is one question only which we are in no way permitted to discuss, and which is taught us as such: *We owe respect and submission to the established authority, the King of Canada.*"[43] Clearly, the students of Brébeuf were being led simultaneously in two opposite directions. They were told that they must be submissive to authority – to the religious authority of the Pope and the political authority of the King of Canada. At the same time, they were made to study the incompatible exhortations of Groulx, of Hertel and other teachers. The message of *Leur inquiétude* could hardly be more precise: they must replace parliamentary democracy by a dictatorship led by a French-Canadian "*chef*" in an independent Laurentie, sheltered from

Anglo-Saxon Protestant values. The students thus lived in ambiguity.

Trudeau was no stranger to Hertel's political ideas, which were, in any case, prevalent in the college environment. If one finds no trace of disagreement with Hertel's views in Trudeau's contemporary notes, it can only mean that he shared them. As a dutiful student, Trudeau had absorbed the nationalist vision communicated by his teachers. He believed that the French-Canadian people needed to be saved from their fallen state. They were in need of an elite. He himself must be part of that elite. He knew that he was up to the challenge, and his teachers, like Hertel himself, knew it as well.

Despite the image that Trudeau projected when he became a federal Liberal candidate in 1965 of being dragged into politics only reluctantly, in fact he early began to think of politics as a noble commitment for which he must prepare himself. In March of 1938, Trudeau dipped into Plato's *Republic* and wrote: "I read some passages at random and others that interested me. . . . I really must return to these writings when I have more time. There are many things which are useful for political or individual development." He was already feeling the need for political development.

Just a month before, on February 10, 1938, Trudeau had given a speech in class which he titled "Considerations on Political Eloquence." He then thanked Father Verest for having taught the class, insistently, this slogan: "Those who can, must become involved in politics." And Trudeau added: "I think that our other teachers were wrong not to initiate us to politics. . . . It is my firmest conviction that those youths who have aptitude for politics commit an act of unforgivable cowardice if they do not engage in active politics from the day that they have the material and intellectual means to do so, that is to say, when they have sufficient means remaining, after they have provided for their family, to ensure their complete independence from everyone." Strong words. They were to be prophetic.

Trudeau knew he would always have the material means to engage in active politics. He set out even then to acquire the needed intellectual resources. At the time, and even four years later when he would study law at the University of Montreal, he conceived of engaging in politics strictly within the terms of French-Canadian nationalism, as a champion of French Quebec. So he set about systematically fashioning his personality and developing his written and spoken style so that he could later express persuasively the ideas that he would be defending. In that, he followed the advice of his favourite teacher, Father Bernier.

———◦———

As he prepared himself to be active in politics, Trudeau encountered a book during his final year at Brébeuf about which he wrote: "It is not a book that one could read profitably before Philosophy II, because it summarizes all the sciences and philosophies. For that reason, it is also hard going, but passionately interesting. . . . The table of contents is perfect. . . . The style is direct, condensed, precise. . . . It is a book that needs to be assimilated entirely."44 This "perfect" book was titled *L'homme, cet inconnu,* by Alexis Carrel.45 Published in 1935, it was written and published in English, while Carrel was in the United States, and a French edition was published in France in that same year. Its extraordinary success was immediate. Translated into some twenty languages, it sold millions of copies. In Quebec, it was particularly appreciated by the Jesuits, who pressed it on their students.

Carrel, born in 1873, had studied medicine at the University of Lyon but spent most of his career in the United States, where he had been conducting research since 1904. He was awarded in 1912 the Nobel Prize for medicine and physiology and was thereafter considered one of France's most eminent scientists. In 1941, Carrel returned to France and he became a star of the Vichy regime. All over France, dozens of streets, public squares, and buildings were named in his honour. In *L'homme, cet inconnu,* written in the midst of the Depression, Carrel examined the causes of the crisis and proposed his solutions. The ideas that earned him such recognition for so many years – and that Trudeau was so elated to discover – are worth examining.

We know a great deal about the physical health of man, Carrel wrote, about the circulation of the blood or the functioning of the kidneys. But we know little about man's mental health. In particular, we are unable to evaluate the effect of technological progress on our psychological balance. And yet, the Depression has its main cause in "industrial civilization," which, with its technical progress, has perverse effects on man: "The enormous dissemination of newspapers, of radio broadcasts and of the cinema has

leveled the intellectual classes of society to the lowest common denominator."[46] People become accustomed to facile pleasures: "The lowest forms
of literature and the counterfeits of science and art are what, in general,
attract the public."[47] For his own undoing, Carrel writes, "modern man
has rejected all disciplining of his appetites."[48] (The Jesuits at Brébeuf were
equally convinced that society had fallen into immorality.)

So it was that modern civilization had effected the physical and
moral weakening of man and the disintegration of the social fibre.
Women were especially responsible: "They abandon their children to a
kindergarten to pursue their careers, their social ambitions, their sexual
pleasures, their literary or artistic fantasies, or simply to play bridge."[49]
The result is a system of education which levels men downward, which
is adverse to their physical or mental health: "Most individuals are now
fashioned in the same mould, with a mix of neurosis and of apathy, of
vanity and lack of self confidence, of muscular strength and susceptibil-
ity to fatigue."[50]

This levelling goes against nature because, according to Carrel, individuals are not, in fact, equal. Nor are the races; the white race is genet-
ically superior to the black. Even among the white races, the inhabitants
of northern countries are superior to those of the South. And so woman,
biologically inferior to man, must be "restored to her natural function,
which is not only to give birth to children, but to bring them up."[51] The
inequality of social classes must also be recognized: "The distribution of
the population into different classes within a country is not merely an
outcome due to chance. . . . It is profoundly based on biology. . . . Those
who, today, are proletarians owe their situation to hereditary defects of
body and mind."[52] In consequence of all these natural inequalities,
Carrel concluded, the principle of democracy is not only unfounded, it is
harmful. "The equality of rights is an illusion. The feeble-minded and the
man of genius must not be equal before the law. The individual who is
stupid, lacking intelligence, incapable of concentration, dispersed, has no
right to higher education. It is simply absurd to give him the same electoral power as to the fully developed individual. The sexes are not equal.
It is dangerous to ignore all these inequalities. The democratic principle
has contributed to the decadence of civilization by impeding the development of the elite."[53] Now, for Carrel, the elite was crucial: "Humanity
never gained anything through the effort of a crowd. It is driven forward

by the passion of a few individuals, by the flame of their intelligence, by their ideal of science, of love or of beauty."[54] And he offered some examples: "Caesar, Napoleon, Mussolini, all the great leaders of people, grew beyond human stature, and they swept along innumerable crowds by their will and their ideas."[55] On the other hand, the democratic principle contributed to the "lowering of the intellectual and moral caliber"[56] of the politicians, who could no longer rise to the demands of their responsibilities.

Carrel, nevertheless, saw hope, "the ill is not beyond repair. There is reason to hope that the very sight of our civilization commencing its decline will force us to question whether the source of our ills is not to be found within ourselves as well as in our institutions."[57] One can understand why the Jesuits were so appreciative of Carrel's theses; his eschatological vision, articulated with all the power of his prestige as a scientist, largely matched the views put forward at that time in the encyclicals and in the teachings of the Church. Carrel was critical of Protestant values. He considered that the Catholic Church alone, "in its deep understanding of human psychology, has placed moral activities high above those that are intellectual."[58] In his view, "Prayer can sometimes precipitate a mysterious phenomenon: a miracle."[59] And so he reached the conclusion that, to emerge from the Depression, what was needed was to foster the development of an elite capable of what he called mystical activity. "It hides within what we see of the visible world. It manifests itself in rare individuals." Although it had occurred in all eras and in all races, "the Christian mystique expresses the highest form of religious activity."[60] Few individuals are capable of attaining mysticism, but "it would not require a great number of dissidents to change modern society to its depths. . . . An ascetic and mystical minority would rapidly acquire an irresistible power over the majority that is blind and wallowing in pleasure. It could succeed, by persuasion or perhaps by force, in imposing on the majority new forms of life."[61]

It is man who must be changed, Carrel insisted, and this would require radical means. "The renewal of individuals . . . is impossible without a revolution,"[62] simply because it means the reversal of the values of the current civilization, "reconstructing our material and mental framework,"[63] and making every effort to produce a true elite. That could only be achieved by remaking man himself. He must reach his

fulfillment through discipline, physical and mental effort, the learning of
a sense of morality, the practice of asceticism and venturing on the path
of mysticism. These representatives of the new elite must also be knowledgeable about all the sciences. But Carrel raised the question: "Can we
find men able to acquire a good knowledge of anatomy, physiology,
chemistry, psychology, pathology, medicine, and at the same time, to have
a deep appreciation of genetics, food chemistry, pedagogy, esthetics,
ethics, religion, political and social economics?" And he provided his
answer: "The acquisition of all these sciences is not impossible for a vigorous mind. It would take about 25 years of uninterrupted study." But
these chosen few must "renounce the ordinary habits of life, perhaps even
marriage and family." Those who found the courage to subject themselves
to such a discipline would be equipped to "direct the construction of
human beings and of a civilization that is fashioned for them."[64]

To achieve the construction of the new man, the new society would
necessarily be antidemocratic: "Instead of leveling down, as we now do,
the organic and mental inequalities, we shall exaggerate them and we
shall construct greater men."[65] It was Carrel's conviction that the full
development and the perpetuation of "a hereditary biological aristocracy would be an important step towards the solutions of the great
problems of the present time."[66] For such an aristocracy to emerge, the
genetic quality of the entire society would have to be improved by preventing, for example, any marriage involving someone who carried
hereditary faults. Carrel recommended at the same time the practice of
voluntary eugenics, which, he said, "would not only bring about the
production of stronger individuals, but also of families in which resistance, intelligence and courage had become hereditary. These families
would constitute an aristocracy, from which were likely to emerge the
elite men."[67] He had a response for those who might find that "eugenics requires the sacrifice of too many individuals. The philosophical
systems and sentimental prejudices must yield, in the face of this necessity. After all, it is the development of the human personality that is the
supreme objective of civilization."[68]

This "supreme objective" required going further still. Society must
get rid of "the immense crowd of the deficient and the criminal."[69]
Imprisonment was too costly a solution. That is why, for the more dangerous criminals, Carrel proposed the whip or even a short stay in a

specialized hospital, where they might be sterilized. For the others, "those who have killed, who have committed armed robbery, who kidnapped children, who despoiled the poor, who seriously betrayed the confidence of the public, a euthanasian institution equipped with appropriate gas could dispose of them humanely and economically."[70]

Such were the views of Carrel which elicited widespread enthusiasm. Such was the book that sold millions of copies in some twenty languages. It remains as a telling testimony to a troubled period. It was not until the early 1990s that researchers focused on the dark, forgotten side of *L'homme, cet inconnu*. The previous adulation that Carrel enjoyed was followed by shock and indignation. In France, a few personalities, such as Jean-Marie Le Pen, leader of the extreme right, continued to defend his views. But numerous groups waged a successful campaign to have Carrel's name removed from public locations that had been named in his honour.

———————

When Trudeau read *L'homme, cet inconnu*, the book that "needs to be assimilated entirely," Carrel's reputation was at its height. Trudeau became lyrical in his appreciation. "It is a study of man that is utterly comprehensive. It brings out the inadequacies and points out the remedies. The chapters on internal time, on the limits of the soul are amazing." He even filled six pages with notes and passages from the book.

From Carrel, he adopted the notion that he must develop all his capacities to the fullest degree so as to join the ranks of the elite. The author also confirmed his own view, acquired at Brébeuf, that saw the source of social dislocations largely in the democratic system. In addition, Trudeau was fascinated by Carrel's views on the mystique of asceticism, and he noted: "The beauty pursued by the mystic is richer and further beyond definition than that of the artist. . . . It requires first the practice of asceticism. . . . Excesses of the body bring on degradation." In June 1944, Trudeau would write an article with the title, "Asceticism in a Canoe." Later, his asceticism – which was often taken for stinginess – would become legendary. Meanwhile, he quoted at length a passage from Carrel on the salutary effects of asceticism and of hard trials: "A man reaches his highest development when he is exposed to harsh weather conditions, when he is deprived of sleep and when he catches up on his sleep, when his food is sometimes abundant and sometimes scarce, when he must by his exertions conquer his shelter and his food. He must also use his muscles, tire himself and rest, fight and suffer, be sometimes happy, love and hate. . . . It is in these conditions, when the adaptive processes function intensely, that he becomes most virile."[71] It was a lesson that Trudeau seems to have retained for life. Later, during his canoe trips, his travels around the world, and in other circumstances, Trudeau would deliberately seek out privations and trials. He would take pleasure in pushing his body and mind to their utmost limits.

He also noted the great value of discipline: "One can see how solid, physically and morally, are those who from childhood experienced an intelligent discipline, who endured privations and adjusted to adverse conditions. . . . Those who were subjected to fasting learn to absorb in one or two days a sufficient quantity of food to last for a week. So it is with sleep." Here we find the young Trudeau learning the importance of developing his own discipline and confronting difficult situations.

He wrote down another thought in which Carrel concurred with what Trudeau had already been taught: "We accommodate ourselves to most of the conditions of modern life. But these accommodations cause organic and mental changes which amount to a real deterioration of the individual." He also noted the advantages of serenity: "Those who have learnt to maintain an inner calm in the midst of the tumult of modern city life will remain inured against disorders of the nerves and of the internal organs. . . . Only an internal life will allow the individual to retain his personality in the midst of the crowd."

Carrel's attack against democracy was also far from unfamiliar, as Trudeau wrote: "The democratic principle has contributed to the undermining of civilization by impeding the development of the elite." This was a sentiment that he had heard expressed many times over his student years. He also noted appreciatively "the importance of the family and of rural society for an individual to preserve his personality." Carrel's values were in large part the same as those promoted by Trudeau's teachers and the Quebec clergy generally. And all agreed that civilization was in danger and that it had to be saved.

For Trudeau, the book was a discovery. It put before him an ambitious project, one that gave him a reason to have hope for the future:

"There is no more beautiful and dangerous adventure than the renovation of modern man. . . . For the first time in the history of the world, a civilization that has reached the beginning of its decline can discern the causes of its rot. Perhaps it will learn to use this awareness and avoid, thanks to the marvelous power of science, the common destiny suffered by all great peoples in the past. On the new path we must from now on advance." The concepts of a "new man," of a "new order" inspired at that time the French-Canadian elite and the Church. The young Trudeau thought that he had, at last, found concrete suggestions for achieving these ideals. He was fascinated by the possibility of being part of the small elite that would lead human beings toward a better world. He knew that he possessed the "vigorous mind" that Carrel postulated for those who would be chosen. At the same time, he expressed some reservations about the long list of scientific accomplishments that would be required of him: "I think that he was carried away when he proposed that a man should become universal in order to save humanity. With the plan of study that he proposed, it would take a miracle for one to survive." But the prospect of taking part in the adventure had Trudeau fascinated.

With these reading notes on *L'homme, cet inconnu*, we conclude the chapter on Trudeau's education at Collège Jean-de-Brébeuf. It must now be obvious that, contrary to a well-established myth that he cultivated, as did others, we nowhere could discover the young man rowing against the current. The student that we did discover was, in fact, much closer to the belated acknowledgement that Trudeau made in 1996. It came in the Foreword to a collection of his writings, and drew little attention: "I cannot say exactly when I became a contrarian, nor why. I do remember, however, that in my early years, far from going 'against the current,' I was more inclined to do and say the conventional thing and to devour gratefully every morsel of knowledge that came my way, whether from my parents, my friends, my teachers, or my Church. My childhood having been a happy one, I felt no need for 'methodic doubt.'"[72]

Why did he feel the need, just four years before his death, to correct the image that had been projected of him over so many decades, and at last to set the record straight? He took the answer with him to the grave.

*Chapter 4*

———◆———

# THE LEADER SHARPENS HIS PEN

*Better a scratchy pen than a pen that has run dry.*

— PIERRE TRUDEAU

*Brébeuf*, November 5, 1938

FROM HIS EARLIEST YEARS, writing in all its forms and fashions fascinated Pierre Trudeau. He read voraciously, both prose and poetry, in
French and English. He also loved the theatre, where he would analyze
the art of the actor as well as the skill of the playwright. In his archives
for the years 1937 to 1939, we found the typescripts for no fewer than
five plays. Did he write them all himself? Were they performed and, if so,
before what audiences? We do not know for sure, except for the one play,
*Dupés*, described earlier. In later life, theatre would remain important to
him; he would take to the stage as both actor and writer, and use the
stage to project his political ideas.

Now we shall consider the budding writer as he published for the first
time in the student paper, the *Brébeuf*. From 1938 to 1939, he authored
five articles. The following year – his last at the college – he served as the
paper's editor-in-chief and produced seven pieces. All twelve were published in the last year and a half of his eight years at the college.[1] Before
then, for whatever reason, he never chose to write for the school paper.

His introductory piece, published in the issue of February 12, 1938,
was headlined "The Snorer and The New Boarder." It was a light-
hearted romp with no serious intent other than to amuse. It evoked an
incident from some years before, when he was a boarder at the college
for the first time. On his first night of sleeping in the dormitory, where

the beds, row on row, were separated only by the width of a washstand, Trudeau's slumber was disturbed by a champion snorer. A few nights later, following the advice he received from a veteran boarder, Trudeau rose, tiptoed to the offensive rumbler and pinched his nose. But a disgusting gooey substance stuck to his thumb and forefinger. Revolted, he took it for snot, only to discover the next day that it was actually Vaseline. The long-suffering snorer had dabbed his nose as a counteroffensive against recurrent nightly raids on his nose. Such was Trudeau's soft entry into the domain of publication, where, later, he would make a name for himself as a cutting polemicist.

His next appearance in the *Brébeuf*, after the summer holidays, was more ambitious. Titled "Brief Praise to All," it appeared in the issue of November 5, 1938. The style this time was more colloquial and terse. Trudeau began by a direct challenge to his readers: "Don't worry, this won't take long for you not to read, for I will be brief." The unusual preamble was apt to catch attention. And brief he was in his praise, though not in the rest of the article, which ran long by *Brébeuf* standards. He praised those who dared to write, even if they wrote badly, because they were willing to lay their ideas out in public, even at the risk of having them ridiculed. They "simply ignore all those who complain that their pen is scratchy," Trudeau wrote, and added: "Better to have a scratchy pen than to have a pen that has run dry."

After the brief praise came lengthier criticism. He scolded those who complained that the school paper contained "too many deep articles." Then he mocked those who thought they were deep when they were, in fact, merely obscure. He insisted that a profound idea need not be expressed in a dense style. Writers who took themselves too seriously, who assumed they were profound when they were merely opaque, he called "Thinkers" with a capital T. "The Thinkers, you see, are people who take everything seriously and, worse, take themselves seriously. . . . Unfortunately, when they hear themselves described as 'heavy and deep,' they fail to catch that what's meant is 'thick and empty.' "

Three months later, on February 24, 1939, he followed up with a kind of manifesto. It was titled, provocatively, "To Rehabilitate Pascal." Why would Blaise Pascal need rehabilitation when his *Pensées* were taught in schools as masterpieces of French prose? There was the issue of Pascal's vendetta against the Jesuits. In 1656, Pascal came to the defence of a Jansenist theologian who was on trial for heresy before the Faculty of Theology of the University of Paris. Pascal launched a series of eighteen public letters titled *Lettres écrites par Louis de Montalte à un provincial*, which fiercely attacked the Jesuits for their doctrines and their morals. The collection, generally known as *Les Provinciales*, was devastating. Jean Lacouture, an expert on the Jesuits, wrote: "Of all the blows to strike the Society of Jesus over more than four centuries, . . . this was the most terrible, attacking its honour as well as its judgment, to the joy of its enemies. . . . The small group of noble adventurers was pilloried for perverting doctrine and for corruption, by one of the greatest writers ever to emerge from Christianity.[2] . . . The Society of Jesus came out of the attack battered in its reputation and its prestige."[3]

This background explains the double provocation of Trudeau's headline. Rehabilitate Pascal? Did that mean taking his side against the Jesuits, even at Brébeuf? In fact, beyond the title, Trudeau did not engage in doctrinal dialectics. His concern was, once again, to teach a lesson to Brébeuf students and human beings in general. A quotation from Pascal was meant to start a discussion on something closer to home. Pascal, in his *Pensées*, had written: "The more one's mind expands, the more apt one is to discover men with originality. The ordinary person can find no difference between men."[4]

Trudeau presented himself as the defence attorney for Pascal: "Recent articles in *Brébeuf* and other important publications have so splendidly contradicted this statement by Pascal, and so completely discredited the man from Port-Royal that it seems there is nothing more to be said in his defence." Trudeau, however, would find words in defence of "this poor man who, by dreaming up his *Pensées* and writing against the Jesuits, was able to ignite a star in the night of knowledge, but who suddenly saw it pale amid the lights of the present century." In fact, Pascal would be used rather clumsily as a cover for developing his own ideas about originality, the True originality – again he used a capital T – and the factitious, which he called the bizarre. He was especially determined to unmask false originality, which he equated with seeking attention.

"Bizarre people are legion throughout history," he wrote. An example: "Benjamin Franklin surprised the women by coming to the salon wearing ski boots." Trudeau then pushed the search for bizarre originality to its extreme, to what must have seemed in 1939 as a *reductio ad absurdum*.

Neither Trudeau nor Brébeuf students at that time could have imagined what would be the bizarre fashions of the 1960s: "Let us quickly evoke some novelties, for instance, wearing the lace from a boot instead of a tie, or appearing in short pants, or shaving our heads or growing a beard."

But what about True originality? He comes to it in the very last sentence for a paradoxical ending: "If all that seems just too humdrum, and if we want to do something truly remarkable, we could be polite towards everyone, we could speak correct French, we could truly think what we say, and we could be Catholic for the entire world to see."

This article must have seemed more than a little precious. The invocation of Pascal had a single purpose, to give a semblance of sophistication and erudition to what was really an exercise in light satire. Once again, Trudeau lectured students for seeking attention by superficial performances rather than by True values. His conclusion, though, was entirely conformist. Was this the young man who could not bear authority? How the Jesuits must have rejoiced that their star student was urging, in a provocative style, the very values that they taught and preached. If he was "rowing against the current," it was by going further than his schoolmates in urging them to live up to these values in daily life. In fact, he sounded like someone preparing to take his place some day as a "*chef*," a leader.

But his preoccupations were clearly not with the great events then taking place in Europe that would soon engulf the planet in a world war. When he published that piece on February 24, 1939, civil war was raging in Spain; Mussolini had already conquered Abyssinia (Ethiopia) and was preparing to invade Albania, which he would do on April 6. Hitler had already annexed Austria and would seize Czechoslovakia on March 15. In August, Hitler and Stalin would sign their non-aggression pact, which would set the stage for the invasion of Poland on September 1, 1939. On September 3, France and the United Kingdom declared war on Germany, followed by Canada shortly after. But Trudeau, at Brébeuf, like most French Canadians, considered these portentous events as remote. For him, what mattered was to be a good Catholic and to speak correct French, avoiding anglicisms. As for the imminence of war, it would get cavalier treatment in the student newspaper.

On April 16 of the previous year, as Europe was shaken by the war jitters that would lead in September to the appeasement of Hitler at

Munich, an article appeared in the *Brébeuf* that proposed an amusing board game to raise money for the charity dispensed by the Fédération des oeuvres catholiques canadiennes-françaises. The author, André Gérin-Lajoie, described the game under the headline, "Will the Humanists Get There Before Hitler?" It presented a map of Europe with swastikas planted here and there. The artist who executed the map was introduced: "Gérard Gauthier, and a few of our classmates, thought it would be fun to symbolize by the various more or less obvious aims of Teutonic imperialism the amounts of money that we suggest the students of Belles-Lettres should donate." Then the rules of the game were explained. "For every five dollars raised, a new country will come under our domination!" The game proposed six theatres for the bidding:

1. To fly the Swastika over Austria, the donations must reach $5.00. A suggestion: The tanks are lined up at the border. It takes 25 cents to send one into Austria.
2. Will we capture Czechoslovakia before Hitler? That will cost $10.00. For a tank in Czechoslovakia: 50 cents.
3. The Swastika over Spain! To send decisive aid to Franco: $15.00. Provide the crew for a battleship for white Spain: 50 cents. Provide the crew for an airplane for white Spain: 25 cents.
4. The Swastika over Africa! To recover the African colonies: $20.00.
5. The Swastika over Asia! For the monopoly over Oriental trade: $25.00. Pay for a wagon on the first train to run on the Berlin–Bombay line!!!
6. The Swastika over Russia! $30.00. For an option on the first oil well exploited by the Nazis in Russia: $2.00.
   Grand Total: $30.00.

Although the author's explanation of the rules of the game is confusing, he helps us to understand how the students of Brébeuf perceived the threat of war. Four of the topics begin with: "The Swastika over . . ." The idea that the swastika could invade three continents inspires the students to create a "fun" game. André Gérin-Lajoie was quite pleased with the invention: "What does the Teacher think of this way of treating contemporary History? In any case, the experiment proved the effectiveness of the means we took to stimulate enthusiasm for the campaign, which went really well." The students of Belles-Lettres raised thirty dollars, while the whole college raised $243.00 for charity.

It has often been argued that the youth of Quebec were at that time simply ignorant of what was developing in Europe. The article proves the contrary. It begins by acknowledging the gathering threat in its first sentence: "At the moment when the Fédération's campaign was launched at the college, all minds were preoccupied by the recent seizure of Austria by Hitler and his provocative attitude towards Czechoslovakia." These students, then in their fifth year at Brébeuf, on average seventeen or eighteen years of age, were quite aware of "the various more or less obvious aims of Teutonic imperialism." What they exhibited was not ignorance, but flippancy. By their game they trivialized the immense tragedy that had begun to descend on mankind.

On April 8, 1939, Trudeau again appeared in the *Brébeuf*, this time with an article titled "Utopie relative." It would be the only one of Trudeau's twelve *Brébeuf* articles to be selected by Gérard Pelletier for the anthology *Against the Current*.[5] In this piece, despite the title's evocation of Thomas More's *Utopia*, Trudeau was not speculating in the realm of political theory. It was, in fact, a very personal exercise, an ode to skiing. Trudeau was at that time the star of Brébeuf's ski team, and he had led it to a first-place finish in an intercollegiate competition. All his life, right to the age of seventy-nine – the year before his death – he would ski in a style that his friend and law partner Roy Heenan would call "breakneck." And that, precisely, would be a highlight of the article: Trudeau did, in fact, break a leg.

In a letter of recommendation for Trudeau written some time after the accident, the prefect of discipline at Brébeuf, Father Donat Boutin, described its aftermath: "A real-life experience tells something about this young man from the point of view of 'moral fibre.' Last year, during a ski outing, . . . Pierre Elliott Trudeau fractured his leg. Instead of withdrawing into the quiet of his home, he chose to become a boarder at the college, he would do his homework in a room at the infirmary, and he would make his way to class in a wheelchair: this decision was his alone; his mother and sister had not yet returned from a trip to Europe."[6]

Trudeau wrote about the accident in anything but a mournful style. "The skier is a god who turns mountains into his toys, who places a bit between the jaws of gravity to do with it what he will, who laughs at the abyss and takes a fierce delight in provoking it." That sentence, surely, with its almost mystical ecstasy at flying into danger, reveals more of the essential Trudeau than anything he had published so far. But, after soaring to the heights came the fall. "It is scarcely believable but true: the skier must fear ecstasy. . . . In this magnificent sport, this incomparable craft, all it took was one mogul to send me soaring. . . . Alas! It is the fate of mortals that we can evade reality only for an instant." His fall brought him back down to earth. He hit a tree and rendered a poetic account of what happened; no lamentation, no cry of pain for him: "One leg encircles a maple lovingly, then remains for 40 days strapped to a pine. Skis made of ash, crutches made of oak. And utopia that is not."

———

Trudeau inaugurated his tenure as the successor to Paul Gérin-Lajoie at the *Brébeuf* with the issue of October 7, 1939. His approach as the editor-in-chief would be very different from that of his more assertive and politically minded predecessor. Trudeau would downplay his own role in determining the quality and pertinence of the school paper, while stressing the individual responsibility of the students. The headline of his first article was deliberately casual, offhand, even anticlimactic: "Entre autres, sur le don de parole" ("Among other things, about the gift of words").

Trudeau adopted a flippant, arch tone, but clearly he meant business. As in that article of the previous November, "Brève louange à tous," he urged his fellow students to break through their inertia and express their ideas in the college paper rather than merely criticize. Writing, he proposed, is a means of pursuing truth. Granted, writing is not easy. But he believed in the familiar French maxim "*C'est en forgeant qu'on devient forgeron*" ("Practice makes perfect"), and he applied that metaphor to writing, in his usual paradoxical style: "You have no ideas? Think up some. You can't think up any? Borrow some; the truth is yours. You can't borrow any? Write without ideas. People will take you for a poet, an editor-in-chief or a politician."

To encourage those who shrank from expressing ideas that might provoke sneers, he defended the principle that the truth best emerges from a clash of ideas. "If you are right to have your ideas, you are wrong to keep them to yourself. If you are wrong to have your ideas, you would be right to expose them to correction." And, to encourage students to come forward with controversial positions, he assured them that he would not impose an official ideology on the paper. "I can promise you that your article will not be rubbing shoulders with ads for brown shirts, black shirts or red shirts." It was shorthand for the ideologies then clashing in Europe: the brown shirts were the Nazi storm troopers, the black shirts were the members of the Italian fascist party, and red shirts referred to Communists.

Trudeau repeated a favourite conviction: you must not be deterred by fear of standing out, of being ridiculed or condemned. "Your ideas might cause people to smile? That's the price of any good deed, and one must learn to pay that price." In his own life, even then, he asserted that principle daily by speaking French with an "international" accent that most students must have considered alien or pretentious. He argued that inertia was the main obstacle to improvement and action was the solution. "You don't want your daughter to be mute? Then teach her the language. You don't want her to stammer? Teach her to speak properly."

Trudeau was developing his own style, writing now in terse, pithy sentences. And he insisted that the paper would not be projecting an ideal image, it would reflect the reality of the students themselves. "In theory, the *Brébeuf* is Catholic, patriotic and artistic. In practice, it will be what you will have made it. If the paper lacks literature, if it lacks religion; if it is flat, round; white, black; short, long; light, serious; don't hold it against us, gentlemen: *Brébeuf* will always be your paper."

Notice the order in which he placed the paper's fundamental values: first priority he granted to Catholicism, followed by French-Canadian patriotism, and aesthetic quality. He also sought to stimulate debate, arguments, or at least, the expression of personal viewpoints. He could have no illusion that he could promise the students freedom of expression. He referred, with a touch of irony, to "la presse (plus ou moins) libre," a free press – more or less. The newspaper was tightly controlled. At the very top of the masthead of the *Brébeuf* was listed the title: "Adviser." The name, while Trudeau was editor: "Père J. Brosseau, S.J." That was where the real veto power resided. And freedom of expression was not a value the Jesuits cherished, unless framed within the limits of "the truth" as defined by religion and patriotism. But Trudeau did strive to bring more spontaneity to a publication that was long on articles that read like prayers, along with reports on sports events, photos of school activities, poems, and reports on the alumni. The paper did not run editorials as such. The editor-in-chief was expected to contribute articles, but they might run anywhere in the paper.

A final comment about Trudeau's first article as editor: it appeared more than a month after the United Kingdom, France, and Canada had declared war on Germany. But Trudeau offered not a word about the war.

———◦———

On November 11, 1939, Remembrance Day, more than two months after Canada had declared war on Nazi Germany, Trudeau brought out his second issue as editor-in-chief. One might have expected a meditation on the First World War, or on this new world war now engaged so soon after the end of the first. But there was nothing of the kind. Trudeau did bring up the subject of war, but only war in general, without reference to any specific war, and only as a small part of a larger discussion. His real objective, in a long article that took up most of the front page, was to castigate those who blindly follow public opinion. The headline was enigmatic, as usual: "De cette autorité,"7 ("About this authority"). He criticized those who feared to express a personal opinion in case they should look foolish. "None but saints and geniuses . . . dare to stand up at the crossroads and cry out as loud as they can that Christ is their King," he scolded. For the same abject reason, "rather few governments take their inspiration from the political program of a certain Jesus, about whom you might have heard. They don't want to annoy anyone or become a laughingstock." As in other articles, Jesus Christ was a reference point. Separation of Church and state was the furthest thought from Trudeau's mind. It was evident to him that governments and the governed alike should look to Jesus to inspire their conduct. If this did not happen, there could be only one explanation: the flock mentality. "You can see all of humanity plodding along, yielding to the most ridiculous styles of living and thinking, all because it is easier to do the wrong thing all together than to react against it alone; no matter that the road is strewn with garbage, as long as it is the road most traveled." Trudeau wrote as a moralist, in no sense as a journalist or a political analyst. He proposed that everyone should be guided by the pursuit of Truth, which he understood to be found primarily in religious teachings. He identified as the main obstacle to the rule of divine Authority "the dependence on a certain vile tyrant known as public opinion."

As one example of people being misled by the fear of public opinion instead of following the true Authority of Jesus, Trudeau described his understanding of the psychology of war: "The explanation of wars is in no way different than that of ridiculous styles. . . . Indeed, rather few people prefer war to peace. Oh, I'm not referring to petty wars between friends, when they get together for a few days to raise their flags and beat the drum. . . . But, when it comes to real wars where the soldiers get angry and bombs kill unto death, those nobody likes. And yet, the soldiers don't dare declare that they would rather stop. . . . And the generals don't dare to sue for peace. . . ."

When Trudeau wrote those lines, Hitler and Stalin had concluded their pact and Hitler had already invaded Eastern Europe. One might have expected that Trudeau would probe this particular war in the light of his Catholic principles. Was it a just war? Did the soldiers really only fight because they submitted to the "tyranny of public opinion"? Instead, he trivialized the issue by making war just one example among many – like odd fashion styles – of people submitting to the tyranny of public opinion. Other examples he gave: the people of Quebec keep voting for the same two old parties out of habit; they shy away from founding a new party because it would look bad. Governments don't take their marching orders from Jesus. Students don't condemn other students when they misbehave, and students fear to submit to the paper an article that offers something different from commonplace sentiments. Why? Because they would look bad.

In fact, like most other students at Brébeuf, and French Canadians generally, he failed to take a stand on the most momentous event of his lifetime. At that same time, while he was working through his thoughts on the "tyranny of public opinion," elsewhere on the planet there was a real tyrant who was in the very act of "leading astray" his people, with dire consequences for all the peoples of Europe and the entire world. But Trudeau never gave Hitler even a passing mention in the newspaper. His reflection remained idealistic, disincarnate, developed on an abstract plane where invoking religion and moralizing on timeless principles replaced looking at the real world.

━━━━◉━━━━

Was Trudeau really unaware of the threat to human and religious values embodied in Hitler? Amid Trudeau's documents in the archives was an essay titled "The Philosophy of Nazism – according to a course given by Father Louis Chagnon, S.J." The seven typewritten pages were signed Léonidas Hudon, Philosphie II^e année. Hudon was a classmate of Trudeau who also contributed to the *Brébeuf*. Father Chagnon was a Jesuit who taught and published under the aegis of the École sociale populaire and also taught courses at Brébeuf. Trudeau, as his notes indicate, had also attended Father Chagnon's lecture on Nazism. In his archives, we found four undated pages of handwritten notes with the heading: "Causerie du Père Chagnon" ("Lecture of Father Chagnon").[8]

Hudon's piece, surprisingly clear-sighted, proves that there was at that time in Quebec a current that was highly critical of Nazism, that understood what it meant and was aware of its implications. Hudon presented Nazism as the greatest danger threatening Western civilization: "A quick look at Europe today brings us face to face with the most horrible devastation ever known. This drama, in which material forces fiercely unleashed confront, in a merciless struggle, our spiritual values, takes its root in the doctrine of *National-Socialism*."[9] Hudon attacked the Nazi doctrine on philosophical grounds, while bringing out the racism and the anti-Semitism on which it fed, and he pointed out its political, economic, and social effects. Already in *Mein Kampf*, Hitler had denounced "violently the avowed enemy of the German people: Judeo-Marxism." Hudon added: "After Hegel and Nietzsche, the third source of Nazi ideology is pagan racism, which is nothing but idolatry of the blood, and it merely exploits a rather natural instinct: the pride of race. The important new factor introduced is the doctrinal systematization of racial superiority. . . . This new idea has been taken up, these days, . . . by Hitler, in the two volumes of *Mein Kampf*. . . . According to this theory, there is a fundamental difference between the races, an inequality that nothing can remove. . . . And so, to restore the glorious German civilization, all the original purity of Nordic blood must be restored and the mystique of the German-Aryan race must be promoted. Consequently, the expansion and the power of the race must be promoted by eugenic sterilization. . . . This explains the merciless persecution of the Jews in the past few years and the struggle waged against the Roman Catholic Church."

Léonidas Hudon clearly identified the utter immorality of the racist Nazi doctrine. He also noted its danger for humanity, and concluded that Nazism must be stopped. "For the German people, the call of the blood represents something divine. In consequence, the German tree must gather in all its branches that have become separated from it in the course of history, at Versailles above all. . . . Hitlerism is therefore, on the international stage, a dynamic without end. Sooner or later, a stop must be put to it, a limit drawn, lest everything be engulfed."

Hudon's piece stands out as a testimony to the period. Clearly, some French Canadians provided a lucid analysis of the Nazi threat, one that stands up splendidly to retrospective scrutiny some sixty-five years later. Only the naive conclusion of Hudon's essay leaves today's reader flabbergasted. It must have come directly from Father Chagnon's lecture, because the same conclusion is to be found in Trudeau's notes. "And so, the conclusion is unavoidable, the world is now threatened by two Bolshevisms, both sworn enemies of true human values, both ferocious de-Christianizers of youth and daunting dangers for civilization. Faced with such monsters, we are left with only one weapon that is stronger than cannons, those destroyers of life, and that is more likely to sway the Master of the universe's destiny, than the ideals claiming to come to the defence of civilization against barbarism: there remains prayer, confident and expiatory prayer." Prayer against the blitzkrieg and Stuka dive-bombers! Prayer to save civilization! Did Trudeau share this view? His notes would indicate that he did; there is no trace of any objection on his part.

The fact that Hudon's article lies among Trudeau's papers seems to indicate that it was intended for publication in the *Brébeuf*. At seven typewritten pages, it was certainly far too long to be published in one issue. There is evidence that Hudon was submitting it for publication in two parts, since at the bottom of page 4 appears: "The critique of this philosophy will appear in the next issue." Yet it never did appear, and we don't know the reason. A plausible explanation is that Trudeau seems to have run into trouble with publishing the paper after Christmas. The

*Brébeuf* sold subscriptions outside the college, advertising that it published nine issues a year. In fact, it had often happened in previous years that nine issues were not published. Trudeau published three before Christmas, and normally should have published six more from January to June 1940. In fact, he brought out only four, and one of the four was a single sheet of four pages that was more an advertisement for a proposed auditorium and gymnasium than a real issue of *Brébeuf*. Hudon's double article could simply have been a casualty of the editor's problems.

Another mystery is that when Trudeau went to Paris to study, he brought along with him his notes on Father Chagnon's lecture. We don't know why. Whatever the reason, both sets of notes on this lecture establish that he was aware of the facts of the Nazi regime. The question remains: why then did he never discuss in the *Brébeuf* the challenge of Nazism, or examine whether the war to which Canada was committed was or was not a just war, within the terms of Catholic philosophy? To that question we have no convincing answer.

On December 23, 1939, just before the students left for Christmas vacation, a lengthy editorial-like statement appeared next to the masthead, titled "A happy New Year to all our readers." It was signed "La Direction," ("The Publishers"), but the writing was in Trudeau's recognizable style. He explained how he would interpret his role as editor-in-chief, which required that he hold the students responsible for the production and the quality of the paper: "We remind you that articles don't grow under cabbage leaves; the students have to write them." He stressed the importance of writing clearly. "We believe more than ever that the more intelligible the article, the better it is." The piece ended with the kind of irony that had become Trudeau's trademark: "We offer thanks to several senior students. But the others should not let themselves become discouraged. If they continue to apply themselves – who knows? – they might even reach the standard of the junior students. And that would grant us our parting wish: that the older students at the college level finally send us something other than their good old destructive criticisms."

In that same Christmas issue, Trudeau published a piece, this time under his own name, with again a jolting headline: "Sea! Christmas!" It was a dialogue of incongruous characters with improbable names, this time set in a lifeboat as their steamer sinks. Why "Sea!" when "Land! Land!" would have seemed more appropriate to the context? Trudeau delighted in this piece in a burlesque of theatrical dialogue. Among the characters tossing in their two cents (or their too little sense) are Rimbaud, G.K. Chesterton, A Conscript, A Voice, A Fish, The Reader, A Young Woman, A Misogynist, Eighty Calories, A Member of the Graduating Class, No One, The Nose, The Essayer – twenty-four characters altogether.

Through the dialogue of the deaf which ensues, some gleanings of meaning occasionally are revealed. A member of the graduating class expressed anguish at what awaited him in a few months when, after eight years of regimentation, he would be faced with a personal choice – much like setting out to sea. And the Second World War had broken out three months earlier: "We prepared for the battle of life; and it is the battle on the Western Front that awaits us." The soon-to-be graduate reflects dispiritedly on the cynicism of the world he is about to join: "If you are a doctor, they take you for an assassin. If you are a monk, they say that you're lazy. If you get into politics, you're considered a thief. Just try to remain enthusiastic: then, you're a scatter-brain; smarten up and you're prematurely aged; try being an artist or a thinker and they will find you impenetrable. I just don't know which way to turn – and you have the nerve to throw me a Merry Christmas! Damn!"

Trudeau might have been expressing his own deep concerns through this kaleidoscope of utterances. Or perhaps he was merely tossing out what he was hearing around him, the good, the bad, and the ridiculous. An Alumnus probably spoke for the author when he addressed the graduating student: "Young people like you, Graduate, become revolutionaries because they want to keep their convictions ardent, and they are right. But you must know that true revolutionaries are optimists, unlike those others, because pessimists all grumble out the same song, even if their notes are different. But the man who has confidence in humanity and who believes it capable of understanding the truth, and who says so to his fellow humans, that man will never give up taking on new struggles. And the proof is that nothing so drives a man to distraction as to remind him of his supreme dignity as a son of God."

No more bantering, there. Whenever he invoked the name of God or of Jesus, you could be sure that Trudeau was speaking from the heart. To lead the good life meant working for a better world, and whoever would do so must become a "true revolutionary." As time would prove, Trudeau's ambition was indeed to become a "true revolutionary."

It has been said by his biographers that Trudeau acquired his faith in human dignity when he came into contact with the "personalist" movement associated with French philosopher Emmanuel Mounier and with the periodical that Mounier founded in 1932, *Esprit*. The story goes that his friends Gérard Pelletier and Alec, Pelletier's wife, introduced Trudeau to *Esprit* in the late 1940s. Others give decisive importance to Trudeau's meeting with Mounier in Paris in 1948. Stephen Clarkson maintains that Trudeau's Catholic political vision was imparted to him, not while he grew up in Quebec, but rather during his encounters – in the plural – with Emmanuel Mounier in Paris.[10] Clarkson is the only biographer to claim that Trudeau met Mounier more than once. Trudeau himself said that he met Mounier just the once, and that was through a chance encounter in a café. Trudeau's close friend, Roger Rolland, present on that occasion, confirms Trudeau's account. According to Clarkson, the personalist critique of the Catholic Church from a left-wing Catholic perspective caught Trudeau's attention and his approval. But the evidence is there in the *Brébeuf* of December 1939 that Trudeau already was committed to the central postulate of personalism, which is the supreme dignity of each human being as the child of God. No doubt, his later contact with personalism enabled him to deepen and broaden his thinking. But the education he received at Brébeuf gave him the theological basis for what would remain a lifelong principle, the transcendent value of every human being. When he eventually came to power, that principle meant to him that political institutions must serve the individual, and not vice-versa. He would entrench that vision in the Constitution through the Canadian Charter of Rights and Freedoms.

Trudeau returned to one of his favourite themes, the rejection of the leadership of the unthinking flock, in an article of February 22, 1940. Again, it offered a provocative title: "Sur les pompiers,"[11] ("About the firemen"). "The cowardly make bad firemen," he began. "They want to mobilize the fire trucks, the hoses and the long ladders to put out a burning match." Trudeau did not appreciate those who ran away from new ideas, as he had made clear in previous articles, such as "De cette autorité." But he was even more incensed when the cowardly wanted to impose their timid standards on others. "We are our own oppressors," Trudeau protests, without identifying clearly who else are the oppressors. The students? The faculty? The Father Adviser, who holds a veto over all that may go into the paper? Trudeau doesn't say. In part, he seems once again to be condemning the tyranny of conventional thinking. "Without realizing it, we have slipped into commonplace judgments and, duped by the illusion of certainty that they bring, we reveled in stereotyped dogmas and outdated fashions. Then, to conceal the shallowness of our concepts, we tarted up our actions with a semblance of originality."

His condemnation seems so sweeping that it could possibly have been addressed to the whole system of education at Brébeuf. Or possibly to some of the teachers. "Let me be clear. I accept fully that the competent authority – and I do mean competent – should evaluate ideas and give advice. But I will not grant that right to someone who considers any innovation a mistake. . . . Let them not pronounce anathemas against us because we move our lives out of the rut." He will accept authority, but insists that authority must be open to innovation, to exploration, to creativity that will sometimes lead to mistakes. But the mistakes can be corrected – the burning match can be extinguished – without cranking out the big firehoses.

Again, his argument will be clothed in ambiguity; but his cry for more freedom will ring clear. "Now that we have had the experience of learning through sports or war or a knock on the head with a truncheon that originality can exist even in the realm of ideas, and that it is essential to the personality; now that we know that leaders must not be afraid of the sound of their own voices, and that they must have confidence in their own importance, we would like to have a turn at the tiller."

That sentence is long and suggestive. What did he mean when he said that "we" learned about originality of thinking from a knock on the head with a truncheon? Was he referring to a personal experience or, as in the reference to war, simply making a general statement? Some authors, such as David Somerville[12], Esther Delisle[13], and François Lessard[14] have asserted that Trudeau did take part in riots, but most biographers have remained unconvinced.

The article led up to an announcement that was also to some degree a declaration of independence. He would create a new section in the paper that would be an open forum for the expression of opinions. "The authors will express their own ideas which will in no way compromise the integrity of the Society of Jesus. They will certainly make mistakes; which is all to the good since they will become aware of their errors. Our essayists will surely blow out their match if they find it burning their fingers." And Trudeau even invoked a mock theological argument to justify his demand for more free discussion: "God would not let us play with matches if his universe were not fireproof. It is not necessary to correct God's work." In other words, God would not have given us the freedom to think without giving us at the same time intelligence. And so to exercise our freedom is in conformity with God's will. And he concluded: "That, at least, is what I think. And I think that I'm right: that's why I published myself."

Trudeau's style during his tenure as editor was typically ironic, unconventional, mannered, and indirect. He rarely wrote a piece where he came right out and said in plain language what he meant. Occasionally, the format he gave to his articles was elaborate, cumbersome: he used the dialogue structure of a play, with many fictitious characters, often with outlandish names, each in turn speaking a sentence or two, often with no visible connection between the various statements. Such was his very long article of March 30, 1940, titled "À propos de style"[15] ("About style"). One character in his little play, The Essayist by name, seemed to speak more for Trudeau himself than did the other characters – who had names like Plain Common Sense, The Shade, The Reader, The Poet, The Navel, Lafontaine. The Essayist seemed mostly confused about what his role was as a writer, and he consulted all these other characters for sound advice. Mostly, they offered a cacophony of conflicting views, except for Plain Common Sense, who does offer one sound statement: "Obscurity is a defect wherever it is found. True, great masters have been obscure. But they are masters, not because of their obscurity, but rather in spite of it. This failing is forgiven them in recognition of their many outstanding qualities."

———◦———

Now we come to Trudeau's swan song as editor, which appeared on June 12, 1940, during his last days as a college student. It had the odd

title "Ceci est l'éditorial" ("This is the editorial"). He had been provoked
to write it by an editorial that had appeared in the publication of the
Catholic youth movement, the Jeunesse étudiante catholique (JEC). The
editorial was signed by one Gérard Pelletier, the "Person in charge" of
that publication. Trudeau did not know him then, though they would
become the fastest of friends and remain so until Pelletier's death in
1997. But, in 1940, Pelletier was not quite twenty-one and he had sent
an editorial message to the editors of all the student papers: "I ask that,
under the auspices of the 'JEC' which joins them all together, each student
paper define its attitude, through the pen of its student in charge, in the
editorial of its next issue." Now Trudeau never wrote editorials and his
"attitude" was only to let the students express themselves. He found
Pelletier's request presumptuous and decided to teach him a lesson.

He wrote that it had been his intention not to reply to the invitation
until, reading other student papers, he saw how solemnly their editors
had carried out the task of "defining" their several publications. So he
resigned himself to doing likewise – with a difference. He did not see
himself, he wrote, as the "person in charge" of imprinting an "attitude"
on the student paper. "We believed that our craft was that of the gar-
dener who sees to it that his garden has all the air, water and sun that it
needs, but who doesn't lose sleep worrying over whether his garden lives
the proper garden life." He protested that the paper's editorial board did
indeed take very seriously the search for the "person in charge." "The
editorial board held an emergency meeting at a quarter past midnight in
the depths of a cave. And, in recognition of my talent for saying very little
in very many words, they appointed me as 'the person in charge.'" Now
that he was in charge, Trudeau felt he had to discover what was the
newspaper's policy. He found it at the top of the front page: "Under
the somewhat sinister letters that spell out an unadorned *Brébeuf*, I discovered our watchword: 'Published by the students of the college.'" So
the attitude of the paper consisted of the sum of the students, or at least,
of those who published in the paper, in all their variegated fashions. "You
will point out to me, Sir, that in the paper's flower bed, few roses have
bloomed and that we mostly grew rhubarb. You are quite correct. We
mostly ended up with rhubarb because what we had available were
mostly rhubarb seeds." And the "editorial" continued on in that vein, in
mock solemn response to Pelletier's self-important invitation.

At the end, Trudeau tried somewhat to soften the satire, urging Pelletier not to take offence. And he explained why he had been irritated: "If we have spoken straightforwardly (after a fashion), it could be that we were less than happy about your words, 'under the *auspices* of the JEC.' Do remember, however, that *Brébeuf* likes nothing better than to receive advice from experienced people. And we are the first to recognize that 'JEC' is experienced." That was the final ironic thrust. Pelletier was all of twenty years old when he sent out his directive to all student newspapers.

Whatever Pelletier experienced when he read the "editorial," time softened the hurt because, decades later, he wrote about it in his memoirs without bitterness. "Trudeau leaped on the occasion to laugh at me, and he didn't miss the target. In an article published in his college's student paper a few months later, he lampooned me, gently, without nastiness, but with enough humour that he made me understand how exaggerated was my militancy at that time."[16]

This incident showed that Trudeau was more attached to individual freedom than was Pelletier. Whereas Pelletier wanted all of Quebec's student papers to speak with one voice, Trudeau believed that such a policy infringed on the freedom of the individual students and the independence of the paper. The divergent approaches of the two men would remain deeply rooted.

Of course, that freedom of expression already had tight limits at Brébeuf and in the *Brébeuf*. Trudeau made an understatement when, in the "editorial," he spoke of his own recent achievement at the paper: "We even inaugurated an Open Forum to allow all the most diverse talents to express themselves, without official ratification. (That, at least, was our personal intention . . .)" And, in that same editorial, he spelled out some clear restrictions on free expression that he accepted: "We were content, this year, to request articles randomly, to correct the style of the most prolix (when our tastes and our capacities permitted), to do the layout of the pages, *to censure what was 'against the faith and good morals.'*" (Italics added.)

So ended Trudeau's tenure as editor-in-chief. He had developed his style and affirmed his whole-hearted commitment to the Catholic faith and to the values taught by the Jesuits. The most frequent theme of his articles, though, was the need to pursue Truth, to resist the pressure of public opinion, to think for oneself. He pressed for more scope for spontaneity, creativity, and freedom in the paper, without challenging the need to exclude whatever went counter to Catholic teaching. At the same time, Trudeau proved himself totally disconnected from the great events happening at the time, notably the beginning of the Second World War and the initial triumphs of the Nazis and their allies. One aspect of his work in the *Brébeuf* must be noted: contrary to his writings as part of his school work or his personal notes during his fifth and sixth years at the college, contrary to his predecessor at the paper, Paul Gérin-Lajoie, Trudeau never sounded the note of Quebec nationalism during the two years he was published in the *Brébeuf*.

Soon after writing his last editorial, Trudeau entered a new phase in his life. He was four months short of his twenty-first birthday.

*Chapter 5*

# LAW SCHOOL – WHAT A BORE!

*Young people equipped to take an active part in politics act as
unspeakable cowards if they fail to do so.*

— PIERRE TRUDEAU
February 10, 1938

IN THE MAY 27, 1939, issue of the *Brébeuf*, Pierre Trudeau published an
article, "Vers la Haute mer" ("To the High Seas"), that filled the whole
front page of the paper. It was a farewell salute to the graduating class a
year ahead of him, a meditation on the joys and sorrows they must feel
as they left the college after eight years to face the challenges of life. His
article could have made a good commencement speech at a graduation
ceremony, combining nostalgic contemplations with a strong affirmation
of the basic values of the college. He wrote that the *"finissants"* had been
well equipped to face the future during their time at their classical
college. "The second year Philosophy students are masters of their spirit
and their soul. They have learnt to study a problem in depth, to reflect
and then to make their choice. They were taught the Truth, and, above
all, the search for the Truth. Now they are anxious to be off because their
success seems assured."

He portrayed them as happy to "come to the end of the beginning,"
just as the athlete in peak condition "is anxious for the game to start."
Because they have been so well prepared during their college years, they
leave with the confidence that they have acquired the right values: "They
stare down those materialistic bourgeois, those complacent Catholics,
and they feel up to any challenge." A generation later, the students would

be less complacent about despising the materialistic bourgeois. But Trudeau, in 1939, echoed the defiant idealism promulgated at the college: "The deeper their dislike of all that is false, the more widely they smile within themselves: because it is easy to overcome if one is beyond reach of the adversary; and because it is sweet to be despised if one knows deep down that one is in the right. Finally, they are about to fight the good fight." We can sense that Trudeau was projecting on the graduating class his own feelings, his own eagerness to fight the good fight. His own conviction of being in possession of the truth inured him in advance against whatever scorn might be directed at him by the complacent. The future polemicist known for his ironic smile could already be glimpsed between the lines.

The following year, when Trudeau's turn had come to leave Brébeuf, he would be awarded two baccalaureates, one in arts and the other in science, with averages of 91.9 and 96.4 per cent respectively. He would at the same time garner an impressive number of prizes. The letter of recommendation that he received from the college stated: "Few students have managed to score such a high average in all subjects as he did during his classical studies."[1] Trudeau's archives also contain a typewritten description of some members of his graduating class. Here is how he was described: "Philosopher, man of science, tragedian, comedian . . . loner, gregarious . . . great athlete. . . . Such are the paradoxes embodied in our vice-president. He is simple where others are conceited, and full of fantasy where others are simple. This ardently ambitious man accepts without arrogance his many successes. . . . His devil-may-care attitude derives from a personal philosophy that considers the dictates of public opinion as pressures to be resisted. So rich a personality, we are convinced, will make him a man indeed, and he will be the champion of all our rights."[2]

His fellow students had already noted the "paradoxes" of his character, as almost everyone would at a later date. Trudeau seemed to embody a combination of almost everything as well as its opposite. His classmates also sensed that they had in their midst the future leader, defender of their rights, that the Jesuit teachers had been praying for. (Jacques Hébert, for instance, recalls that, at Collège Sainte-Marie, Father Mignault would constantly grab boys by the shoulder and with a shake, challenge them: "Boy, your *patrie* needs you. Boy, you must

become a leader. Tell me, boy, do you want to become a leader?"3)
Trudeau seemed unusually well prepared to face life's challenges. The
range of abilities he had demonstrated meant that he could have taken up
almost any career. The fortune inherited from his father meant that,
whatever he chose to do in life, money would not be an object. If he
opted for further studies, he would have his choice of universities. But
which would it be?

On that same document with a description of all the students in the
graduating class, Trudeau wrote by hand the career choice of each student.
Beside the name of Pierre Vaillancourt, for instance, he wrote: "Medicine."
For Blaise Turcotte: "Jesuit." Pierre Vadeboncœur: "Law." Beside his own
name he wrote: "Economics." Now, at the time, Quebec's two French-
language universities, Université de Montréal and Université Laval, had no
department of economics or of political economy. That meant that
Trudeau, in his final months at Brébeuf, must have planned to go outside
of Quebec to study. And yet, in September of 1940, he was to be found
studying law at the Université de Montréal. What had happened?

In his *Memoirs*, Trudeau wrote that he had long hesitated between
"law, psychology, sociology and political science."4 On other occasions,
he said that he had considered law as well as more purely intellectual
subjects, such as psychology or philosophy.5 Quite possibly, he was
drawn to the latter subjects by his reading of Alexis Carrel's *L'homme,
cet inconnu*. But his experience of studying on his own a 1928 textbook
published in Paris, *Traité de psychologie*, by Georges Dwelshauvers,
soon cooled his interest in that subject. Methodical as usual, he filled
sixteen pages with notes from that book before writing: "At first, there
were ideas and theories that I took the trouble to transcribe. But eventually it became mind-numbing."6

Looking for direction in the choice of a career, he went with his friend
Pierre Vadeboncœur to consult Henri Bourassa, then five years retired
from active politics, but who had been for decades Quebec's most eminent
nationalist. Elected as a Liberal to the federal Parliament in 1896, Bourassa
had split with Wilfrid Laurier in 1899 over Canada's participation in the
Boer War and later helped Borden defeat Laurier in the elections of 1911.
Bourassa had sat in both the federal Parliament and the Legislature in
Quebec City and, in 1910, had founded *Le Devoir*. When the two students
came by to consult him in the spring of 1940, he was seventy-one years old,

but still much admired by the Jesuits for his past ardent defence of Catholicism, of the French language, and of Canada's autonomy within the British Empire and Quebec's autonomy within Canada. Trudeau did not keep a record of what the great man told him, but he did express his amazement that Bourassa would agree to meet with two students. Another person he consulted about his career path was André Laurendeau, whose articles he had admired in *L'Action nationale*. Laurendeau, editor of the nationalist publication, advised Trudeau that French Canada "was terribly lacking in economic expertise. . . . It was urgent that young people establish themselves in that field." Trudeau added: "That's why I took the joint degree in economics and political science."[7]

From his account, one would conclude that his meeting with Laurendeau took place in early 1944. But how to reconcile that with what he wrote beside his name in 1940: "Économie"? It suggests that the meeting occurred during Trudeau's last months at Brébeuf rather than at the Université de Montréal, and that it was Laurendeau's recommendation that inspired his resolution to become an economist. Trudeau's *Memoirs* were published half a century after these events: his memory about the time of his meeting with Laurendeau might have become confused. This hypothesis is strengthened by an important document that demonstrates beyond a doubt that, during that last year at Brébeuf, Trudeau was planning to study political economy as a prelude to a career in politics.

———— ⚙ ————

On January 5, 1940, having ascertained that the Rhodes scholarships were not suspended for the duration of the war, Trudeau obtained the application forms and, on January 7, submitted his application.[8] His submission was in French, but he wrote at the bottom of his covering letter, in English: "Being a French-Canadian student at a French-Canadian college, I imagine it to be the preference of the committee that I write this paper in French. However, should such be their wish, I would gladly rewrite it in English."

The draft of his letter reveals facts about Trudeau's career ambitions that have remained unknown to this day. After acknowledging that it was not easy for him to be singing his own praises, he laid out his ambitions and described his interests with remarkable candour. He declared immediately the paramount importance of religion in his life, and how seriously he had taken his studies: "After religion, which obviously transcends all my activities, since it is of universal application, I can say that my studies constitute my essential activity, and that is so for the simple reason that I have a very great confidence in the education imparted by the classical course." Indeed, even many years later, when he would angrily denounce the inadequacies of university education in Quebec, he would retain a fond memory of his classical studies. Trudeau admitted to the selection committee that he had sometimes wondered whether he would not be better advised to neglect some of the subjects on the curriculum in favour of giving more time "to reading, to philosophy and even to activities outside the scope of the college." But he did not regret the choice he had made because the general culture he had received gave him "the capacity to choose the profession towards which I am most inclined and for which I have the most natural aptitude."

Each applicant was asked to describe "his general interests and activities (including athletics)." Trudeau responded: "Everyone must have some pastime. My hobby is to have them all. 'Jack of all trades, and . . .' I am a founding member of the Académie Sciences-Arts (Academy of Sciences and Arts). I delve into French and English literature out of personal interest; I am a regular at the symphony; I took a course in the History of Art with Mr. Gagnon. I love the piano; I dabbled at pastel and oil paintings. I was the recipient of a general prize in human biology. I earned a diploma from the St. John Ambulance Association. In sports, I enjoy trying everything. I have a great love for skiing; I swam for the team of the Central District Sea Scouts; I always was on my class's team for softball, hockey and track and field. During the holidays I also box, sail, go horseback riding and practice archery. Now, I know that it would be pretentious to lay a claim to mastery in all of these pursuits; I can only assure you that I enjoy them all."

The list of his "hobbies" is staggering. He scarcely exaggerated by saying that he enjoyed them all. It has often been said of Trudeau that his individualism kept him from enjoying team sports and that he only cared for individual competition. That assumption is now untenable. He explained that the reason he rushed from one activity to another was because of his temperament. "In my leisure activities, I need the element of surprise, of variety, of action; I love to understand human beings and to evaluate their ideas."

This last sentence made the bridge between his account of his activities in general, and the very heart of the letter, his career plans for the future. Trudeau then made an astonishing revelation: "I sought a profession where all my inclinations and all my tastes would find satisfaction, and so I chose a career in politics." He wrote that in 1940, at the age of twenty, when he was just graduating from college – he, the very man who later cultivated an image as the reluctant politician. He added that he would leave it up to circumstances to determine what form his involvement with politics would take, and that he might opt "for government, for diplomacy or for journalism." So he really did believe and apply to himself what he had written in 1938, namely that young men should be active in politics as soon as they were in a position to do so, and to do otherwise would be an act of cowardice.

He went on in his letter to make other surprising revelations: "For some years now, while not neglecting my general education, I have sought out activities that prepare one most immediately for public life. And so I took diction lessons; I acted in several plays, originally with the Scouts, then at Camp Ahmek and in college; finally, I am currently taking singing lessons with Mr. Roger Larivière. In addition, I published a number of articles in the college paper, the *Brébeuf*, of which I am the editor."

Trudeau spells out what he takes to be the requirements for succeeding in politics: a good general education, a proper diction, the control of the voice that comes with singing lessons, the ability to act and to write. Already, he understood that politics would require more than good ideas and good policies, that one must also know how to communicate them. Long before universities established departments of communication, he understood the range of abilities that would be required of a good communicator. Trudeau, when he eventually became a political leader, would also understand that theatre had a definite role to play. This might explain his sliding down banisters, his pirouettes, and his recurrent dramatic entrances.

His letter also makes sense of his decision to abandon his milieu's French pronunciation to take up the more prestigious "international French," for which so many different explanations have been put forward. It was said that he did so to stand out, because he was a snob, or as a way to reject his French-Canadian identity, or to distance himself from his father's colloquial speech. The reality is simpler: he considered

proper diction to be part of the accomplishments appropriate for anyone
seriously aspiring to become a statesman. And since Trudeau made it a
personal imperative to put his principles immediately into practice, he
chose while still at school to raise the quality of his speech.

In his letter, having first presented his many qualifications, Trudeau
then acknowledged that they alone were not sufficient. More was needed
to rise above the tawdry level of politics that he considered typical of the
times. "All this is quite superficial and could merely serve the interests of
a demagogue or a time-server. What is needed today, what so many have
been calling for, are leaders endowed with a profound understanding of
human beings, with a proper appreciation of their rights and their
responsibilities." Trudeau had internalized the lessons of his Jesuit teachers. And so he explained his plans to prepare himself for politics at a
higher level. It had been his intention, after graduation, "to study law,
history and the social sciences," which would deepen his understanding
of human nature. But now he proposed an alternative. "If I should be
granted the immense privilege of studying at Oxford, I would probably
take the combination of 'Philosophy-Politics-Economics' and, if that
would not be taking on too much, also 'Modern History.'"

Trudeau's application for the Rhodes was backed by a letter of
recommendation signed by J.A. Thouin, chief officer of the Montreal
Recorder's Court (a lower level court now known as the Municipal
Court of the City of Montreal). The letter was dated January 10, 1940.
Why Trudeau chose Thouin as a reference is unclear, but Thouin did
summon up all of his literary powers to sing the praises of the young
man. He devoted a full page to listing his outstanding academic results
and his many extracurricular activities. He then described his character:
"Without wishing to exaggerate, I would be remiss if I failed to speak of
the personal qualities of this college student in whom one can already
discern a man who is serious and wanting to get ahead. Gifted with an
enquiring mind, he has long been thinking of his future and of how to
achieve it. . . . I know that his fondest hope is to complete his studies in
Europe and that he will be daunted neither by work nor sacrifice. What
are his faults? No doubt he must have some, but I have to tell you in all
honesty that I know of none, and if that is so, it means that they can be
neither numerous nor serious, for I often see him and I have the opportunity to observe him and so to know him well. . . . In conclusion, it gives

me great pleasure to state with all possible honesty that Pierre Elliott
Trudeau is one of our all too rare young men who has it settled in his
head and in his heart to make something of himself and also to work
without stinting to achieve his ideal."9

Trudeau wanted to "make something of himself." Yes, we suggest,
what he wanted was to develop into a leader, and he wanted it with his
head and all his heart. A myth has it that Trudeau was dry and distant.
"He was the least sentimental of men," wrote Stephen Clarkson.10 On
the contrary, he was a man with a heart. His sensitivity, well known to
those who were close to him, was expressed in his private notes as well
as in his letters to his friends. His involvement in politics would reveal a
passionate young man. He would remain sensitive for the rest of his life.

In addition to writing a covering letter, each Rhodes scholarship
candidate was required to write an essay. Trudeau had a choice of eight
topics and chose "Des possibilités d'une paix universelle," ("On the
Possibility of Universal Peace"). At the top of the first page of his rough
draft, he wrote, as usual, A.M.D.G., then jotted down ideas that he
intended to develop. "Intelligence: to think for one self; admit the truth.
Peace means living in harmony, recognizing the rights and responsibilities of others. To do that, one must do one's own thinking, freed from the
yoke of public opinion." These are the favourite themes that he had
expressed in the Brébeuf. But, as in those articles, he now surprisingly
wrote not a word about the war then raging in Europe, a war that
Canada had joined. Universal peace, he wrote, would only become possible when "Humanity is freed from the egotists, the recklessly ambitious
and the impious."

The Trudeau of 1940 recognized that a perfectly moral society
cannot be achieved and is "worthy of appearing in Thomas More's
Utopia." That is why the best we can do is "to teach men to beware of
those who are guilty of leading them astray." And how did Trudeau think
that could be done? By teaching them "to use their intelligence."
Trudeau, then and thereafter, would always insist on the importance of
intelligence. When, a decade later, he would publish his very first piece in
Cité libre, he would write: "Let us be intelligent!" But, in his essay for
the Rhodes, he recognized that he could not put his faith in intelligence
alone because "it sometimes happens that the most intelligent are precisely those who are most willing to lead the people into disorders." For

that reason, it is "absolutely necessary to develop, along with intelligence, a moral sense in this new civilization. . . . The government of a country must give a good example and ensure that no seriously harmful influence be permitted to distort the natural tendency towards what is true." According to his moralistic thinking, a good government must hold up the Good as an ideal.

Years later, upholding a liberal vision, he would assert that the state's function is not to defend morality, but to uphold justice. But, in 1940, Trudeau was committed to the ideal of a Christian society in a Christian state that was the official doctrine of the Roman Catholic Church and was promulgated by his teachers at Brébeuf. He warned against those who "lead the people into disorders." Now, even as he wrote those lines, there was indeed in Europe someone who was doing precisely that, crushing the countries that he conquered. But the prospective Rhodes scholar never raised the factors that provoke wars and constitute obstacles to a universal peace. The political and economic problems then ravaging the peoples of the planet seemed to leave him indifferent. His thinking was developed within the cocoon of his little religious universe where he moralized on an abstract salvation resulting from making human beings perfect.

In retrospect, the narrowness of his vision is stunning. The same young man who declared that he wanted to pursue a career in politics, who chose to write an essay on the possibilities of universal peace, seemed utterly oblivious to world conflicts and their origins. On January 25, Trudeau was invited for an interview. A week later, on February 3, he requested the return of the documents he had submitted, notably his birth certificate and his academic report cards. In what was probably his first important experience of failure, he had been turned down for the Rhodes scholarship. Why? In the absence of documentary proof, we can only conjecture. But it seems plausible that, despite his outstanding qualifications, it was the disconcerting naïveté of his essay, reflecting his Brébeuf education, that was decisive in his rejection in favour of students educated elsewhere, at institutions such as McGill University.

Failing to win the Rhodes, Trudeau decided to continue his studies in Canada. For him, that necessarily meant Quebec because, at that time, like many of Quebec's French Canadians, he gave little indication that the rest of Canada meant anything to him. Of course, even while remaining in Quebec, he could have registered at McGill in political economy, a subject unavailable in the French universities. McGill was then unquestionably Quebec's most prestigious university. But instead, Trudeau chose law, and at the Université de Montréal. Why?

In his *Memoirs*, Trudeau wrote that his father had always advised him to get a law degree as a basic education, and afterward to pursue the career of his choice. So he was following the advice of his father, it seems. But there was another possible explanation: law was the usual training ground for future politicians. When studies in political economy at Oxford were excluded, law became a logical choice. Still, the question remains: why not McGill? His familiarity with English meant that he would have had no particular difficulty studying there. But his Brébeuf training might have made him resistant to registering at an English-speaking and essentially Protestant Quebec institution like McGill. Its materialism, in contrast to the idealistic religious vocation that was assumed to be the providential design for French Canadians in general and Brébeuf students in particular, would have made McGill a distasteful choice. Moreover, with a political career in prospect that might one day make him a Quebec leader, the Université de Montréal, French and Catholic, was a choice more appropriate to his own sense of identity. Even though the study of law was not his first choice, and the practice of law not his ultimate career destination, his three years at the Université de Montréal would be a stage on the way to where he aimed to go.

He began his new course of studies in the fall of 1940, just one year after Canada had declared war. For the most part, the content of his law courses does not seem to have had a marked effect on his intellectual development. Still, it is worth noting the treatment that was given to the institution of democracy in a course on constitutional law given by Professor Bernard Bissonnette. In notes dated November 1941, Trudeau wrote down the defects of democracy: "Ignorance, credulity, intolerance, hatred for superiority, the cult of incompetence, an excess of equality, versatility, the passions of the crowd, the envy of individuals."[11] Democracy, it seems, had rather a bad reputation in the Quebec of the 1940s.

Trudeau audited two lectures on the history of Canada that were given by Lionel Groulx and that were not part of his program.[12] He wrote, or perhaps merely kept, just four pages of nondescript notes on the second lecture. But on the first lecture, which dealt with the rebellions of 1837–38, he kept lengthy notes. This happened near the beginning of his first months in law school. It will be recalled that the rebellion occurred both in Lower Canada – a smaller version of today's Quebec – and Upper Canada – the ancestor of today's Ontario. In both provinces, the insurrection followed years of complaints about abuse of power and corruption on the part of the respective governors and their cliques, and fruitless demands for responsible government. In Lower Canada, Louis-Joseph Papineau and his Parti patriote led the insurrection. The Catholic hierarchy condemned the revolt and threatened with excommunication those who took up arms. There were violent clashes between the insurgents and the British Army. The rebellion was put down; several of its leaders were hanged or sent into exile. Papineau, still considered one of the greatest French-Canadian heroes, fled the country to spend some years in the United States. In 1937, the centennial of the insurrection had been celebrated with enthusiasm in nationalist circles and in the classical colleges.

In his university course, Groulx faced a dilemma in dealing with the insurrection. As a priest, he advocated submission to authority. As we have seen, in *Brébeuf* Paul Gérin-Lajoie protested, in defence of the college, that it never fostered the spirit of separatism but rather inculcated submission to the King of England and of Canada.[13] But, as an ardent nationalist, Groulx looked kindly on the insurrection, which he considered an important event in the history of the liberation of the French-Canadian people. How could he reconcile submission and uprising? It was no easy question for this priest.

In a section titled "Moral Rules for Any Insurrection," Groulx began by establishing a certain number of principles and criteria which, taken together, would morally justify an insurrection. As might be expected, his very demanding system would only accept political violence in very special circumstances. To be legitimate, it had to meet the four following conditions, as Trudeau the student wrote down: "a) a truly tyrannical government; b) that all peaceful means should have been exhausted; c) the moral certainty of success rather than making the situation worse; d) the consent by reasonable public opinion to this extreme remedy." By these criteria, Groulx went on to consider the insurrection of 1837–38. He recognized that it met only two of the four criteria. Logically, he should therefore have concluded that the insurrection was unjustified from a moral standpoint. But he did not draw that conclusion. Instead, he merely observed: "A difficult judgment to make because of the complexity of the question."

Groulx's application of each of the four criteria to the insurrection, as noted by Trudeau, is revealing. The two criteria that he considered not met were c) and d). With respect to c), Groulx recognized that success had not been assured. As for criterion d), he recognized that the consent of reasonable public opinion had not been given. But with respect to the first two criteria, Groulx was satisfied that they had been met. The first was the existence of a tyrannical government. On this point, Trudeau wrote: "There was a tyrannical government: it was opposed to the policy of the common good since seven-eighths of the population were experiencing constraint." Presumably, by seven-eighths, he was referring to the proportion of the Lower Canadian population that was French and Catholic. This hardly corresponds to the commonly accepted definition of a "tyrannical government." The *Petit Robert* dictionary gives this: "The absolute and oppressive government of a tyrant considered especially in the light of its unjust, arbitrary, and cruel aspects." Groulx offered no evidence of unjust, arbitrary or cruel acts perpetrated by the legitimate government. He raised only the "constraint" experienced by those seven-eighths. But no society exists without a degree of constraint. Groulx offered no evidence to back up the statement that seven-eighths of the people lived under constraint. Perhaps it was self-evident to him that a French and Catholic people were necessarily under constraint when ruled by an English, non-Catholic power. One might have expected more robust proofs. But, presumably, the students were satisfied by the demonstration.

The second criterion was to establish that all peaceful means of obtaining justice had been exhausted. Trudeau wrote: "There was reason to believe that all constitutional recourse had been exhausted. Cf: Gosford Report, Grey. . . . Above all, England at this time was evolving toward democracy." This argument is startling, if argument it is. Can one possibly evoke the evolution of England toward democracy as an argument to justify the morality of an insurrection? It seems incredible, but it might be possible, to judge by the teaching of the professor of constitutional law, among others. Quebec at that time, as will shortly become evident, often considered democracy as a misfortune for mankind, as a very bad system of government. As for proving that constitutional means had been exhausted, Groulx was content with saying, "There was reason to believe . . ."

It seems surprising that such weak arguments could have satisfied skeptical students. One must assume that most of them were not skeptical, but ready, rather, to accept Groulx's views, since they were nationalists like him. They chose not to consider the fact that the insurrection was definitively condemned by the Church. Even Groulx's moralizing approach made it difficult for him to justify the insurrection. As a priest and the grand champion of the nationalist cause, Groulx put himself in an equivocal position when he called for a French and Catholic state. He was forced to resort to pirouettes to withhold condemnation of the doomed insurrection. If the twenty-two-year-old Trudeau gave no sign in his notes of skepticism when offered such weak arguments, it could only mean that he, too, wanted to believe in the legitimacy of certain insurrections. Like much of the university community, it seems that he had begun to dream of a radical change to be brought about in his own contemporary society.

---

As for Trudeau's other courses at the university, they offer no particular interest, and we will skip over them to look at Trudeau's marks. With a few exceptions, they were brilliant. He received a perfect score of 20 out of a possible 20 in constitutional law, and a perfect 40 out of 40 in civil law. In three subjects, history of the law, municipal history, and administrative law, he obtained mediocre scores of 11 out of 20. It is obvious that he performed brilliantly precisely in the subjects that were more closely related to his interest in politics. One might also notice in passing that the two last subjects in which he received low marks were given by the same professor, a Mr. Baudoin. Presumably the man was a strict marker, or, alternatively, Trudeau found him or his subjects uninspiring.

After three years in law school, Trudeau obtained his Bachelor of Laws degree "with great distinction," and other important marks of recognition as well. On June 25, 1943, the daily *La Presse* listed the results of all the graduates in law and published a photograph of Trudeau, who had won both of the medals awarded: that of the governor general for excellence, and that of the lieutenant-governor "for the student who came first in the examination for the bachelor's degree." Of the seven prizes that were awarded, Trudeau walked off with three: the prize of the Chamber of Notaries, given to "the student who achieved the best results on the exam for notarial procedure"; the Jetté-Campbell prize for "the student who, during his studies, obtained the highest examination marks in civil law"; and the Larue prize, "for the student who, having demonstrated a satisfactory attendance and application during his courses, obtained the highest cumulative marks for all the exams." He was showered with congratulatory messages and replied to each one. Always frugal, he wrote the rough drafts of his replies on the back of the envelopes or of the letters. He did not boast of his triumph. His sister Suzette, who happened to be at Old Orchard at that time, only heard of it from someone else. She wrote him in English on July 1: "In one of his letters, Pierre R.[14] sent me a clipping of *La Presse*. That was the first I heard of your most recent successes. It is good to know that your efforts were so rewarded." And yet, despite his brilliant performance, Trudeau never had a high regard for his studies at the Université de Montréal. In contrast to his high appreciation for Collège Brébeuf and for the quality of the education he received there, he had nothing but contempt for his law school. In all his interviews later, and again in his *Memoirs*, he would bring up his experience there only to contrast it unfavourably with what he experienced at Harvard.

This does not mean that, between 1940 and 1943, little happened with respect to his intellectual development. That conclusion would likely be drawn if one relied only on his *Memoirs*, where he granted so little space to those years, or on other accounts elsewhere. Here and there, the comment recurs that he was bored by his law courses. As a relief, he went motorcycling, played tricks on his friends (one recalls the incident of the Prussian helmet with Roger Rolland), he went on long canoe trips, and wrote "L'ascétisme en canot." He published a few light articles in the student publication *Quartier Latin*, with little connection to politics. In a word, to all appearances, Trudeau the student led a carefree life with little connection to what was happening at the time in the world outside the university.

In contrast, though, a few authors, such as François Lessard,[15] Esther Delisle,[16] David Somerville[17] and François Hertel,[18] did come out with troubling allegations: that Trudeau had participated in student demonstrations, that he had been involved in a secret society, that he had stored weapons in his basement, but these discordant voices went unheard in a media desert. Their assertions, considered extravagant, did not fit the now classic image of Trudeau as an apolitical young man. The fact that entire peoples were falling under the yoke of a tyrant had, somehow, escaped his notice. History recorded only a single intervention by Trudeau in politics, one that was reported by each and all, including by Trudeau himself, namely his speech in favour of the anti-conscription candidate, Jean Drapeau, which was reported by *Le Devoir* on November 26, 1942.

———✦———

Before discussing that speech, a reminder: in Quebec during the Second World War, as in all of Canada, students who did not go overseas had to belong to the COTC – the Canadian Officers Training Corps. Trudeau was no exception, and his archives contain many documents dealing with such items as his appointments for medical tests or his orders to report to training camp. A photograph shows him as one of seven men in casual dress at the military camp where they trained in the summer, Camp Farnham, Quebec. Trudeau wrote on the back of the photo: "Farnham. From June 21 to July 4, 1943. The 'commando types' of the 'no zeal' tent." And Trudeau wrote down their names: "Charles Lussier, Gabriel Filion, Robert Pager, Jean-Baptiste Boulanger, Pierre Trudeau, Jean Gascon. And the citizen neighbour: Jacques Lavigne."[19] Charles Lussier would later work closely with Trudeau on important projects, notably the magazine *Cité libre*, of which he would be on the board of directors in 1950, and on the book which Trudeau edited in 1956, *La Grève de l'amiante*, for which he contributed the seventh chapter, "La grève dans nos cadres juridiques." In 1976, Trudeau would appoint him to a five-year term as chairman of the Canada Council. Jean-Baptiste Boulanger would later become a psychiatrist, but when this photo was taken, he and Trudeau were already working on a great secret project that we shall describe in detail in Chapter 9. Jean Gascon would become, as is well known, a giant of Quebec's theatre, co-founding the Théâtre du Nouveau Monde, becoming the first director of the National Theatre School, and, from 1968 to 1974, he would serve as artistic director of the Stratford Shakespearean Festival.

Another photograph taken that same summer shows several young men clad in shorts, stripped to the waist, with gas masks covering their faces. The photo gives a definite suggestion that they took their military training rather casually, as Trudeau confirmed in his *Memoirs*: "You were either conscripted into the army, or if you were a student you had to join the Canadian Officers Training Corps. This required us to go to an armoury in the city twice a week to do drills and learn how to handle weapons. Each summer, in addition, the COTC sent us to Camp Farnham for a few weeks of additional training. Nearly all former students who are my age remember the COTC, whether fondly or otherwise. For my part, I recall a run-in with an officer who was giving us orders in English. Since he was addressing French-speaking recruits, I wanted to know why he wasn't commanding us in our own language. But, as you might expect, my request had little effect. Neither the times nor the army favoured bilingualism in federal institutions."[20] There Trudeau appears already as the champion of French he was to remain all his life.

Strange to say, Trudeau's military training in the 1940s did not seem to convince him of the need to fight in this war against Nazism. "The war was an undeniably important reality, but a very distant one. Moreover, it was part of current events, and as I have explained, they did not interest me very much. . . . I am sure I was vaguely aware, at the start of the war, that it might constitute the most dramatic adventure the men of my generation would ever confront. But if you were a French Canadian in Montreal in the early 1940s, you did not automatically believe that this was a just war. We still knew nothing of the Holocaust and we tended to think of this war as a settling of scores among the superpowers."[21]

By his own account, Trudeau devoted little attention to a war that threatened to destroy Western civilization, until he attended Harvard University in 1944 at the age of twenty-five. The young man who could hardly wait to engage in the *real* struggle of life let himself be carried along by public opinion. But what deeply concerned him and the people around him was that Prime Minister Mackenzie King had broken his 1939 promise not to impose conscription for service overseas. *That* was worth fighting over. Trudeau explained: "I remember that at the beginning of the war a Mr. Gourd, a family friend, took me to the Forum to hear a speech by Ernest Lapointe, who was Prime Minister Mackenzie King's right-hand man and Quebec lieutenant. And so I heard this politician solemnly promise this huge crowd that his government would 'never' impose compulsory military service on Canadians. French Canadians still remembered the 1917 conscription crisis, with its riots and its deaths. Lapointe's promise was therefore seen as enormously important, and it led Quebeckers to feel certain that re-electing the Liberal Party would ensure that the next government would never introduce conscription."[22]

In the event, enacting conscription was exactly what the government did, following a plebiscite held in April 1942. The French-Canadian population felt that it had been betrayed. Of the entire six years of one of the most horrible wars ever experienced by the human race, what most French Canadians were to remember best was the so-called conscription crisis.[23] And Trudeau shared fully this obsessive sense of betrayal. It motivated what would be, in his own account, his only political activity. "When the Liberals subsequently decided to get Major-General Léo La Flèche elected in a by-election in Outremont, a young lawyer named Jean Drapeau ran against him as the 'candidate of the conscripted.' I participated in it by speaking at one of his rallies. That was, I believe, my only participation in the politics of that era."[24]

In that speech of November 25, 1942, Trudeau uttered the cry that, the next morning, would resound in the headline of a very detailed story in Le Devoir: "Finie la flèche du conquérant, vive le drapeau de la liberté!" ("Out with the Arrow of the Conqueror, Long Live the Flag of Freedom!") The pun was perfect. La Flèche, the name of the pro-conscription Liberal candidate, meant, literally "the arrow." Drapeau, the name of the anti-conscription candidate, meant "flag." Trudeau combined their names into a deadly anti-British, anti-colonial thrust. Was this, really, as he said in his Memoirs and as people have believed, his only political activity during the war? We shall let that unlikely claim pass for the moment. But first, back to his speech.

On that evening of November 25, 1942, in anticipation of the by-election that had been called for November 30, in the constituency of Outremont, a political rally was held at Outremont's École Lajoie in support of a young lawyer still articling named Jean Drapeau. It was the beginning of a public career that would later make him famous as the mayor of Montreal. He was the only candidate running against a war hero, Major-General Léo-Richer La Flèche, who had been recalled from overseas to become Assistant Deputy to the Minister of National War Services and was then named to the cabinet as minister. He was on a mission to defend the Liberal government's new policy of conscription for service overseas. According to the account in *Le Devoir*, the rally attracted such a crowd that loudspeakers were set up outside for all the people who had been unable to make their way inside the hall, so that they, too, could "participate in the enthusiasm that reigned all evening."

The newspaper account conveyed a sense of the high tension and the anger of the participants, notably the six pro-Drapeau speakers whose interventions were noted in the report. The first to denounce La Flèche was Michel Chartrand, a fiery orator who would later become an incendiary labour leader. After him came D'Iberville Fortier, and then Pierre Trudeau, followed by two others. The last would be Jean Drapeau, the "candidate of the conscripted."

With the torrent of words and the slashing irony that would become his trademark, Michel Chartrand made a show of great generosity in granting General La Flèche "the right to think that his *patrie* is in England," while ours, he said, is in Canada. Chartrand spoke for the orators who would come to the microphone after him, and, no doubt, for a majority of Quebec's French Canadians, when he declared to the crowd: "It is false to say today that we are fighting for Canada." If it were so, he would not hesitate one minute to defend and protect "the soil which we inhabit, the soil where our parents live, the soil which we know." Only, this war was not about protecting Canada: it was a conflict between England and its allies against its enemies of the moment. So, if English Canadians were backing the war, that was not because they thought that Canada was threatened, but quite simply because they were more British than Canadian. Blinded by their imperialist patriotism, they forgot the promise that Mackenzie King had now betrayed. They were free to define themselves as British if that was their choice, Chartrand conceded. But that in no way gave them the right to put "great pressure" on French Canadians so as to compel them to sign on to an imperialist policy. "They call us cowards and claim that we do not speak for Canada," Chartrand said, referring to the massive "No" vote in that year's plebiscite by Quebec's French Canadians. The fact was, Chartrand said, that the plebiscite was a political fraud devised to allow King to go back on his solemn promise. Chartrand, the future far left-wing union leader, was so carried away by his eloquence that he accused Ottawa of wanting to impose on Quebec "a centralizing and reductive socialism."

D'Iberville Fortier, who would later take on prominent federal positions, including ambassador to several countries and Commissioner of Official Languages, took the stage after Chartrand. He, too, waxed ironic. French Canadians, he recalled, had often been called "the spoiled children of Canada." He appealed to the crowd: "Have they spoiled us enough?" Presumably the crowd responded with heartfelt boos. This time, he continued, the federal government had outdone itself: "At the instigation of our own dear *Gazette*, of the *Globe and Mail*, and of Toronto's Two Hundred, they are sending us a traveling salesman with a mission to sell conscription to the Province of Quebec . . . and, if Quebec will not buy . . . *to give it to us anyway*." (The italics were in *Le Devoir*'s account.) In other words, according to Fortier, if Quebeckers would not buy into conscription, the government would impose it anyway.

D'Iberville Fortier then took up the same arguments put forward by Chartrand. "If English Canadians, because they had been in this country barely a few generations, wanted us to fight all of England's battles on land and sea across the globe, wherever the British Empire was engaged in military action, we, on the contrary, would accept conscription only for the defence of our Canada." He perceived English-speaking Canadians as newcomers compared to French Canadians, and gave that as the explanation for their eagerness to fight overseas. "While we understand that civilization, democracy and Christianity are endangered, we also understand that our own national freedom is at stake."

That surprising statement deserves a moment's consideration. It has often been said that French Canadians opposed participating in the war because they did not understand what was at stake. But here was Fortier stating quite candidly that the war was waged in defence of "civilization, democracy and Christianity." Yet, when the national freedom of French Canadians was in the picture, those values somehow became secondary.

Trudeau spoke next, and then a teacher by the name of Jean-Louis Arbique, who complimented French Canadians for their exemplary patriotism, ready as they were to defend their country. "The French Canadians have behaved in this war as in all the preceding wars, in a manner that deserves the fullest praise. . . . They know that their first duty, one which they will never shirk, is to defend Canada."

Drapeau himself, the "candidate of the conscripts," also took up that theme when his turn came to speak: "We are not against anyone, we are for Canada, we want to live according to our principles. While it is true that we are proud to be *Canadiens*, let us go back to our tradition of knowing when to fight for the superior interests of the nation." And so for Drapeau, as for the other speakers, "the superior interests of the nation" were not at stake in this war, since the country was not threatened. So many fervent declarations of willingness to defend Canada would suggest that the war was being waged far away, on the other side of the Atlantic.

And yet, even as the speeches unfolded, German submarines had already torpedoed several merchant ships in the Gulf of St. Lawrence, causing many casualties. The Nazi high command had decided to prevent provisions shipped through the St. Lawrence from Canada and the United States from reaching Great Britain. To protect the shipping, the government of Canada had built or expanded naval bases in Halifax and Sydney, Nova Scotia, and in Gaspé, Quebec. A few days after the inauguration of the Gaspé base, on May 1, 1942, a German submarine penetrated into the Gulf of St. Lawrence and sank two merchant ships, one British, the other Dutch. On July 6, 1942, three ships of a convoy of twelve were torpedoed, one of them Greek. The losses rose month by month. On October 14, 1942, the month before the meeting in Outremont, the ferry *Caribou*, plying between Sydney and Port-aux-Basques, Newfoundland, was attacked and sunk. Of the 237 on board, only 101 passengers survived.

The battle in the Gulf of St. Lawrence, and notably the tragic loss of the *Caribou*, convinced English Canada that the fighting was not restricted to Europe: the German submarines had sunk twenty-one ships in the St. Lawrence, and several others had been badly damaged, and the number of people who had lost their lives was nearing three hundred. Airplanes had been reported missing, precious cargo had been destroyed. Some of the battles took place barely three hundred kilometres from the city of Quebec.[25] But, on that November 25, 1942, at l'École Lajoie, all the speakers stated with firm conviction that this war being waged on the other side of the Atlantic was not Canada's concern. Were it to be so, they would unhesitatingly fight to defend their country.

Oddly, Trudeau would write in 1993 in his *Memoirs*: "At the time, Canada was in the grip of a real war hysteria. Is it true that the Gulf of St. Lawrence was swarming with enemy submarines? I have no idea (although I know that one Canadian ferry, the *Caribou*, was torpedoed, with heavy loss of life), but a lot of people were absolutely convinced of it at the time."[26] Why, fifty-one years after that meeting, did he still have no idea? And who were these many people who were in the grip of war hysteria? Clearly, on that night in Outremont, the speakers were not among them.

When Trudeau's turn came to speak, he gave the evening's most passionate speech. Not only did he provide *Le Devoir* with its headline, but the reporter commented about the speaker who succeeded Trudeau: "The teacher Jean-Louis Arbique was less fiery than the man who spoke before him." Fiery, indeed! Trudeau launched into his tirade by insisting that the people owed it to themselves to cast their ballot, not so much for Drapeau, as against General La Flèche, who had the indecency to campaign while wearing his soldier's uniform. "In a democracy, I learned that a candidate should come forward as a citizen and not as the representative of a military clique." He then denounced the "disgusting dishonesty" of the King government, which resorted to wiles to force conscription for overseas service on an unwilling French-Canadian people. In a democracy, Trudeau said, the people are never wrong. "And if we are not in a democracy, let the revolution begin without delay."

The revolution? Was Trudeau speaking rhetorically, or did he really mean revolution? We can't tell just yet. But he left no doubt about his contempt for the members of the King government, whom he divided into two categories, "the big shots who are traitors," and "the big shots who are honest." The reporter did not record whether Trudeau had more to say about the "traitors," but he did stigmatize the "honest big shots" who illustrated their "stupidity" by accepting conscription. They were stupid because they accepted that Canada was under attack; Trudeau joined the chorus of the previous speakers to scorn that notion. "The best example of imbecility is the argument about the house on fire," he said. The proof that the government in Ottawa was following a policy that was "imbecilic, when it wasn't disgusting," was that this government had declared war "at a time when America was not threatened with an invasion, at a time when Hitler had not yet won his staggering victories."

Those last words deserve a pause. Hitler had not yet won his staggering victories? So Trudeau by now was fully aware of Hitler's vast conquests. He might surely have concluded that the threat was real, that the declaration of war had been neither "imbecilic," nor "disgusting," but justified. Like D'Iberville Fortier who recognized the threat to "civilization, democracy and Christianity," Trudeau and the other anti-conscription speakers were aware of the serious stakes. And yet, belittling the Nazi threat, Trudeau considered only the affront to the French-Canadian people. He suggested that the King government's policy on conscription for overseas service justified revolution. Was it a hyperbole? Not quite. The final words of the speech suggest a call to revolution: "Citizens of Quebec, don't be satisfied with belly aching. Long live the flag of liberty. We've had enough of band-aids ("*cataplasmes*"), the time has come for cataclysms." Moreover, his words, raising the flag of freedom against the arrow of the conqueror, sounded like a call to separation.

How did it happen that a young man who claimed to have so little interest in the war was able to give so fiery a speech? Why did he evoke revolution and cataclysms in a speech meant to help elect Drapeau, the "candidate of the conscripts"? And, when he suggested that reforms would be merely band-aids, what did he have in mind when he spoke of cataclysms? Did he really mean to advocate overthrowing the established order – a genuine revolution? And, if so, what replacement regime did he have in mind? This impassioned speech clearly went far beyond the single issue of conscription. The five paragraphs devoted to it in *Le Devoir* raised questions that have so far remained unanswered.

The speakers that evening clearly were confident that they spoke for all French Canadians. But history is not that simple. When the vote was counted the following week, General La Flèche won the election easily with 12,378 votes, while Jean Drapeau received 6,948. But, to understand where Trudeau was coming from at that time, and what were his political views and extracurricular activities, one must take a broader view of the social and ideological context. In particular, given the ascendancy of the Roman Catholic religion in Quebec generally and in Trudeau's mental makeup in particular, it is time to take a close look at the Church's position on the Depression, on its attendant social and economic crisis, and on the Second World War.

*Chapter 6*

# CORPORATISM, A BLESSING!

*Here and there we find a few fragments of social justice. We need more than that; we need full-scale corporatism.*

— CARDINAL VILLENEUVE

*L'Ordre nouveau,* April 17, 1937

THE DEVASTATING DEPRESSION of the 1930s provoked in almost every Western country a fundamental reconsideration of the established order. For some, the objective went no further than reforming existing institutions. Such was U.S. president Franklin D. Roosevelt's intention with his New Deal of 1933. Others, in far greater numbers, envisioned the radical refashioning of society itself. In France, for example, a movement encompassing intellectuals and politicians sought a "New Order," vague in outline, that could provide a middle way between liberal democracy, which they considered to have failed, and various totalitarian options, which they also rejected.

In Quebec, as might be expected, the Catholic clergy led the way in the search for solutions. Priests and bishops agreed that the root causes of the crying social problems were planted in Protestant Anglo-Saxon individualism and materialism: they led to the "excesses of capitalism" and to the liberal democratic mentality. These imports, alien to traditional French Catholic Quebec, were judged to be the "fruit of the Reformation." As the solution to the grievous problems of society, Quebec's men of the cloth preached the "revival of the soul," which would begin with the repudiation of "pagan doctrines" and the collective return to "true Christian philosophy," so that there might emerge, at last, "the New Man."

In 1891, Pope Leo XIII issued his encyclical *Rerum novarum* ("About the new realities"), dealing with the new relations between capital and labour. On May 15, 1931, forty years to the day later, Pope Pius XI issued a new encyclical, *Quadragesimo anno* ("On the fortieth year"), subtitled "On reconstruction of the social order." Both encyclicals were attempts by the Holy See to come to terms with the new urban industrial societies. Pius XI's attempt to find a spiritual solution to the Depression gave a powerful new impulse to the quest for a "new order." In Quebec, the Jesuit priest, Joseph-Papin Archambault would become its chief herald. He had already established himself as a pioneer of social Catholicism for having been one of the founders of the Jesuit-run École sociale populaire – the social school of the people – which had been born in 1911 in the spirit of *Rerum novarum*. Its objective was to bring Catholic social doctrine and Catholic action to the urban masses, particularly by training a lay elite and encouraging participation in closed retreats. Fr. Archambault was appointed the École's chief executive officer in 1929, two years before *Quadragesimo anno*, and he would remain at the helm until 1959. Worth noting, as well, was that he had been the chief initiator in 1913 of the French-Canadian nationalist Ligue des droits du français and became its first president under the pseudonym of Pierre Homier. In 1917, the Ligue founded the right-wing nationalist monthly *L'Action française*, which would be the predecessor of what is today the most influential nationalist-separatist publication, *L'Action nationale*,[1] and he acted as its co-editor from 1917 to 1921. In 1921, through the École sociale populaire, he also founded the "Semaines sociales du Canada" (the Social Weeks of Canada), which, every year, brought together for a week members of the Church hierarchy with lay Catholics to discuss from both a religious and social perspective selected topics of current relevance. His ardent Catholicism and his aggressive French-Canadian nationalism were fused into a single conviction and made him a force to reckon with. Raymond Laliberté, a political scientist at Laval University, wrote that it was under Fr. Archambault's influence that "a genuine theory of political restructuring of French Canada"[2] slowly emerged.

On October 21, 1931, just a few months after the publication of *Quadragesimo anno*, Fr. Archambault gave an important lecture on it and on *Rerum novarum* at Quebec's Laval University.[3] He began by denouncing the evil that afflicted Canadian society. "The social order, at the present time, is badly shaken. Its economic underpinnings are giving way under the multiple shocks of a Depression that no legislative or financial measure seems able to control. . . . Just look at the immense army of the unemployed, an idled and worried crowd that is tormented by hunger and that revolutionary propaganda has already penetrated."4 But Fr. Archambault was able to bring tidings of reassurance amid the gloom: "Fortunately, in this stormy sky, a sign of hope has flashed. It rises from Rome."5 The light of hope was the social doctrine of the Catholic Church, as enunciated by *Rerum novarum* in 1891 and just renewed and expanded by *Quadragesimo anno*. Fr. Archambault stated that it would not be enough to read and meditate over these directives of the Pope: "We must also act. We must attempt to achieve the Papal program; we must work to bring to fruition the economic and spiritual reforms that he advocates."6 And what action was required? The priest gave his answer: listen to the Pope. "The restoration of the social order is impossible, Pius XI tells us, without a complete renewal of the Christian spirit. Because the present difficulty is more than a technical question, it is a moral question. At its root what it reveals is the failure of the soul."7

For Fr. Archambault, for the Church in Quebec, to speak of the Christian spirit meant to speak of the Catholic spirit – which, therefore, excluded the rest of Canada, mostly Protestant, from being part of the solution to the Depression. The conclusion of Fr. Archambault's address left no room for ambiguity: he invited "each Catholic to get resolutely to work." Implicitly, he was proposing a true revolution that could only be carried through in Quebec, as it was the only Catholic province of Canada. In this sense, Fr. Archambault, like other members of the Church hierarchy in Quebec, was sending out an equivocal message. Without explicitly championing the separation of Quebec, he was insisting on the urgency of a new social order that could, in fact, only be achieved in a Catholic country, and so in a sovereign Quebec. The young Trudeau, who would begin his studies at Brébeuf within a year, would prove responsive to that message and draw its logical conclusion.

Fr. Archambault then turned his attention from the spiritual to the temporal domain. For a solution to be found to the Depression and to restore the social order, the existing liberalism and individualism must be fought, but without falling into the false remedies of communism and socialism. Instead, he proposed a rather simple alternative for restoring the social order: the creation of industry-wide associations. "In the place of class struggle, which has caused so many evils, [these associations] would substitute a sincere collaboration and would put the society on its way to a felicitous transformation."[8] The political crisis could also be resolved if only the state properly fulfilled the role that was outlined in the papal encyclicals. The state must "direct, supervise, stimulate, contain, all in accordance with what circumstances suggest or necessity dictates."[9]

Fr. Archambault's proposals for dealing with the worldwide crisis, abstract as they were, gradually were taken up across Quebec. On November 16, 1931, not four weeks after that speech, the bishop of Chicoutimi, Monsignor Charles Lamarche, sent out a circular letter to the clergy of his diocese along with a copy of the encyclical, *Quadragesimo anno*. He, also, attributed the Depression to God's anger. "For too long, now, the attempt was made to organize the society without God and against God . . . But, despite the ingratitude and blindness of His children, this God, who is also a Father, did not forget his mercy: He punishes the world, but only in order to save it."[10] The Quebec hierarchy would return often to this interpretation of the Depression as a well-deserved punishment for sin, along with the implication that the Depression could only be ended if the people turned back to God.

On January 4, 1932, the Archbishop of Montreal, Monsignor Georges Gauthier, also sent out a letter to his clergy, and he, too, sought for a solution to the Depression. But he was most concerned to warn his faithful against the dangers of communism, which the Pope had denounced as "intrinsically perverse." For French Canadians, he insisted, the choice should be simple: "Rome or Moscow. We have reached the crossroads and we must make a choice. For us, any hesitation will be short-lived, if there is any at all. We shall turn towards Rome because Rome means Catholicism, and Catholicism is our salvation."[11] He was, in fact, conveying the exact same message as Pius XI: "We can truthfully say that the Church, imitating Christ, has passed through the ages doing good to all. There would be neither socialism nor communism if the leaders of the nations had not spurned the Church's teachings and her motherly warnings."[12] In consequence, Mgr. Gauthier concluded, Catholics must implement the social system proposed by Pius XI: "To the extent that we achieve this harmony among all the branches of economic activity, it will become possible to establish 'a policy with respect to salaries' which will ensure for the greatest possible number of workers that they will be able to rent out their labour and so purchase all that is needed for a decent living."[13] This prelate's remedies, be it noted, were rather more concrete than merely conversion, since they included a policy on salaries and "harmony" between capital and labour.

In the two encyclicals dealing with modern economic conditions, not much attention is paid to the theme so familiar in Quebec of leaving the city to return to the land. But the Church in Quebec was particularly responsive to this solution. At their meeting of June 3, 1932, the bishops and archbishops gave their enthusiastic approval to "the return to the land." This would constitute, they maintained "the most profoundly humane solution to the current problem. . . . That is why We strongly recommend an exodus towards the countryside."[14] This single remedy was recommended over and over. Mgr. Gauthier, for example, stated in a letter of February 4, 1934: "Industry uproots the man from the countryside; it tends to create in the cities what is called the proletariat, or even pauperism. . . . Meanwhile, the land remains our essential wealth and the condition of our stability."[15]

---

The Church urged young people to become involved in social action. Answering that call, while adding to it a strong streak of nationalism, a score of university students, including the future noted ecologist Pierre Dansereau and two future publishers of Le Devoir, Gérard Filion and André Laurendeau, together founded a movement that they called Jeune-Canada. In December 1932, they read out publicly in a hall of Collège Sainte-Marie the "Manifesto of the Young Generation." "French is an official language of Canada just as much as is English," they proclaimed. They demanded equal treatment for French and English, both for the languages and for those who spoke them. They expressed strong support for "the campaign which is presently waged for the refrancisation of the Province of Quebec." Going beyond the issue of language, they criticized the state of the economy. "The French Canadians are in the process of becoming, in their own homeland, a vast people of proletarians," they warned. "We cannot accept that foreign capitalists who exploit our national resources and the French Canadian work force should be forever authorized to practice a veritable ostracism against our engineers and our technicians while attributing to us in our own country's economic life the role of labourers and servants." They ended their manifesto with this appeal to the youth: "Let us remember that we will not be '*Maîtres chez nous*' ('Masters in Our Own Homes') unless we become worthy of being so."

The slogan, "*Maîtres chez nous*," here making its first public appearance, was to have an important future. The manifesto provoked a great deal of interest and was published by many newspapers and magazines in the following months. Patriotic associations, like the Société Saint-Jean-Baptiste, got behind the youth movement, encouraging their members to sign a petition in support of the manifesto. It is reported that more than one hundred thousand people signed. The movement left behind "an important imprint on the social and political scene of Quebec in the 1930s," wrote historian Louise Bienvenue in her doctoral thesis.[16] The movement, as it became more successful, also became increasingly radical. Over the next five years, it attempted to awaken the collective consciousness of French Canadians. Its defence of a Catholic and French Quebec eventually led it to propose Quebec's economic and political independence. On December 3, 1934, in a lecture titled "Who will save Quebec?" André Laurendeau declared: "Catholics and French Canadians, that is what we are. . . . And our patrie, ladies and gentlemen, is Quebec."

---

Meanwhile, elsewhere in Canada, socialism was taking institutional form, winning adherents and offering more down-to-earth solutions to the Depression. In August 1932, a socialist party was born in Calgary, called the Co-operative Commonwealth Federation (CCF). In anticipation of that event, the bishops of Quebec and of Ottawa met in Quebec City on June 3, 1932, and issued a pastoral letter to their clergy, to the religious communities, and to all Catholics, to warn them of the threat.[17] Putting forward once again the view that the current general suffering of the people was willed by God to "bring them back into the paths of virtue,"[18] the bishops recommended that the faithful turn to prayer, attend "all the liturgical ceremonies," and do "penance in order that their sins be erased."

But the prelates did not limit themselves to spiritual remedies. They put everyone on notice regarding the dangerous seductions of socialism and called for its repression: "It is up to the public authorities to put a stop to the proselytizing by these agents of spiritual and temporal desolation."[19] At its convention of July 1933, the CCF would elect the Methodist clergyman J.S. Woodsworth as party leader and adopt the celebrated Regina Manifesto as its anti-capitalist, non-communist program. But, in anticipation of the convention, an article in the April–May issue of the monthly *Pour la Restauration sociale au Canada*, published by the Jesuits' École sociale populaire, delivered a severe criticism of the new party.[20] Its author was the Dominican priest and sociologist Georges-Henri Lévesque, who would later go on to fame as the founder of Laval University's School of Social Sciences and one of the instigators of the Quiet Revolution.

On October 5, 1933, the archbishops and bishops of all of Canada – most of them French Canadians – met in Quebec City to condemn the CCF.[21] They quoted the warning pronounced by Pius XI in *Quadragesimo anno*: "It belongs to Our Pastoral Office to warn these persons of the grave and imminent evil: let all remember that Liberalism is the father of this Socialism that is pervading morality and culture and that Bolshevism is its heir." The Pope also declared Bolshevism to be "the sworn enemy of the Holy Church and of God Himself." Socialism, then, was to be feared religiously because it was on the slippery slope to bolshevism. So it was that, on February 4, 1934, Mgr. Georges Gauthier, the archbishop of Montreal, issued a pastoral letter and ordered that it be "read during the sermon at all the parish masses, on the Sunday after its reception." The letter was long. And what was its message? While communism was not a threat in Canada, he conceded, "socialism – which is communism in the long run – is very much to be feared, and it is in the process of establishing itself among us."[22] And so the archbishop went on to condemn the CCF. Mgr. Gauthier also recommended that the faithful return to the land. But, above all, he joined the other Canadian bishops and archbishops in calling for the establishment of a new social order, rather vaguely defined, that would foster co-operation between the social classes: "We must hasten with our prayers the moment when, in accordance with the thinking of Pius XI, these pressing questions will be regulated by collective agreements, with owners and workers establishing by mutual consent a regime that takes into account the common good and that favours the collaboration of the several occupational associations."[23] It is noteworthy that a new expression had entered the vocabulary of the Church in Quebec: it now called for the *collaboration of the occupational associations.*

———◦———

On February 1, 1933, shortly before his elevation to the title of cardinal, Rodrigue Villeneuve, the Archbishop of Quebec, had delivered a very long discourse, issuing a call for French Canadians to mobilize in response to the Pope's summons: "The course of our history will not be changed tomorrow by fruitless protestations nor by frights. It is by action, the action of everyone, the action of you, the faithful, as well as the action of your leaders."[24] The cardinal-designate invited the laity to take part in two areas from which Catholic action "will be able to study and draw up an *economico-social* program that conforms to Catholic principles and that will form, from a religious and social point of view, the leaders and the propagandists of the economico-social organizations that will be animated by its spirit."[25] In addition, Villeneuve announced, "if political questions have a religious and moral dimension, [Catholic action] can and must intervene directly."[26] The Church in Quebec thereby took on a radical new direction: in the name of Christ, and in conformity with the messages of the Vatican, it would henceforth become involved in the economic, social, and political spheres: "Well, gentlemen, the Pope teaches us how to save the world, how to drag society back from ruin, how to follow the Church and raise the standard of Jesus Christ. It is by Catholic action."[27]

The answer to the bishops' summons was not long in coming. The April–May issue of the periodical published by the École sociale populaire was titled "Pour la Restauration sociale au Canada," almost the identical title that Fr. Archambault had given to his speech of October 1931, and that itself was the subtitle of *Quadragesimo anno*. This issue was intended to give direction for future action. It contained three articles: the first two offered a critique leading to the rejection of, respectively, capitalism and, as already mentioned, of socialism – the CCF. The third

article, by the Jesuit Louis Chagnon, was titled "Catholic Social
Guidelines," and declared the source of its inspiration: "These few
pages are nothing but a brief summary of the Catholic social guidelines, an outline of the guiding principles derived from the encyclical
*Quadragesimo anno.*"[28] It put forward in little more than two pages a
thirteen-point action program that would enter Quebec history as "The
1933 Program for Social Restoration." We summarize the most interesting items in the order in which they appeared:

- The state must subject to severe regulation all financial institutions and joint stock companies so as to put an end to abuses and
  speculation.
- The true Christian spirit must replace a spirit of dominating and
  greedy egotism.
- It is the duty of the state to impose an overall direction on the
  national economy and to establish a National Economic Council
  which will express a *corporatist organization,* and make it possible for the authorities to act in close collaboration with the
  authorized representatives of all the branches of production.
- We must aim at establishing a *corporatist order* through the
  complete and legal organization of the different occupations or
  industries.
- In order to re-establish a proper population balance, we must
  foster the family farm, restrict industrialized farming, and
  promote colonization systematically.

Let us linger for a moment on the words that we have italicized.
Here, in May 1933, we see for the first time the appearance of the words
*corporatist organization* and *corporatist order.* The state is given the
responsibility to set up the institutions required for the proper functioning of this new order. Indeed, the model proposed makes important
demands of the state; its role and its power will be progressively defined
in the following years. What remains unspecified is which order of government, federal or provincial, is to carry out these new responsibilities
of the state. The program does maintain, however, in its thirteenth and
last point that "the state must respect the rights of the provinces and the

principle of the equality of the two races." That would seem to imply that the corporatist model could be implemented right across Canada, even though it would seem obvious that infusing a "truly Christian spirit" in the majority Protestant Canadian federation would be an impossibility, given that it involved transforming the society in accordance with the exclusively Catholic vision of Pope Pius XI.

The program thus put forward was to inspire the creation of a new political party, the Action libérale nationale (ALN), which came into being in 1934. Its founder, Paul Gouin, was the son of former Liberal premier Lomer Gouin, and grandson of former premier Honoré Mercier. Gouin had become convinced that the current Liberal Party led by Premier Louis-Alexandre Taschereau was given over to precisely the economic liberalism which the Church condemned, and so he broke with it dramatically. His new party was calculated to bring comfort to the Church, and especially to the Jesuits. Its Manifesto, published in 1934, echoed in its first paragraph the strictures of *Quadragesimo anno* against economic liberalism and the need for a new order: "The current Depression is largely due to faulty distribution in the economy, to the cupidity of high finance and to abuses of all kinds which have crept into the functioning of the democratic system." The policies announced were also calculated to please the Church in Quebec: "We, like so many others, firmly believe that the task of economic restoration comes down mainly to one of rural restoration, based on the family farm and on cooperation. That is why we place agrarian reform at the very heart of our plan of action." In fact, the ALN went considerably farther in its program than just agrarian reform. Expressing both its nationalism and its bias against capitalism, it proposed "to break by every possible means the grip in which the provinces and the municipalities are held by the great financial institutions, the electricity trust and that of the pulp and paper industry."

In the provincial elections of November 1935, thanks to its strategic alliance with Maurice Duplessis's Conservative Party, the ALN succeeded in electing twenty-six members of the Legislative Assembly, including Gouin. But the ALN was to be short-lived. Duplessis soon merged the two

parties to create the Union nationale. Feeling betrayed, Gouin struggled
for four years to recreate the ALN. The elections of 1939 turned out to
be a total disaster for him as the ALN was wiped out. Despite its failure,
there is no doubt that the ALN, like the Jeune-Canada movement, helped
to spread in Quebec, especially in the colleges and universities, reform
ideas inspired by the Church.

The Church continued in its search for a solution to the Depression.
On November 30, 1937, all of Quebec's bishops, headed by Cardinal
Villeneuve, issued a pastoral letter on "the rural problem." It was to be
read during mass in all the parishes of Quebec. It is beyond question,
they affirmed, that "there exists among us an *agricultural question.*"
The bishops recommended that "our rural populations should remain
attached to the soil."29 They explained that farmers had been abandoning their land "more for moral reasons and for a state of mind
rather than because of the Depression or of temporary hardships."30
The letter ends by proposing a solution to present difficulties: "If you
want to lighten your earthly trials, be deeply pious and generous
Christians, and both the social problem and the crisis in agriculture will
be substantially resolved."31

———————◈———————

The proposals to resolve social problems by economic, social, and political measures had an important place. But it must not be forgotten that for
Pius XI and for the Church, desirable social and political changes were
impossible to bring about "without a complete renewal of the Christian
spirit," because the Depression was caused largely by spiritual transgres-
sions. But how was the spirit, the soul to be set right? Part of the remedy
was to be found in the Spiritual Exercises of Saint Ignatius and by the
spread of the practice of closed retreats, such as those that were held in all
the classical colleges. A "closed" retreat was one where the "retreatant"
spent twenty-four hours a day on premises dedicated to spiritual renewal,
away from home and isolated from all outside influences, most of the time
in silence, meditating and praying, and receiving spiritual instruction
from a retreat master.

Here, for example, was how Pierre Trudeau recorded his agenda on
November 4, 1935, when he was on a closed retreat in Boucherville.

6:00   Wake up time

6:25   Visit to the Chapel

6:30   Angelus – Prayer

       Instruction in the Chapel

       Meditation in one's room

7:30   Mass

8:00   Review of the meditation (in one's room)

8:15   Breakfast – Rosary outside

9:30   Instruction in the Chapel

       Meditation in one's room

10:45  Review of the meditation in one's room

11:00  Free time

11:45  Examination of conscience in the Chapel

12:00  Lunch – Recreation

1:30   Stations of the Cross

2:00   Free time

2:45   Instruction in the Chapel

       Meditation in one's room

4:00   Free time

4:30   Instruction in the Chapel

       Meditation in one's room

5:45   Benediction of the Blessed Sacrament

7:45   Supper – Recreation

       Prayer in the chapel

       Instruction – Bedtime

The Church was convinced that from these closed retreats would emerge a new elite, and Fr. Archambault was their most zealous proponent: "Like the apostle emerging from the upper chamber, it is a new man who goes down into the fray, his spirit ignited by the light of the Gospel, his will bent on the Gospel's diffusion. No matter what events he may encounter, he will face them as a Christian. If only 10, 20, or 50 leaders of industry or of finance, union leaders or statesmen, were to put themselves through this strong discipline, they would be transformed and would then act on society like the yeast in the dough; they would fashion it and renew it."[32]

The Jesuits saw it as their own special mission to foster that elite. From its ranks they hoped to see a leader emerge who would reflect his Christian education and its values. In 1935, the young André Laurendeau, who was soon to become an outstanding opinion leader in Quebec, prayed that Heaven would send a *pure laine* French-Canadian leader: "We ask Providence to send us this man who will lead us out of social and national dislocation, who will wrench us from the claws of the moneyed powers, of the grasping trusts; we need a real one hundred per cent French Canadian, one who loves his *patrie*, and who will save it. At the call of this leader, we will be ready for every sacrifice and, when he appears, we will recognize him, we will place ourselves under his orders, because we will be ready to struggle and to vanquish."[33]

Assuming that God were actually to answer these prayers, how would the leader come to power? To that question, there was no answer. What if this leader should turn out to be a dictator? No problem! That is even what some were calling for. As an example, a classmate of Trudeau named Robert Labelle published an article in the college paper with the revealing headline: "In favour of dictatorship." He invoked the authority of St. Thomas Aquinas to argue in the *Brébeuf* of April 16, 1938, that "the best government is that of a single person." Without the need to deal with the demands of a parliament, he argued, a dictatorship could act more quickly and more effectively, and so make it possible to emerge from the Depression. And the young scholar concluded: "A dictatorial regime . . . would be the best possible system of government" for Canada. A drawing of Mussolini illustrated the article.

Was this merely the opinion of one hare-brained student? Not at all. The very next year Lionel Groulx drew the portrait of the leader he hoped to see appear: "And you, young people, who have so often disappointed us, but who always then rekindled our hopes, do make sure, through all your efforts and all your prayers, that we shall see happen to us what is an essential condition of restoration for any people that has slumped too low; do make sure that there shall happen to us what has happened in Portugal, in Spain, in Ireland, in Poland, in Italy and even in Turkey: the arrival of a leader, someone who can draw others along, someone who can inspire enthusiasm and determination, someone, as well, who can calmly mobilize energies, a man who understands what organic and persevering policy is needed to save a country . . ."[34]

Is this what Fr. Archambault meant by "the apostle descending from the upper chamber"? Take Italy for example. Beginning in the early 1920s, Mussolini gradually put in place a regime that was totalitarian and fascist. He eliminated ruthlessly all opposition by closing down newspapers critical of the regime, by assassinations, by torture, by publicly humiliating or exiling those who opposed him. All other political parties were banished. The state became all-encompassing, as Mussolini expressed it in his often cited slogan: "Everything in the state, nothing outside the state, nothing against the state." (*Tutto nello Stato, niente al di fuori dello Stato, nulla conto lo Stato.*) Laws were passed whereby loyalty to the regime became a condition for employment in the public service. Immigrants were deprived of Italian citizenship. Reprisals became legal, not only in response to political actions, but even to words, ideas, and the merest intentions that were considered undesirable.[35] To all intents and purposes, the legislative and executive powers fused together as the Grand Fascist Council became the single most powerful organ of the state. Mussolini described accurately in a single sentence his vision of the corporatist state: "We control the political forces, we control the moral forces, we control the economic forces, and thus we are in the midst of the corporative fascist state."[36] Corporatism was a system which placed "the labour force at the disposal of its leader, as a 'mass which obeys.'"[37]

So this was the kind of leader so much admired by Groulx and so many others, the leader who, it was prayed, would come to save the French-Canadian people. Similar disturbing facts could be recalled from other countries lauded by Groulx. While their regimes varied somewhat from country to country, all were run by a strongman who was not subject to the vagaries of people's votes. And that was precisely their appeal, as Groulx explained: "In the domain of politics, two apparently insurmountable obstacles block the road to any reform: universal suffrage and financial dictatorship. The first chooses badly the representatives of the people, the second debases them."[38] This attitude was shared by most members of the French-Canadian elite.

The Church, closing its eyes to the danger posed by too powerful a leader and convinced that faith alone could save the world, prepared the youth by inculcating in them "a profound religion" and initiating them to the social doctrine promulgated in the encyclicals. As a student Trudeau attended many of the Church's training sessions – today we would call them indoctrination sessions – such as the "Semaine sociale" which was held from November 28 to December 4, 1937. We found forty pages of notes that he had carefully compiled in the course of the week. Among the distinguished speakers who addressed the audience were the inevitable Fr. Archambault, the nationalist philosopher, journalist, and critic Victor Barbeau, as well as Gérard Filion and André Laurendeau. Barbeau, ardent defender of the French language, would be instrumental in 1944 in the creation of the Académie canadienne-française. Filion was then the editor of the Catholic farmers' publication, *La Terre de chez nous*. He would later have a distinguished career as the anti-Duplessis publisher of *Le Devoir*. Laurendeau had just returned from two years in Paris, where he had studied philosophy and literature, at the Sorbonne and at the Institut catholique de Paris. He was then the just-appointed publisher of the nationalist publication *L'Action nationale*, succeeding his father, Arthur Laurendeau, and would later be outstanding as a journalist and publisher of *Le Devoir*. From 1963 to 1968, he would co-chair the Royal Commission on Bilingualism and Biculturalism.

One talk given that week was titled: "The errors of economic liberalism." Another, "The just demands of capital and of labour," was given by Alfred Charpentier, president of the Confédération des Travailleurs catholiques du Canada, who described the misdeeds of liberalism and of capitalism. Léon-Mercier Gouin, the brother of Paul Gouin and later a Liberal senator from 1940 to 1976, gave a talk on "The illusion of communism and socialism." The title of yet another talk was "The abuses of modern capitalism." A lecture under the revealing title of "The necessity of corporatism" was offered twice. None of the speeches went against the prevailing doctrines of the Church. Clearly, developing a critical judgment was not on the program that week.

*

March 11, 1941, would be an important date in Quebec for the teaching of the Church. On the occasion of the fiftieth anniversary of *Rerum novarum* and the tenth anniversary of *Quadragesimo anno*, the bishops of Quebec issued an important "Collective pastoral letter." They praised as always life on the farm, but in a somewhat muted fashion in comparison with past practice. Their emphasis now was on cooperation. "Those who can should prefer to earn their living in the country rather than in the cities! They will have a better life there, as long as they agree to get organized and cooperate together."39 This new cooperative social spirit of the Church should be taught in the family, the prelates urged, but especially in the schools: "It is at school above all that it will develop, that it will receive its doctrinal basis and that it will be translated into concrete actions. . . . All the time that is required should be devoted to this teaching."40 The pastoral letter insisted on the importance of "impregnating" the students with "the doctrine of the encyclicals."

Turning to the problem of the class struggle, the letter, invoking the Pope, recommended what it now called explicitly the *corporatist institution*: "We cannot attain a perfect cure unless we substitute, to these opposed classes, well-constituted organs, 'orders' or 'occupations' that bring men together, not according to the place they hold on the labour market, but according to the different branches of social activity where they have chosen to work. Consequently, the Church these days, through the voice of its Head, expressly recommended the *institution of corporatism*."41 In this collective pastoral letter of the bishops, the word *corporatism* makes its first direct, enthusiastic appearance. It informs us that the concept is already popular in Quebec: "As we learn from the encyclical *Quadragesimo anno*, the organization into labour unions is only a first step. It must lead us towards *corporatism*. It pleases us to see that some of our most distinguished citizens, motivated only by their Catholic and social spirit, have chosen to become apostles of this salutary reform. Convinced as they are of its moral and legal value, they now endeavour to plant the seed in the terrain of the occupations."42 Trudeau, as we saw, had the praises of corporatism sung to him by 1937, if not earlier. To spread the reform, the bishops counselled, people should join existing associations "and they will infuse them with the true corporatist spirit, they will turn them into single and homogeneous bodies." Their efforts should be supported by the state which "will confer on the corporation its powers, it will give it a legal structure and turn it into a true professional organism endowed with the authority to govern its members."43

The pastoral letter expressed optimism about the future of corporatism: "That is not, dear brothers, only a dream. We think the day will come – and it will be soon, We hope – when the Province of Quebec will offer the world the example of having a corporatist organization inspired by the encyclicals, without requiring any change to our Constitution, that is adapted to our spirit and our traditions, and that will play a most beneficial economic and social role. This would, indeed, be the *new order*, based on justice and charity, which all good citizens are demanding. We hope that its advent will be soon and we bless with all Our hearts the courageous apostles of this salutary restoration."44

The bishops equated *corporatism* with the advent of a *new order*. The search for a third way between capitalism and socialism – for a new order – was commonplace during the 1930s. In France, two intellectuals, Robert Aron and Arnaud Dandieu, had described in general terms in their book, *La révolution nécessaire*, the kind of fundamental change that they envisaged. They founded a periodical to promote their vision and called it *L'Ordre nouveau*. In 1936, inspired by this concept of a corporatist "new order" in Quebec, Cardinal Villeneuve promoted the launching of a periodical that would also be called, like its French counterpart, *L'Ordre nouveau*. History was later to record that only fascist regimes established such a new order. In 1939, the name of the periodical, now entrusted to the Jesuits, was changed from *L'Ordre nouveau* to *Relations*, probably because the words *New Order* had become so firmly associated with fascist regimes. By 1941 when the bishops spoke in their pastoral letter of "a new order," the association with fascism was even stronger.

The fact is that the Church hierarchy, like most of the French-Canadian elite, had a positive opinion of the fascist dictators. Jean-Louis Roux, the noted actor and director, recalled what people in his circle said at the time, for example, about Portugal's Salazar: "There was much enthusiasm among (young French Canadians) over the fact that Salazar had shown such zeal in applying to his whole nation the teaching of the encyclicals with respect to social questions and turned Portugal into a corporatist state."45 Antonio de Oliveira Salazar had used the occasion of his being appointed prime minister in 1932 to seize power and establish a dictatorial regime that was nationalist and Christian. He called it the New State (*O estado novo*). He then imposed on the country a single party, called the "National Union," and relied on the omnipresent police to suppress all opposition. (It is worth noting that, in 1935, the new party created in Quebec by the coalition of the Conservative Party of Maurice Duplessis with Paul Gouin's Action libérale nationale was also called the Union nationale, just like Salazar's party.)

Jean-Louis Roux writes that another fascist regime was also much admired by the French-Canadian elite: "Some of our teachers often spoke with undisguised enthusiasm of the accomplishments of Mussolini in fascist Italy. How often were we not serenaded with accounts of the draining of the Pontine Marshes and of trains running on time since the Duce took over! About Hitler we were more reserved, but the fact remains that we did not condemn him outright. In that respect we shared the ambiguous attitude of the Vatican and of Pius XII."[46]

And so the bishops knew what they were saying when their collective letter called for a corporatist new order in Quebec. The founder of *Le Devoir*, Henri Bourassa, the man who had inspired a whole generation, declared that this Episcopal letter was "one of the most important [documents] ever to appear in our country"; and he invited his audience to "let themselves be permeated by this doctrine and to incorporate it in their lives, wherever they may be."[47] Cardinal Villeneuve was equally supportive: "The pastoral letter has the great merit of offering a faithful summary of the social doctrine of the Church, then of applying this teaching to our own situation. It traces a program for the reconstruction of Canadian society, one that should rally the support of all men of good will, whatever their political allegiance. It will now be up to them to settle the technical details and to prepare for the realization of this new order."[48]

The principles having been established, there remained to develop a plan of action.

———◦———

The École sociale populaire undertook precisely this task. To apply to Quebec the particulars of the Church's social doctrine, the ÉSP called on a young Jesuit scholastic, Richard Arès, to put together a document that could be used as a study guide on the subject. In 1941, it was published under the bulky title, *Plans d'étude sur la restauration sociale, d'après la Lettre pastorale collective de l'épiscopat de la province de Québec sur les encycliques "Rerum novarum" et "Quadragesimo anno."*

There can be no doubt that Trudeau was familiar with the doctrine contained in this study guide. Like all his fellow students, he had been imbued with the social teaching of the Church while he was a student at Brébeuf. Fr. Arès had been Trudeau's teacher there for a course in political economy in 1939–40, at the very time when Arès was engaged in his work for the École sociale populaire, which had begun in 1937. The guide is worth studying because it provides the clearest and fullest exposition of how the Catholic Church in Quebec understood the Papal encyclicals and adapted them to the situation of French Canadians, even as late as 1941, when Canada had been at war with the fascist powers for nearly two years.

Following closely the plan of the pastoral letter from Quebec's bishops, Fr. Arès began by analyzing the main existing social systems. He gave this section the evocative title, "Current disorder and false solutions." He had not the slightest doubt that the society was sick and that all current models were flawed. Liberalism and capitalism were denounced in terms that evoked the Vatican. And socialism? He recognized that some of its demands, such as the call for greater social justice, were not dissimilar to the teaching of Catholicism. But he hastened to add, quoting *Quadragesimo anno*: "No one can be at the same time a good Catholic and a true socialist."[49] He then applied that stricture of the Pope to the situation in Canada, recalling that Mgr. Gauthier had warned Catholics about the dangers of the CCF.[50] As for communism, unsurprisingly, Fr. Arès insisted that it was a duty "to fight it immediately by preventing its propagation among us."[51]

There are striking omissions in Fr. Arès's treatment of "Current disorder and false remedies." Nowhere is there mention of fascism or of Nazism. Could they not be classified as "false remedies"? This study guide was offered to Catholics in 1941, while war raged and the Western world was opening its eyes to the horrors of the fascist and Nazi regimes. Was this strange silence peculiar to Quebec, or did it, in fact, originate in the Vatican?

A debate has raged for decades now on the degree of responsibility of the Vatican, and more particularly of Pius XI and Pius XII, with respect to the catastrophic events of the Second World War.[52] Without wanting to become embroiled in the controversy, we think it useful to recall a number of international events that can shed light on the climate in Quebec in 1941.

In 1929, Vatican City was recognized as an independent entity under the "sovereign jurisdiction" of the Holy See by the Treaty of Conciliation, usually called the Lateran Treaty, signed on February 11, 1929, by Benito Mussolini and Cardinal Pietro Gasparri, Secretary of State to Pius XI. In exchange for the Pope's recognition of the fascist regime, of the Italian state and of Rome as its capital, Mussolini recognized Catholicism as the official religion of Italy. The Pope gave a token of his gratitude on January 9, 1932, when he conferred on Mussolini the papal Order of the Golden Spur. Accordingly, when Mussolini attacked Ethiopia on October 3, 1935, the Holy See uttered no condemnation of this act of war in spite of the previous speeches in favour of peace by Eugenio Pacelli, the favourite cardinal of Pius XI, who was also to succeed him as Pope Pius XII. The Pope did not curb the militaristic outbursts of some of his bishops, such as this prayerful invocation by the Bishop of Terracina: "O Duce! Today Italy is Fascist and the hearts of all Italians beat together with yours. The nation is ready for any sacrifice to ensure the triumph of peace and of Roman and Christian civilizations. . . . God bless you, O Duce."53

Whatever the Pope's strategic reasons for signing the Lateran Treaty with fascist Italy, the effect was to send to the world, and certainly to the Church in Quebec, the message that Mussolini, the fascist, enjoyed the Pope's blessing. Hitler, a canny observer, quickly drew the appropriate lesson. On February 22, 1929, only days after it was signed, Hitler published an article praising the treaty, which, he said, showed the world that the Vatican preferred fascism to liberal democracy: "The Vatican trusts the new political realities far more than it did the former liberal democracy with which it could not come to terms. . . . The fact that the Catholic Church has come to an agreement with Fascist Italy proves beyond doubt that the Fascist world of ideas is closer to Christianity than those of Jewish liberalism or even atheistic Marxism."54

History soon did seem to prove him right. Four years later, in 1933, following lengthy negotiations, the Pope signed with Hitler a Concordat according to which the Nazi regime made some concessions to the Catholic Church, in recognition of which the Church committed itself to abstain from pronouncing itself on subjects dealing with Germany that were deemed political. In an article in the *National Catholic Weekly*,[55] Robert Krieg, a professor of theology at Notre Dame University and author of *Catholic Theologians in Nazi Germany*, published in 2004, explained the problems, the ambiguities, and the effects caused by this agreement with Hitler. The consequence was, according to Krieg, that Hitler was granted in the eyes of the world the legitimacy for which he yearned, while German Catholics were demoralized, they who, with the support of their bishops, had fiercely opposed National-Socialism from the 1920s to the signature of the Concordat in 1933.

Whether because of the Concordat or, as some experts maintain, for other reasons, the Vatican kept silent when, on June 30, 1934, during the night that Hitler cynically referred to as "the night of the long knives," the Führer, abetted by the SS, eliminated his potential rivals within the Nazi party in a bloody purge. In the aftermath, many scientists and intellectuals, notably Albert Einstein, fled the brutal and totalitarian regime. There then occurred during the night of November 9 to 10, 1938, the pogrom to which cynical Nazis gave the poetic name of *Kristallnacht*, "the Night of Broken Glass," a reference to shattered windows and dishes. Across Germany, Nazis torched about one hundred synagogues, smashed and looted thousands of businesses, and assassinated many Jews.

Still the Pope kept silent. "It seems that Christian anti-Semitism played a huge role in the Holocaust,"[56] wrote John Shelby Spong, the former Episcopal bishop of Newark. In fact, during the whole course of the Second World War, Pope Pius XII never publicly condemned Nazism or fascism, even while there is evidence of secret efforts on his part to save Jewish lives. To the contrary, the Holy See's relations with fascist Italy and Nazi Germany, and the papal silence in the midst of atrocities, lent to these regimes a degree of respectability, especially among practising Catholics.

This background explains the silence of Fr. Arès. The École sociale populaire, placing its full confidence in a Pope who seemed on such good terms with these regimes, chose not to include fascism and Nazism on its list of current false solutions. We are inclined to believe that the only reason its 1941 study guide did not come right out and praise some fascist regimes, such as those of Marshal Pétain, of Salazar, Franco or Mussolini, was that Fr. Arès knew full well that Canada was at war with the countries of the Axis and that praising the enemy would be found offensive.

Having identified the causes of social disorder, the document went on in a second section to deal with social reconstruction. As might be expected, Arès designated the Church as the primary agent of reconstruction. The second role was assigned to the state, and in third position were the professional-occupational bodies. The Church, as Fr. Arès recalled, invoking the authority of Leo XIII and Pius XI, proclaimed through the encyclicals its right and even its duty to intervene on economic and social questions. From its position above all regimes, the Church summoned them all "to its tribunal in order to approve of them or condemn them in accordance with the rules of faith and morals."[57] Interestingly, Fr. Arès insisted that the workers must accept social inequalities: "These inequalities are necessary for order, they are in order."[58]

Fr. Arès also recognized the appropriateness of family allowances that had been introduced by the federal government. But, in accordance with Quebec's distinctive nationalist tradition, he suspected as dangerous whatever came from Ottawa: "The law, which is good in principle, . . . constitutes a serious infringement on provincial rights and will cause serious drawbacks, especially for the Province of Quebec."[59] It is surprising to find, in a document dealing with the reconstruction of the social order, a critique of the division of powers between Ottawa and Quebec. On the face of it, constitutional niceties have nothing to do with the objective of social reconstruction as elaborated in the encyclicals. But, when the École sociale populaire applied the social doctrine of the Church to Quebec, it felt obliged to defend provincial autonomy.

Fr. Arès then turned to the second agent of social reconstruction: the state. In addressing the issue of unemployment among young people, the document required the state to come to the aid of agriculture, because French Canadians were not ready to take control of heavy industry. "The agricultural profession has always been more appropriate to our aptitudes, our talents, our needs,"[60] Fr. Arès proclaimed. As a consequence, the state had the obligation to elaborate and implement a policy for colonizing unoccupied lands in Quebec. In 1941, the Quebec Church used the encyclicals to promote an enterprise of its own, the return to the land. In the face of the obvious industrialization of the province, the myth of the soil was systematically promoted in much of Quebec's literature and in its schools. In summary, the state's main function was to act as principal executor in the task of social reconstruction, as conceived by the Church.

Fr. Arès then discussed the third agent of social reconstruction, the professional associations, of which he sang their praises. The Church, he said, recognizes the right for employers and workers to form protective associations, but on condition that they be "initiated by Catholics for Catholics, and set themselves up between Catholics." He gave his blessing to agricultural associations which, also, "have the right and even the duty to be Catholic."[61]

For the École sociale populaire, Catholic unions were not intended as ends in themselves. Rather, their true function was, in the words of Pius XI, "to prepare the way for better bodies, for these corporate associations."[62] And so the corporation bringing together all the participants in each occupational sector would constitute "an element of order and of organization in the sphere of the economy."[63]

When Fr. Arès then applied the concept of corporatism to conditions in Quebec, he wrote as a nationalist. For "us," he maintained, corporatism offered "the means to liberate ourselves, to reconquer our national heritage."[64] To attempt such a reconquest right across Canada was unthinkable, because Canada was simply too diverse a country to lend itself to an operation of such complexity. In fact, though he did not come right out and say it, Fr. Arès excluded Canada as a whole because its majority was Protestant and English-speaking. This would become even more explicit six years later when he would go beyond the argument of complexity to propose limiting to Quebec his intended campaign. He would simply deny that Canada was really a nation. He would write in 1947: "There is, of course, a Canadian people, but this people is so heterogeneous in its makeup, so divided in its affections and its objectives, and, with less than a century of shared life, it does not seem to have attained that psychological and moral unity that would be required for Canada to be qualified as a nation." On the other hand, he would add, "for the French Canadians of Quebec, this province truly qualifies as a *patrie*, and that from the triple point of view of geography, nationality and politics."[65] In 1941, though, he merely explained that only within Quebec could corporatism be adopted as an instrument of "national" liberation. Repeating verbatim the words of the pastoral letter, Fr. Arès expressed his hope that the day would come "when the Province of Quebec will give the world the example of a corporatist organization that was inspired by the encyclicals."[66]

Why was there so much enthusiasm in Quebec for corporatism? Fr. Arès explained it by "the achievements of modern corporatist regimes and, especially, the approval of the Church."[67] Indeed, already on April 17, 1937, Cardinal Villeneuve echoed the Pope when he issued a watchword that expressed his enthusiasm: "Here and there we find a few fragments of social justice. But these semblances of a remedy will not do. We need more than that, we need full-scale corporatism."[68]

It would not be amiss to recall that, in 1941, when the École sociale populaire published its praise for the virtues of corporatism, Marshal Pétain's government had joined the ranks of the fascist governments that had adopted the corporatist mode. And yet, Fr. Arès dared to assert that corporatism was possible "in every form of government that respects natural and divine law. Only totalitarian dictatorship is detrimental to it, because of its excessively centralizing character. And so, far from being incompatible with democracy, corporatism suits democracy. Corporatism will protect our democratic system against the abuses to which it is exposed."[69] But the facts of history, by 1941, contradicted his assumption: none but the fascist regimes had adopted the corporatist model; not a single democracy had done so. That was not mere coincidence. A glance at the role and the power of the state in corporatist regimes is revealing.

Fr. Arès echoed Fr. Archambault's views on the subject. The state, he explained, "must help, support and stimulate private initiatives aimed at establishing corporations and provide the corporations with what they need if they are to fulfill their mission."[70] In effect, it is up to the state to decide what powers the corporations will need, thereby itself determining the extent and limits of its own power. Furthermore, we are told that the corporations will bring about social peace. But how? In such a regime, how will conflicts be settled when they arise within a corporation? *Quadragesimo anno* had its own answer to that question at article 94: "Strikes and lock-outs are forbidden; if the parties cannot settle their dispute, public authority intervenes." What this means is that corporatism takes away from opposing groups any means of exerting pressure. This leaves the state as the unchallenged and unchallengeable arbiter of all conflicts. And the state itself is beyond the control of the citizens. There simply exists no mechanism for exerting pressure on the state.

It must be obvious that corporatism runs counter to any liberal and democratic concept of the relationship between individuals and the state. In a liberal democracy, society is perceived as bringing together autonomous individuals who pursue their self-interest. Through universal suffrage, they have ultimate control over the institutions and the legal systems that rule them. Those who favour corporatism maintain that, in a system of liberal democracy, individuals are only interested in achieving their selfish interests, while their participation in the political system is purely formal. By contrast, they say, the corporatist system creates "organic" links, first between the individual and his group or his corporation, and then between the several corporations which themselves are, in turn, organically linked to the whole, that is, to the nation. In a corporatist system, the occupational association is to be the central axis for the activities of individuals. They are to derive pride and a sense of worth from their work carried out within the ambit of the corporation. It is through the corporation that they act on the larger society. All individuals, setting aside the perspective of conflicting interests, recognize that the group is more important than the individual, they accept their position in the social hierarchy and they willingly subject their own interests to a powerful state ruled by a benevolent and wise leader who is not, himself, submissive to the will of the people.

Corporatism is the very antithesis of democracy, because it requires the people to be submissive to the state. It is the antithesis of liberalism, because the will of the leader replaces the rule of law. On July 6, 1933, *Le Devoir* published a translation of a letter which the German Catholic hierarchy had issued; and which demonstrated how the organic concept of the nation could lead to admiration for a fascist regime: "Our era stands out for the uniquely energetic affirmation of authority and for an inflexible will to unite organically the citizens and the corporations to the great Whole embodied by the state. It springs from a principle of natural law, for it is impossible for any social life to prosper without a supreme authority."[71] To a large extent, the French-Canadian intelligentsia shared that point of view.

So, contrary to what Fr. Arès asserts, this corporatist new order is well-suited to regimes that are dictatorial, authoritarian, or fascist. Its compatibility with democracy, though, has no theoretical or practical foundation. However, when Fr. Arès referred to corporatism's modern accomplishments, he naturally evoked in the minds of his readers thoughts about the accomplishments of European fascist regimes which were all the more admired because they favoured the Catholic Church. The Pope had publicly shown his appreciation for these dictators by decorating Mussolini, by congratulating Franco "for his Catholic victory," and Pétain "for the fortunate renewal of religious life in France."[72]

This document, *Plans d'étude sur la restauration sociale*, put together by Fr. Arès, stands as the logical conclusion to the search for a new order, started in 1931 under the influence of Fr. Archambault, responding to the appeal of the Pope. Moving beyond the promotion of corporatism, it presented the practical means of implementing it. The fact that this model of social organization had been used in authoritarian and fascist regimes has led more than one analyst to conclude that, during the Second World War, the majority of the members of the French-Canadian elite was not only opposed to conscription, but also sympathetic to fascism.

In 1962, André Laurendeau tried to explain the conscription crisis and the position of French Canadians during that war. With courage and candour he took up the events of the period one by one, as he had lived through them from the inside. Even as the Canadian media were saturated with reports on the atrocities committed by the Nazis, French Canadians continued to believe that it was all propaganda. We were "deliberately deaf,"[73] Laurendeau explained. Or, as Jean-Louis Roux put it, we were "very naïve and properly brainwashed."[74] Blinded by their resentment toward *les Anglais*, French Canadians refused to believe anything *les Anglais* said or wrote about the war. "What reached us about the war had the stamp of propaganda and we did not believe it,"[75]

Laurendeau wrote. Even the few French Canadians who supported the position of the federal government – like Cardinal Villeneuve, Jean-Charles Harvey, and a few others – were themselves considered to be victims of propaganda, and lost any credibility.[76] Only such blindness could account for the fact that Henri Bourassa spoke one day of "Pétain, greater at Vichy than at Verdun."[77] Laurendeau claimed that few people in his circle listened to the propaganda broadcasts from Vichy over short-wave radio. True, they might not have listened to them over the air waves, but he failed to mention that the speeches of Pétain were read regularly in the classical colleges. They were published in the Province of Quebec by Éditions Fides, which at that time was operated by the Frères de Sainte-Croix. Roger Varin, who had collaborated with Trudeau in some political activities, was in charge of this project.[78]

But even André Laurendeau went only halfway toward explaining the causes of this collective misjudgment. Yes, French Canadians were "deliberately deaf" to the messages beamed by *les Anglais*. But, at the same time, as good Catholics, they were most receptive to the messages coming from the Pope and the Church. For them, what corporatism represented was the defence of Christian values, and so it seemed preferable to the values represented by Anglo-Saxon liberal democracy. In their enthusiasm for the messages of the papal encyclicals, a large proportion of the clerico-nationalist elite dreamed of establishing in Quebec a splendid corporatist regime where a strong leader would restore order, Christian values, and human dignity. A collective blindness due to mistrust of British propaganda does not come near to explaining why, for example, a Henri Bourassa could express such boundless admiration for the Maréchal.

When the *Plans d'étude sur la restauration sociale* was published, Trudeau was a twenty-two-year-old student at the Université de Montréal. This document merely restated and confirmed the message of mobilization that the Pope had issued to all Catholics in 1931 and the consequent lessons that Trudeau had been taught at Brébeuf and at the Semaines sociales. He had routinely been told that liberalism and democracy were at the root of social disruption. At the same time, many of his teachers had been openly praying for the appearance of an authoritarian leader, one who was inspired by the Christian faith, a man on the model of Mussolini, Salazar, or Pétain. This long-awaited leader, a *pure laine* French Canadian of course, would restore order and social peace in Quebec by establishing corporatism in a Catholic and French state. Until 1944, when Trudeau would leave Quebec for Harvard University, this was the predominant ideological and social setting within which he developed his own vision and committed himself for the first time to political action.

*Chapter 7*

——◦——

# READ TO LEAD

*Sure of themselves, [the mystics] turn out to be great men of action. [They experience] the need to radiate around them that which they have received, they experience it as a force of love.*

— HENRI BERGSON
*Les deux sources de la morale et de la religion,* 1932

PIERRE TRUDEAU, now in his early twenties, was enrolled in law at the Université de Montréal, but he was decidedly unenthusiastic. In the fall of 1940, he had moved less than a mile up Mount Royal, from Collège Jean-de-Brébeuf to the university campus dominated by the high tower of its library. The world was at war, the Depression and its aftermath still gripped the country in a sense of insecurity, and French Canadians, remembering the First World War, were determined there could be no conscription for service overseas. In Quebec, the clerico-nationalist elite maintained its faith in the papal encyclicals, its admiration for European authoritarian regimes, its prayers for the emergence of a new order, and its hope for the appearance of a strong *chef* who would lead French Canadians to their redemption.

The clues to the progression of Trudeau's thinking during those student years are to be found in the notes that he kept as he reflected on what he read. He engaged in a virtual dialogue with the authors who had caught his attention, jotting down his response to their views. Some of his comments were so personal that, reading them now, one feels embarrassed at intruding like a stranger on the intimacy of his soul.

Trudeau obviously knew his way around the copious world of his own notes. He must have had a system for classifying them: periodically he referred back to them and seemed to know exactly where to find what he had previously written. For example, it was likely in 1940 that he read Léon Bloy's 1886 novel, *Le Désespéré*. In August of 1944, he read another Bloy novel, *La femme pauvre*, published in 1897. On the very page where he had written down his thoughts about the first Bloy novel, he now wrote four years later: "Everything I said about *Le Désespéré* I now repeat about *La femme pauvre* and I erase every thing else. It is a *great* novel. [Bloy is] the writer of pain and destitution." Few readers could claim to be so well organized.

We now accompany him through his reading, beginning with the summer of 1940. During the holidays between college and university, he chose books mostly for his own enjoyment. In July, he read two plays by Shakespeare. He found in *A Midsummer Night's Dream* "enough beauty to charm the soul of a child." He was less impressed by *The Tempest*: "It has neither the power of the great dramas (*Macbeth* and the others) nor the fairy-like fantasy of the comedies." Trudeau, it should be noted, wrote these comments in French even though he had read Shakespeare in English. He would do this regularly. Despite his fluency in English, he was really a French Canadian who could speak another language. And, though he spoke English without difficulty, writing English was a different matter. All his life, when it came to writing, he was more at ease in French than in English.

In August, he read *Le pain dur*, a play by Paul Claudel, who was at that time the favourite author of French-Canadian Jesuits. Trudeau read five works by Claudel between 1940 and 1943 and filled thirteen pages with notes that express great admiration for the ardent Catholic poet-moralist. Of *Le pain dur* he wrote: "Read on the return trip through the arid Western countryside (August 1940)." Such circumstantial comments pop up periodically in his reading notes and prove quite helpful to biographers as they reconstruct his intellectual journey. He described Claudel's play as "a gripping drama," with "admirable" writing so charged with meaning that it must be read and reread. He showed no sign of recognizing the anti-Semitism explicit in Claudel's writing. In that respect he was typical of his time and place. He noted without a qualm:

"A dark and deep drama, . . . the whole plot is psychological. Our attention is fascinated by scenes where [Jewish] beings act out their fate as
though compelled by all their atavism, all the power of their heredity. . . .
Sichel, this shameless Jewess, is willing to put up with absolutely anything to escape her race, and is at last freed from the yoke that weighs on
Israel, but, despite everything, she displays a certain nobility even in her
depravity." With nothing but praise for the author, Trudeau wrote: "I find
that Claudel is the only one who comes close to the richness of thought,
the exuberance of style, the splendour of imagery, the human philosophy
of Shakespeare."

During his first year of studies at the Université de Montréal, he devoted
much of his reading to other authors inspired by Catholicism, including
François Mauriac, Léon Bloy, Paul Bourget, Ernest Psichari, and Blaise
Pascal. Trudeau declared Mauriac's novel, Le Nœud de vipères, The Nest
of Vipers, to be a masterpiece.[1] François Mauriac (1885–1970), who was
awarded the Nobel Prize for Literature in 1952, projected in his novels a
dark vision of human beings caught between their passions and their
search for God. Unlike most of the authors that Trudeau was reading,
Mauriac became active in the Résistance and supported de Gaulle.
Trudeau also jotted down a comment that tells us more about himself than
about the book. "Novels would have no interest if the characters did not
in some way resemble the reader." And he proceeded to point out some
character traits in the book that he recognized in himself. "Whether out of
shyness or pride, I have taken with women that superior and condescend-
ing tone that they just hate. . . . I hastened to displease deliberately, out of
fear that I might displease naturally. . . . That ability to deceive oneself,
which makes life easier for most men, has always eluded me. . . . Silence is
my way out and I always take refuge in it."

These notes reveal young Trudeau as someone who observed himself
without complacency and without false modesty. As a fervent Catholic,
he appreciated especially the books that helped him to find words to
express his Christian ideals. While reading Thérèse Desqueyroux,[2] for
example, he wrote: "One must have read Mauriac's novels if one would
acquire Charity, Love and Pity for Humanity." As for Paul Bourget's
novel, Le disciple,[3] he found it "superb" because, he said, it illustrated

marvellously God's presence everywhere and, contrary to what one found in psychology, it demonstrated that "the movements of the soul cannot be studied like those of a watch. . . . The lesson that emerges is that, yes, one can enclose oneself within theories that take us far from common sense. But all it takes is to observe human beings to feel the presence of a God, the presence of a mystery from the beyond."

Trudeau was not taken, however, with François Hertel's novel of 1940, *Mondes Chimériques*. He wrote that "the several episodes are presented with some originality, which saves them from the dryness of an essay. Some of them offer hardly any interest and others are quite simply tall tales built around a joke that you could see coming."4 Trudeau had known and appreciated Hertel from his years at Brébeuf, but this did not prevent him from criticizing his writings.

On social questions, Trudeau read only one book during this period, titled *Le souverain captif*.5 The author, André Tardieu, had followed an unusual career path that is worth considering. Born in Paris in 1876, he was first a diplomat, then a correspondent for the liberal Parisian daily *Le Temps*, and then an author. But he attained fame above all as one of France's most eminent politicians between the two world wars. From the end of the First World War, he held various important portfolios in the government. In 1929 and 1930, while he was president of the Council – the equivalent of today's prime minister – during the Great Depression, he proposed policies of social security, free tuition, and the public financing of major public works. But then, as France experienced a series of weak and unstable ministries amid a crisis of authority and legitimacy, Tardieu lost confidence in its political institutions and became a severe critic, not only of leading politicians, but of the parliamentary system itself. Convinced that the Third Republic was headed toward its downfall, he concluded that its political institutions must be rebuilt from top to bottom, and to achieve this he allied himself with the Action française of Charles Maurras, an extreme nationalist and monarchist, as well as other similar movements. In 1934, when he was mandated to carry out a study to reform France's Constitution, he proposed an authoritarian state.

In 1935, he withdrew from active politics to concentrate on studying political institutions and social questions. He began publishing his new ideas for fundamental reform in 1936 in *Le souverain captif*. There,

Tardieu mounted a vehement attack against democracy and parliamentary government, proposing instead an elitist and authoritarian system. A professor of political science at France's Université de Versailles–Saint Quentin, Yves Pormeur, published in 1999 an article that was generally favourable toward Tardieu, but with serious reservations: "His hostility towards the parliament, which he saw as castrating government leaders and rendering impossible the policies that Tardieu judged to be absolutely necessary for the country, was strengthened by his contempt for the lower class status of most members of parliament whom, as they represented rural constituencies, he considered incapable of thinking in terms of the common good, and unable to rise to the high standards required when dealing with affairs of state."[6] Tardieu was convinced that an effective government required a political system that "allows competent men, drawn from the elite, to exercise their talents."

Trudeau, quite taken, wrote about Tardieu's book: "It is well done, concrete, mostly non-partisan." Tardieu's authoritarian and elitist view did not disturb Trudeau for the good reason that they were totally compatible with the positions of the Church and of the French-Canadian elite, which both were calling for a revolution to restore the social order. Tardieu also spoke of revolution and stressed its link with Christianity: "It is Christianity that, by separating the individual conscience from the state, made modern revolutions possible."

The Jesuits, of course, had little regard for the French Revolution or for democracy. So also with Tardieu: "All the governments since 1789 have been against freedom and equality. . . . The sovereignty of the people simply does not exist: The Chambre des Députés represents a majority neither of the nation nor of the voters." He found the democratic principle to be fundamentally faulty: "The system of majorities rides on a presupposition, that of the infallibility of great numbers. Just prove to me that this presupposition is truly a principle."[7] To this, Trudeau reacted: "Whatever may be the case, one can see the weakness of democracy which is incapable of reforming itself on its own. . . . The more you wish to have an idea gain wide acceptance, the more you are forced to compromise." Trudeau had only one criticism of the book: "Obviously, it is a little annoying to see this demolition of the entire current system, without being told what is proposed to replace it." Trudeau was not satisfied with mere analysis. Reflection, for him, was to be a prelude to action. He read in order to act. And so, left unsatisfied by Tardieu, he continued to search for whatever could provide him with a solid, concrete foundation for political action. It happened that the authors he turned to were all inspired by Catholicism.

In March 1941, Trudeau read *Le voyage du Centurion*, in which the author, Ernest Psichari, chose the medium of an autobiographical novel to describe his spiritual development as a soldier and his conversion to Catholicism. It was published posthumously in 1916. Psichari was the grandson of Ernest Renan, the French philosopher of religion and an apostate Catholic who had studied for the priesthood. His best friend was philosopher Jacques Maritain, also a convert to Catholicism. When Psichari was killed at the front in an early First World War battle in 1914, his intention was to study for the priesthood. Paul Claudel dedicated some of his writings to him. In 1940, the Vichy government held him up as a very model for its right-wing Catholic "Révolution Nationale," and he was also highly regarded by the Jesuits in Quebec. Trudeau was full of admiration for what he had read, and wrote: "What is of great interest in this book is seeing how this young man, disenchanted with the world, is brought by hard but firm stages to convert. . . . He recovered his fidelity towards the France that he had cursed. But this fidelity leads him to that other, also holding a claim to his fidelity, that other which is the very soul of France: Christendom. This great mystic writes sublime pages, admirable prayers. . . . Several passages cast a new light on our beliefs, on passages of the Gospel. . . . Above all, this beautiful soul seems to realize the importance of Jesus, the link between God and us."

During his entire first year at the Université de Montréal, religion continued to govern his choice and his appreciation of the books that he read, in either French or English. His reading of G.K. Chesterton's 1908 suspense romp, *The Man Who Was Thursday*, brought out this comment: "It is part of human nature to search for the good and the true." Chesterton, of course, was a convert to Catholicism, the most prominent Catholic British author of his day. Then, when Trudeau read Aldous Huxley's satirical novel *Point Counterpoint*,[8] in which the author expressed his disenchantment and his skepticism, Trudeau's attention was caught by the references to Christianity. "The book is an admirable creation. . . . The author is a kind of humanistic free thinker. His heroes . . . idealize the whole man, who fully develops his body and his mind, who finds Christianity revolting because asceticism is contempt for the body. Still, one has to say that he thinks that Christ is an excellent model because he was fully human. . . . All told, a deep work, sometimes obscure. Perhaps dangerous for a mind that is not prepared: both because of some sensual scenes and heterodox theories."

Trudeau was able to appreciate the qualities of this work, even if it rejected his faith. And yet, his comment about the danger for unprepared minds showed that he had internalized the principle of banning books through the Index. He submitted to it himself for so long because he found such a control to be reasonable.

Trudeau looked for religious significance in the literary works that he read, but he also sought practical lessons for his own life. His reading of *Point Counterpoint* suggested to him a defence mechanism that he might use. "An impressive spectacle, if it is broken down into its component parts, can easily be made to look ridiculous. In the same way, if I found someone intimidating or overawing, all I would have to do is to take pictures of his gestures, of his mouth in a sneer, of a poorly constructed sentence; or, if that did not do it, I would only have to think of the horrible skull camouflaged only by a thin layer of skin to regain my composure and, at the very least, to return defensively a contemptuous look."

That stratagem reminds us that Trudeau, the polemicist and then the politician, would often be accused of looking contemptuous or arrogant. Here we catch him in the process of developing that defensive weapon. Significantly, only his adversaries denounced what they considered to be arrogance.

In March 1941, Trudeau read Blaise Pascal's *Pensées*. His notes on the *Pensées* are so self-revealing that we will quote from them extensively. He began: "One hesitates to give one's opinion of Pascal if it should turn out to be rather negative, because we have been told so often that he was a genius. And so, if one comes across a *pensée* [a thought] that is badly expressed or superficial, one is hesitant to say so." Even when we are certain that we are right, Trudeau continued, we feel obliged to justify our criticism, which "would require long explanations, a host of subtleties, many references to other axioms, and also assurances that we are not silly enough to assume that Pascal was entirely wrong."

Then Trudeau asked himself, what is it that keeps us from writing exactly what we think, without such convolutions and reservations? His answer to himself struck us as also directed to ourselves, his future biographers. Without these convolutions and reservations, he explained, we are afraid that someone reading what we write will consider us ridiculous. "And so our reticence has its root in pride," he wrote. "And this pride presumes another that is much more presumptuous, because it assumes that people will take the trouble to read what we write on scraps of paper, that some day biographers will delve into all that we have written down to follow therein the development of our thinking. One knows instinctively just how foolish that assumption is. And so, rebelling against oneself, one picks up the pen and writes. But even that rebellion is rooted in pride: it is inspired not so much from believing impossible our future greatness and the need for biographers, but rather from thinking it very unlikely that these biographers (who, we hope, will have to exist), will ever take the huge trouble to study the immense accumulation of paper that we are gathering (as though it were on purpose, to provide them with material!!!)

"When I criticize Pascal, I tell myself quite rightly that there is no harm, that I should not be thought too conceited just for that. Since I have no reason to think myself the equal of Pascal, therefore what I write is simply a harmless means of improving my writing style, of freeing up my thinking, of strengthening my own judgment by putting it in contact with that of a genius. But when Pascal writes that Descartes is ridiculous and insipid, is he not in somewhat the same position as myself? . . . The parallels are obviously not the same, since Pascal arrived at a time when the centuries had not yet confirmed the greatness of Descartes (while I arrive at a time when Pascal is known to be a genius); what's more, Pascal, writing down his thoughts, was more assured of surviving than I am (more assured because of his previous success, but not more convinced! Such is my assurance.) (I have this assurance because I'm role playing, and not so much because it's definitely within me.)"

Remarkable! Nowhere else do we get so clearly the impression that Trudeau was speaking to posterity, asking to be judged at his true worth. He wanted to give his future biographers the opportunity to follow the reasoning that had led him to some conclusion or other – assuming, of course, that biographers there would be. Is this the true explanation for the "immense accumulation of paper" that has found its way to Library and Archives Canada and which we have been able to consult? The question stands. And when he said that he was convinced he would be famous, was he really, as he claimed, just kidding? Or did he already consider the possibility, now that he had decided to devote himself to public affairs, that some day he was to become an important person? Was he already practising his pirouettes, his theatrical stunts, his winks aimed at the audience?

In that same March of 1941, Trudeau discovered Henri Bergson's *Les deux sources de la morale et de la religion*.9 Enchanted from the very first page, he jotted down: "Now, there's a great book!" He filled five pages with admiring observations. That might be why, on April 7 of that year, he would write to the archdiocese of Montreal for permission to read two other works by Bergson. Dazzled by Bergson's genius, he wrote of *Les deux sources*: "The sole and priceless lesson that this master gives is to search impartially for the Truth, to see beyond the 'axioms' of common sense. This essay on Morality introduces an entire critique, a whole philosophy based on previously unknown foundations. When you listen to this great mind, you get the benefit not only of his teachings, but above all of his method of working and thinking."

In those few lines, Trudeau evoked three elements of Bergson's philosophy that echoed the ideas promoted at Brébeuf by the Jesuits: the search for truth; the need to go beyond common sense; the search for principles of philosophy that can found a system of morality. We can't be sure whether he had already been given a foretaste of Bergson at Brébeuf, whether he had read some selections from Bergson's book. What seems likely is that he was now dazzled because this "master" brilliantly communicated the ideas that were Trudeau's own.

Another factor probably added to his enthusiasm. Trudeau was exposed to a thinker of great repute who presented a defence of Catholicism from a scientific perspective. Now Bergson, as is well known, was of Jewish origin. How could Trudeau fail to be delighted by the fact that the very religion Bergson came to – and attempted to prove was "scientifically" superior, both spiritually and morally – was also the religion that Trudeau adhered to with such passionate conviction? Bergson's philosophy, as developed in *Les deux sources*, could only confirm Trudeau in his own faith. We now sketch out that philosophy in broad strokes.

All his life, Bergson attempted to develop a philosophy of morality based on scientific principles. He received the Nobel Prize for Literature in 1927 for his master work, *L'évolution créatrice*, published in 1907, but it was only with his last great work, *Les deux sources de la morale et de la religion*,[10] published in 1932, that he achieved his objective. Here, his admirers and his followers agreed, he laid out at last a "science" of morality which gave a decisive role to God, to religion, and to Christianity. It was only to be expected, then, that Trudeau would describe the book as a "magnificent theodicy," that is, a treatise justifying God's treatment of humans.

Whence do we acquire the notion of the Good, Bergson asked? And what are the foundations of Morality? Morality has its first and earlier source in "the closed society" and it is based on reason, Trudeau writes, summarizing what he read. On the other hand, the second source of morality is that of "the open society." Transcending reason and linking us to God, it extends to all humanity and "was brought out by great mystics who grasped that He loves all men."

According to Bergson, reason as the source of morality can take human beings quite a distance but it cannot suffice. Even Plato's "just society," Bergson explained, was confined to a specific society, whose members were "bound to one another by strict obligations."[11] Plato rose by reason alone to a concept of morality quite close to that of the "open society," but he never achieved it. "His understanding was only a step away from the idea that all have an equal value from the fact of being human. But that was a step that he never took. It would have meant condemning slavery, repudiating the Greek idea that foreigners, being barbarians, could invoke no right."[12] Indeed, that "step," according to Bergson, could never be taken by reason alone, because "reason can only advance reasons, which can always be contradicted by other reasons."[13]

Bergson maintained that the Jewish people, though fundamentally different from the Greeks in their approach to morality, still retained the sense of morality and justice that derived from a "closed society." The justice preached by Israel's prophets "concerned Israel above all; their indignation against injustice was the very anger of Jahveh against his disobeying people or against the enemies of this chosen people."[14] Nevertheless, Bergson maintained, Judaism had progressed almost to the morality of an open society. "Israel . . . rose so high above the rest of humanity that, sooner or later, it would have been taken as the model."[15] And that is precisely what Christianity did by becoming the natural successor to Judaism, thereby achieving a qualitative leap for morality and justice.

For Bergson, this transition from the group to humanity, from respect for the law to love for others, required transcending not only particular interests but also human reason. "It was only with the advent of Christianity that the idea of universal brotherhood, which implies equal rights and the inviolability of the person, became activated. Someone might object that this activation was long in coming. It is true that 18 centuries passed by before the proclamation of the Rights of Man by the Puritans of America, soon to be followed by the men of the French Revolution. Nevertheless, the process began with the teaching of the Gospel, to carry on indefinitely. It is one thing for an ideal to be merely presented to mankind by wise men worthy of our admiration; but it is quite another for that ideal to be carried across the world in a message laden with love and which evoked love."[16]

Universal brotherhood, equality of rights, inviolability of the person: these concepts would be associated with Trudeau all his life. He probably encountered them here for the first time within the context of a political and moral philosophy that had received worldwide recognition. For Bergson, whom Trudeau was reading with such enthusiasm, it was through the channel of Christianity that these abstract ideals became "activated." It seems irresistible to conclude that Trudeau in turn "activated" these underlying concepts through the Canadian Charter of Rights and Freedoms, which he bequeathed to Canadians along with the patriation of the Constitution in 1982.

There has been a tendency among his biographers to attribute such central concepts as the primacy of the individual and the inviolability of rights to Trudeau's encounter with the personalism of Emmanuel Mounier. But it is clear that he had already encountered them in his religion classes at Brébeuf and that he found them again in the pages of Bergson's book, which so excited his admiration. Personalism did enrich and focus his thinking, but most of its basic ideas were already familiar to him. He confirmed this in his *Memoirs*: "My adherence to personalism was not the result of a sudden flash of insight. Quite the contrary, it was the outcome of a long reflection."[17]

How were these ideals of the inviolability of the person and of social justice to be "activated," according to Bergson? They required transcending what already existed to create something new. This process, which Bergson called "the vital force," involved "supposing as possible that which is actually impossible within a given society."[18] In order to conceive of an "open society," a society encompassing all of humanity, it was necessary to transcend reason, which was cloistered in what already existed. For this to happen, it was required that men emerge who had the exceptional capacity to "suppose as possible what is impossible," and who acted accordingly. Bergson called them "mystics," whom he described as "privileged souls who felt a kinship with all souls and who, instead of remaining within the limits of the group, reached out to humanity in general through a surge of love."[19] These exceptional beings, these "mystics," inspired us to follow them, to imitate them. How did they do it? "It is not by a compulsion that is more or less attenuated," Bergson wrote. "It is by a more or less resistible attraction."[20]

What was the source of the power of these mystics? "Sure of themselves, [because they sense something within them that is better than themselves,] they turn out to be great men of action, to the great surprise of those for whom mysticism amounts only to vision, to rapture, to ecstasy. [They experience] the need to radiate around them that which they have received, they experience it as a force of love. . . . A love which elicits a return of love for the mystic, but, through him, for him, other men will allow their souls to extend love to all humanity."[21]

Bergson's theory of the mystics raises an interesting question: does it apply in some way to Trudeau himself? At different times he exerted on many people – not all – a strange fascination. During the 1968 election campaign, a few months after he was chosen Liberal leader, the phenomenon was so extreme that it was called "Trudeaumania." No one could recall an equivalent enthusiasm for a leader in the annals of Canadian politics. Large, enthusiastic crowds came out to hear him speak; young women squealed with delight when they sighted him. Even his enemies had to acknowledge that Trudeau as a political leader had "charisma." Was it the equivalent of what Bergson called "the vital force"? When Trudeau died, sixteen years after leaving power, a wave of love and gratitude swept across much of the country, symbolized by the people who stood in line for hours before the Peace Tower to spend a few seconds reverentially before his coffin. It seemed that Canadians sensed his humanism and his determination to implement a different vision, one that made Canada a more "open society," more inclusive and generous, with less scope for hatred or discrimination. This resembled what Bergson called "the force of love." Trudeau might never have been considered a "mystic," but most people sensed that he belonged in a class apart.

Reading Bergson confirmed in Trudeau the conviction that, in the search for the True and the Good, reason alone was not enough; it must be complemented by faith. Bergson also confirmed his sense, conveyed repeatedly at Brébeuf, that the true leader must express his own ideas, even if they should be an embarrassment to everyone else. That was the most common theme of Trudeau's articles in the *Brébeuf*. But what Trudeau did not yet grasp was Bergson's central concept, that of the "open society." The mystic acts for the benefit of all humanity, and not solely for the good of his people – such as the French Canadians. It would be some years more before Trudeau learned to transcend the nationalism of his circle, which, despite its essential religious content, had expressed the morality of a "closed society." Rejecting and combatting the nationalism of his youth, he would apply the morality of an "open society" to Canada, which was the framework of his direct political action. There, he would struggle for the recognition of the dignity and the inviolability of each person. But he would also pursue peace, disarmament, and the rights of the individual everywhere in the world, thereby urging all of humanity toward the morality of an "open society."

After he put down Bergson's book in March 1941, it would be several months, February 1942, before Trudeau again took up the systematic reading of a book dealing with politics and philosophy. In between, he mostly read books of literature. He wrote appreciatively of Marcel Proust's *Du côté de chez Swann* and Lewis Carroll's *Alice's Adventures in*

*Wonderland.*[22] About the first, he commented: "Whoever has never read Proust is to be pitied. . . . For he will never learn that one can be a spectator of one's own soul." In *Alice*, he was drawn, not for the first time, to what is extraordinary. "You have to hand it to the English, they are where you find works of 'nonsense.' They have imagination. . . . At any age you can appreciate a book that despises the trivia of what is real . . . and which twists words into new meanings."

In September 1941, after completing a remarkable canoe trip, he read with delight a travel story titled *Équipée ou Voyage au pays du réel.*[23] The author of this 1929 book, Victor Segalen, conveyed his passion for untamed nature and strong emotions, and his distaste at returning to city life. "Bravo, now here is truly a book with sensational feelings! And I couldn't have found a better moment to read it than on my return from our Adventure to Hudson Bay. . . . Each chapter reveals and conveys a new sensation that poets of the trivial never explored: . . . the bath in the torrent, the sensation of the skin in contact with the kisses of the water, shooting a rapid. And what is truly extraordinary is that this masterpiece reveals a host of joys, disgusts that are experienced by every real voyageur of the unknown. Like the distaste for the return, . . . the contempt for all the 'So! You haven't changed' that you get when you are back."

The trip that Trudeau referred to was, in fact, an expedition of more than one thousand miles that he undertook during the summer holidays of 1941. There were six in the party, travelling in three canoes. They included his two Desrosiers cousins and his former Brébeuf classmate, Guy Viau, of whom Trudeau was to write in his memoirs: "I owe to Guy Viau my appreciation of art."[24] They retraced the journey made in the seventeenth century by Pierre-Esprit Radisson and his brother-in-law, Médart Chouart-Desgroseillers, coureurs de bois and founders of the Hudson's Bay Company.[25]

Trudeau's party left Montreal in their canoes, paddled up the Ottawa River, crossed Lake Temiskaming, then went down the Harricana River to James Bay, where they canoed on to Moosonee, at the bay's southern shore. Three years after the event, Trudeau would write an account of the trip that was also an ode to friendship, to the cleansing virtues of communing with nature, and to the strenuous life. Titled "L'ascétisme en canot," it would be published in the Catholic youth movement's periodical *Journal JEC.*[26]

But, right after his return from the trip, he gave an altogether different account, in an eight-page letter dated September 5, 1941, to his
friend François Hertel.[27] "Mon cher Monsieur Hertel," he began. "So
you don't read the newspapers, do you? Or is it possible that your place
of exile is in a region so far out of the way that you have not heard of
that voyage of adventure that the whole civilized world is talking about."
Trudeau was making a friendly joke about the fact that the priest had
been transferred from Montreal to teach at the Jesuit college in Sudbury,
in northern Ontario. His claim that the whole civilized world was discussing his canoe trip in fact rested on a brief account in some local
newspaper that he did not name. But he did make clear that he was outraged by the piece because the reporter had treated their expedition as no
more than a student's lark. Trudeau wrote: "'Students went on a pleasant voyage' was the headline, grandiose, unbelievable but true. 'They
went on a pleasant excursion.' (That was the brilliant sentence of the
journalist. Do you feel that it describes adequately the sublime undertaking, the incomparable daring of our pleasant excursion?) No, really,
did you ever see anything so stupid? And what makes me boil over each
time, is that the last sentence is more monumentally inept than the whole
article (the part is greater than the whole). I can understand why the
journalist writes like an idiot: those are his instructions."

The letter continued with more attacks in the same vein. But
Trudeau's disappointment was not directed only at the reporter. Their
whole marvellous adventure that he had long dreamed about had nearly
turned out badly. "I almost choked to death when David, who had found
it impossible to find someone to share the paddling (you have to be two
to a canoe), decided to hire an Indian. That was the last straw . . . I had
left Montreal with the intention of slaking at last my extraordinary thirst
for the extraordinary. So you can imagine how I felt when I found out
that this 'pleasant excursion' that I had so long dreamed about and
which was rather *my* undertaking (sh! Don't tell the others) was going to
turn into a bourgeois outing. Merde!"[28]

It was a letdown. The would-be adventurer who, perhaps inspired by
Alexis Carrel, had sought privations and had driven his body to the outer
limits of its capacity in order to become truly a man, who thought that a
future leader must develop to the utmost his body and mind, and who
had dreamed of this trip as an opportunity to face dangers and brave the

elements, saw in the hiring of an Indian guide the frustration of all his expectations. He considered quitting. But he changed his attitude, and for a revealing reason. "Thanks be to heaven which, after two days, began to send us a pack of troubles. First of all, it turned out that the Indian had only crossed 60 of the 280 miles between Amos and Moosonee; so he wasn't a guide. Woe to the man who claims that we had a guide; he will feel the blade of my dagger. And then, as the ultimate lucky break (how cynical can you get!), the poor Indian after two days came down with a terrible flu. During the whole trip he was feverish, he even became delirious. And so we were able to match him in daring and craft. So it happened that Guizot and I shot the rapids while the others portaged. The food began to give out, the portages were impossible, the rapids dangerous, the rain oppressed us, the storm never stopped blasting. In a word, life was becoming beautiful."

How could Trudeau revel in so many miseries? We might have expected that, after he and his friends had managed to overcome adversity, he would be quite proud of himself. Not he. After telling Hertel about his other exploits on the trip, he explained why he wrote such a long letter. "I probably thought that, by writing freely, I could finally justify myself, finally show that the enterprise was worthwhile and prove that I had not failed wretchedly. And yet, I have to conclude scholastically that I am no more a man than I was before, and that is so despite my beard. . . . But really, what am I complaining about? That our adventure turned out well? That we got back in one piece? You know what, I really think that I left with the conviction that we would get lost in the woods, that we would be forced to live two years with a marvelous tribe in unknown country. What an idiot! Those things just don't happen. There is only one extraordinary, non-trivial thing that one can experience in life: that is death."

Such a statement boggles the mind. In his search for extraordinary adventures like those found in books, he found that life falls short of expectations. Was he taking his clue, once again, from Carrel, who had written: "Death itself takes on a smile when it attaches itself to a great adventure, to the beauty of sacrifice, or to illumination of the soul that loses itself in the heart of God"?[29] Was it a sign of a lack of maturity? Or did he need to prove to himself that he could face anything fearlessly, even death? Was this part of his training to become a leader? Or merely the posturing of a student? Whatever the reality, this letter displays none of the serenity that will be in evidence three years later in "L'ascétisme en canot."

As he came to the end of his letter, Trudeau showed little enthusiasm over returning to university for his second year of law. "Forgive my going on. I will lose the habit two days from now: my professors will once again make sure that I am disgusted with travel under whatever mode."

---

With his courses leaving him cold, Trudeau looked elsewhere for intellectual stimulation. Soon after the start of his second year at law school, his friend Roger Rolland invited him to submit an article for the periodical that he had just founded, *Amérique française*. Trudeau chose to do a book review of *Voyages de Marco Polo*, by the French-Canadian writer Alain Grandbois.[30] The book had just won a "prix David," one of three monetary awards then given annually by the Government of Quebec to the three books judged to be the best published that year. Trudeau was just back from his thousand-mile canoe trip. He had just read Victor Ségalen's true adventure book, *Équipée*, which had moved him to enthusiasm. But this new book, which purported to relate the voyages of one of history's greatest explorers, repelled him utterly. He condemned it from the start of his brief review: "A work that no man of culture can afford not to have in his waste basket."[31] Then he backed up his judgment: "All told . . . it was considered that all you had to do was to throw everything together, mention the Polos now and then, quote them at great length, fill in the blanks by anachronistic quotations from Mohammed, and there you would have your book. That is how chocolate is whipped up. . . . When the story is already seven centuries old, it is hardly acceptable to serve up the same twists and turns, unless one can add a new historical dimension; unless one infuses it with a literary quality, and discovers new feelings. (I have in mind the splendid *Équipée* by Victor Ségalen.)" The rest of the critique was in the same vein. Trudeau was willing to concede that the author had shown some qualities. "I won't say that he failed miserably: the narration of anecdotes about these strangers from long ago proceeds in a clear and always natural style." But Trudeau insisted that this rather insipid production did not deserve a first prize: "A first prize carries with it the promise of a new work, of something that has been molded and shaped." And so he arrived at his devastating conclusion: "The author brought not a breath of original inspiration. The artist created nothing. And so what we are given to stare at is a vulgar vulgarization for the vulgar."

This was Trudeau's first publication outside of a student paper. This might be why he first submitted a draft to someone for critical feedback.[32] The written comments on Trudeau's draft, in a hand that is clearly not his, leave us perplexed as to the critic's identity. Could it be Vadeboncœur? In his memoirs, Trudeau would write: "It was Pierre Vadeboncœur who, towards the end of the classical course, truly introduced me to the art of writing well in French."[33] But when we asked him whether he was the critic of Trudeau's review, he replied that he had never edited any writing by his friend, adding that he did not know what Trudeau was referring to.[34] Was it Roger Rolland, the publisher of the periodical? When we asked him, Rolland replied that he had never seen a draft copy of the review. Could the critic have been Jean-Baptiste Boulanger – who died in 2000 – of whom Trudeau wrote in his memoirs: "In school, this precocious boy amazed me"?[35] Whoever the corrector was, the tone of the comments leaves no doubt that they were made by a close friend, someone who felt he could be brutally frank. But he did offer an apology: "Forgive the rather arrogant tone, which is brought on by the role that you are imposing on me."

Indeed, although he found Trudeau's phrase, "breath of original inspiration," to be "very good," he found "vulgar vulgarization" to be "weak." (That did not deter Trudeau from retaining the phrase in his final version.) In the margins of the draft, the critic wrote such observations as these: "You're trying to say something here but your words are up in the air." There was also the occasional encouraging note: "good" and "excellent." Sometimes, too, he lectured Trudeau about his character: "I can see now how your pride could cause you to fail! . . . Your main problem: that you did not sufficiently muzzle the haranguer within you; your words sometimes carry you away to the detriment of your observations – your model here is La Rochefoucauld, who never did impress me. I also would have preferred that you not play so obviously to the reader – one senses that you are intent on a success." After lecturing him on three rules for good writing, the critic concluded on an encouraging note: "The best thing about your article, and that is something, is that it shows that you have grasped what style is all about." It has often been said about Trudeau that he was from earliest childhood extremely proud of himself and could brook no criticism. Here we have an example suggesting that he was open to learning from others.

———◆———

On November 13, 1941, Trudeau wrote out a draft on a quite different subject. He was writing five months before the plebiscite on conscription of April 27, 1942. It does not seem ever to have been published, but it is worth our attention because it is probably his first piece of writing motivated by a political commitment. He gave it the title, "Mûrs,"[36] meaning ripe. It denounced both *les Anglais* in Ottawa who wanted to impose conscription for overseas service and the French Canadians who remained passive. The point of the title is clear from the first sentence: "The gourmets of Ottawa have prodded us, sniffed us, kneaded us and found us ripe." Then he switched languages to write in English: "Now is the time for conscription." He had caught on to the stylistic impact of alternating between French and English: French when speaking for himself or French Canadians, English when supposedly speaking for Ottawa. The federal government, he said in French, pretended to be defending freedom, when in reality its only objective was to join ranks with England when it was under threat. Then, switching back to English, he explained, ironically: "The pledge of 'no conscription' was given in the days of the Maginot Line. Today things have changed, and we are not held to our promises." So the federal government had been dishonest in its about-face on conscription. But we French Canadians are also to blame, he wrote: "We are the first to forget those promises that we extorted from the government." French Canadians are only courageous in the absence of danger. "In the past, those who opposed conscription won election, not because the people hated conscription, but because conscription seemed so unlikely. The people admired the brave promises that required no effort to be fulfilled. But, now that the danger is real and getting closer, the people like conscription and the government can move towards implementing it without consulting the people."

He criticized French Canadians who took part in the war effort and who thereby became Ottawa's accomplices. The government was then able to pretend that French Canadians were in favour of conscription. "And so we want to go off and fight. And so we want compulsory military service.

Oh, what great logicians we have in our governments. The big shots have become psychologists. . . . They know what we think before we utter a word. . . . They pretended that the other Canadians loved the war, and it turned out well; since the others didn't respond, it must have been true." Then, in English: "The brave French-Canadians are as anxious as any to have conscription."

Trudeau wanted to demonstrate that he, at least, had the courage of his convictions. That is why he announced emphatically – and repeated it in English to make sure the government understood – his opposition both to conscription and to the war in all its dimensions. The conclusion of his piece reverberates with his anger: "Now here's a surprise: they got me quite wrong. . . . In my own case, they happened to get it wrong. And since I don't take it well when someone puts words in my mouth without consulting me first, I wish to point out their mistake. I am a French Canadian and I am not in favour of conscription. Please allow me to make myself clear: 'I am a brave French Canadian and I am not as anxious as any to have conscription.'" This last sentence was written in English. Then he repeated in French: "I am a French Canadian and I am not in favour of conscription. Allow me to make myself clear. I am not only against conscription, but I am also against mobilization, against participation, against rearming, against aid to the belligerents. I am *against the war.* Is that quite clear now, or are you again going to play on words?"

It has been generally accepted, and Trudeau wrote it himself, that the war was, for him, "an important reality, of course, but a very distant one," and that "It was part of current events, and they did not interest me very much."37 What is true is that he, like the majority of French Canadians, seemed indifferent to the stakes and the horrors of this war. The real war even then being waged so cruelly in Europe, the real tragedy striking so many millions of human beings, were only distant events – like the Trojan War. As he would later write in his memoirs: "Was the war in Europe important? Sure, I told myself, but ancient campaigns like the Trojan Wars also deserved to be learned about."38 But conscription, on the other hand, now there was a truly major issue. And so, a year before the speech that he was to give supporting Jean Drapeau as candidate in Outremont, Trudeau, in his first *engagé* writing, revealed his vehement opposition, not just to conscription, but to everything connected with the war.

By the end of 1941, Trudeau had already taken a forceful position on the issue of conscription. Meanwhile, in the process of developing his own political philosophy, he had read only two germane books that year, Tardieu's *Le souverain captif* and Bergson's *Les deux sources de la morale et de la religion*. Both books, the one dealing with politics and the other with philosophy, were calculated to strengthen the outlook that he had absorbed at Brébeuf, notably the need to struggle for the advent of a new society founded on Christian values. He was delighted to discover "scientific" confirmation of his convictions, but he still had not arrived at concrete proposals to bring into being this new social order.

The coming year of 1942 would prove a turning point for the development of his political philosophy and his commitment to political action.

# Chapter 8

## 1942: LONG LIVE PÉTAIN!

*The real traitors are neither Pétain nor Maurras, but "the leftist government . . . the Front populaire . . . here are the traitors of the métèque Léon Blum."*

> — JEAN-BAPTISTE BOULANGER
> *Maurras a-t-il trahi?*, 1945

IN 1942, Pierre Trudeau's political militancy surged and crested. For us, his biographers, 1942 was also the most difficult year to be following him because we found our discoveries to be so disconcerting. He was a full-time law student, and he was busy with a range of activities that went from reading books on political theory to drawing up strategies and tactics for revolution. Sometimes he worked alone, sometimes he plotted with his friend Jean-Baptiste Boulanger, and at other times he worked with a group. As we reconstructed his movements, it was hard to believe that this burst of activity took place within a single year. It was a little like watching a movie played in fast motion. And what was the object of so much frantic activity? To plan a revolution.

As we carried out our research, two nagging questions persisted: Why did Trudeau, usually so direct, maintain until his death an almost total silence about this particularly explosive period of his life? And why did those of his contemporaries who were in the know, and who had become his most determined adversaries, choose to be his accomplices in covering up what he and they did together back then? To answer these questions would take us into divining intentions and so we will limit ourselves to tentative suggestions that are based on the documents at our disposal.

Between 1941 and 1944 the young Trudeau espoused with conviction and enthusiasm the very ideological commitments that the post-1950 Trudeau would despise. When he arrived at Harvard University, a new cultural universe opened up before him and he used his new perspective to scrutinize his past assumptions. He would try to understand how he, so determined to search for the Truth, could have embraced such gross errors. He would then come to realize that he had been blinded by the entire cultural complex in which he had grown and had been educated. That cultural complex, as he came to realize, operated to the detriment of all French Canadians. Little by little, he would throw off the ideology that had governed him during the most formative period of his life and come to adopt the universal values of liberalism. He would then devote the rest of his life to promoting those values, to searching for concrete solutions to the real problems of all Canadians, but in particular, to the problems of French Canadians, of aboriginals, and of the country's several minorities. And he would carry on this struggle without ever turning his back on his identity as a French Canadian from Quebec. Trudeau did, then, transcend the legacy of his youth. But there is a sense in which he never faced up to it. He would attack those who propagated and tried to impose a narrow nationalism and the secession of Quebec. But he seems to have repressed from his memory his own past as a narrow nationalist and a separatist. He retained a selective memory of his own war years, recalling almost exclusively his own justified struggle against conscription. But he remained silent about so much of his buried past.

And what about his contemporaries who had conspired with him and later turned into his adversaries? Why did they choose not to expose his past? Perhaps they shared his reasons for discretion. If they had denounced Trudeau, they would have had to reveal their own wartime activities and the values they then espoused. "With a common accord, we [French Canadians] stopped talking about it, as if we were not proud of what we had done," André Laurendeau was to write in 1962.[1] The French-Canadian elite, recalling the war, chose to focus almost exclusively on the conscription crisis. But it would seem obvious that, had Mackenzie King's "broken promise" not existed, it would have had to be invented.

The war forced the elite to choose between their hereditary enemy, England, which had imposed on them such false values as liberalism and

democracy, and the revered Marshal Henri Philippe Pétain who proposed a "Révolution nationale" under the slogan of "Travail, Patrie,
Famille" – the solid values of work, country, family. Pétain represented,
it was felt, the partial restoration of the Catholic France beloved by the
Quebec clergy, the old France that had existed before the Revolution of
1789 and before the anti-Catholic secularizing laws of the nineteenth and
early twentieth centuries. Could the French-Canadian elite side wholeheartedly with England when the Marshal was collaborating with
Germany, England's enemy? And yet, how could they side openly with
Pétain when Quebec was part of the Dominion of Canada and still recognized the British Crown? "Whatever the peace turns out to be, it will
be made without us and against us."[2] Trudeau's friend and closest collaborator, Jean-Baptiste Boulanger, wrote in 1943, while a medical
student at the Université de Montréal.[3]

Caught in this dilemma of contradictory allegiances, one can understand that the elite clung to the struggle against conscription as a noble
alibi, both in their own eyes and the eyes of the world, for refusing to recognize the horrors of Nazism and for refusing to commit themselves to
the war against it. Aware that they were condemned by "the others" in
Canada and abroad, they did not know how to explain that they were
neither heartless nor cowards, but the victims of an all-too successful
collective indoctrination. In the final analysis, it seemed the more con-
venient solution for much of the elite – including notably Trudeau – was
to develop a collective amnesia that was given a welcome cover by the
struggle against conscription. Even Laurendeau, when he came to write
his own *mea culpa*, was content to recall the sequence of political events
in Canada that had given legitimacy, he felt, to French-speaking
Quebeckers' opposition to conscription, while passing over the French-
Canadian elite's attitude toward Pétain, toward the authoritarian and
fascist regimes of Europe, and toward democracy itself.

But the written documents do not suffer a loss of memory. One
wonders why Trudeau saved his writings from 1942 when he could so
easily have destroyed those stubborn witnesses to his troubling past. He
could have maintained forever the mythical version of his life. We believe
that he had failed to face up to the follies of his youth, but was unwilling
to cheat with history. All his life, he had made it a point of principle to

search for the truth. He intended that someone, someday, should discover and bring to light his own attitudes and actions, and those of the majority of the French-Canadian elite during those dark years.

And so it is our task to retrace Trudeau's movements in 1942, guided for the most part by documents that have remained unknown to this day. Since he did not keep an exhaustive record of all of his important activities, we will also sometimes make use of credible secondary sources to follow him through his lectures, conferences, meetings, demonstrations, and the like. But Trudeau left behind such a wealth of documents, and they are so revealing, that our account will rely primarily on them.

———※———

As always, even as he was busy elsewhere, Trudeau managed to read an impressive number of books, both fiction and non-fiction, in French and in English. He worked his way through works by Jules Romains, Paul Valéry, André Malraux, Panaït Istrati, André Gide, Virginia Woolf, Emily Brontë, and many others. Most of the time, he delighted in what he read. We shall skip over his notes on these authors to concentrate on just a few books that played a significant role in his political development. At times, we shall also take notice of occasional articles, especially those that appeared in the *Quartier Latin*, the publication of the students of the Université de Montréal. Trudeau read it regularly, even during those years when he was away at Harvard.[4]

In January 1942, he read Robert Hunter's *Revolution (Why, How, When)*. The choice of this book demonstrates his continuing interest in revolution, one that would increase steadily until June 1942, when he read with enormous enthusiasm *La révolution nécessaire*, by Robert Aron and Arnaud Dandieu.[5] But Hunter's book left him cold. "A hybrid book where the excellent can be found right next to the mediocre," he observed. Convinced as he was of the superiority of the French culture that he claimed as his own – a viewpoint he maintained for a few more years – he wrote: "The American mind is very different from that of the French: the composition is slack . . . it is hard to find the overall viewpoint." He did, though, make a concession: "Still, this work would be valuable even if it did nothing but put forward the theses and the techniques of the great revolutionaries." It was from Hunter's book that he learned that the communists had been initiated to the techniques of revolutionary action by reading Karl Marx's treatise on the French Revolution. They learned there, notably, that "Republicans and moderates should be put out of the way; representative governments can't be relied upon." Lenin had his own advice to offer, Trudeau noted: "The surest means of overturning the existing basis of society is to debauch the currency."

Revolutionary and military strategies were clearly on Trudeau's mind. He noted, for example, that Lenin kept two books by his bedside: Carl von Clausewitz's classic work, *Concerning War*, and Marx's *The Civil War in France*, in which he examined the abortive Paris uprising of September 1870 aimed at creating an autonomous workers' republic. Trudeau was also interested in Trotsky's strategic thinking. He noted: "Trotsky, the master technician of Revolutions, said that Revolution should not be carried out by fighting mobs, but by small trained forces: Lenin, Mussolini, Hitler used his tactics." His admiration for Trotsky would be reinforced when he read works by Tharaud in March, by Malaparte in April, and, finally, by Sorel in May 1942.

On January 30, 1942, *Le Quartier Latin* published an article by Trudeau's friend Jean-Baptiste Boulanger, three years his junior, but who had made a strong impression on him. In 1993, Trudeau would write: "In school, this precocious boy amazed me. At the age of ten, he had written a biography of Napoleon that had earned him a medal from the Académie française." Trudeau also recalled sharing a pedagogical adventure with Boulanger: "We decided together to read over one summer the great works of political writing – Aristotle, Plato, Rousseau's *Social Contract*, Montesquieu, and others – and to exchange letters giving each other our impressions and our comments on each of the works we read. Boulanger knew more than I did in this field, and that was why I hung around with him."[6] Boulanger confirmed Trudeau's account: "I also remember that studious summer that we devoted to the 'great political works.'"[7] Neither gave the date or the reason for such a studious summer. In fact, it was the summer of 1942, and their motivation was peculiarly political. We can be sure that Trudeau had read this and other articles published in *Le Quartier Latin* by his friend, and we can even safely assume that he shared most of his views.

In his article, "Sous le masque d'Otto Strasser," Boulanger was reviewing a book, *L'aigle prussien sur l'Allemagne*, written by the German Otto Strasser. The author had originally intended to title his

book *Sous le masque d'Hitler*. Strasser developed the thesis that Germany
could never be at peace "without the complete annihilation of Nazism
and Prussianism." Boulanger, in his review, disagreed. He considered the
struggle waged against Hitler by Otto Strasser and his brother Gregor –
whom Hitler had ordered assassinated – to be nothing more than a
"mask" for "a family quarrel. Otto summons his brother back to life to
avenge him and fulfill himself." Boulanger also observed contemptuously: "Some of Strasser's passages sound like the complaints of a
servant who has been fired."

Boulanger never explained the circumstances of Gregor Strasser's
death. In fact, he died during that "night of the long knives," June 30,
1934, when Hitler annihilated his opponents and the members of the
Nazi party who had criticized him. Gregor Strasser, a proponent of socialism within the National Socialist Party, was the leading figure of the
party's left wing and he fell victim to that night's political assassinations.
This was the historic conflict that Boulanger reduced to nothing more
than a family quarrel. His own pro-Hitler bias came out in his conclusion.
After warning his readers that they would not find in Strasser's book
"what is behind and what is within National Socialism," he informed
them that "all the inner structure of the party was analyzed by the master
who had founded it; the explanation constitutes the second volume of
*Mein Kampf*." Boulanger had not only read the notorious work of the
"master," but he recommended it to the students of the Université de
Montréal through their paper, the *Quartier Latin*. Incidentally, *Mein
Kampf* was not on the Vatican's Index of prohibited books.

In a postscript to his article Boulanger raised a different subject.
Newspaper editor and novelist Jean-Charles Harvey, one of the rare
liberal voices in the Quebec of the early 1940s, had rebuked Boulanger
in his paper, *Le jour*, for the distinct lack of enthusiasm with which he
had discussed a speech given by Churchill on a visit to Canada.
Boulanger replied: "But is it not Churchill, rather, who is the attacker?"
And Boulanger expressed his indignation that "in Canada it is the love
of France that is rationed, and not the insults against her. What we are
forbidden to write under the National Defence Regulations, that we
must keep in our grieving hearts so as never to forget." His heart grieved
at being forbidden to publish his admiration for the Pétain regime, the
collaborator of Nazi Germany.

But he was particularly outraged that Harvey had had the indecency to write: "I see nothing *miraculous* about that old man in Vichy."[8] Boulanger responded: "The miracle of Pétain, like that of Joan of Arc, is quite simply to have saved their patrie." For Boulanger, Pétain and Joan of Arc represented one and the same cause. Nor did his fervour for the Vichy regime abate as the war progressed. On January 23, 1943, he wrote again in the *Quartier Latin*: "Defeat saved France from suicide. . . . The Latin soul will live again. . . . This new soul is full of foresight and it is industrious, it feeds on life itself and on life's sublime realities. This soul is that of our French ancestors who transmitted to us, along with their blood, the honour of their race so that we might perpetuate it on American soil. It is because that soul is immortal that we have faith in our *work*, that we have built our lives around the *family*, which is the source of our hope made flesh and the cradle and the justification for the *patrie* which embraces our human charity, and also that we await the resurrection of our people in the Roman Peace of the universal Church."

Boulanger put in italics the three words, *travail, famille, patrie*, which were the very slogan of Pétain's Vichy regime. Enthusiasm for a France returned to official Catholicism under Pétain was widespread in Boulanger's world. As we saw, Trudeau's teachers insisted that their students were not the children of Voltaire, who was called the "spirit of evil incarnate" by Adolphe-Basile Routhier, author of the lyrics of "O Canada."[9] When, in 1905, France adopted the law separating Church and state, France "dishonoured itself in the eyes of the civilized world."[10] This idea was expressed recurrently in the *Brébeuf*. Similarly, on December 19, 1941, an article in the *Quartier Latin* declared: "After having broken in 1789 with the Christian tradition, the France of the Revolution and of the Freemasons fabricated and paraded around the world a distorted and diminished culture. . . . This was the France that repudiated itself, the France whose sons we are no longer and the France that we have no wish to reproduce in ourselves."[11]

Pétain, on the other hand, who was handed full powers by the National Assembly on July 10, 1940, when the republican Constitution was abolished, found favour among French Canadians who responded to his praise for rural life, his rejection of "cosmopolitanism" – meaning Jewish influence – and his exaltation of the French nation. Again, as the article in the *Quartier Latin* declared, French Canadians could once more declare their pride in their French origins: "The actions of Pétain and of his team plunge the French spirit once again into the very source of its baptism and of the most authentic values of the Greco-Roman tradition. . . . And it is a joy for us to see France recover its eternal traits. . . . France is restored to us because it is the pre-revolutionary spirit that continues to inspire our cultural and religious life."[12]

France, restored to pre-revolutionary values, was now ironically among the enemies of England, and so of Canada. That explained, according to Boulanger, the love that French Canadians had to nurture in secret in their grieving hearts. The love was, in fact, not all that secret. For the entire duration of the war and despite the censorship, the *Quartier Latin* published with few exceptions nothing but articles full of admiration for the France of Pétain, and without notable concern for its collaboration with Nazi Germany.

So it happened that the entire issue of December 20, 1940, celebrated the French spirit in all its manifestations. François Hertel's article, titled "Charles Lepic et la France," expressed such sublime admiration for the country that it became ridiculous. "All the French have a sense of humour," he wrote. "When France laughs, the very breast of the earth heaves, and when it weeps, both poles grimace under the glaciers." In the same issue, the editor of the paper published a passage of a speech by Marshal Pétain himself, in which the great man had sung the praises of the French peasant who drew his strength "from the very soil of the patrie."[13] Those words echoed what Quebec's priests and politicians, poets and novelists, had been celebrating for years. They were all delighted to recognize that, at last, Quebec and France were singing from the same hymn book.

By contrast, Jean-Charles Harvey's skeptical comments about the Marshal took real courage. Boulanger's response treated the writer to the most insulting of put-downs: "Why should I bother to answer Mr. Harvey? He hates us because we want to be French . . . he is unworthy of writing in the language of France." What could explain so much vindictiveness against Harvey? His offence was that, from the beginning of the war, he propounded in his weekly *Le jour*, liberal and democratic ideas. He vehemently criticized Marshal Pétain and backed the allied forces. However, *Le jour* didn't have much of an impact. As the historian Éric Amyot notes, Harvey's vehement critique "is a double-edged sword.

Because of his radical views, *Le jour* was a marginal publication. By flaunting a violent anti-clericalism he disturbed, to say the least, the great majority of French Canadians."[14]

Boulanger, by contrast, was an unconditional admirer of Pétain and Charles Maurras. Maurras, the journalist, poet, author, and politician, is remembered for his leadership of the extreme right. He was a pillar of the nationalist movement l'Action française, and of the periodical that it published under that name, from its founding in 1899 in the midst of the Dreyfus affair. It began as a pro-republican review, but soon moved to monarchism. It also became increasingly anti-liberal, anti-democratic, and anti-Semitic, under his influence. Maurras's major work, titled *Enquête sur la monarchie*, was published in 1900. In 1941, the year following the fall of France and the establishment of the Vichy rule over the part of France that was not occupied by the Nazis, he published *La seule France* to defend the regime of Marshal Pétain. At the end of the war, Maurras was found guilty of collaboration with Nazi Germany and imprisoned.

This did not deter Boulanger's admiration. In 1945, after the liberation of France, after his two heroes had been judged and condemned, Boulanger came to their defence by publishing a sixteen-page pamphlet in which he reprinted articles he had published during the war in the *Quartier Latin*. It was titled *Charles Maurras a-t-il trahi? de Maurras à Pétain*,[15] and in the preface he vented his indignation at seeing how public opinion in Quebec had turned against the two. "There was a time when being a disciple of Maurras was quite in style," he recalled.[16] Boulanger argued that the true traitors were not Pétain or Maurras, but rather "the pacifists, . . . the leftists in power who introduced the 40-hour week, . . . the Popular Front . . ., these are the traitors brought in by that métèque, Léon Blum."[17] *Métèque* is a racist term that was used to designate a foreigner. Blum had been born of a Jewish family in Alsace in 1872. He had been the architect of the Popular Front, which took power in 1936, and he was premier of France from 1936 to 1937, the first Jew to lead the country.

Boulanger was particularly resentful toward the "false-French" and "the left-wing propaganda that corrupts our newspapers."[18] Unfortunately, he bemoaned, "in the Anglo-Saxon countries, as ours is still, those who are on the right are subject to anathema: there is no salvation except in democracy, and Maurras spent his whole life denouncing the democratic fallacy as 'a sin against the mind' and the 'inversion of all principles' dealing with government."[19]

As late as 1945, Boulanger expressed his immense admiration for Maurras by quoting him extensively, especially from his *La seule France* and *Enquête sur la monarchie*. (These are books that Trudeau would read, probably because his good friend recommended them, and they, and Maurras, are described in detail later in this chapter.) Boulanger concluded his apologia by declaring his gratitude toward "the Master who taught us the use of the organic laws of thought and who tutored our youthful minds."[20] He used the evocative word *organic*. During that era, a central concept of authoritarian ideologies, whether corporatist, fascist, or Nazi, was that of the "organic" relationship between the individual, the nation, and its leader. He then spoke directly to the Master: "I thank you, Charles Maurras, for having awakened in me a French consciousness; for having initiated me into a world of clear ideas and the harmony of their interrelationship, of Order which begets Progress and of Tradition, which is the guardian of Hope. May you be forever blessed."[21]

———※———

So this was the Jean-Baptiste Boulanger with whom Trudeau would be closely involved in political plotting. Not that Trudeau necessarily shared all his views. Though generally favourable to Pétain's Vichy regime and what it represented, Trudeau did not surrender altogether his critical sense. Searching for the truth as was his wont, he read books that took an opposite view to his own. For example, in August 1942, he read *France: 1940–1942*, by Frank Rice,[22] in which the author presented a whole series of documents detailing how the Vichy regime came into being. Trudeau recognized that the account was fair. "This book's value is that it allows us to come to our own conclusions, by providing testimonies from all sides. The author, of course, is Gaullist and against the Axis, but he does not compel us to share his views." At the time, and till nearly the end of the war, de Gaulle was mostly rejected in Quebec. This book did not change Trudeau's partiality for Vichy, but it did leave him with a degree of respect for its opponents. "As for myself, I came away from the book with a great sorrow for France, a great sympathy for Pétain and those who remained behind, but also some admiration for those who left their patrie, wanting to fight to the end." His admiration did not extend to the leader of these fighters, General de Gaulle. His brief comment: "I know nothing about the wisdom or the sincerity of their leader."

———◆———

In February 1942, Trudeau read *Les conséquences politiques de la paix* by the right-wing historian and friend of Charles Maurras, Jacques Bainville, also one of the prominent personalities of L'Action française. Trudeau commented: "A remarkable example of what wisdom, perspicacity, strategy can accomplish in the area of politics."

What Trudeau found remarkable was that, as far back as 1920, Bainville had been able to predict by a penetrating analysis that "Germany would be the first of the vanquished nations to recover" and to become once again a great power; that it "would seize Poland (which is now its territory) while Russia would expand so as to claim its former possessions in Poland." Unquestionably Bainville's analysis, carried out only a year after the Versailles treaty, impresses by its perceptiveness of the consequences that would follow the treaty. Bainville died in 1936 and so was prevented from presenting additional causes to his analysis of the coming world war. Still, it is surprising that Trudeau, in 1942, did not recognize that Bainville's analysis was incomplete, since it did not include the stunning rise to power of Nazism, with all the catastrophic events that followed.

We found no evidence that Trudeau consulted other authors on the causes of the war. But reading Bainville alone would have confirmed the analysis shared by most of Quebec's intellectuals at the time. They considered that this war was quite simply the logical consequence of the First World War, since it followed inevitably from the great errors committed by the European powers at Versailles. As a consequence, in their view, Canada had no obligation to join in cleaning up the mess left by the imperialist European powers in 1919, nor in paying a price for their miscalculations.

———◆———

As he pursued his self-education, Trudeau read in February 1942 a problematic biography titled *Léon Degrelle et l'avenir de "Rex."* Its author, the French journalist and writer Robert Brasillach, had begun his career as a literary columnist for Charles Maurras's *Action française.* Over time, like so many other French intellectuals of the traditional extreme right, Brasillach moved closer to Nazism. In 1937, he was appointed editor-in-chief of the weekly *Je suis partout*, in which he expressed his growing admiration for Nazism. In 1941, he published *Notre avant-guerre*, his largely autobiographical memoirs of the period between the two world wars, in which he expressed his racism and anti-Semitism as part of his fanatical vision. During the Vichy regime he celebrated Franco-German collaboration. After the Liberation, in February 1945, he was executed by a firing squad as a collaborator.

Trudeau was enchanted by Brasillach's biography of Degrelle and expressed not the slightest reservation over the author's extremist views. On the contrary, he felt inspired by what he read in 1942, as he acknowledged: "This biographical essay is all too short, but it is long enough to fire me up with enthusiasm. Degrelle, the leader and founder of the Rexist party in Belgium, is a young man who must be imitated. Dynamic, a cheeky *gamin*, given to practical jokes, but also idealistic, Catholic, courageous, mystical."

A young man who must be imitated. The qualities of Degrelle noted by Trudeau were, in fact, the very qualities that Trudeau possessed or to which he aspired. In addition, Degrelle acted as a true mystic, according to Bergson's definition. He spent himself utterly in pursuit of ideals that transcended his own self and sacrificed himself for the benefit of the collectivity. There was another parallel. Degrelle's inspiration for his political action, his vision for restoring the social order, was largely derived from the papal encyclicals, notably *Quadragesimo anno*. Like the Jesuits in Quebec and, to a lesser extent, like Quebec's bishops, Degrelle dreamed of transforming Belgium into an officially Catholic corporatist state. Not only Degrelle's corporatism, but his emblematic cult of Christ the King, was apt to appeal to the Jesuit-trained Trudeau who, while engaged in Loyola's Spiritual Exercises, had mediated on the "Two Standards," that of the Devil and of Christ the King, each summoning their supporters to their cause.

After travel in America, a young Degrelle returned to Belgium and became active in politics to counter the ills of his people. Like Bergson's mystic, Degrelle demanded justice, and when he spoke, Trudeau noted, people listened attentively and many wanted to follow him because they sensed that he spoke the plain language of truth. "His party grew in support day by day, had the government trembling, unmasked ministers, demanded justice everywhere and obtained it. They swept (figuratively and literally) the garbage in front of the minister's door. And Degrelle continued his campaign . . . he spoke to his audience as if in conversation, spoke to them about his projects, laughed and cried with them."

Degrelle also fought for something that Trudeau appreciated: he wanted to preserve both French and Flemish, which increased his popularity with both the Walloons and the Flemish, as Trudeau observed: "The young and the old, the Walloons and the Flemish come running, because to the first he preaches the preservation of French, to the second the preservation of the Flemish language. It is pointless to attempt to melt together these two nationalities, bilingualism cannot be applied everywhere: for it to be applied in the capital is enough." In effect, Degrelle was proposing what is now called "territorial bilingualism," the model that has been urged by a number of Quebec's intellectuals and nationalists. The young Trudeau was attracted to this model in 1942, but he would later change his mind and repudiate it when he passed the Official Languages Act. As he explained to us in 1997, "Canada must be bilingual. We must learn from the Belgian experience. They chose a language policy based on territory. And things did not get better, they became worse: the country is more divided than ever. We must draw lessons from this experiment."[23]

Trudeau's two pages of enthusiastic notes on Degrelle seem to describe a knight errant who founded a legitimate party to work for the good of the country. But what was this Christus Rex party whose leaders fired Trudeau with enthusiasm in 1942 as "idealistic, Catholic, courageous, mystical"? The Wikipedia encyclopedia thus describes Degrelle's political movement: "Rexism was the ideology of the Rexist party, officially called Christus Rex, and was founded in 1930 by Léon Degrelle, a French-speaking Belgian. The name was derived from the Roman Catholic social teachings concerning Christus Rex (Christ the King). It was also the title of a conservative Roman Catholic journal. The ideology of Rexism called for the moral renewal of Belgian society in conformity with the teachings of the Roman Catholic Church, by forming a corporatist society, and abolishing democracy." Rexism exploited in its propaganda the many financial scandals linked to Belgian politicians during this troubled period. In 1936, as Degrelle moved closer to the fascist movements that were growing in different parts of Europe,

Rexism lost part of its moderate support. In July 1937, Degrelle was condemned to a four-month suspended prison sentence for libel. In June 1940, following the invasion of Belgium by the German armies, Degrelle did what collaborationist parties in France were to do as well: he advocated collaborating with the Nazi Reich. In August 1941, together with the most extreme Rexists, he created an anti-Bolshevik force, the Légion Wallonie, a paramilitary organization modelled on the SS, which fought alongside German forces on the Russian front. After the war, the Rexist movement was outlawed in Belgium, and several of its leading figures were shot, while Degrelle fled to Spain, condemned to death in absentia.

So this was "the young man who must be imitated," as Trudeau wrote in 1942, the man who wanted so much to help his country and who caused corrupt politicians to live in fear. Was Trudeau simply unaware of the record of both Brasillach and of Degrelle, whom Brasillach so lauded in his biography? For a young man so determined to pursue the Truth, Trudeau demonstrated either surprising carelessness or insensitivity toward disturbing facts about both the biographer – shot by France as a collaborator – and his hero – condemned to death by Belgium as a collaborator three years later.

Trudeau's other readings during that same period, and his comments on them, are not reassuring. In March 1942, he read *L'envoyé de l'archange*, published in 1939 by the brothers Jean et Jérôme Tharaud. Though they had won the Prix Goncourt in 1906 for another of their books, and would later both be elected to the Académie française, the brothers had published works that were considered anti-Semitic, such as *Petite histoire des juifs* (1927) and *Quand Israël n'est plus* (1934). The book that Trudeau read was a biography of Corneliu Zelea Codreanu, a Romanian terrorist who led the Nazi-inspired Iron Guard terrorist militia and who openly displayed his hatred for the Jews. Trudeau commented that the book "is far from being a masterpiece of its kind," but he still found it "objective with respect to the facts." He then wrote: "Codreanu is a hard man, the son of immigrants who is deeply committed to the flourishing of Romania. But he is particularly opposed to the Jews who seem to be ruining the country. . . . From the time of their graduation from secondary school, the Twenty [a secret society] swear to fight to the death against the Jews. [At the university, Codreanu's] professor teaches him to hate the Jews. Then, there follows the Jewish reaction: the police manhandle him, insult him. He swears that he will revenge himself and, at the next provocation, he shoots the chief of police point blank, killing him. . . . The 'Captain' [Codreanu] has but to suggest an assassination for it to take place."

Trudeau, be it noted, offered no criticism of Codreanu's primitive anti-Semitism. He made no comment about his murderous hatred of the Jews, nor of the assertion that the police manhandled him because of "the Jewish reaction." He said nothing about his trivializing of assassination. Rather, what Trudeau noted was that, despite all of Codreanu's misdeeds, "the government tried in vain to condemn him: everywhere the people showed their sympathy for him." What was the secret of his success? "He is a mystic, a man regarding whom legends spring up spontaneously; who attracts the people as does a miracle-worker; because he intuits the inner thrust of the Romanians: hatred of the Jews, suppression of the parties, moral rebirth."

Trudeau had discovered another mystic, in addition to Degrelle. At this point in his life, Trudeau seemed completely fascinated by the biographies of "true" flesh and blood mystics. He was so full of admiration for those ardent and idealistic personalities who wanted to redeem their people and were willing to pay any price in the name of Christ or of a nationalist mystique, that he seemed blind to their dark side. That is why he could be unconcerned about the vile character of this terrorist who assassinated innocent people without a qualm and waged a battle to the death against the Jews. Drawing an overall conclusion about Codreanu, Trudeau wrote: "I think that this man had more enthusiasm than intelligence. And yet he was able to fashion a new man; he awakened the ideal. But he alienated many of his supporters." This, surely, was a rather limp judgment on a merciless terrorist who was anti-Semitic to the depths of his soul. Codreanu the mystic ended his days serving a ten-year sentence at forced labour in prison, where he was assassinated.

Are we to conclude from his admiration for Degrelle and his respect for Codreanu that Trudeau was himself anti-Semitic? One recalls the anti-Semitic play, *Dupés*, that he wrote as a student at Brébeuf. He also expressed enthusiasm for a number of authors who considered the collective guilt of the Jews to be an irrefutable fact. Nowadays, such an attitude would be considered shocking. But it must be remembered that, during the 1940s, anti-Semitism was a given in most Western countries, including Canada, among people who would then go on to prestigious careers. Although a few courageous Canadian voices were raised here and there against anti-Semitism, we were unable to find a single one in all the issues of the *Quartier Latin* published during that period. But, during that same period, its anti-Semitic and xenophobic articles were legion. Let us quote just two, written by students who would later achieve celebrity, Michel Chartrand, the future union leader and grand orator, who could hold an audience for hours at a time, and Jean Drapeau, the future perennial mayor of Montreal.

Chartrand, no Codreanu, did not accuse the Jews of destroying Quebec, but he did reproach them for monopolizing the clothing industry. He did not raise the question why French Canadians were unable to compete with Jewish immigrants who usually arrived with little money, rudimentary education, and no knowledge of either of the country's two languages. All that counted for Chartrand, in his November 1940 *Quartier Latin* article,[24] was that "these factories employ 26,633 individuals in Quebec who are forced to become members of unions led by Jews on behalf of Jewish bosses." In consequence, no less than $100 million are "grabbed by these foreigners whom no one can stand except immigration officers." In fact, when Chartrand referred to "foreigners that no one can stand," he used the verb "sentir" which means "smell" as well as "stand." He played on the stereotype that Jews stank. For him those Jewish workers were "foreigners" and would always remain so.

As for Jean Drapeau, he was unable to stand – or to stand the smell of – such "foreigners." His article was titled "Au sujet de nos hôtes"[25] ("About Our Guests"). He began by repudiating the common assumption that French Canadians knew little about the war. In fact, he countered, they were being bombarded with war news to the point of "nausea." Moreover, even without such news, they would be aware that "Canada is at present used as a refuge by a considerable number of immigrants," for the simple reason that, each day, "we see them, we hear them, we rub shoulders with them, and sometimes, too, we can smell them." He went on in the same vein: "So we have refugees from war in Canada. And it seems to be fashionable in some circles to grieve over the lot of these unfortunates." He made clear that he did not count himself among those bleeding hearts by adding: "Each time that Canada, and particularly French Canada, has deigned to accept immigrants in the name of some grand principle, we have always had occasion to regret it. . . . What did it serve us to open our doors wide to the refugees from the Russian Revolution? How did those 'poor unfortunates' who had to flee the fires of the revolution show us their gratitude?"

Drapeau's answer to his own question must today seem disconcerting: "Why, they thanked us by transforming the great commercial artery of our city – the former 'Main Street'[26] – into a disgusting bazaar where some slab of stinking meat lies beside dirty loaves and where the sidewalks are used as garbage containers for rotting fruit and vegetables; they enriched our metropolis with repellent neighborhoods where we can't even walk without a violent urge to vomit." And that is not all, according to Drapeau. Not satisfied with spreading their stench on Saint-Laurent Street, they also used "clearly dishonest" business practices that ruined French-Canadian trade. Drapeau then extended his observations outside Canada, echoing a point of view typical of Charles Maurras: "If the Canadian experience were not enough, we could point to the innumerable trials that France is currently [in October 1940] enduring and which are simply the consequence of its policy of hospitality towards refugees from Russia, Austria, Czechoslovakia, Spain."

There you have it. Why did France go to war, suffer a defeat, find itself partitioned into an occupied zone and a zone controlled by the Vichy government? It was all caused by the foreigners, the alien residents! This sort of perception was already projected in 1938 by the French-Catholic nationalist novelist, Émile Baumann, when he wrote a preface to André Laurendeau's book on Lionel Groulx: "The French of continental France have been suffering for too long now when they see the face of their patrie deformed by the intrusion of the métèques."[27] Georges Pelletier, then director of Le Devoir, was also openly anti-Semitic. Éric Amyot writes: "As early as August 10, 1940, he [Pelletier] condoned the measures taken by the Vichy regime, underscoring the fact that it was the foreigners' treason that led to France's catastrophic defeat. He went on to warn his fellow French Canadians against the danger represented by Jewish immigrants fleeing Europe."[28] In a lengthy editorial written on October 18, he approved the anti-Semitic laws of Pétain's regime claiming that "in no way are these measures meant to humiliate these people, they are essential to the security of the state."[29]

Clearly, the University of Montreal's students merely reflected the beliefs of opinion leaders. We could have quoted many more articles from the *Quartier Latin* that were just as offensive, or even worse. We did not choose these two examples for their extremism, but for the future prominence of their authors. Indeed, as André Laurendeau, the future co-chair of the Royal Commission on Bilingualism and Biculturalism, was to maintain, such sentiments as those expressed by Drapeau and Chartrand were predominant at that time among French Canadians, especially the young people. He himself awakened to the enormity of his prejudice in February 1963, when he met a Jewish woman whose grandfather had escaped Nazi Germany to find refuge in Canada. During their conversation, Laurendeau came to realize with shame and regret that her grandfather had been able to save his life and the lives of his family members, now living in Canada, not *thanks* to Laurendeau's own efforts and those of other French Canadians, but *despite* their best efforts to keep out Jewish immigrants: "In 1933 . . . I belonged to a group of nationalists – of Young Turks under the name of Jeune-Canada. Jews at that time were protesting everywhere against the treatment of Jews in Germany. They had held a meeting in Montreal attended by French Canadian politicians, including Senator Raoul Dandurand. So we held a counter-demonstration . . . which we called 'Politicians and Jews.' I still don't know what got into us. . . . I took part in the meeting, at which I spoke at length about the politicians and a little – but that was too much – about the Jews. Because we gave some terrible speeches. One of us went so far as to declare that 'it is impossible in Germany to step on the tail of this bitch of a Jewry without our hearing the barking in Canada.' 'Forgive them, Lord, for they knew not what they said.' Really, we did not know. Those speeches by 20-year-old boys reflected the ideas that were common in their surroundings; those that you heard there were not always pretty or intelligent. And that is precisely what scares me. [My companions were] good guys. None, as far as I know, turned into a thief or an anti-Semite. They were sincere and passionate. At the very time when Hitler was preparing to kill six million Jews, they spoke sincerely about a 'so-called persecution,' or 'alleged persecutions,' which they contrasted with the mistreatments – 'and these are real' – which French Canadians were subjected to here. I can still see and hear myself complaining as loud as I could at that meeting, and meanwhile a German Jew saved his family from death by going into exile. . . . There are days when human progress seems terribly slow."[30]

This confession helps us to understand the attitudes that prevailed during that period. Blinded by their clerico-nationalist indoctrination, French Canadians considered the reported suffering of the Jews to be much exaggerated compared to their own. This was the cultural atmosphere in which Trudeau lived until he left for Harvard in 1944, as he was about to turn twenty-five. So it is hardly surprising that anti-Semitic writings and speeches had left him unmoved.

Even his friend François Hertel, with whom he was in close contact and whom he admired, would express undisguised prejudice against Jews in 1944 – yes, in 1944 – shortly before the war ended and after the Allies had liberated the extermination camps and so revealed to the world the appalling horrors of the Holocaust. He deplored the excesses of past generosity shown by French Canadians toward the Jews. "What can I say, to take but one example, about those unwise favours that, in the Province of Quebec, we lavished on a certain race that is not notably favourable towards us and that has become a threat to our businesses and even to our vacation resorts?"[31] Hertel was referring, no doubt, to Ste Agathe des Monts, a vacation village in the Laurentian mountains north of Montreal, where Jewish families had congregated in large numbers. What he failed to explain was that, at the time, many resort areas deliberately excluded Jews. For example, at Lac-des-Quatorze-Îles, also in the Laurentians, at that very time there was an understanding among all the owners of cottages on the lake that they would not rent or sell to Jews.

Hertel dissociated himself from the extreme hatred of Jews expressed by French journalist Édouard Drumont in his 1886 bestseller, *La France juive*. "Certainly, anti-Semitism such as propounded by Drumont is foolish and nasty; but is it not equally foolish to set the stage for anti-Semitic crises by allowing the Jew to take advantage of our people until the day comes when muffled hatreds break out into spectacular pogroms?"[32] This was the same François Hertel of whom Trudeau said in his memoirs that he "influenced a whole generation of students."

Neither in his published articles nor in his private notes did Trudeau give the slightest sign of opposition to the hateful prejudices so prevalent in his world. All told, in comparison to what others were saying and writing we find that Trudeau could be criticized less for his anti-Jewish writing than for his silence, for his lack of any critical reaction to all the anti-Jewish tirades made by his peers, his teachers, and by the authors and the "heroes" for whom he expressed so much admiration.

———•———

Meanwhile, Trudeau continued in his attempts to build up an expertise for the future political action that he had in mind. He wanted practical direction. That was what he had found lacking when, in 1940, he read Tardieu. Trudeau had appreciated Tardieu's claim that a Christian revolution was a necessity in order to put an end to the abuses of democracy. But he regretted not finding there concrete proposals for the society that was to be constructed. What he had particularly appreciated when he read Hunter's *Revolution (Why, How, When)* was to learn about "the theses and techniques of the great revolutionaries," notably Trotsky. Now that he had made up his mind to undertake that same Christian revolution, true to his methodical character, he searched for the means to carry it out.

His personal notes record that in "April? 1942" – he inserted the question mark – he read Italian pro-fascist journalist Curzio Malaparte's 1931 book, *Technique du coup d'État*. He found it, despite some weaknesses, "supremely interesting." He appreciated the way Malaparte examined "the development of tactics for a coup d'État as formulated by Trotsky." Trudeau filled four pages of notes detailing the theories of that tactical genius of the Bolshevik Revolution and examining the success or failures of various coups depending on whether or not they had applied Trotsky's lessons. He wrote: "To seize control of the state, Trotsky proved that there was no need to capture the government, to surround the ministries, to lay siege to the Parliament. It can be done by teams of 10 technicians who have rehearsed their plan of attack again and again and who, when the time comes, take control of the electric power plants, the railway stations, the post and telegraph offices, the telephone exchanges, the water supply and public services. They will paralyze the state's economic, political and social infrastructure. The government would be reduced to impotence. The technique required neither an impressive armed force nor the support of the masses, it needed only their complicit inertia."

In his autobiography, Jean-Louis Roux[33] acknowledged that he had belonged as a student to a secret revolutionary movement that aimed at making French Canada an independent state. This was toward the end of his studies at Collège Sainte-Marie, and so circa 1942. The group called itself "les X," or "LX." Roux recalls receiving a document in which "we were told what to do when the day came to besiege the police and fire stations and to occupy Montreal's radio stations." It would seem that someone in that underground movement had studied Trotsky. We shall revisit "les X" in Chapter 9.

---

In May 1942, Trudeau, while a law student, read *La seule France: chronique des jours d'épreuve*. He noted that the book had been "smuggled into Canada, was mimeographed and sold by stealth." Trudeau, who would not read a book on the Index without permission, had no qualms about violating federal wartime regulations. As an admirer of Maurras, he filled four pages with his comments on *La seule France*. In the fall, he would read Maurras's *Enquête sur la monarchie*, and would return to read it again in 1944, when he would cover thirteen pages with his comments and praises.

As an opening remark on *La seule France* Trudeau wrote: "Baptiste (Boulanger) wrote me that Maurras is 'the most French of all the French.'" That accolade, according to Maurras's biographer and close associate Pierre Boutang, was bestowed on the author by Marshal Pétain himself when, on November 22, 1941, he wrote on a copy of *La France nouvelle*: "To Mr. Charles Maurras, the most French of all the French."[34] Trudeau's comment: "Well, I almost have to agree, and much could be said about the style, which combines a perfect fluidity with a very great limpidity and purity. . . . But what truly counts is his thought. . . . Maurras is relentlessly logical, and it is sheer delight to see how he starts with an observation about some fact and then draws from it the most rigorous and the soundest of consequences." So, even as late as 1944, Trudeau remained dazzled by Maurras's style and intellectual rigour, both, as he thought, so French. "No one can deny that Maurras's doctrine is firmly based on the facts of history," he wrote. From that perspective, we must consider some of the ideas that Maurras propounded in *La seule France*.

The title of Chapter 1, "French unity first," conveys the general thrust of the book. The French have finally got rid of the *legal country* and have rediscovered, with Marshal Pétain, *the real country*, with both countries italicized. Then, in Chapter 2, the author explains the causes for France's defeat in 1940. Trudeau reflected accurately Maurras's arguments when he inscribed in his notebook: "He condemned relentlessly the republican government in general; specifically, he demonstrated accurately that its behaviour from 1918 on was typically and stupidly republican. All the phony French, the international clique of aliens [*métèques*] who had settled in France, constantly pressured France towards peace; then, in 1935, as soon as France was perfectly weakened and disarmed, they began the war. They did everything they could to provoke it, and they committed the unforgivable crime of *declaring* war, that is, of launching an offensive war when the people were prepared at most to defend the patrie. The government was also to a large extent responsible: this republican government, blindly romantic, in the grip of international Jewry, of Freemasonry, of communists and of the English."

The causes of the war, as put forward by Maurras in explanations that Trudeau found "relentlessly logical," deserve a closer look. There was, in the first place, the government that acted in a way that was "typically and stupidly republican." Maurras condemned everything that could be called republican, because, as he wrote, in italics, *"the Republic of France is the reign of the Foreigner."*35 From that premise, Maurras easily identified the authors of those blunders committed in France: they were all part of the "phony French," that international clique of *"métèques"* and international Jewry. First they weakened France, Maurras explains, then they provoked the war: "I know, I see, I verify, that we were thrust into the abyss where we find ourselves spinning, by the politicians of the parliamentary regime and of Judeo-masonry. That is what they wanted. Really wanted. They prepared it consciously, at length, minutely. . . . These men had only to say: *We do it*, and, consequently, *we want it*. . . . So how can this firm intention, this clear plan, be reconciled with the results that they could not fail to foresee, given the strength of the enemy and their own weakness?"36

Maurras argues seriously that the Jews and the Freemasons set out to weaken France, then chose war even when they knew that defeat was inevitable. So preposterous a thesis does not seem to have given Maurras a moment's pause as he analyzed the causes of the war. How could he explain a behaviour so irrational? Maurras's answer is unanswerable: it is a mystery. "*You can never know what goes on inside the head of a Jew . . .* The nervousness of the race, its long migration, the contradictions of its historic status, have all had the natural effect of creating a barrier when we try to penetrate by pertinent psychological reasoning into the secret labyrinth of their impulses and their motives. . . . So let no one ask us to explain the behaviour of the Western Jews at the time when war was declared."37

Trudeau's notes followed Maurras as he developed his "logical" argument on the causes of the war. "What a blunder: a war fought over principles, over democracy, when France had not yet even recovered . . . from the last war." How could Trudeau possibly agree that to defend principles was a blunder? Such a stance, for him, was paradoxical. He admired mystics who were willing to sacrifice themselves to defend high moral "principles" in order to bring about a social order based on Catholic values. Yet he repudiated as a blunder any thought of going to war for "principles." Obviously, he was referring only to "false principles."

When Maurras spoke of "false principles" or of a "war for ideas," he was referring to a so-called Jewish plot "for an offensive war," against which he tried to warn all the members of the government: "Whether they be Jews or Jew lovers, these fine gentlemen keep in close touch with London's Jewish clan, which is all-powerful."38 As Maurras saw it, Neville Chamberlain, the British prime minister from 1937 to 1940, let himself be taken in by international Jewry. The man thought he was leading Britain into a "war for prestige which was at the same time a war for ideas," when in reality he was only serving the interests of the Jews of France and England. In the eyes of history, Chamberlain has been condemned for having gone too far to "appease" Hitler's Germany in the hope of avoiding a war. But Maurras accused him of being a warmonger.39 And Trudeau, swayed by the anti-English, anti-Jewish attitudes rampant in his surroundings, was unable to see through Maurras's fallacies.

So, again, how did it happen that France was plunged into this war? Trudeau found the answer in *La seule France*. "Maurras demonstrates that it was England's constant policy to weaken France: just as England carried out the (so-called) *French* Revolution, so it was England that prevented, on September 2, 1939, the mediation arranged by Mussolini between Hitler and the democracies. Then, when the blow fell, England wanted France to bear the full impact." So now it was England that caused France's monstrous blunder. But what happened to the previous explanation that it was all the fault of the aliens, the *"métèques"*? Trudeau does not seem to have noticed the contradiction. Trained by his teachers to consider "perfidious Albion" as the source of all evil, Trudeau went on to write that England caused both the war and, earlier, the "French" Revolution. Maurras used harsher words. He described it as: "That most cosmopolitan of Revolutions, the one that is still ineptly called French . . ."[40]

Why was the "French" Revolution not really French? Because Maurras, like his allies on France's extreme right, and like so much of Quebec's clerico-nationalist elite, believed that the *real* values cherished by the *real* French people could not possibly be those of the 1789 Revolution, or of the Republic, or of democracy, or of sordid aliens like the Jews and the Freemasons, or of those eternal enemies, the English. In this conflict opposing two standards, Marshal Pétain raised the standard of Christ, of "la vieille France." Trudeau recorded his unqualified admiration for Maurras's mythologizing: "The inflexible royalist wrote here pages full of confidence in the future, and full of bitterness over the past. He has at last his authoritarian state. He endorses totally the actions of the great Maréchal Pétain." And Trudeau added a testimony to his complete acceptance of Pétain's Vichy: "[Maurras] is full of a wise enthusiasm for [Pétain's] National Revolution and its slogan, 'Travail, Famille, Patrie.'"

Indeed, Maurras was immensely grateful to Marshal Pétain because he had, at last, restored "France to the French." He did so in many ways, including, for example, through the Raphaël Alibert law of October 3, 1940, on the "statute of the Jews." One of Pétain's closest associates and friends, disciple of Maurras, viciously anti-Semitic, Alibert was appointed Under-Secretary of State to the President of the Council in the very first days of the regime. Then, as *garde des Sceaux*, that is Minister of Justice, he was responsible for this law on the "statute of the Jews." Marc Ferro, a well-known French historian, claims that no German pressure whatsoever had been exerted on the Vichy government. Pétain, who participated personally in drafting this law, "proved to be one of the strictest."[41] Maurras welcomed this statute and, taking as an example the medical profession, from which Jews were henceforth excluded, claimed that this was only right because "no profession had been so invaded by cosmopolitanism as the medical profession."[42] The new law simply put an end "to abuses that had become intolerable."[43] As Maurras explained, the medical profession had, at one time been passed on from father to son. But something happened. "Cosmopolitanism in the liberal professions had the effect of destroying that admirable and precious *continuity of the elites* which had constituted the underlying strength of our country. . . . The family provided support to the corporation and this harmonious construction continued to the very summit. So what the new law encourages is truly the restoration of the national, familial and corporatist spirit, simultaneously with a restoration of the elites."[44] Maurras also had a ready reply for anyone so bold as to raise a complaint that the law violated human rights. "We are the masters of the house that our fathers built and for which they gave their sweat and their blood. We have the absolute right to set our conditions for the nomads whom we receive under our roofs. And we also have the right to set limits to our hospitality, which we could also withhold."[45]

Such were the principles of the author, Maurras, for whom Trudeau as a young man had the very highest regard. How could he, at the age of twenty-two, be carried to the heights of enthusiasm for Maurras's vicious, xenophobic, and paranoid ravings? How could he find them "inexorably logical"? At that stage, Trudeau believed in the superiority of an authoritarian state, as did so many French Canadians in Quebec. He shared not only Maurras's admiration for "the great Maréchal Pétain" and his National Revolution, but also his suspicious contempt for the man that Maurras called "the ex-general de Gaulle," and for the "Free French." Trudeau, like Maurras, was still convinced that any French person worthy of the name would back Marshal Pétain and consider that he had taken the only honourable course. Like Maurras, Trudeau believed that to go to war to defend such false "principles" was a blunder.

Trudeau's reading was not motivated merely by the wish to expand his general knowledge. He was looking for enlightenment that he could apply to his own society. And so, as he came to the end of his notes on *La seule France*, he wrote a half-page of conclusions under the heading, "Applying to Canada." There he drew the lesson that Maurras taught with respect to the war: "If the French territory is threatened, if our frontier is invaded, all our efforts, even the most powerful, must be mobilized against the invader. But that is a far cry from our wanting war, from launching it: the war for ideas, the war for principles, the war of grandeur, to these I say no, thanks; it is far beyond our remaining means. . . . To charge, now, just because England charges or because English principles demand that they charge is a romantic policy."

Trudeau now had a new argument against participating in the Second World War, in addition to Mackenzie King's notorious "promise betrayed." Convinced by Maurras, he had no intention of agreeing to a war for "English principles," or for a "romantic" policy. What did Maurras mean when he attached so much significance to a "romantic policy"? That word, *romantic*, needs some attention, since Maurras gave it negative connotations, far from ordinary usage, when he spoke of a "romantic policy," or, earlier, of the "romantic blindness" of the republican government. Similarly, Boulanger derided Otto Strasser as a "romantic hero." Maurras, in fact, devoted much of his writing to a contemptuous critique of romanticism, both in its literary and its political form. So it was when he described Victor Hugo, an eminent romantic writer: "The very essence of mediocrity, Hugo's 'thought' is almost nil." He considered Hugo's writing to be "the ideological club of the republican school, with its progressivism, pacifism and humanitarian religion."[46]

Maurras despised romanticism because it symbolized for him "the primacy of passion over . . . reason."[47] Maurras, like most of those supporting extreme-right policies, considered that giving prime importance to passion meant losing sight of the true interests of the community. Those he called "romantics" were those we would now call "liberals," and he saw them as bleeding hearts who chose to blame the criminal's social circumstances rather than the crime, and to feel more pity for the criminal than for the victim. Maurras objected: "The pity that is true pity is, in fact, the reason which enjoins us not to forget, as our century is so · apt to do, the justified protection that is owed to the seed of the Strong. Because, in addition to Initiative and Invention which, nine times out of ten, belong to them, it is only their seed which creates the capital which makes everything move forward. There is no progress without it. . . ."48 Maurras's most serious reproach against the romantics was that they neglected the vital role of the elite. As he wrote in *L'Enquête sur la monarchie*, "Will, decisiveness, enterprise are the work of the few; assent, acceptance characterize the majority. It is to minorities that we owe virtue, daring, power and innovativeness. . . . And so our concern should not be to rally the majorities. In any event, they will come around on their own."49

It is startling to discover that Trudeau's later well-known slogan, "Reason before passion," was one that he first encountered in 1942 in reading Maurras. He was to apply it as part of a vision that would be quite opposite to Maurras's repudiation of liberalism and of democracy, or his celebration of the strong and of the authoritarian state.

While Trudeau succumbed to the charm of Maurras, his notes show that he did not agree unreservedly with all his themes. In fact, he had two reservations. One dealt with the appropriateness of going to war: "However, he [Maurras] gives rather short shrift to some of the problems raised by his theories: the attitude of Russia in June 1941, the reason why the government of France wanted a weak France in the time of danger. . . . But he promises that he will clear it all up some day and I believe him." On the other hand, when it came to Maurras's defence of the monarchy, Trudeau found it lucid, but still "somewhat one-sided . . . because Maurras wants to turn everything into an argument in favour of his royalist commitment." Still, he found Maurras's arguments so convincing that he wondered why all the French were not, then, monarchists: "I am not French and I can't say whether or not Maurras has observed the facts correctly. But if one accepts his facts as reality, it would follow that the French should hardly be anything other than royalists. To tell the truth, there is only one thing that bothers me with respect to Maurras: it is the fact that France is not royalist even after almost half a century of such intensive propaganda."

His admiration for Maurras was, nevertheless, so generally uncritical that he was able to write without comment or any hint of criticism the following: "The hatred that he nurses towards the foreigners (the *métèques*) who prostitute France is something to behold." He also wrote: "This master of politics, the father of contemporary nationalism, deserves to be known for this reason alone that he places the salvation of his patrie above all else." And he added approvingly: "For better or for worse, the future belongs to nations." He did remark a few pages later, however, that Maurras's excessive nationalism and his "gallicanism" had been condemned by the Church. (In Quebec, Henri Bourassa had been criticized by Rome for similar reasons.) And Trudeau added that Maurras "did not seem to understand that, for a Catholic, *it is the reign of the Church that counts above all.*" He was caught in a paradox, admiring greatly Maurras's nationalism while recognizing that his nationalism, since it had been condemned by the Pope, was contrary to the universal mission of Catholicism. He seemed unaware of the contradiction, perhaps because he, like most of the Quebec elite at the time, was living the same ambiguity of wanting to reconcile his Catholicism with his French-Canadian nationalism.

It is worth noting that the Pope's condemnation of Maurras in 1926, and his placing of *L'Action française* on the Index, encouraged the emergence in France of a Catholicism that was less nationalistic, less authoritarian, less corporatist, less anti-liberal and anti-democratic, a Catholicism that turned more toward social action. Unlike Maurras, these "left-wing" Catholics, such as Étienne Gilson, Nicolas Berdiaev, Jacques Maritain, and Emmanuel Mounier – who was to found in 1932 the periodical *Esprit*, model of the future *Cité libre* – placed the emphasis on the "person" rather than the nation. These "personalists" were opposed to a Maurras–style nationalism, and appealed instead to universal values embracing all humanity.

In Quebec, personalism would take root only much later, with the birth of *Cité libre*. In the 1930s, it evoked only a weak echo. Jacques Maritain gave a few lectures there, and the *Quartier Latin* published accounts of his visits. In August 1942, Trudeau read Maritain's *Humanisme intégral*, but without much enthusiasm. Nationalism so occupied the cultural space that, even when the likes of André Laurendeau and François Hertel, claiming to be personalists, introduced the movement to Quebec, their personalism was so tainted by nationalism that the progressive element of the Christian left disappeared almost entirely, to the benefit of ideas that closely resembled those of Maurras.

Trudeau was not in any respect the exception. He accepted without demur the rejection of democracy and the assumption that an authoritarian and hierarchical structure was required. Maurras, he wrote, "exposes the ineptitude of democracy and of the republic in France [since] the very idea of organization excludes that of equality." As a consequence, Trudeau saw nothing unjust in a regime where "one man alone commands all the others." He gave this vindication, underlining the words: *"Since, in any case, we will always be governed, what justice requires is that we be well governed*: what is the difference in obeying one, one hundred or one thousand? The worst inequity would be to lack the necessities for the lack of a good government."[50] Trudeau did not share Maurras's commitment to monarchism, but he accepted the principle that authority should be vested in a single person. He seems not to have been concerned by the possible abuse of power that could result from such a structure. "The dangers that derive from power are less threatening than the risks that arise from the lack of power." No doubt he had in mind Maurras's critique of the impotence of the Third Republic. In Trudeau's view, for the administered to enjoy more freedom required that the administrators wield more authority. What was required, as he put it, underlining his words, was *"Authority above, liberties below."*[51]

It was Maurras's contention that democracy led to chaos by causing rapid changes of government: "What enterprise would not go to ruin if its management were shaken up every 10 or 30 months? No minister is granted the time to study the department that he is supposed to lead."[52] He had then concluded between 1900 and 1909 to the unquestionable superiority of a political system comprised of strong local communities and a strong central state (a system that would be called, a few years later, "corporatism.") Trudeau quoted Maurras: "It goes without saying that the cities, provinces, associations – all these sovereignties would be represented. Their elected councils (and it is an established fact that elections within an occupational structure give far better results than do political elections) thus become sovereign councils. They are true local senates. . . . And the powerful state will be weak when faced with citizens supported by free and strong communities."[53]

Trudeau was won over by that concept of governance. But how could it be attained? By acting at the source of the ill. And so Trudeau explained: "Because the ill is in politics, Maurras invents the slogan: 'Politics first.'"[54] And how will the change come about that will do away

with the existing regime so as to establish the desired new one? Maurras's
answer: by revolution. It was a proposal that Trudeau found congenial:
"Will we be accused of organizing sedition? That would be true, in a sense.
Indeed, since this regime provokes revolts of all kinds, we *organize* them:
we transform revolts which would be fatal in such a way that they work to
the benefit of a public order which saves and which restores everything."[55]

In fact, what Trudeau most appreciated in *L'Enquête sur la monarchie*, that he described as "a big brick of a book," were two sections:
"The masterful 150-page introduction [that] demonstrates the impotence of democracy and of the French Republic," and " '*Si le coup de
force est possible*,' which is a truly daring essay on the assault that would
be required to overthrow the Third Republic." Trudeau admired
Maurras's prescience: "Around 1909, Maurras discovered the logic of
modern revolution that will later be perfected by Trotsky and which will
be put to use in all countries: it is the seizure of the nerve centers of the
country by small daring groups. There is no need to defeat armies, it is
enough to paralyze the brain of the country." Trudeau was encountering
again a revolutionary tactic that he had already appreciated when he read
Malaparte's book. Another parallel: Maurras, like the other authors that
he had been reading, condemned democracy and asserted the obvious
superiority of authoritarian regimes under the rule of a powerful leader.
This was a theme that Trudeau heard repeatedly in his daily life. This
concordance of messages reflected the fact that, almost until the time he
left for Harvard, he exposed himself almost exclusively to influences
emanating from a right-wing ideology most often inspired by the teachings of Charles Maurras.

We say "almost exclusively," because there were a few rare exceptions, and we shall now consider some of them.

---

In his search for appropriate models and for ethical arguments to justify
the revolution that he had in mind, Trudeau read in May of 1942 a book
with a very different ideological perspective, *Réflexions sur la violence*,
published in 1908. Its author, Georges Sorel, was a leading theoretician
of Revolutionary Syndicalism. In this book, his masterwork, Sorel cited
Marx, Proudhon, and Nietzsche to develop a severe critique of parliamentary democracy, of the bourgeoisie's immorality, and of the corruption of

politicians. He was also critical of socialists, like the politician Jean Jaurès, who advocated replacing the capitalist system by democratic means. Sorel considered these democratic socialists as his worst opponents. There could be no progress toward the new society, he believed, if existing bourgeois institutions were accepted. Only violence at the hands of workers could put an end to the corruption of the existing regime. But how could the working class be rallied? Sorel saw in the general strike the necessary myth that could mobilize the workers and bring them to power. Ironically, this left-wing syndicalist, by his critique of parliamentary democracy and bourgeois decadence, but above all by his promotion of violence, would contribute more to the success of fascism, particularly in Italy, than to the socialist left. Though they were ideologically at opposite poles, Sorel shared with Maurras the same rejection of democracy, of liberalism, and of parliamentary government; both decried the corruption of the bourgeoisie and of politicians seduced by the power of money. Not surprisingly, Sorel drew closer in 1906 to *L'Action française*, but the alliance proved to be temporary. The Bolshevik Revolution of 1917 attracted his support and, in 1920, he published *Plaidoyer pour Lénine*, a defence of the Russian revolutionary leader.

Trudeau, in his quest for tools that would make possible a radical change in the society, was willing to go exploring far afield from his familiar ideological terrain. He wrote down no less than thirteen pages of notes on Sorel which began: "According to Tharaud, this is the book that most influenced Lenin and Mussolini." Trudeau had read the Tharaud brothers' biography of Corneliu Codreanu, noted earlier, which might well have inspired him to read Sorel.

His notes indicate that Sorel caused him some consternation. This was his first exposure to a major Marxist author. For the first time, he was confronted with "the class struggle," with a new social order that was proposed without Christianity as its very foundation, with the idea that the ideal historic protagonist to bring about this new society would be, not a person, not a "mystic," but a social class, the working class. Despite some misgivings, Trudeau did not condemn the book or its author. On the contrary, he commented: "For certain, this book belongs in the restricted category of works that bring something new, that spring from a deep and personal reflection. There may be errors, there certainly are gaps, but at least Sorel developed a line of thought and dared to put it down on paper." He complimented Sorel for daring to think outside of the beaten paths and for avoiding "the prudent and crowded 'juste milieu'" – the golden mean of those that Trudeau called, contemptuously, "the innumerable repeaters and regurgitators" of this "*juste*" milieu. And that was not all. "Sorel is a self-taught man whose thinking owes much to Bergson. He has – though not as much as Bergson – that admirable intellectual asceticism that allows the discovery of new ideas. . . . But he lacks the incomparable style of Bergson, that inconceivable capacity to create."

For Trudeau to compare Sorel to Bergson was high praise, especially given that Sorel was a non-believer. Moreover, Trudeau granted that some of Sorel's criticisms of the Catholic Church were valid. "It is true that he occasionally falls into monstrous errors, but it can't be denied that, in general, he is a clear-sighted and useful critic of our faults." Trudeau agreed particularly with Sorel's claim that "the mass of Christians does not follow Christian morality." And with this other comment: "Morality must be driven by the sublime. That is the case among Catholics when they have to struggle in a Protestant country." How could Trudeau not be impressed, as a French Canadian struggling against "Protestant Canada"? But then, Trudeau could hardly approve of Sorel when he wrote that this "spirit of the sublime can be found among workers who are passionately in favour of the general strike." That is to say, he could not approve it then, in 1942. In 1949, when he would commit himself passionately to supporting the striking workers at Asbestos, he might have thought differently. Sorel held that, to achieve the sublime, it was "necessary that each person in the party consider himself as being in the army of truth having to fight the armies of evil." The Jesuits at Brébeuf would have put it no differently. The evocation of the army of truth against the armies of evil would have recalled to Trudeau Loyola's meditation on the Two Standards, even if he could not share Sorel's concept of truth, of the good or of evil.

As to the concrete means for carrying out his future revolution, even while he criticized Sorel's Marxist model, Trudeau accepted his teaching about the mobilizing power of myths as well as the morality of the use of violence. "One can talk forever about revolts without ever provoking a revolutionary movement, in the absence of myths accepted by the masses," Sorel wrote. It is the myth, by stimulating the imagination, that leads to action. Now, after having been convinced by his reading of Maurras that reason must reign over passion, Trudeau was intrigued by Sorel's doctrine about the mobilizing power of myth, as he wrote: "Today, the experience of the past 35 years enables us to appreciate at the same time Sorel's perspicacity and his errors. The importance of '*myth*' has been demonstrated in the seizing of power by Lenin, Mussolini, Hitler." In his search for a mobilizing myth that could apply to his own society, Trudeau wrote down a prophetic thought: "The myth of separatism could very likely succeed in the land of Quebec."

*He wrote that in May 1942!* The referendums of 1980 and 1995 would bear out his analysis. Trudeau fought so hard against the Yes in the 1980 referendum on sovereignty-association precisely because he had recognized nearly forty years earlier the mobilizing power of the separatist myth. In 1942, he was considering how to use it himself for his own revolution. In 1980, with the benefit of decades of reflection, he would understand its perverse effects.

As for the morality of violence, it goes without saying that Sorel's approach violated Trudeau's values. And so he wrote: "Obviously, a doctrine based on the principle of the class struggle seems fundamentally wrong and anti-Christian." But he qualified that statement immediately: "This obviousness could be remarkably limited. . . . Sorel demonstrates that the current system is not without violence." And so Trudeau asked: "How, then, would a general strike be more immoral than a war or a revolution carried out in pursuit of justice? Sorel replies by quoting Proudhon: 'To feel and to assert human dignity first in all that pertains to us, and then in the person of our fellow-men, without falling into egotism, as well as not paying the slightest reference to deity or to society: *this is what is right.* To be ready under all circumstances to rise energetically in defence of this dignity, even against oneself if need be: *this is justice.*'"[56] Though Trudeau as a young man could clearly not accept a morality that excluded "the slightest reference to deity or to society," yet he found in Sorel concepts that were entirely compatible with the Christian values that he had assimilated during his years at Brébeuf, notably the respect for human dignity in oneself and in others, without any self-seeking, and the obligation to defend human dignity in the name of justice.

There was one more book that Trudeau studied, after Sorel, before he plunged wholeheartedly into planning for a revolution. In June 1942, he read *La révolution nécessaire*, published in 1933 by Robert Aron and Arnaud Dandieu.57 His notes on the book filled twelve pages. Robert Aron, as was said of him when he died in 1975, was one of "all those young men in search of an intelligent order or of a more humane model of society."58 In their search for an alternative to the worldwide Depression, to the chronic instability of the French parliamentary regime, and to Bolshevik collectivism, these French intellectuals, Catholic for the most part – though Aron was Jewish – proposed a form of corporatism that was inspired by social Catholicism. Aron became a regular contributor to the periodical *L'Ordre nouveau*, which was founded by his friend Dandieu and professed to be neither on the right nor the left. By contrast, the well-known periodical *Esprit*, founded by Emmanuel Mounier, defined itself as both Catholic and left wing. This entire group of committed intellectuals found supporters from the left as well as the right, and even from such extreme left-wingers as the "revolutionary syndicalists," or such extreme right-wingers as the disciples of Maurras. What they held in common was the conviction that a "new order," one that would be different from everything known, had urgently to be invented.

For Trudeau, *La révolution nécessaire* came at exactly the right time. He still had the sense that he was lacking ideological and strategic weapons for launching his revolutionary project, despite all the ideas that he had culled from his reading, despite the moral philosophy that he had borrowed from Bergson, despite the principles of political philosophy that he had acquired from Maurras, and the revolutionary strategies that he had learned from Malaparte and Sorel. But as he read *La révolution nécessaire*, he found that everything came together. He found there what he considered to be the synthesis of everything he had read and appreciated so far, but also a revolutionary model of society based on moral and spiritual principles that he shared. He found the perfect model for carrying out his proposed personalist and Christian revolution. "The revolution that is needed is the humane revolution. What must be accomplished above all is to see that man recovers his rank as a person, that is to say, as a free, autonomous and intelligent being. The only acceptable system is anarchy. (See Larousse: Political and social system where the individual develops himself freely, emancipated from all governmental trusteeship.) Besides, for all the 19th Century revolutionaries (Marx, Bakhunin, Proudhon), the same anarchic conception of the individual provides the fundamental drive of the revolutionary spirit. The inspiration is shared, the tactics vary: the only common objective is – to organize anarchy."

This was an unusual use of the word *anarchy*. Etymologically, the word means absence of government. Nowadays, it has different meanings according to one's political views. For its proponents, anarchy suggests "society without a state," and so, complete individual liberty. For its critics, it is synonymous with chaos. Trudeau gave the word an entirely positive connotation. However, by giving to three such fierce adversaries a common objective in anarchy, Trudeau displayed his unfamiliarity with Marx's biting critique directed against the anarchist perspective of the two others. Reading those twelve pages of notes, one is left with the impression that Trudeau had found at last what had been missing to build his revolutionary project: a critique of the existing social order, a set of theoretical principles to guide the revolutionary action, and a sketch of the social order to emerge from the revolution.

The co-authors of *La révolution nécessaire*, as they developed their critique of the social order, invoked Marxist notions to explain why the capitalist must always increase the tempo of production and lower his cost by replacing workers by machines in order to maximize his profits. This, they maintained, had disastrous effects on human beings: "If the consumer loses confidence or reduces his needs, capitalism goes bankrupt. Simultaneously, unemployment becomes inordinate. That is why all eyes then turn to consider the Managed Economy. And what follows is the collective tyranny of Stalin, of Mussolini, of Hitler."

At this point Trudeau was exploring the Marxist critique of capitalism, first with Sorel, now with Aron and Dandieu. This discovery would prove to be a first step toward what would later become his embrace of left-wing Catholicism and of the personalist movement. For the time, though, he agreed with Aron and Dandieu in denouncing the managed economy that leads to "collective tyranny," of various forms: "If the proletariat, once in power, sets up a state that is as centralized and rigid as other states, whether monarchical, fascist or bourgeois, its fundamental flaw will be the same: to oppress the individual in the name of abstract structures." Like the co-authors, he was convinced that "the solution must be found elsewhere, not in tyranny, but rather in freedom."

Trudeau, like Aron and Dandieu, criticized "statism," including that of the proletarian state, yet for the co-authors, as for Hertel and the Quebec elite, the statism they deplored was that of communism above all, sometimes that of Nazism, and, only rarely, that of fascism. It was never the statism associated with authoritarian rule or with corporatism. Trudeau agreed with Aron and Dandieu in pronouncing the same stricture against liberalism as against Marxism, as he wrote: "The construction of the new order [must be based on the] refutation of Marxism and of liberalism, which both make the same mistake of reducing the person to economic man, . . . as though conflicts did not sometimes originate from psychological or spiritual causes!" For Trudeau in 1942, only corporatism such as that proposed by Pétain and Maurras could be acceptable.

Trudeau was impressed by the economic analysis of Aron and Dandieu, who considered unemployment to be an endemic flaw of the capitalist system. They also focused on the phenomenon of what they called "a servile class." Its members not only performed the most repellent tasks in a society, but they were the most vulnerable to unemployment. And so, they wrote, this class must be eliminated from the post-revolutionary society that they envisaged. Would their cure be better than the disease? That would soon become apparent.

From their critique of capitalism, the authors moved on to their "Outline of a general theory of revolution." Trudeau agreed with them that a state should be founded on respect for "the supreme value of the human person," so as to foster individuals who will be "free, autonomous, intelligent." But, in reality, what model of the state would be most apt to realize these laudable but vague values? For some people, liberal democracy is the most appropriate regime to promote these values. For Charles Maurras, on the other hand, only an authoritarian state – monarchical, ideally – could enshrine them. Trudeau, however, did not seem aware that almost all regimes, be they authoritarian or otherwise, claim to uphold this ambiguous notion of respect for the individual. And so he concluded, along with Aron and Dandieu, that to reform existing institutions was impossible because they "were not conceived in relation to the human person," and therefore "what is needed at all costs is revolution and not evolution."

His reading of *La révolution nécessaire* only confirmed him in his convictions. Following Aron and Dandieu, he wrote that "this revolution must be anarchic, that is to say that all institutions must be conceived as a function of the human person." Secondly, it must "encompass all spheres of human activity." Finally, "with respect to the economy, the revolution must foster technological progress and put it in the service of the person." And how will these wonderful objectives be attained? The third section of the book gives a glimpse of the projected post-revolution social order.

In order to abolish degrading servile work to the extent possible, the authors advocated that a maximum effort be devoted to the mechanization of labour. They who had blamed the working class's unemployment and penury on the "extreme" replacement of man by machines now expected a benign impact in the new order from those same machines, because of corporatism – and something else. They envisaged a new arm of government, the "creation of a civil service on the analogy of military service, which would involve calling up for service in the factories all those who would be needed for production." Clearly, if the state undertook to decide which citizens must work, and where, that would mean a managed economy – exactly what Trudeau, and Aron and Dandieu, had denounced as contrary to the freedom and dignity of the individual. How would the corporatist managed economy be different from the "collective tyranny of Stalin, Mussolini, and Hitler"? Neither Trudeau nor his authors discerned a contradiction between their ideals based on human dignity and their proposed social structure in which the state, omnipresent, exercised in reality what they had called, when referring to totalitarian regimes, "a guardianship by government."

History has shown that such a model for organizing the workforce flourished in fascist and corporatist regimes, notably those of Mussolini, Salazar, and, later, Pétain. Under Vichy, for example, Pierre Laval, as "head of government," promulgated the law titled "Service du Travail Obligatoire," which entailed a conscription of all French males between the ages of twenty-three and twenty-five, who were then sent to Germany to work in the factories. Hundreds of thousands of men were thus recruited for forced labour. Did they rejoice in their freedom expanded under Pétain? In fact, a great number showed their gratitude by choosing the Résistance (the French underground) rather than Germany. Only an authoritarian regime could have been capable of enforcing such a law. Mackenzie King, pleading at that same time with Canadians to release him from his conscription promise, offered quite a contrast. But Trudeau was not conscious of his double standard.

In pure theory, the concept of corporatism could be considered compatible with individual freedom. The reconciliation of the two was attempted during the 1930s and 1940s by a number of these "personalists" who advocated a left-wing Catholicism. In the reality of history, however, the corporatist regimes with which Trudeau and his contemporaries in Quebec were familiar included, on the one hand, Hitler's unpopular Nazi Germany – which they considered too anti-Christian and which won the approval of only a tiny minority of Quebeckers – and, on the other, the popular regimes of Salazar, of Mussolini, and, above all, of Marshal Pétain's France. It was to these three models of "successful" corporatism, especially that of Pétain, that Trudeau turned as he prepared to start his own revolution and read *La révolution nécessaire*, oblivious to the discrepancies between the fine ideals of freedom and individual dignity, and the way they actually were put into practice in these regimes.

As he was coming to the end of his observations on the book, Trudeau wrote down his overall impression of the "author" – he used the singular. He had a single negative comment: "He has only one unpleasant tendency: he philosophizes," that is to say, he tends to deal in abstractions that "take him far afield" or he tends "not to let the reader know where he wants to lead him." But this criticism did not detract seriously from what he considered a great book. "These are minor flaws because, altogether, the author carries off a magnificent presentation of what a humane Revolution means, and he lays out the fundamentals of a system that can have marvelous consequences, beyond calculation. Unfortunately, he did not live to develop the economic and concrete plan which would be required. It is up to others to take up the torch. . . ."

Arnaud Dandieu died in 1933, just before the book was published. Robert Aron lived until 1975. As a Jew, at the very time when Trudeau was reading his book, Aron was suffering all the consequences of France's defeat and had to escape in order to survive. In 1954, he would publish *Histoire de Vichy*, which established itself as essential reading on that regime.[59] Why did Trudeau refer only to Dandieu as the author of

*La révolution nécessaire?* Whatever the reason, he concluded as he closed the book that the torch had to be taken up by others. The others, he resolved, would be himself and his companions at arms. Indeed, he had no sooner reached the end of the book than he threw himself into drawing up the plan for the revolution that the author had been prevented by death from carrying out. The book had done more than ignite Trudeau's admiration: it incited him to "take up the torch."

As he reached the end of his preparation through the study of theory, and the beginning of his commitment to political action, Trudeau had been most deeply influenced by two authors: Bergson for moral philosophy and Maurras for political philosophy. He found Maurras's slogan, "politics first," both pleasing and convincing. All his reading converged to buttress his long-held conviction that political action was an obligation. His concept of political action was strongly influenced by Maurras, whose priorities were "the idea of authority, the idea of heredity, the idea of order, the idea of local and occupational autonomy, the idea of the political primacy of Catholicism."[60] All of these ideas, with the exception of "the idea of heredity," were expressed in his reading notes and confirmed that Trudeau was undeniably a disciple of Maurras as he picked up the torch.

# Chapter 9

## LA RÉVOLUTION NATIONALE

*The Patrie to be reborn from the Revolution will be Catholic, French and Laurentian.*

— PIERRE TRUDEAU

IN THE SUMMER OF 1942, Pierre Trudeau's life became an intellectual whirlwind. His writings, his activities, became so numerous that to follow his trail took us into a labyrinth. He was deeply involved in putting together a secret revolutionary organization. Had he already been involved earlier in clandestine activity? And if so, for how long? We can give no conclusive answer. But, among his papers, we found an intriguing manuscript written, we would estimate, in the fall of 1942. It was titled "Document for the leaders only." It offered the following account.

"One day, several years ago, there were three guys who were tired of hearing themselves lectured to with proposals for half measures, repetitions about the futility of any effort, or counsels of suicide; tired of seeing our forces divided and energies wasted while our entire people slid toward the crevasse, and of waiting for the signal that never came from those who could have given it. They decided to make a start and then never to stop. . . . From the tumult of brainstorming there emerged a clear consciousness of la Patrie. They began, then, to discover themselves. Finally, having analyzed themselves, they were able to define the true motives of their determination and give a definitive direction to their action."[1]

In the fall of 1942, Trudeau was already a member of a threesome determined to change their world. And who were the three? Because theirs was a secret society, their names were never given clearly. But the document itself provides clues that reveal their identity. "They had nothing, they knew nothing, they were nothing. One of them was acquainted with Freemasonry; the two others, with nothing yet, *ma foi*! The second's daring was just about limitless and his tenacity relentless. The third escapes characterization, except for his intelligence, which was extreme."

Who, then, were the three? In 1979, François Lessard published a book, titled *Messages au Frère Trudeau*.[2] He stated there that he was familiar with Freemasonry: and so it is reasonable for us to assume that the first member of the triumvirate was François Lessard. Unlike other friends from Trudeau's youth, he was later to have a rather undistinguished career, as an investment broker. In the early 1940s, however, he worked closely with Trudeau within their secret society.

Who was the second member? The reference to "limitless" daring and "relentless" tenacity points directly to Pierre Trudeau. As for the third shadowy figure, Trudeau indicated in later writings how much he had admired the intelligence and the culture of Jean-Baptiste Boulanger. So there, arguably, was the third member, the one with "extreme" intelligence.

Who, then, were those "leaders" for whom the document was "exclusively" intended? And what were the objectives of the movement? The various strands of the enterprise were so interwoven that, to establish who was who, who did what, when, and why, we sometimes felt that we had taken on the hat, and the role, of Sherlock Holmes!

For clarity, we shall divide into two chapters our account of the revolution that Trudeau and his companions were plotting. This chapter will explore the drafts they worked on for their intended manifesto, then the manifesto itself, and finally the reading program that Boulanger and Trudeau assigned themselves in order to give their undertaking theoretical depth. At the same time, alongside these theoretical and organizational pursuits, Trudeau was also taking part in political activities. These will be described in the next chapter.

This period of intense activity extended over ten months, from February to December 1942. Its various elements and moments did not fall neatly into an orderly progression but overlapped, intersected, and interacted, with reading, drafting, exchanges of letters, meetings, and political actions all swirling turbulently throughout the period. This dizzying plunge into the underground will accordingly sometimes leap forward and look backward, take up a topic then set it aside only to return to it later.

---

In a notebook,[3] toward the bottom of the same page which concluded the draft of his article, "Mûrs," described earlier, Trudeau had scribbled: "Baptiste, 10018, 102nd Avenue, Edmonton." This was the address of Jean-Baptiste Boulanger. He and Trudeau had developed a close relationship since Boulanger had arrived at Brébeuf in 1939 from his native Edmonton. When Boulanger returned home to Edmonton for the 1942 summer vacation, the two friends had agreed on a program of reading and writing on the subject of statecraft, with a timetable for exchanging their thoughts. And so Trudeau wrote down the following:

| Letter leaves | July 14: | Plan |
|---|---|---|
| Thursday | July 24: | Republic |
| Monday | August 3: | Politics |
| Monday | August 10: | Contract |
| Friday | August 20: | Maurras Enquête |

Trudeau would later write in his *Memoirs* that his friend Boulanger knew much more about politics than he did. Certainly, his article "Sous le masque d'Otto Strasser," which we reviewed in Chapter 8, showed an awareness of what was taking place in Germany as well as in Marshal Pétain's France. Trudeau's published articles, by contrast, had dealt only with local issues.

The two friends agreed that they would come up with a "plan" by July 14. Then, just over a month later, they were to have read and commented on Plato's *Republic*, Aristotle's *Politics*, Rousseau's *The Social Contract*, and Maurras's *Enquête sur la monarchie*. These books, with the exception of Charles Maurras's *Enquête*, were then, as now, recognized classics of political philosophy.

Most biographers, and even Trudeau himself in his *Memoirs*, have left the impression that this summer's reading program was simply about how two serious university students continued to educate themselves during summer vacation. In fact, they were searching for the theoretical foundations that could guide them as they planned their future post-revolutionary society.

We found no trace of Boulanger's comments on these works, but that he did read them is clear from the dialogue that he carried on with Trudeau. Methodical as ever, the latter kept detailed notes of his reading. He even met the deadlines they had set, except when external circumstances prevented him. When he couldn't find a copy of Aristotle in time, he substituted a letter commenting on Rousseau. However, he did not submit his comments on *L'Enquête sur la monarchie* by the agreed date. We do know, as pointed out in the last chapter, that he read this book in the fall of 1942, and would read it a second time in March of 1944. And we know that he had already read with enthusiasm Maurras's *La seule France*.

Between July 7 and 14, they worked on the "plan." It was, in fact, a political manifesto which announced the launch of a new political movement. Though its authors never actually called it a "manifesto," that is the term we will use, for clarity. Every word, every idea of the manifesto was minutely dissected and reviewed again. For example, here is how they went about choosing the title.

Trudeau first called the text "Principles of the Revolution," then changed that to "Plan" in the second draft. By the third draft it was called "Our Plan," and he explained the change to Boulanger as follows: "We had to get across the fact that these five absolute and ontologically true principles, when they were combined, formed not just some chance plan, but 'the plan' of the undertaking that we are drawing up, 'our plan,' for us, a specific group of Laurentian revolutionaries. That explains why you saw that 'Plan' was replaced by 'Our Plan' or 'The Plan.' (I have to admit that, if all were to agree on the complete suppression of the word 'our,' I still prefer just 'Plan')."

Who are the "all" who had to give their consent? We shall endeavour presently to identify some of them, at least.

Three pages further, in a section of his letter titled "Explanations," Trudeau took up again his argument in favour of calling the manifesto simply "Plan."

PLAN

A destructive word. Plan, the first measure of a drum tattoo: plan, plan, plan, rataplan. Plan, an explosive monosyllable; through suddenly opened lips, the brusque ejection of a meaning; the sound that one hears; the breath and the saliva which follow; a cannonade. (*300 yards. Target in front, one sound* . . . Ah! My dear Baptiste, those were the days!).4

A constructive word. Plane, a surface which serves as a foundation. Plan, architectural sketch of the future society.

After all, what does it mean to revolutionize but to destroy and build? But, paradoxically, the word becomes diminished if we join it to another word: "Our plan," "the plan," "plan of la Laurentie," etc. Moreover, these additions are pointless in every instance that we envisage: the book as a whole, the context, the place of publication, the distributors of the pamphlet will all contribute adequately to individualize the plan.

At every stage of the production of the manifesto, Trudeau's passion for precisely the right word and for the concise expression was always in evidence. It turned out, though, that despite all his elegant arguments, his proposal did not prevail. The final version of the "Principles of the Revolution" – or at least the last that we saw – had become: "The principles."

We will not follow each of Trudeau's words, each idea, through all their several evolutions and refinements. But the example just given demonstrates the complexity of our task, as we worked our way through a succession of drafts, a proliferation of sections such as "Comments" and "Explanations," and ever-changing headings.5

The twenty handwritten pages that include the three drafts of the manifesto are dated July 7 to 14 and are intended for Boulanger alone. But we know already that other people were involved in the project. For instance, in a letter that François Lessard wrote to Trudeau, dated June 29 of that year, he asked him to remind Boulanger that he was to come by to pick up documents intended for "Thomas (S.J.)." This refers, without question, to Father Thomas Mignault. Jean-Louis Roux recalls: "For many young men who attended Collège Sainte-Marie and who came under the influence of its prefect of discipline, Father Thomas Mignault, French Canadians would fulfill their destiny in a Laurentie from which all English domination would be banished."[6] In a similar vein, François Lessard wrote about this Jesuit that "it will only become known some day just how important was the role that he played in the history of Quebec."[7] Father Mignault was aware of the revolutionary project from the start and very probably took part in its development.

With the exception of this evocation of Mignault, no other name was mentioned in Trudeau's letters before July 14, when the first version of the manifesto was distributed. The final version, though, which was typed out, makes clear that other people had had a hand in it. It seems that this version was to be discussed and adopted in the fall, as implied by Trudeau's comment to Boulanger: "Here you have my most recent wording; you can reject it immediately or wait until the fall to demolish it, it really doesn't matter which."

---

The manifesto, in its first version, included six articles; the final version, only five. To illustrate how the drafting evolved, we shall compare the first three articles of the first version with the two corresponding articles in the final version:

FIRST VERSION:

1 – Our Revolution will be the permanent struggle that the French Canadian will wage to ensure the triumph, then the maintenance, of the Good in French Canadian society.

2 – The existence of a sovereign French Canadian state is the essential condition for ordering all reality in function of the French Canadians' own interest.

3 – The nation thus constituted will have three fundamental characteristics, which are nothing more than its confused but quintessential tendencies: it will be Laurentian, French and Catholic.

1 – The national revolution is a permanent struggle aimed at the human excellence of the community.

2 – The Patrie to be reborn from the Revolution will be Catholic, French and Laurentian.

The wording of the final version had become more pithy. Trudeau explained the change in one of his comments: "To express in a succinct and imperative formula a concise and inexorable logic: in this way alone can we hope to achieve the dynamism and truth which are essential for a declaration of principles. . . . We have taken care to use precise words without an overlap in meaning. (That is why we don't speak of a state that is 'free and sovereign,' for that is the very nature of the state to be 'free and sovereign.') Because we were formulating a statement of principles, and not a medley of considerations, advice, commentary and principles."

As we compare the two versions of the manifesto, it is worth noticing that the revolution of "the French Canadian" has mutated, in the very first article, into "la révolution nationale." Given the care with which they chose their words, it can be no coincidence that they selected the very slogan – "la Révolution nationale" – which the Vichy regime adopted on June 26, 1940, following the Armistice that Nazi Germany granted to France.

It was also noteworthy that the words *French Canadian*, found four times with slight variations in the original version of the first two principles, were replaced by the single word *Laurentian* in the final version. For our revolutionaries, the inhabitants of the projected new state are to be identified only by their citizenship in their new *patrie*, "la Laurentie," breaking every link of identification with Canada. In the 1960s, the secessionists would adopt the same strategy, but substituting for *Laurentie* and *Laurentien*, the words *Québec* and *Québécois*.

What links did these revolutionaries of the 1940s anticipate between their future state and Canada? And what responsibilities would *la Laurentie* undertake toward the French speakers in the "rest of Canada"? As a Franco-Albertan, Boulanger could not remain disinterested, and he proposed: "We are separatists, if by separatism [it] is meant that the current Quebec will become a *sovereign* state, within or outside of a Confederation, no matter for the time being; and with a constant solidarity with all the French minorities who live on the former territory of New France."

Trudeau replied: "On the subject of the solidarity of the French minorities, we do not think it appropriate to take a stand in the declaration. . . . Let us remember, however, that we cannot at the same time withdraw from the Federation and propose to exercise a control there." He was already convinced of this in 1942. Later in his career he would repeat it unfailingly to the separatists, reminding them that they could not have it both ways, withdrawing from Canada, yet at the same time making demands regarding Canada's treatment of its French-speaking citizens.

Boulanger's proposal was that the new state should become sovereign and then decide whether or not it would be part of Confederation. Trudeau countered: "Political constraints and justice will determine the immediate significance of our autonomy. And if it seems to be in our interest not to break *immediately* all links, confederal or American, we shall not hesitate. The revolution will not be carried out for the word, separatism, but for the improvement of the peoples, properly understood."

Before the referendum of May 1980 on the secession of Quebec, Claude Morin, then minister of intergovernmental affairs in the government of René Lévesque, would leave the impression that he had "discovered" a new strategy, which would be called "*étapisme*," meaning that secession would be carried out one step at a time. Trudeau had thought of it four decades earlier. He recognized already in 1942 that politics, being the art of the possible, made it necessary to adjust to circumstances and to compromise – namely, not to declare immediately the independence of la Laurentie. The question arises: how can one adjust to circumstances without betraying one's principles? Trudeau's answer was to distinguish what is fundamental from what is secondary. He considered that the main objective was not the victory of "separatism" but the Good of the people, and he was ready to postpone a declaration of independence until the time was ripe.

But that did not make him any less of a separatist. For the Trudeau of 1942, a sovereign state "was the essential condition" for the triumph and the maintenance of the Good. And that required a revolution. Now, an insurrection went counter to the principle of obedience to authority preached by the Church. It could only become ethical if it met specific criteria, as Professor Groulx taught. So how, then, did Trudeau and his companions-at-arms justify the morality of their revolution? The answer is that they simply accepted a postulate which they would never try to prove, namely that the triumph of the Good demanded a nation that was simultaneously "Laurentian, French and Catholic." It followed, therefore, that since la Laurentie could only come about through revolution, then that revolution was necessarily morally justified.

---

A Laurentie that was Catholic and French would ensure that the Good would triumph for French Canadians. But what about the Good for English-speakers, Protestants, Jews, and all others who were not Catholic French Canadians? The manifesto did not raise the subject, because those people were not considered to be truly part of the *patrie*. "La Patrie . . . is a living framework, created by God, where men pursue Happiness in a community of faith, of mentality, of blood, of language," the manifesto proclaimed. This racist definition of *la patrie* truly reflected the spirit of the age. It revealed, for example, the influence of Groulx, who made much of racial purity, or that of Hertel, who stated that, to achieve a personalist revolution, it was required "to be ourselves," that is, French and Catholic. Our revolutionaries subscribed without qualification to this ethnic definition of the nation.

So it was that, in the section on Comments, Trudeau and his partners raised the question: "What ideal state would be appropriate, given who we are?" The answer: "In accordance with our Catholic, Latin and French character, we recognize the necessity for order in the state and the primacy of the human person."

In effect, for them, the necessity for order and for the primacy of the person derived from the Catholic, Latin, and French character of this ethnic group, with all its unique attributes and needs. Outside of this collectivity, presumably, order and the primacy of the person were not to be found. We saw in Chapter 6 that this anthropomorphizing of the nation was to be found in the social doctrine of the Church, in the encyclicals of Popes Leo XIII and Pius XI as well as in pastoral letters of the bishops of Quebec. Since each nation was thought to possess its own distinctive nature and its personality, it could not possibly have a normal development if its unique characteristics were ignored. The Trudeau of 1942 fully subscribed to this model. He wrote: "The liberation of the patrie, the establishment of institutions and of disciplines which are concordant with its nature, will make it possible for it to achieve the normal development of its personality."

The revolution had as its objective the Good. But, between the first and the final version of the manifesto, a change occurred: instead of aiming at the triumph of the "Good in French Canadian society," the revolution would instead "strive for the human excellence of the community." Trudeau explained: "We think that we have found in the human excellence of our community the 'Myth,' or, if Plato is to be preferred to Sorel, 'the ideal' of our revolutionary action. That is to say, an objective that is always desired, constantly brought closer, but never attained."

We have here the reappearance of Sorel's mobilizing "myth." Combining rather awkwardly Sorel and Plato, Trudeau in fact adopted the Platonic notions of the absolute True and Good. According to Plato, to achieve this Ideal required the wisdom of a God. A mere human could only make every effort to come closer to it. One could not ensure once and for all the triumph of the Good because, as Trudeau wrote, "human excellence is fleeting, not that the Good is capricious, but that it exists in time." That is why, "so as not to lose the fruit of a successful political revolution, we establish the permanent Revolution (and that, with a much broader meaning than is understood by Trotskyism). We don't want a revolt that would prove incidental and temporary only to degenerate into a new 'established order' that would be as odious as its predecessor."

This last comment might seem surprising. How could their "permanent revolution" have "a much broader meaning than is understood by Trotskyism" when, as is well known, for Trotsky, socialism could only succeed in Russia if it spread across the planet? Yet Trudeau and his companions never intended to export their revolution beyond the boundaries of la Laurentie. And so, what was this "much broader meaning"? While Trotsky's aim was a proletarian revolution, their aim was a Christian struggle of good against evil. They knew that the nation, like human beings, could never eliminate sin once and for all. So it would be impossible to retain permanently "the fruit of a successful revolution." And that is why, relying on the Bible, Trudeau and his comrades projected a permanent revolution so as to take into account the weakness of humans and their original sin.

———◦———

What would be the character of the state which achieved this revolution? Trudeau's answer largely reflected his reading: "The constitution of the Laurentian state will be, in principle, authoritarian and unitary. But decentralization, corresponding to the economic characteristics of the territory and countering any tyrannical aspirations, will ensure the interests of collective liberty and personal anarchy." In its final formulation, that wording would be modified to read: "The Nation will find its expression in a state that will be at one and the same time authoritarian and the guardian of freedoms." Trudeau would add his own comment: "We believe that the state cannot pursue effectively the common good of the nation unless it answers to a single leader. . . . We must remember that authority comes from above, not from below: we condemn parliamentary democracy and liberalism."

This condemnation, as well as the juxtaposition of contradictory concepts such as a state that was both authoritarian and the guardian of freedoms, were in no sense peculiar to Trudeau. The book by Aron and Dandieu, *La révolution nécessaire*, Charles Maurras's *Enquête sur la monarchie*, the pastoral letters issued by the Church hierarchy in Quebec, the *Plan d'études* put out as a pedagogical guide by the École sociale populaire du Québec, all converged to convey the same message. Trudeau merely proposed to put into practice what the French-Canadian elite was praying for.

Boulanger proposed to go even further in this direction than Trudeau: "We want a monarchical state, a state whose head – king, regent or president – will be for life, along with the right to choose his associates and his successor, responsible to the Revolution alone." An absolute monarch, responsible only to an abstraction like "the Revolution"? Such was Boulanger's astonishing contribution. And yet, it did not upset Trudeau. He merely observed: "We have not yet dealt in our deliberations with the issues of responsibility and the method of succession." The two companions had obviously been won over by Maurras, who propounded just such ideas in *Enquête sur la monarchie*: "We conceive [the monarchical regime] as the regime of order. We conceive of this order as in conformity with the nature of the French nation and with the rules of universal reason. In other words, we see this regime as the polar opposite of that to which we are presently subjected."[8]

Within a political system in which a powerful leader, a king no less, was appointed for life and then was even given the right to choose his successors, how could the threat of dictatorship and tyranny be averted? Trudeau saw no problem. He offered this assurance: "Political and economic decentralization, corresponding to the diversity of our territory, will limit the power of the monarch and will ensure the safeguarding of personal freedoms. . . . We consider that a state so conceived will respect the human personality of its citizens and will recognize that, while social anarchy is fatal, individual anarchy is a necessity!"

He was echoing the idea of individual anarchy that had been advocated by Aron and Dandieu. He was also espousing Charles Maurras's conviction that only hereditary monarchy had a vested interest in promoting decentralization: "The hereditary Monarchy, freed from the yoke of election . . . will have the *power* to decentralize. The national interest, and consequently its own interest, will obviously transform that into a *duty*."[9] Trudeau's readings had obviously registered.

But even decentralization requires an organizing principle. "Given who we are, what social and economic organization would we obtain from an ideal state?" After raising that question, the would-be revolutionaries gave their answer: "The economic and social organization will be corporatist. Each of the collectivities which make up the society will attend to settling individual problems, and a central council will take on the responsibility for establishing harmony among the parties." With corporatism as the panacea resolving all economic and social problems, the authors felt no need to press on with their thinking. Nowhere is there any sign of a discussion on the principles that underlie the functions assigned to the state: the organization of the army, of the police, of taxation, of the currency, of education, of health, and so forth. Faith in corporatism substituted for economic, political, and social science. "The society on which our state will be founded will be organized on the corporatist principle, so as to bring together those common interests that form a bond: they will thus be enabled to choose for their own purposes the means which they alone can discuss pertinently. The delegations of the corporations to the regional assemblies will constitute the base of the Government, and a national assembly, constituted along similar principles, will form the unitary bond of the state."

The revolutionaries had no doubt that their corporatist system would work. After all, it had been urged by the omniscient Maurras, by the Pope, the Catholic Church, and even by Aron and Dandieu, though in a somewhat different form. To this model they joined Plato's idea that, in a just and well-ordered society, each individual must be assigned to the lot and the social function that best corresponds to his talents and his capacities. The individual, then, would want to excel through his occupational association and would not waste his time on other people's business or on politics. To the objection that this model failed to provide equality of opportunity, our two political philosophers replied: "Since perfect equality among individuals is neither desirable nor possible, a social hierarchy will establish itself naturally." And, as a consequence, they could declare: "The social and economic constitution will be hierarchical, familial and corporatist."

At the apex of this hierarchy would be a "philosopher-king," who alone would possess the competencies and the capacities required to deal with the questions that would arise in the political order. This hierarchical structure would be consistent with the natural order or, as Maurras put it, it would be consistent with "the rules of universal reason." And so its members would raise no protest against it. In accordance with Plato's philosophy, moreover, the "hierarchy" proposed by Trudeau and Boulanger would not be founded on wealth nor would it confer social privileges. They wrote: "Division within a nation is deadly, especially when it arises from the arbitrary frontiers of fortune. A better alternative is to tolerate a 'social ladder' with rungs corresponding to the human values of culture and morality, of family and work. By taxing wealth and even setting its upper limits, we would encourage a greater number within the ranks of the elite to achieve their full potential, and we would locate elsewhere than in lucre the goals of the ambitious."

So would it come about that the elite would be recognized, not for its wealth, but for such virtues as its faith, its culture, its morality. The elite would claim no privileges. Quite the opposite: it would feel honour-bound to ensure the happiness of the people. This, of course, corresponded to the morality that the classical colleges strove to inculcate in all their students, consistent with the social doctrine of the Catholic Church. For that reason, Trudeau and his band of brothers could take for granted that they were part of the proposed aristocracy, without the slightest self-consciousness.

Among all the many facets of the revolution that Trudeau and Boulanger explored, one is worth noting: their conception of the role of women in the Revolution and in the post-revolutionary society. Boulanger proposed that "as spouses and as mothers, the women of our country have a role to play in the Revolution, and no one is better able to define it than a few of them." But Trudeau rejected this culturalist perspective which implied that only women could speak in the name of women. In 1942, Trudeau was already able to comment: "Not a useful principle. We shall not insult women by restricting them to some particularist style of action, outside the general principles of the revolution. It goes without saying that the human excellence of a community cannot be achieved without them. We shall discuss this further when we come to the topic of family and corporatist organization." Unfortunately, we found no writing where that topic was further discussed.

———◆———

Without retracing further the complex discussions that preceded the final draft of the "plan," we shall close this section by reproducing at some length both the first and the final version of the manifesto.

First draft of the manifesto, handwritten:

## PRINCIPLES OF THE REVOLUTION

1. Our Revolution will be the permanent struggle that the French Canadian will wage to ensure the triumph and then the maintenance of the Good in the French Canadian society.
2. The existence of a Sovereign French Canadian State is the essential condition for the existence of a social order reflecting the distinctive interests of the French Canadians.
3. The nation so constituted will have three fundamental characteristics, which are nothing else than the categorical affirmation of its confused but quintessential tendencies: it will be Laurentian, French and Catholic.

4. This State will have its own territory, determined by historic and demographic necessities and by an international policy focused on order and justice.

5. The constitution of the Laurentian State will be authoritarian and unitary in principle. But decentralization, corresponding to the economic characteristics of the territory and countering any tyrannical aspirations, will ensure the protection of collective liberty and personal anarchy.

6. The economic and social organization will be corporatist. Each of the collectivities which make up the society will be responsible for settling individual problems, and a central council will establish harmony among the parties. Since equality among individuals is neither desirable nor possible, an aristocracy or an elite will arise naturally; its virtue will not rest on wealth – to which legislation will set limits – but on the more human qualities of moral and intellectual excellence.

Final version of the manifesto, typewritten:

## THE PRINCIPLES

1. The national revolution is a permanent struggle which strives for the human excellence of the community.

2. The Patrie which will be reborn from the Revolution will be Catholic, French and Laurentian.

3. The Nation will express itself in a State that is at the same time authoritarian and the guardian of freedoms.

4. The social and economic constitution will be hierarchical, familial and corporatist.

7. God approves.

In the final version two anomalies stand out. In the first place, one notices that principle number four is immediately followed by principle number seven. Then, the seventh, "God approves," is not a principle, but a statement. To make sense of this, we must look back at previous drafts of the manifesto. In the second draft, the number of principles was reduced from six to five. Nevertheless, Trudeau wrote down, right after the fifth principle, the number 7 and the words: "Dieu a dit," God has spoken. In the third draft, the same formula was kept, but Trudeau added an explanation: "The last proposition (Dieu a dit) was written for the reasons which you all know. But even when these reasons become obsolete, we would like to see the custom established of always writing as a 7th item: Dieu a dit, because we find so appealing the definitive pride of this short sentence, rather emphatic as it is." The Lord, having created the world, rested on the seventh day. This subtle reminder of God's work must have appealed to the group, because Trudeau's explanation is found verbatim in the Comments section of the final version, with this difference that "God has spoken" was replaced by "God approves." God, in effect, no longer dictates the principles of their revolution, he simply approves them. This example shows the extent to which religion permeated these documents. It also shows how thoroughly the final wording of the manifesto bore Trudeau's signature. He was its driving spirit. Was he also the group's leader? We leave that question aside for the moment.

Now, with their plan in place, the group turned to determining the organization of the revolutionary cell. We found only one text on the subject, and we believe it is incomplete. Once again, it seems that it was Trudeau who was put in charge of this section, as the handwriting is recognizably his. "The central power will include several people," he wrote. "First of all, the five (though not necessarily all of them) who are in the know. Then the others who will join and who are competent."

Who are the five? We already know with some certainty the identity of three, namely Trudeau, Boulanger, and Lessard. Father Thomas Mignault was most likely one of the other two – it will be recalled that Boulanger was instructed to bring him some documents, and he clearly shared the revolutionary and separatist commitments of the group. As for the fifth, two documents lead to the conclusion that it was Father Marie-Joseph d'Anjou, who was a teacher at Brébeuf. Among miscellaneous documents in Trudeau's archives we found a typewritten letter with the signature, "M.-J. d'Anjou, S.J." The letter was addressed to M. Antonio Boisclair, C.E.C.C. of Brébeuf College, and was dated November 7, 1941. It was intriguingly enigmatic, full of innuendoes and veiled meanings. Here are some excerpts from it:

After discussion about the "cases" that you put to me, I believe that the answer must be *negative*, that is to say that the one who has already involved himself (in the ways that you indicated) should not try to involve himself elsewhere if that would absolutely require of him that he swear that he is not already committed. . . .

It is only normal that, to bring about a superior good, one will encounter greater difficulties than in the ordinary and mediocre pursuit of virtue and of the apostolate.

Good day. Pray for me.

Why speak in such a roundabout manner about a "case"? And for a Jesuit, what could be this "good" that is "superior" to run-of-the-mill virtue and to a "mediocre" apostolate? Clearly, he was referring to a heroic undertaking, and one that could only be discussed in a kind of code. The Revolution, which was to establish a Catholic and French-Laurentian state, could quite likely be that superior apostolate to which he referred. And why would he ask Mr. Boisclair to pray for him? Could it be so that a difficult and important project with which he was involved could be carried to a successful conclusion? These are questions that cannot be answered definitively. But, along with other evidence, they suggest to us that Father d'Anjou occupied a central role in the organization.

The letter indicates that, as of its date of November 7, 1941, the undertaking to form a militant secret society had already been underway for some time. In fact, François Lessard maintained that Trudeau had been involved in underground societies since 1937.[10] Trudeau himself, in his article "Sur les pompiers," published in the *Brébeuf* of February 22, 1940, alluded to the fact that he could have taken part in activities involving physical confrontations with the police. He made no mention of having taken part in demonstrations, either in his *Memoirs* or in interviews. But an incident occurred in the House of Commons on April 5, 1977, which deserves attention. *Hansard*, the official verbatim transcription of proceedings, records this exchange:

**Mr. René Matte (Champlain):** Would the right hon. Prime Minister tell the House whether he has already been a militant, or more specifically, whether he has been or still is a member of a secret association which recommends a conciliatory attitude towards independence in Quebec?

**Mr. Hnatyshyn:** The Prime Minister nodded yes.[11]

So it was that, as prime minister, Pierre Trudeau acknowledged in the Commons that he had been part of a secret society. Moreover, through the process of drawing up the plan we have seen that he must have been one of its most active members. His signature is everywhere. Was he the group's leader? Yes, according to François Hertel. In 1977, Hertel told a journalist for *La Presse*: "Trudeau had set up a secret society."[12] That seemed to imply that he was its leader. But we think not. While his particularly active participation is beyond doubt, there is no evidence establishing him as the leader. Who, then, really was?

According to Jean-Louis Roux, rumour at the time designated François Hertel himself. But we found no documentary evidence in Trudeau's archives to support the claim. That Hertel was an active participant seems clear, almost certain. How could he otherwise have known of its existence? Lessard even calls him the group's "best recruiting agent."[13] But Hertel had neither the toughness nor the taste for actual leadership. He was a man of ideas, not a man of action.

In a document in which Trudeau laid out a proposed cell structure for the secret society, he wrote that the "central power" – P.C. in French – would be made up of the five "in the know," to which others would be added who were "competent." Some were to specialize in gathering information, others in recruitment, others in propaganda. This central power would be headed by an elected president who was to be called "the Speaker." He would hold discussions with "all the branches." In case of disagreement, Trudeau wrote, "it will be necessary to consult the ultimate power [P.U. in French], who is unknown to the P.C., and with whom secret communications will go through a lieutenant (e.g., Gagné or someone else who is not suspected by the other gang)." Now, who is this ultimate power (P.U.)? A new clue suggests, once again, the central role played by Father d'Anjou. Trudeau wrote: "The P.U. will consist of only d'An. And he will be replaced if someone should demonstrate incomparably stronger leadership qualities. D'A will remain as his adviser." So it seems likely that Father d'Anjou was the Ultimate Power, or supreme leader, of this secret society. His letter of November 1941, quoted above, could even suggest that he instigated the secret society.

This leader with the ultimate power headed an organization that was radically hierarchical. On the rung below him were the five members of the Central Power: Trudeau, Lessard, Boulanger, Mignault, and Hertel. Below them, the section heads and the secretaries who were to pass on the orders to "the heads of the three bands [the head of Propaganda, the head of Information, and the head of Recruitment]: they pass them on to their subordinates to ensure that all the L.X. members are instructed."

And there you have the code name whereby its members designate this secret society. These "L.X." are to be organized in accordance with the corporatist model. "We must see to it that we group together those who have the same aptitudes (anarchy): they will have to know each other as they will be acting in common. . . . In this way leaders will be formed who will be able to raise up around them a secret society, seize power in their neighborhood, keep track of hostile bands and so forth. But these leaders will remain under our orders; they could be promoted."

The concern for secrecy and the fear of betrayal were always in evidence. "All the people in the P.C. must be absolutely dependable, to make sure that one of them does not betray the others. Moreover, we must instil in them a fear of the P.U., who will order very severe reprisals (temporary kidnapping). . . . The decisions taken will be passed on by someone from the P.C. (Lessard, because he is known) who will pretend to have received them from persons unknown."

The panoply of secrecy to guarantee the members' anonymity reflects Trudeau's constant taste for theatre as well as his preference for keeping apart his several social roles. "It would even be advisable that the people on the P.C., when they meet, should come in disguise and call each other by pseudonyms, so as to acquire the habit of keeping separate their secret business and their social life."

After settling the organization of the cells, the L.X. members were to proceed with recruitment and projected actions. A dummy recruitment form was made up that included, not only the usual entries, such as name, address, birthdate, but others quite out of the ordinary that the L.X. considered important, such as "recommended by . . . ," "recruited by . . . ," "physical description: beard, mustache, eyeglasses, birthmarks." A married recruit would have to list the number of children. Not only was the recruit's current employment to be given, but also all previous employment, including the names of the employers. They were to declare their technical competencies. The L.X. took their business seriously. Oddly, though, the single filled-out form that we found did not comply with these directions. It lists the name of the recruit, Bernard Boivin, and, at the bottom of the page, his code number: MI 498 I. This could indicate that he was member number 498. Lessard makes the claim that they were a few hundred.[14] The letter I in his identifying number could mean that he was part of the "Information" band, particularly so since, under the heading of "*au courant*" – knowledgeable about – these details are given: "Re: civil information, police, our stations, the number of police officers, etc."

Jean-Louis Roux, an L.X. recruit, cast the recruiting process in a revealing light. He recalls in his memoirs that he briefly belonged to a "perfectly loony" secret society "that was called the X." (Our documents suggest that the name was really the L.X.) Roux explained how it functioned: "Within the X hierarchy, we were supposed to know only two people: our immediate superior, who brought us orders, and our direct subordinate, to whom we transmitted them. The X took themselves very seriously. Within their ranks a document was passed around which explained the tactics to be deployed when the day came when it was decided to capture the police and fire stations as well as to occupy the city's radio stations. Each member of the X was expected to recruit a certain number of new members. On my list there appeared the names of Jean-Marie Gauvreau, founder of the École du meuble, and of Édouard Montpetit, secretary general of the Université de Montréal. When Pierre-Louis Gélinas, my immediate superior in the hierarchy, gave me these names, it confirmed the doubts I had been having about whether the X were to be taken seriously. . . . One Christmas night, the identity of the Grand X, the supreme leader, was to be revealed in the course of an important assembly. Rumour had it that François Hertel was the one. . . . A student who was older than I, François Lessard, gave me notice of the meeting. . . . So I announced to him that I intended to resign from the movement. There was silence on the line. Then, his voice dropping to basso profondo, Lessard declared that 'the X is not something that you can just drop out of like that,' with his solemn tone implying that severe repressive measures awaited me. Then he hung up. I was not unduly alarmed, but rather curious about what treatment would be meted out to me. The days, the weeks, the months passed by. Nothing happened. I'm still waiting."

Roux's experience bears out that the planned procedures for recruitment were, in fact, implemented. The name of the secretary general of the University of Montreal, Édouard Montpetit, on Roux's list could reveal the movement's immaturity. But it also raises the possibility that prominent people may have joined the L.X. We are unlikely ever to know for sure because, according to Lessard, a membership list was never drawn up.[15] As for the "reprisals" with which Roux was threatened, it seems clear that the "temporary kidnapping" evoked in the document remained a dead letter.

⸺◉⸺

These events, these documents, take us beyond the "Plan" that was to be readied by July 14, 1942. The timetable that Trudeau and Boulanger had set for themselves that summer listed the manifesto as only their first item, to be followed by letters in which they exchanged their comments on a list of books.

Trudeau managed, in addition to getting through the reading list, to read other books for his own enjoyment. In July, he read André Malraux's *La voie royale*, in August, Emily Brontë's *Wuthering Heights*, as well as *La beauté sur la terre* by Swiss novelist Charles-Ferdinand Ramuz; then, in September, *Thunder on the Left*, by Christopher Morley and *To the Lighthouse*, by Virginia Woolf. Oddly enough, three of the books that he read for pleasure were by English authors, even as he went about preparing a revolution to create a French and Laurentian country. He waxed enthusiastic about *To the Lighthouse*, which he called "a jewel of suggestion, a model for its mastery of style and ideas." We shall not linger over these readings, which were marginal with respect to his main activities, but we shall return later to just one book that was outside of his set program: Jacques Maritain's *L'Humanisme intégral*, which he read in August 1942.

Ten days after sending off his "plan" to Boulanger, Trudeau was scheduled to send him his comments on Plato's *Republic*. Between the two dates, he treated himself to a second-hand Harley-Davidson motorcycle, at a cost of $450. The circumstances of the purchase are a reminder that Trudeau was not off on some other planet as he toiled at preparing his revolution. The world war constantly impinged on daily life. The insurance policy on his motorcycle carried this warning: "The government has imposed restrictions on the sale of new tires and inner tubes. Take all precautions to avoid the theft of your automobile's tires and inner tubes. To replace them will prove difficult and perhaps impossible."[16]

These cautions did not diminish Trudeau's joy in his new acquisition. He wrote to his friend: "You and I had equal opportunities, and the past two weeks went by quickly for both of us. But there was a difference in that I bought a motorcycle. I won't describe for you the general consequences of owning a bike; it will give you enough of an idea if I tell you that, a week ago, it ran me up to Lac des Pins where I stayed with a charming family, but where reading and writing were much less accessible than in my room." That is why, he explained, "the time available was shorter than I could have wished, because my letter is on the lookout for the last train to Montreal." Despite the distractions, he still managed to send off his comments on Plato precisely on the date they had agreed upon, July 24. But he wrote: "Ouf! Baptiste, I am drained. About all I am up to is my friendship and my blessing, and I send you both without hesitation."

We do not have the letter that Boulanger sent in reply. But, in acknowledging it, Trudeau wrote: "The vigorous simplicity of your text could put to shame the men of letters." Trudeau admired Boulanger, as he later announced in his *Memoirs*, and it would seem that he aspired to reach his level, as he added: "And I told myself that I must at all costs muzzle the haranguer within me." That expression, "muzzle the haranguer within you," was used by the person who did a critique of Trudeau's article reviewing Alain Grandbois's book on Marco Polo.[17] Was Boulanger, then, the critic?

———◆———

Before he wrote down his comments on Plato, Trudeau put his friend on notice: "I want you to know in the first place that I am slow and hard to move to enthusiasm." But he admitted that Plato had taken him by surprise, because of his simplicity. "Naively, . . . I had imagined who knows what, perhaps a towering grand metaphysician, a thinker bristling with abstractions, given to impenetrable dialectics. And so I was astonished to make the acquaintance of this philosopher who was so human, so vulnerable." Trudeau wondered how he should approach him so as to derive the greatest benefit. "I can see only two ways of judging Plato fairly. The first would be to read him (in the original Greek) with a precise understanding of his life and of the philosophy of his contemporaries. The second, which of course has much less value, would be to read all the major dialogues in an excellent translation. Outside of that, there is no salvation. . . . Now, instead of pursuing either of these inquiries, I spent my time reading essays on the life, the works, the philosophy of Plato, an analysis of the Republic. . . . This reading wasn't wasted; but it gives me no right to claim a *personal* opinion."

And so, within a ten-day period, Trudeau read not only *The Republic*, but also a range of analyses dealing with the philosopher and his work. There are some who might have felt authorized thereby to claim some expertise on the subject. Trudeau rather downplayed his feat: "About Plato I know just enough to dare to write nothing about him. . . . There is nothing I could assert about Plato but that the opposite could equally be argued." Still, that did not prevent him from sending fifteen pages of comments to his friend.

Consider his criticisms, for a start. The most important dealt with what he called Plato's "statism." "The political idea that you find everywhere, in the ideal Republic, is surely statism. I won't spend time on that doctrine, which we have denounced at length. To measure its worth, all you have to do is to see the exaggerated consequences to which it leads even Plato's moderate mind. Can there be anything less human and more antisocial than his famous family communism? . . . I think it was inexcusable of him to have failed to understand the fundamentally human character of those social conventions that are essential not only to the free expression of the personality – because children 'express' their parents – but also to the healthy development of the race. (This question deserves that we take it up again once you are back.)"

We saw in Chapter 8 what a negative perception Trudeau and his companions had of statism, thus agreeing with Aron and Dandieu. So his negative reaction to Plato is understandable. His rejection of family

communism is in conformity with the Church's teaching on the impor-
tance of family. But we are left with a paradox: why would he condemn
Plato's extension of state power, when he himself proposed, for his ideal
Laurentie, an authoritarian state ruled by a powerful leader? Moreover,
Trudeau even granted that, "in Plato's defence, if ever anyone could have
justified statism by keeping it within just limits, it was he."

Plato, Trudeau observed, had "relegated the arts to the third rank."
That hardly was apt to please this great lover of the arts and of literature,
which Trudeau was to remain all his life. But, even there, Trudeau
forgave him "because of his nice distinction between the theatre which
purifies, ennobles, and the theatre which merely exploits the sentimen-
tality of the crowd. He sacrifices the first to more surely kill the second,
which is bad." Here Trudeau had adopted the attitude of his Jesuit teachers and of the Church; he also was probably reflecting the influence on
him of Alexis Carrel, who attributed "the dissolution of family and
social units to the enormous presence of newspapers, of radio and of the
cinema." Like his teachers, Trudeau approved of classical theatre and
condemned more recent entertainment media for having, in Carrel's
words, "levelled down the intellectual classes of society to the lowest
common denominator."[18] As for Plato's style, Trudeau also found
something to criticize. "I have to admit that the gimmick of philosophical dialogues finally got on my nerves. I know that it occasionally can
be useful to provide variety and interest, . . . but most often I found exas-
perating the statements and the stupid 'I surrender,' uttered repeatedly by
the dim conversationalist."

But these criticisms were inoffensive in comparison with his broad
approval, which surprised even Trudeau himself. "Did I not start out on
this task full of prejudice towards Plato? But then, I didn't write to you
for nothing; indeed, unless I'm mistaken, here I am sliding towards a
raging Platonism." He now considered the philosopher to be "a peerless
educator and professor." When he discovered that Plato was at one with
the two of them in proposing the division of society into occupational
associations, he exclaimed: "For that I have nothing but praise. In the
well-ordered society, the citizen is not the slave of his craft, he loves it."
In addition, Plato proposed that society should have the structure of a
pyramid, with, at its apex, an authoritarian leader, a "philosopher-king."
Seeing their own social vision confirmed, Trudeau wrote: "Let me just

point out, Baptiste, that if we fail totally, it will be a wonderful comfort to read again those passages where Plato also proposes an authoritarian and aristocratic politics."

Even on the subject of style, Trudeau came to recognize that Plato's irony was so subtle and pleasing that he had missed it altogether. In short, he was dazzled by all of the philosopher's qualities. "I have rarely come across . . . a man with so constant a concern for the triumph of the good. There is truly a just man who feared God. . . . He is outstandingly sincere and his pre-eminent characteristic, surely, was his magnificent virtue of justice. His purpose was to discover and teach what would lead men to perfection and please the gods." His reflections on Plato's ideas led him to think of his own next life and he confided to Boulanger: "Isn't it sublime to assert that, even if the rewards of virtue are not always obvious, too bad: once we are in heaven, it will be useful to have been just."

———— ◆ ————

Their timetable required that Trudeau send his comments on Aristotle's *Politics* by August 3. As it turned out, he mailed on August 4 six pages of commentary on Rousseau's *Le Contrat social*. He explained that he had been disappointed by his disorganized notes on Plato and had resolved that his next mailing would be "something to see." But circumstances had forced him to change his plans. "I spent more time searching for Aristotle's 'Politics' than it would have taken me to read it; and, in the end, I had no choice but to send away for it from somewhere, perhaps the United States. In the meanwhile, I threw myself into Rousseau's politics, and so our timetable has been reversed." He then added, with a touch of humour: "Too bad, but, in the absence of other qualities, I at least provide you the pleasure of a surprise."

At the very end of the draft of his letter, a brief note refers to his "marginal notes on the *Contrat social*." Unfortunately, we were unable to locate these notes. The year before, it will be recalled, that is in 1941, Trudeau had requested and obtained the bishop's permission to read Rousseau's book, which was on the Index. We do not know whether he actually read it then, but now, in 1942, he was full of enthusiasm about it: "First, Rousseau delighted me by his style. . . . I now think that *Le Contrat social* . . . has been most unjustly denigrated by most of the 'thinkers' whom I had honoured with my attention."

Despite these words of praise, however, Trudeau often distorted Rousseau's ideas to find in them support for his own point of view. Take, for example, the relationship between freedom and obedience. When Rousseau wrote that "force is a physical power. To yield to force is an act of necessity, not an act of will,"[19] he was only stating the obvious fact that the weak must obey the strong because to do otherwise is impossible. In Rousseau's model, the legitimacy of the state depends not on force, but on what he calls "the general will." Trudeau, however, interpreted this as follows: "When a government has been imposed by force, after a conquest, that government is illegitimate, because it was not established mainly for the well-being of the conquered people. And so no accumulation of years can ever make that government legitimate: for that to happen, the people would have to consent unanimously to accept such a government. And if a part of the population dissents, it is entitled to form a distinct people."

So did Trudeau, when he was not quite twenty-three, interpret Rousseau to justify creating an independent Laurentie. In the process, he failed to note that the French-Canadian people had, for more than a century, enjoyed the same political rights as the rest of the population. So Trudeau was unjustified in maintaining that the government continued to be illegitimate. Moreover, nowhere in Rousseau's work is there to be found the slightest reference to the right of a dissident faction of a population to form a separate people.

Trudeau was convinced that corporatism would improve on the weaknesses of Rousseau's model. He granted that, in the abstract, Rousseau "proposes quite respectable institutions," but they did not work in practice. However, he did exclaim enthusiastically: "What delighted me at every page was to see that corporatism, a humanist aristocracy and the curb on wealth, as we have proposed in our plan, stood out as the obvious and only means of achieving the ideal order."

While one can indeed find in Rousseau proposals for limiting wealth and propounding the advantages of a meritocracy, one would be hard-pressed to find an argument in favour of corporatism. Quite the contrary. In Rousseau's ideal society, in order for the general will to assert itself, the requirement is "that there be no partial society within the state and that each citizen express only his own opinion. . . . When factions are formed, when partial associations contest the greater society, . . . then there is no longer a general will, and the view that carries the day is nothing more than a particular view."[20] Manifestly, Rousseau would consider the corporation, a partial society if ever there was one, to be an insurmountable obstacle to the expression of the general will.

In fact, according to Rousseau, in order for the general will to express itself, it is an absolute requirement that the citizens participate actively in political life: "As soon as public service ceases to be the citizens' main business, . . . the state is well on its way towards its ruin."[21] Rousseau explains: "Since the sovereign has no other power than that of legislating, . . . and since laws are nothing but the authentic acts of the general will, the sovereign cannot act but when the people has assembled."[22] It is quite obvious that Rousseau's model was the antithesis of corporatism, since the members of the corporations deal only with their own affairs, and have no means of acting politically.

Putting aside Rousseau's basic argument, Trudeau drew the following conclusion: "It is the corporation that will meet Rousseau's requirement." Without showing why, he simply declared that the very existence of the corporations would solve the problem of the political participation of the citizens. This enabled Trudeau to interpret Rousseau's *Contrat social*, just as he had done with Plato's *Republic*, as confirming the excellence of what he and Boulanger had in mind.

―――――◉――――――

When Trudeau mailed his comments on Aristotle's *Politics* on October 12, his eight-page letter made it abundantly clear that he did not take to Aristotle. He had read him in an English translation which he had found clunky, without literary merit. This might explain his negative reaction. "I found Aristotle complicated, indirect, repellent. The truth is that such translations place obstacles in the way of those who want to grasp the substance of the thinking."

Beyond these criticisms Trudeau gave vent to his sense of satire: "He was in every respect the very model of those who today teach Aristotelianism: a dry professor who is categorical, erudite and a merciless logician. . . . The ideas that he teaches no longer hold, either because they are obsolete or already well-known. . . . Never before did I grasp so clearly the difference between a thinker and a logician."

Trudeau was fascinated by the thinker, bored by the logician. But he still found a few ideas that held some interest for him. And, once again, his own perspective coloured his understanding. He wrote in English: "The state exists for the sake of the good life, not merely for protection and intercourse. *Therefore the absolute right to power is the ability to contribute to the good life.*" The first sentence was a direct quotation from Aristotle. For Aristotle, the good life encompasses not merely the intellectual and moral sphere, but also, and necessarily, participation in political life. Trudeau thought he had discovered in the Greek philosopher support for the legitimacy of the revolutionary project that he and Boulanger had embarked on: he concluded that a government that was dedicated to the "good life" of its citizens had an unqualified right to power.

On August 20, Trudeau was scheduled to send to Boulanger his reaction to Maurras's *Enquête sur la monarchie*, but he failed to do so. It is quite possible that he read the book without writing down his comments. What is certain is that, in August, he did read a book that was not part of their program *L'Humanisme intégral*,[23] by Jacques Maritain, one of the greatest Catholic philosophers of the twentieth century.

Maritain had participated in the creation and the promotion of the "personalist" movement, along with Robert Aron and Arnaud Dandieu, Nicolas Berdiaev, and Emmanuel Mounier. But, unlike most personalists, Maritain supported liberalism and democracy and did not indulge in anti-Americanism. He was, in fact, well acquainted with America. He had taught since 1932 at the Pontifical Medieval Institute, affiliated with the University of Toronto, and had occasionally lectured at the Université de Montréal. In 1939, when war broke out, he happened to be in Canada and decided not to return to France. He was a professor at Princeton University in 1941–42, then at Columbia University from 1942 to 1944.

So it was that Maritain was living in New York at the very time when Trudeau read his *L'Humanisme intégral*. He was in the process of developing the principles of a Christian humanism founded on natural law; he was also an active supporter of the war effort and a promoter of human rights. Maritain had already written, among other works, *Le Crépuscule de la civilisation*, published in Montreal in 1941, in which he praised American democracy and expressed his pleasure at discovering in the United States signs of "the reconciliation, now well under way after more than a century of destructive conflict, between patriotism, liberty, democracy and religion."[24] In that same year, he also published – this time in New York – *À travers le désastre*. Instead of attributing the fall of France to the failures of parliamentary democracy, he blamed it on all those who "counted on totalitarian dictatorships and invested their confidence in them."[25]

In May 1942, Maritain published in New York *Les droits de l'Homme*,[26] which had first appeared in France in an underground edition in 1940, at the beginning of the Occupation. As a result of this book, he was invited to participate actively in the drafting of the United Nations' Declaration of Human Rights, which would be adopted on December 10, 1948, by the General Assembly.

Ideologically the polar opposite of Alexis Carrel or Charles Maurras, Maritain considered human rights as fundamental: "We know that an essential characteristic of a civilization that is worthy of the name is the recognition and the respect for the dignity of the human person; we know that, to defend the rights of the human person just as to defend freedom, one should be ready to give one's life."[27]

But Trudeau had read none of these books in which Maritain defended those profoundly Catholic values that were quite at variance with what prevailed at the time in Quebec. In the one book that Trudeau did read, *L'Humanisme intégral*, which was to become a classic, Maritain reflected on the Christian's response to pressing social problems such as questions of justice, the relationship between the spiritual and the temporal, and between the person and the state. He proposed an "integral" humanism, one that takes into account the whole person, including the material and spiritual dimensions. The title was evocative of the *"nationalisme intégral"* propounded by Charles Maurras. Was Maritain's title meant in mockery, or was he deliberately offering a counter-philosophy?

To our knowledge, this was Trudeau's first encounter with a profoundly Catholic thinker who also defended liberalism and democracy. The similarity between Maritain's vision and that which Trudeau would project as an adult is striking. Both would agree that the primacy of the person and the notion of human dignity, carried as a corollary respect for the inalienable rights of the person. For both, such rights must be protected by law.

One might have expected that Trudeau would react to so masterful a work with the same excitement that he displayed when he read Bergson's *Deux sources*. But no, his six pages of notes are rather restrained: "With little originality but with considerable clarity of vision and spirit of synthesis, Maritain summarizes the evolution of humanism down the ages and discovers the wellsprings of culture. . . . In brief, Maritain speaks the language of reason (inspired by St. Thomas). He discerns rather successfully the golden mean."

Trudeau found in this book support for a needed Christian revolution: "[Maritain] believes that only a new Christianity can save the world . . . He brings out its dimensions: communitarian, personalist, peregrinational."[28] But Trudeau drew a bizarre conclusion: "And therefore, decentralization" – an idea that did not follow from Maritain's main premise.

Finally, Trudeau was appreciative of the importance that Maritain conferred on the rights and the freedom of the person, and recognized that corporatism did not automatically guarantee such rights. He concluded that this was something that must be taken care of in the governance of their future society: "To defend the person against the corporatist collectivity. . . . To guarantee within these bodies the right and the freedom of the person." He noted that Maritain, just like his own revolutionary group, considered that "one must not rebuild a privileged moneyed class, but one must make it possible for every man to enjoy in fact his status as heir to previous generations."

Out of all 311 pages of this major work by Maritain, Trudeau selected for mention only these few ideas. Nothing seemed to move him to enthusiasm. He left the impression that he found little that was useful. He did not like the style: "He is not the world's clearest writer. His sentences are repetitive and often poorly put together. His style does not adequately distinguish the several strands of thought and he presents them to us all tangled. What saves him, fortunately, is that he always announces his different topics, takes them into account and knows where he is headed."

But as for practical and political guidance, he found that Maritain's ideas had little relevance: "As soon as he gets into practical questions, he is right out of it. His political action would be perfectly unrealistic; he hangs on to a backward-looking democracy, to a capitalism that does not clearly distinguish itself from corporatism." Trudeau does not even bother to back up his severe criticisms, as he often did with other authors.

In reality, Maritain was defending before his very eyes the same propositions that he would be defending himself many years later. But, in 1942, the young revolutionary rejected almost out of hand Maritain's ideas for the simple reason that they went against the stands taken by the great majority of the French-Canadian elite. Moreover, when Trudeau was reading *L'Humanisme intégral*, the great Catholic thinker had a bad reputation in Quebec, and for obvious reasons.

Maritain denounced all the totalitarian regimes, notably the France of Pétain. In the name of Christianity, he condemned anti-Semitism and the persecution of the Jews. "Our era offers to the homicidal demons incredible banquets. Stalin gave them the Kulaks; Hitler gives them the Jews. And both give them the Christians as well."[29] To explain France's defeat, he condemned Maurras and the French extremists with their "stunning indifference to the common good and to the reputation of their country. To tell the truth, the France that they loved and wanted to serve was not France, but their France, the *right* France." He accused the collaborators of being blind or else accomplices. He flayed "what German propaganda calls the reconstruction of peace in Europe and . . . a 'new order' which, if it did truly and durably become established, would mean that Europe had become the vassal of Nazi totalitarianism."[30]

For Maritain, this war was "not a mere national war, not a mere police action war, not a holy war, nor an ideological war, but a war of civilization,"[31] that is, a total war against the fascist and Nazi regimes, which did not deserve the name of civilizations. Unlike Trudeau and Laurendeau and most of the French-Canadian intelligentsia, Maritain backed unreservedly the position of the Allies: "That the common effort of the British Commonwealth and of the United States should win this war, there, at the present time, is what is of greatest importance for freedom and for civilization. Of course, the defeat of Germany will not suffice to overcome all the problems obstructing a freedom to be conquered, a civilization to be saved and restored. But it is a condition for these problems to be resolved, and for the world to be saved from the slavery which today threatens each and everyone."[32]

Maritain condemned the Vichy government's collaboration with the fascist and Nazi regimes. He accused Pétain, friend of Franco and admirer of his accomplishments, of wanting to establish a "Catholico-dictatorial regime of the same kind"[33] in France. The only reason one could not describe the Vichy regime as fascist, he maintained, was "that there is no regime at all there, and there cannot be one as long as Germany governs and France is a prisoner of war."[34]

France, he said, must rid itself of this rotten regime: "[If the people of France] are to benefit from some of the initiatives currently attempted in France . . . it will be because they sweep away the autocratic regime, the pseudo 'national revolution,' the scenery of Moral Order and of a decidedly fascist 'reconstruction' that the government of the armistice is determined to impose on the country."[35]

In 1962, André Laurendeau attempted to justify the French Canadians' opposition to the war by claiming that they considered the disastrous news from Europe to be mere British propaganda. To defend Henri Bourassa, who sang the praises of "le Grand Maréchal," Laurendeau stated that Bourassa knew nothing about what was really happening in France.

Even granted that Quebec's intelligentsia was blinded by deep-seated anti-British prejudices, how can one explain that it ignored the poignant and clear-sighted message of this renowned Catholic thinker, a personalist publishing in French, living in North America, and frequently visiting Quebec? Why would the thesis of *À travers le désastre* have remained unknown even while Maurras's *La seule France*, condemned by the censorship in Canada, circulated clandestinely? Why was Maritain rejected?

In 2005, André Burelle, Trudeau's speech writer for several years while he was prime minister, offered the following explanation: "In Quebec, the Church authorities and the nationalist intelligentsia of the 1930s and of the post-war years treated Maritain as a dangerous left-winger and found fault with him because he had dared to speak out against Franco during the Spanish civil war."[36] Bizarre. Burelle mentioned the 1930s and the post-war years. But what was their opinion of Maritain during the war? And why give as sole explanation for the rejection of Maritain his opposition to Franco, and say nothing about his support for democracy, his fierce opposition to fascism, his total support for the cause of the Allies, and his unqualified condemnation of Maurras, of Pétain, and of the Vichy regime?

When Trudeau read *L'Humanisme intégral*, Maritain's perspective ran counter to almost everything espoused by the Church and the intelligentsia in Quebec; Trudeau scarcely picked up on any of the important ideas that he could read there in black and white.

According to Maritain, in the modern polity, the Christian must recognize and accept the fact that the citizens come together in communities that have quite different conceptions of the Good. "In contrast to the several totalitarian concepts of the state that are currently fashionable, we are dealing with a *pluralist* polity. . . . Civil society is not made up solely of individuals, but of sub-societies composed of these individuals; and a pluralist polity recognizes for these sub-societies as far-reaching an autonomy as possible, and it varies its own internal structure for adaptations according to the nature of the sub-societies."[37]

Maritain asserted that there was no alternative: willy nilly, pluralism already was an established fact in the polity. That is why a just society had to make allowances for it both in its structure and in its governance. "One must abandon the idea of finding in a common confession of faith the source and the principle of unity for the social entity."[38] A quarter century later, Trudeau, as minister of justice, would arrive at precisely the same conclusion. He would insist that the law must distinguish between crime and sin and punish only crime. Later, recognizing the obvious and inevitable pluralist nature of Canada, Trudeau as prime minister would vest the principle of pluralism in the Constitution. But, in 1942, he was a long way from such a perspective.

Maritain assailed the absence of pluralism in totalitarian regimes and insisted that they were anti-Christian. "In the polity of modern times, the faithful and the infidels are found together. And, of course, today the totalitarian polity insists on forcing once more on everyone the same rule of faith, in the name, this time, of temporal power: but this solution is unacceptable for a Christian."[39] By this standard, Maritain would have qualified the project for a Catholic Laurentie as "totalitarian." But Trudeau apparently noticed nothing.

Maritain also condemned the very idea of an authoritarian leader that young French Canadians had been brought up on from childhood.

"The leader is simply a companion who has the right to give orders to others."⁴⁰ He opposed, as well, the hierarchical system advocated by the proponents of corporatism. But Trudeau was not there yet. It would be several more years before he would adopt liberalism as a philosophy, and democracy as a political system.

Blinded by the ideological atmosphere of his surroundings, which he had so fully internalized, Trudeau could not recognize that *L'Humanisme intégral* condemned almost the entire Maurassian structure on which he and his companions proposed to build their "national revolution." Trudeau apparently didn't even notice that the Christian revolution advocated by Maritain would bring with it democracy, freedom, respect for minorities, and moral pluralism. Their revolution, by contrast, would bring authoritarianism, corporatism, indifference to the needs of minorities, and the imposition of a single state religion with a single conception of the good. Trudeau failed at that time to keep an appointment with his destiny.

As he reached the end of his preparatory reading, which he interpreted through the prism of his convictions and beneath the dominant ideas of his surroundings, Trudeau found no argument to shake his confidence in the ideological soundness of his project. Quite the contrary. He was ready to plunge heart and soul into political action. Meanwhile, the Second World War took a distinctive turn in Quebec. There was adamant opposition to conscription for service overseas. This fierce fight was led by the League for the Defence of Canada, which would later convert itself into a political party, the Bloc populaire canadien. It was in this frantic atmosphere that Trudeau, as a young man, prepared to launch his revolution for the triumph of the True and the Good.

*Chapter 10*

————◦◦————

# NOTHING MATTERS NOW
# BUT VICTORY

*We were deaf, deliberately, immured in our refusals. It could be*
*that we were blind and deaf by choice rather than let ourselves*
*be swayed.*

— ANDRÉ LAURENDEAU
*La Crise de la conscription, 1942, 1962*

WHAT WERE THE L.X. UP TO, once they had completed the task of final-
izing their manifesto? More importantly, what were they actually doing
in pursuit of their revolutionary goal? Again, it is a mystery. Esther
Delisle recounted a few anecdotes about them in her book *Essais sur
l'imprégnation fasciste au Québec.* Her information was gathered during
the 1990s, by telephone or by interviews, but accounts recalled from
memory many decades after the event often prove to be notoriously
unreliable. She also had access to Lessard's personal collection of letters,
but unfortunately it did not include a single letter to or from Trudeau, or
any reference to his involvement in an activity, or anything beyond the
mention of his name.

We don't know when Trudeau parted company with the L.X. We
don't even know when the group went out of existence. There is a letter,
though, which seems to establish that Father d'Anjou was still discussing
revolutionary strategy with some of its members as late as March 1943:
"We have to say *how* we will go about getting rid of the political parties.
Will we do it suddenly, or in stages? . . . We must suppress the Legislative

Council in the province. . . . If it is our intention to set up a corporatist regime as Hertel proposes in his last book, we have to decide how we plan to do it. By a radical coup d'état, as was done in Portugal, or by a more gradual evolution, as would seem to be the requirement here?"[1] As the Pétain regime did in France, Father d'Anjou and his co-conspirators wanted to do away with the parliamentary system and they considered a coup d'état, following the lead of Salazar. When did they put a stop to their planning for a future corporatist state that would be Catholic and French? We don't know. All that we can know for certain is that the national revolution in Quebec never did take place. There was not to be even an attempt at a coup.

This does not imply that Trudeau abstained from any involvement whatsoever in a public demonstration. Up to this point in our account we have followed only his intellectual activities: he read prodigiously, took down notes, and published articles in the *Brébeuf*. Even while he was engaged in drawing up plans for the revolution, he found time to do some writing. It seems unlikely that a man who was so committed to political action should have taken no part in the many demonstrations in which French Canadians protested against conscription for overseas military service. History has recorded nothing but his speech in support of Jean Drapeau. But reality was not that simple. Hertel has asserted that "Trudeau fought with the police in 1937 and 1938, when French Canadians celebrated the one hundredth anniversary of the revolution of the Patriotes."[2] Trudeau himself has dropped hints which may confirm Hertel's assertion. In his article in the *Brébeuf* titled "Sur les pompiers," it will be recalled, he evoked the night sticks of the police. The centenary of the insurrection had been exploited to stimulate the nationalism of French Canadians, especially in the classical colleges. There is a strong possibility that Trudeau took part in the attendant demonstrations.

The year 1939 had established a new and distinctive climate in Quebec. Opposition to this war that Canada had joined began to polarize public opinion. André Laurendeau offered an explanation for the reluctance of French Canadians to support the fighting. The people, he said, "lost no love on England, feared to be drawn into England's quarrels, had no sense at all that they had a duty to fulfill and, more than anything, they abhorred conscription which would force their sons to join up and go abroad to fight."[3] This attitude was criticized as early as June 1940, not only by English-speaking Canadians, but also by intellectuals in France, such as Father Doncoeur. This French Jesuit, also a friend of Laurendeau, wrote him: "Your attitude at this time is without magnanimity. I consider it unintelligent. I understand why you have no wish to be submissive towards the English. . . . But you must be aware of the price in blood that must be paid today for neutrality. As for Canada, don't let yourselves be deceived into thinking that you are safe from this hateful Hitlerian power."[4] Laurendeau wrote back: "Just as during the worst moments of the last war, our dearest French friends could no longer understand us. . . . If it should be true that our attitude is without magnanimity – it is not up to us to decide – it has not been the easy way out."[5] French Canadians were overcome with a sense of being totally isolated.

The fall of France shook them and provoked an immediate surge of support for the decree instituting national mobilization in Canada. But soon, other factors arose, such as their admiration for the Pétain regime, which strengthened their determined opposition to conscription. The Liberals of Mackenzie King had been re-elected in 1940 with 178 out of 245 seats nationally. In Quebec they did even better, taking 64 out of 65 seats (three of which were taken by "Independent Liberals"). An independent Conservative won the only other seat. Politicians, both in Ottawa and Quebec, remembered only too well what price the Conservatives were made to pay after Prime Minister Robert Borden implemented conscription for overseas in 1917 after promising he would not do so. They were driven from power and rarely able afterwards to win appreciable support in Quebec. The Liberals did not want to suffer a similar fate, and so they made the promise – and reaffirmed it repeatedly – that they would never impose conscription for service overseas.

But circumstances changed as more countries were crushed under the boots of Hitler's victorious armies, and more became known about the atrocities perpetrated by the Nazis. The call for conscription became more insistent among English-speaking Canadians. As a result, the chasm deepened between Canadians who spoke French and those who spoke English. That division became a crisis in 1942, as Laurendeau indicated by the very title of his book: *La crise de la conscription, 1942*. To justify the attitude of French Canadians, he wrote: "In retrospect, we consider the war of 1939–45 as a world war, and in fact it did become so. In 1939, though, it was European, strictly European."⁶ But Laurendeau correctly gave the date of 1942 for the conscription crisis. Was one meant to conclude that, in 1942, which he correctly identified as the critical year for the struggle over conscription, the war was still strictly European? To put the question in context, we shall sketch out the state of the Second World War in 1942, and the policies adopted by the King government to deal with the pressures to which it was subjected.

———————

After the fall of France in 1940, Great Britain alone maintained the struggle against Hitler as his armies went from victory to victory, invading one European country after the other. The non-aggression treaty that Hitler had signed with Stalin in 1939 bound the two powers together. But Hitler was only awaiting the moment when he could repudiate this agreement with the country of communism, which he hated, describing it as "the result of a Jewish plot to dominate the world." On June 22, 1941, confident of a swift victory, he ordered the Wehrmacht to invade the Soviet Union.

Half a globe away, on Sunday, December 7, 1941, Japan's air force delivered a surprise attack on Pearl Harbor, destroying in a few hours the American fleet and killing close to 2,500 soldiers and sailors. The next day, the United States declared war on Japan. On December 11, Germany and Italy in turn declared war on the United States. So it was that, by the end of the year 1941, the world was engulfed in war. Few countries were able to remain uninvolved in the conflict.

On the very day of the attack on Pearl Harbor, Hitler set in motion the operation called *Nacht und Nebel* – Night and Fog – intended to create an atmosphere of terror and so break the resistance to Nazi occupation. Henceforth, there were just two forms of reprisals: the summary execution of those presumed to be guilty or their disappearance into "the night and the fog," that is, their removal to concentration camps. At the same time, the better to deal with his enemies who had become powerfully reinforced with the entry into the war of the Soviet Union and the United States, Germany appropriated for its own use the resources of the countries they had occupied and initiated there a system of compulsory service for the benefit of Germany. Accordingly, the head of the Pétain government, Pierre Laval, passed a law compelling seven hundred thousand French citizens to be taken to Germany to work there as slaves for the benefit of the Nazi regime. It was not long afterward, namely on January 20, 1942, that German authorities met at Wannsee, a suburb of Berlin, to draw up their plan for "the final solution" of the Jewish question. Once again, the Pétain government followed suit. On July 15 occurred the notorious "roundup of the Vel' d'Hiv," during which thousands of Jews were gathered in this Paris sports complex, to be deported to concentration camps. Most of them were to perish, a great number exterminated in the gas chambers.

How, then, could Laurendeau credibly suggest that in 1942, the year of the conscription crisis, the war was strictly European? In reality, it was a fight to the finish between two civilizations, one of which was convinced that it could dominate the world for a thousand years, eliminating in the process the "inferior races." At Nazi rallies, the crowds, carried away by emotion, clamoured: "One hope, one people, one nation, one destiny for a thousand years." The other civilization fought back with total commitment, knowing that its very survival was at stake.

These circumstances had a major impact on politics in Canada. From the start of the war, Canadian volunteers had joined up to serve alongside the British army. In April 1942, partly to respond to the Soviet demand that the Allies open a second front, they attempted a landing at the French port of Dieppe. Of the 6,000 troops engaged in the action, 5,000 were Canadian. The venture ended in a disaster for the Allies, both from the human and military points of view. The force invading by water, ineptly backed up by the air force, was cut to pieces in less than ten hours. Casualties among the Canadians included 900 killed, 1,000 wounded, and 2,000 taken prisoner. Mackenzie King was aware of the political repercussions of the Dieppe rout, as he wrote in his diary: "I am still not too sure of the wisdom of what was attempted. It goes back, I feel, above all to the time when it was felt it was necessary to have the Canadians do something for a variety of reasons. . . . It makes me sad of heart. . . . I now regret it."[7]

In Quebec, the event was taken as proof – and it would long be remembered as such – that the British used the Canadian troops as cannon fodder. Accordingly, after the war was over, on January 19, 1946, the publisher of the weekly *Notre temps*, Léopold Richer, was to write:

"It is as though Canada was born to be the world's saviour, and then its laughing-stock. That is what the imperial link means for us."

————◦◦◦————

The pressures kept increasing from the rest of Canada for a more robust participation in the war effort. Mackenzie King felt compelled to find a way to free himself from his promise. Caught between that pledge and the call for "a total war which requires a total effort," he sought to win over the assent of French Canadians by making all Canadians aware of the seriousness of the international situation. And so his Speech from the Throne of January 22, 1942, announced that a plebiscite on freeing him from his promise would be held on the following April 27.

In Quebec, the announcement was followed immediately by the creation of the Ligue pour la défense du Canada (League for the Defence of Canada). It was backed by the lion of French-Canadian nationalism, Henri Bourassa, by its leading theoretician, Lionel Groulx, and by Georges Pelletier, publisher of *Le Devoir*.[8] From the start, the League vented its contempt for the established political parties and took it as its objective to prevent conscription. It rallied immediately all the nationalist leaders and their associations, notably the youth movements represented by the young law student Jean Drapeau, who was to play an increasingly important role in the League. Within months, Drapeau would be running in a by-election as the unofficial candidate of the Bloc populaire, and Trudeau would make his dramatic speech in his support.

André Laurendeau was given the title of secretary of the Ligue pour la défense du Canada. In reality, he would become its most important organizer and guiding genius. He was only thirty years old, but, as may be recalled from Chapter 6, his record as a nationalist and a disciple of Lionel Groulx had prepared him for this role. In 1942, when he was appointed secretary of the Ligue pour la défense du Canada, he had been the publisher of the nationalist periodical *L'Action nationale*, since 1937.

The League attracted tens of thousands of nationalists from all parties and staged many public events. We do not know whether the law student, Pierre Trudeau, actually signed up as a member, but he certainly took part in at least some of its activities. The *Quartier Latin*, at the Université de Montréal, gave extensive coverage to each appearance of the League and constantly urged the students to take part in every demonstration. So it was that, in its edition of February 6, 1942, the editorial lectured the students: "The Ligue pour la défense du Canada will be holding on Wednesday, February 11, a great public meeting in the St. James Market. This meeting, to be chaired by Mr. Jean Drapeau, *must* be a success. . . . We must turn out in impressive numbers so as to make clear our determination to support the leaders who are motivated by concern for the interests of the people – of all the people – and not by tawdry party interests or their own personal interests. . . . The students are unalterably opposed to conscription for overseas."

This appeal was heard. On February 11, at the St. James Market, nearly ten thousand people filled the hall and spilled out on the street to hear speeches by Jean Drapeau, Henri Bourassa, and others. The meeting ended with a riot when young men, after leaving the hall, broke the windows of streetcars, wandered about in gangs, cleaned out a house of prostitution, and chanted: "Down with the *Gazette*! Down with the Jews!"[9] Some witnesses claim that Trudeau took part in the riot. Gaetan Robert, who was his friend at that time, said that they were in it together not only on that occasion, but on other occasions as well. He recalled that they often went with others of their fellow students to disrupt demonstrations in favour of conscription: "Trudeau and I and some other friends would come prepared, with bits of metal inside our hats in case police hit us. Once we tried to smash the windows at the *Gazette* building."[10]

Jean-Louis Roux, a medical student at the time at the Université de Montréal, also remembers this riot: "A great gathering was organized at the St. James Market to protest against the threat of conscription. Thousands of demonstrators came in answer to the call. . . . Michel Chartrand, sitting atop a newspaper kiosk, defied the police officers who tried unsuccessfully to order him down. . . . The crowd soon wearied of the speeches and the demonstration then turned into a parade. It advanced westward on Sainte-Catherine Street, shattering along the way the shop windows if the owners had a foreign-sounding name, above all if it was Jewish. . . . This combination of latent anti-Semitism, of resentment towards Great Britain and of blindness in the face of the rising power of National-Socialism largely reflected the tone of the newspapers that we read and of the education that we received. . . . We were taught the history of Canada according to the textbook of the Christian Brothers. . . . Everything in it was impregnated with hostility towards the Anglais."[11]

At the end of February, another protest meeting was held, and Jean Drapeau was, once again, a featured speaker. On March 20, in an issue of the *Quartier Latin* that was entirely devoted to the coming plebiscite, the student council – the Association générale des étudiants de l'Université de Montréal – took up the entire front page to explain why everyone must vote No. It issued this summons: "On Tuesday evening, March 24th: *ALL* must be there at the Jean Talon Market." That night, as well, the meeting turned into a riot. To the cry of "Down with the Jews!" youths vandalized Jewish shops along Saint Lawrence Street.[12] Police and demonstrators clashed. In his account, Laurendeau denied that the vandals were from the League: "I have always been convinced that these young anti-Semites were the former blackshirts of Adrien Arcand."[13] Maybe. Somehow, we find Jean-Louis Roux's account to be more convincing.

François Lessard relates that, during the riot, a law student named Maurice Riel was arrested and charged. Two other students, Pierre Labrecque and Pierre Trudeau, testified in his favour and he was eventually acquitted, according to Lessard. Many years later, in October 1973, Prime Minister Pierre Trudeau would appoint Maurice Riel to the Senate. He would be named Speaker of the Upper Chamber in 1983–84. When he was questioned about the riot by Esther Delisle, Maurice Riel recognized that he was at that time a friend of Pierre Trudeau, but he did not recall the incident.[14] That, too, is possible. As Laurendeau described it, the French Canadians, by common agreement, stopped talking about the war.[15] None but a handful ever acknowledged that they had been pro-Pétain, pro-corporatism, or ever participated in these riots.

On April 22, just five days before the plebiscite, the League organized its last protest meeting, held at the Jean Talon Market. "The crowd was estimated to number more than 20,000," Laurendeau wrote. "What was spoken that night is of no importance now. The crowd came out to attend a big party."[16] The Ligue succeeded in playing on all the nationalist heartstrings of the French Canadians, drawing on all their past collective frustrations to focus them on the fight against conscription.

When the votes of the plebiscite were counted, the Ligue had scored a dramatic victory: in the other provinces, the Yes vote exceeded 80 per cent; in Quebec it was the No vote that rallied 71.6 per cent of the population as a whole, but 85 per cent of French Canadians. "So it was that, together, we experienced a moment of unanimity such as we have rarely seen in our entire history,"[17] Laurendeau recalled. Needless to say, this struggle against conscription heightened among French Canadians a xenophobia and an anti-English sentiment that verged on hatred. It also further discredited the established parties and possibly contributed to the rise of anti-clericalism within the nationalist intelligentsia. Some members of the Church hierarchy who had supported the position of the federal government were subjected to scorn by the Ligue and its supporters. According to Mason Wade, "Cardinal Villeneuve's zeal won him the nickname of 'Kid Villeneuve' and 'Newtown, O.H.M.S.' (On His Majesty's Service) It was felt that he was true neither to his people nor his cloth."[18]

Canada was more divided than ever, as each side nursed its resentment against the other. Improvising in his efforts to keep the country from the breaking point, Mackenzie King amended the law on mobilization to make conscription permissible, but without actually imposing it. Thus was born the slogan, memorable for its calculated ambiguity: "Conscription if necessary, but not necessarily conscription."[19] The Ligue lost no time before it reacted. On May 19, 1942, it held another rally, this time to protest against the new law.

The university students were caught up in the frantic atmosphere of the times. That Trudeau took part in the Ligue's demonstrations, we can have no doubt. His own opposition to the war reflected the views of everyone in his circle. He shared their political assumptions. The Church, like the French-Canadian elite, had for the past decade been demanding fundamental change, sometimes even an independent country. The French Canadians, it was thought, needed such changes to fulfill themselves, to protect their language and their faith, to protect themselves against *les Anglais*. Trudeau, as a young adult, simply took these demands to their logical conclusion: only a revolution could bring about the required change. And so it was up to him to prepare himself and to bring the people to a realization of what was needed. In the meanwhile, with the Ligue as a cover, he and his like-minded companions would begin to spread their message.

So it came about that, perhaps swept along by the rally of May 19, 1942, they staged an allegorical play which they called "Dollard" or "the Dollard Play," according to the account given by François Lessard.[20] The name referred to Adam Dollard-des-Ormeaux, a controversial figure from the history of New France who died in May 1660, during a battle

with the Iroquois at the Long Sault rapids on the Ottawa River, roughly
where the boundary between Quebec and Ontario is now drawn.[21] For
nationalist historians such as Lionel Groulx, Dollard and his companions died as martyrs in the defence of their faith and of New France.
Other historians give a different interpretation to this incident in the
early wars of the colony, even suggesting that Dollard and his sixteen
French companions had set out from Ville Marie to plunder. Depending
on the school of thought, Dollard was either a national hero or an adventurer who met his death through miscalculation.

Lessard stated that their modern re-enactment of the battle of the
Long Sault was staged under the stars at the foot of Mount Royal, "on a
warm evening" of 1942, before a large crowd.[22] Given the subject matter
and the place, the event must have occurred on the weekend of May 24,
when nationalist Quebec celebrated "Dollard's holiday." Lionel Groulx
had been promoting this celebration for several years with the intention
of replacing the "Victoria day holiday," or "the Queen's birthday," celebrated as an official holiday in Canada since 1845. Victoria had reigned
for sixty-four years, and her birthday on May 24 had remained ever since
as the official birthday in Canada of the subsequent monarchs. And so
the play carried implicitly an anti-British, anti-colonial message. It was
written, according to Lessard, by two people whose names began with V.
One of the two was almost certainly Roger Varin, very active in the
Ligue, who since early 1941 was planning to publish in Quebec works
by Catholic and nationalist French authors.[23] The play, Lessard related,
was staged by "a handful of Quebec separatists, women and men, who
belonged to a secret society."[24] Jean-Louis Roux played Dollard. Jean
Gascon personified the St. Lawrence River. (Both men would leave their
mark on theatre in Canada.) Trudeau, wearing a feathered headdress,
played an Iroquois. At one moment during the play, just when one of
Dollard's surviving companions was being tortured, a voice cried out to
the torturers: "Make them wear spectacles, red or blue!" Red, of course,
was the colour of the Liberals, blue the colour of the Conservatives. The
implication was that the Iroquois, torturing the French Canadians of
New France, had now been replaced by the two established political
parties. So did the young people of the Ligue express their contempt for
the politicians. Trudeau would soon use again the image of the torturers
when he gave his speech backing Jean Drapeau: the savage Iroquois were

succeeded by more recent savages – the *Anglais*. Lessard explained how putting on this play was intended to advance their revolutionary aims: because of the War Measures Act, they had to cloak their words and their actions under apparently innocuous covers, such as the Ligue pour la défense du Canada, or a play.[25]

---

While Trudeau and his companions busied themselves with putting on plays, thrashing out the wording of the L.X. manifesto, and making plans for revolution, the war was devastating the planet. The pressure was on the government to make ever increasing contributions to the war effort. To raise the required money, both to invest in armaments and to support the Allies, the government issued at various times treasury promissory notes that were called "Victory bonds." On October 16, 1942, Mackenzie King launched the third such subscription campaign by giving a speech that was broadcast from Montreal.[26] He urged Canadians to lend the government $750 million, the largest objective set so far. To make persuasive his pitch for funds, he took as the theme of his speech a sentence uttered by Winston Churchill: "Nothing matters now but Victory!" That slogan would be repeated seven times in his urgent appeal. "Whether we like it or not, we do well to realize that this is a fight to the finish, and that upon its outcome will depend, for good or ill, the future of all countries and of all continents. . . . From the day Hitler achieved power in Germany, the concentration camp became a symbol of Nazi domination. In the conquered countries, as in Germany itself, the unspeakable tortures of the concentration camp have been used by Hitler to end opposition to the single master race." Referring to a recent event in which Jews and others were seized in their thousands and guarded temporarily in a sports stadium, King added: "A typical example is what occurred as recently as last July when 15,000 alien refugees in France were rounded up by the Nazis to be shipped to concentration camps in Poland."[27] He denounced the perversion of the Nazi "New Order," the reduction of entire peoples to slavery, and enumerated all the reasons that compelled the Allies to fight until they achieved a final victory.

Trudeau, like the nationalists generally, considered this speech as nothing but propaganda. He decided to respond. In a draft dated "end of October," he wrote out a parody of a speech and gave it the title

"Nothing matters now but victory!" Supposedly, a fatuous French-Canadian dignitary was addressing a meeting of students. The parody would actually be published in the *Quartier Latin* on November 20, with the author's name given as: "Pierre Elliot Trudeau, Chevalier True de la Roche-Ondine." It turned into derision Mackenzie King's patriotic plea.

The supposed dignitary began: "My venerable profession, together with my exalted personal merit, give me access to the distinguished circles of our Dominion. Whenever I want, I am welcomed by well-heeled refugees, by statesmen, business tycoons and the like. . . . Ah, we love you, you beautiful young people, you beautiful young university students! Experience teaches us that you will be tomorrow's elite, the cream and the very cheese of our race." After delivering these introductory compliments with ridiculous pomposity, the orator went on to say that he was disappointed with the students: "More than once, you have caused us deep pain. . . . But last year, you went altogether too far, and a twisted mentality was on general display at the university. . . . Why, you even stooped so low that you applauded some jailbirds."

The students at that time would have understood the reference: it was to Montreal's mayor, Camillien Houde, and to fringe party leader Adrien Arcand, both imprisoned under the War Measures Act, as we will see presently.

The orator continued: "You have ridiculed and treated with contempt our great politicians, in defiance of their wisdom which has been so appreciated by our powerful Allies. You showed your rebelliousness during the plebiscite. Young people, this can't go on. I would go so far as to say that this has to stop." He warned that the government might take action against them. "We could put an end to the publication of that subversive *Quartier Latin*, in which the ignominy of the editors exceeds even the cynicism of its readers." After evoking all the punitive actions that could be taken, the orator changed his tone: none of these measures would be carried out because the government chose not to disturb "those gentlemen in your midst who remain blindly trustful and respectful towards the establishment." The good man was on a reconciliation mission. He wanted to promote "the rebirth of *bonne entente* [understanding] between the peoples of our great Canada." He then uttered the slogan of Mackenzie King: "My friends, nothing matters now but victory." He urged his fellow citizens to set aside their childish grievances.

"Let us suppose for a moment what is impossible, namely that England has at times treated us badly, us French Canadians. Let us imagine, as the nationalist cry-babies do, that we might possibly have some justifiable grievances against the majority race. So what? Even the greatest peoples are not perfect . . . and besides, when the house is on fire, . . . is that the right time to bring up childish quarrels? How can you possibly be thinking of minority rights? Or speak of economic discrimination? And throw up questions of decentralization, education, religion? My dear friends, my dear good little friends, you already know that the elite is looking out for you: if all these trifles amounted to anything, we would be the first to be on the case."

Always tongue-in-cheek, Trudeau was, in fact, enumerating the legitimate grievances according to the nationalist canon, while at the same time satirizing French Canadians who lined up with the government, thus abandoning the true interests of their own people. He then turned his scorn on the usual arguments brought up to justify conscription for service overseas, by putting them in the mouth of this pompous fraud: "Is it possible that you have time for such nonsense, at the hour when the Freedom of the righteous peoples is threatened, at the minute when democracy and liberalism are wobbling, at the very instant when our magnificent economic structure is crashing?"

Trudeau's sarcasm was patent. For him, it was not the traditional grievances of French Canadians that could be dismissed as nonsense, but rather democracy, liberalism, and capitalism. His puppet orator was now reaching the point of his speech. "Nothing matters now but victory," and he would tell the students why: "French Canadians, just think of it. If the *monster of Berlin* should be victorious, our life would not be easy. Colonials of perfidious Germany, we should find in her a ruthless mistress who would attempt to assimilate us by every possible means. To destroy our religion, impose the German language and bastardize our culture: these aims would be her sole preoccupation. She would dominate our economic life, she would confine us in industry to the menial jobs. Our countryside would be emptied, our natural resources taken over. That is when we would be exposed to the disgusting mockery of a press that betrays, of an oligarchy that crushes, and of a government that exploits the people it is supposed to protect. Take a close look at this horrifying picture and be aware that these abominations could befall us if we don't instantly annihilate the *Nazi hordes*."

The reference to *"perfide Allemagne"* is an obvious evocation of "perfidious Albion," the classical hostile description of England. Nothing would really change for French Canadians since the threatened "abominations" were already part of their daily life. (Many a French Canadian at that time maintained that there was little to choose between the Germans and *les Anglais*. On March 6, 1942, an editorial in the *Quartier Latin* made the point: "In Germany, of course, the cult of the mind has been abolished and science itself has been brought down to only what is needed for the war economy. . . . True. But the perennial Anglo-Saxon materialism is no less of a surrender.")

It was in the name of a futile victory, Trudeau implied, that French Canadians were being asked to set aside for the duration their true values. "As for your national pride, students, it is a commendable virtue. But in good time. After the Victory of right over violence, of justice over inequity, we will take up again, if you so insist, these questions dealing with God, with integral humanism, with corporatism, with autonomy, with the employment of women, with the conscription of children, and what not. But what is important at this moment is to save what truly counts, that is, our material wealth which is threatened, because defeat would debase our currency. For heaven's sake, I pray you, drop everything and be governed by just this one thought: that nothing matters now but victory!" In other words, Trudeau was saying, what this war really boils down to is money. That was the only real issue.

Let us go back to Trudeau's reference to students applauding jail-birds. What was he referring to? In his personal papers, we found the answer: the draft for a play which he wrote, titled: *To concentrate or not to concentrate.*[28] It was played before a student audience. Among the main characters of the play one finds the guard of a concentration camp who is named Fritz Von Korn Flakes. There is also an unnamed visiting minister of the government and two "jailbirds" named Camillien and Adrien. They obviously represent Camillien Houde and Adrien Arcand. Houde had been arrested on August 5, 1940, and then interned for having urged the population not to register for possible mobilization as was required by a law passed on June 21, 1940. A great number of

French Canadians admired his courage and approved of his conduct.
When he was eventually freed on August 16, 1944, he would be greeted
as a national hero and re-elected as Montreal's mayor from 1944 to
1954. As for Adrien Arcand, he was an unrepentant anti-Semite and bitterly anti-communist. In 1938, he became leader of a Nazi, anti-separatist
party called Parti de l'unité nationale. His party was outlawed at the start
of the war and, from 1940 to 1945, he was interned in New Brunswick.
In *Dangerous Patriots: Canada's Unknown Prisoners of* War, the authors
related that, while he was interned, Arcand would sit on a makeshift
throne and explain to the other prisoners how he would govern Canada
after Hitler won the war.[29]

Trudeau's play treated its subject farcically. For instance, on the wall
of the concentration camp, a sign read: "Concentrate, concentrate,
something will always come of it" – a play on a famous saying: "Lie, lie,
some of it will always stick." The minister asks the guard whether he is
German. His reply: "Yes, Mr. Minister. Heil Hitler! Oh! I mean, Heil
Mackenzie King!" Trudeau had filled four typewritten pages with such
gags. For example, the minister wants to know what the prisoners do all
day. The reply: "They fabricate concentrates of Rita wine, concentrates
of aspirin, concentrated milk . . ." The two jailbirds appear before the
minister, each singing a song to the tune of a ditty that every French-
Canadian child learns by the age of five, "La bonne aventure." In their
refrain, though, "the good adventure" becomes "the sad adventure." The
Camillien Houde character sings (we have not attempted to replicate
the French rhymes): "I wanted to make a hit with the dames, and so I ran
for the job of Fuehrer. But I was told, we have enough of one Fuehrer,
and Adolf is the one." In another scene, the two jailbirds make their
escape from the camp with the complicity of the cook. On their way out
they meet Santa Claus, who has been interned because "on his costume,
in big letters is written *Made in Germany*."

The audience must have enjoyed the play because "they even stooped
so low as to applaud the jailbirds." This was what many students found
funny during one of the most terrible years of the war when Hitler still
seemed invincible.

Five days after the *Quartier Latin* published Trudeau's "Nothing matters now but victory," he gave his speech in support of Jean Drapeau in the Outremont by-election. When we examined in Chapter 4 *Le Devoir*'s report on the evening event, much remained unclear, questions remained unanswered. Now, in the light of Trudeau's private papers, we can put his speech in its proper context.

During the demonstration of May 19, 1942, which we mentioned above, one of the leaders of the Ligue pour la défense du Canada, René Chaloult, was charged with having spoken out subversively against conscription. He was jailed, but eventually acquitted in August. The Ligue celebrated his release from jail with a great banquet. The celebration attracted so many people that the intended venue proved too small and the banquet had to be moved to the Atwater Market.[30] André Laurendeau recalled the atmosphere: "On that August evening of 1942, everyone had the feeling that a new party was about to be born."[31] And so it happened; the following month, the Bloc populaire canadien was founded, and it rallied all of Quebec's patriotic and nationalist associations. As was already true of the Ligue, the Bloc populaire won the support of nationalist stalwarts Henri Bourassa, Lionel Groulx, and Georges Pelletier, as well as of his newspaper *Le Devoir*.

The new party planned to be active on both the federal and provincial scenes. Its slogan, "Canada for Canadians, Quebec for Quebecers,"[32] summarized its program: it demanded that Canada act in full independence from Great Britain, and that Quebec be autonomous within the federation. In the *Quartier Latin*, the Bloc populaire announced that it was the only party to put the family at the forefront of its policies, the only party to demand "economic liberation both federally and provincially," and the only one to put up "an effective wall against the increasing threat of a bureaucratic and centralizing state socialism." (Indeed, when Michel Chartrand reproached Ottawa with having a socialist and centralizing policy in his Outremont speech as reported by *Le Devoir*, he was in fact merely stating the position of the Bloc.) Maxime Raymond became the movement's leader and its popularity increased by the day. The same major figures who led the Ligue were now to be found in the Bloc, and they continued their struggle against conscription, in the aftermath of the plebiscite.

Anyone who backed the federal government on the issue or who opposed the Bloc was treated with contempt, no matter what the individual's social position. So it was with Father Arthur Maheux, a professor of Canadian history at Laval University. Between September 1942 and January 1943, he presented a series of radio broadcasts on Radio-Canada under the general theme "Pourquoi sommes-nous divisés?" This brought down on his head "personal attacks of a virulence never known in Quebec in the case of a priest."[33] Lionel Groulx published a scathing tract in reply titled "Pourquoi nous sommes divisés." Fr. Maheux asserted in *Ton histoire est une épopée* that the history textbooks in Quebec's schools taught children to hate *les Anglais*: "Such textbooks, slowly and surely, inculcate hatred." That brought an angry rebuttal from André Laurendeau.[34] Father Sabourin, a chaplain in the armed forces, gave a speech in which he spoke favourably of England. He was made an object of ridicule by Michel Chartrand in that same speech that he gave in support of Drapeau.[35] However, several members of the Church hierarchy, including Cardinal Villeneuve, Archbishop Joseph Charbonneau of Montreal, and Archbishop Alexandre Vachon of Ottawa, withheld their support from the Bloc.

Shortly after the Bloc was founded, the federal government announced that two by-elections would be held in November, including the aforementioned one in Outremont. Laurendeau explained the dilemma that was faced by the new party. The Bloc "did not want to be put to the test before it was ready. . . . In Outremont, a nationalist was certain of defeat because of the presence there of an English-Jewish majority. In the plebiscite, the riding had voted Yes by 60 per cent."[36] What made defeat even more certain was that the Liberal candidate was Major General La Flèche, the newly appointed Minister of National War Services. The Bloc's leaders decided that, instead of putting up a candidate running under the label of the party, they would use the occasion to gain some experience. The young Jean Drapeau, who was making a name for himself because of his activities under the aegis of the Ligue, had offered to run as the Bloc's unofficial candidate. He would announce that he was the "candidate of the conscripted." Henri Bourassa bestowed on him a weighty endorsement. In his excellent study devoted to the Bloc, Paul-André Comeau wrote: "Almost all the leaders of the Bloc populaire made an appearance in the Outremont riding, supposedly in a private capacity. . . . The daily *Le Devoir* fell in behind the founders of the new party. In effect, it became a dress rehearsal in the course of which most of the main figures of the Bloc populaire had their first taste of political action."37

This by-election had special importance for the Bloc. We have no evidence proving that Trudeau was a member at this time, but everything suggests that he was at least a sympathizer. The fact that he was chosen to give one of the campaign speeches shows that he was already known and well regarded. It is odd that Laurendeau, in describing the climactic meeting, makes no mention of Trudeau, even though it was Trudeau's speech that provided *Le Devoir* with its headline. But Laurendeau was writing his account of the conscription crisis in 1962, and by then the two former companions-at-arms were already fighting on opposite sides of the "national question." Trudeau had acquired a reputation for his hostility toward French-Canadian nationalism. Their ideological divergence could well have provoked Laurendeau's lapse of memory. On the other hand, he recalled perfectly the speech given by Michel Chartrand. "In his caustic style, he brought up every last historical grievance which we hold against *Mother England*, with a bitterness, a violence that left us breathless."38 That, however, was not exactly how *Le Devoir* reported on the evening's speeches.

Trudeau and Drapeau knew each other well. They had been active for some time in the same nationalist movements. At the time when Trudeau gave his speech, he had already worked hard on the manifesto for the National Revolution, together with Boulanger and possibly others. Some cells of the L.X. had most likely been formed already, with recruitment already started. And so it should come as no surprise that Trudeau injected calls for revolution into his pro-Drapeau speech. They are to be found there clearly in the draft of the speech Trudeau had prepared,39 which we have already summarized in Chapter 5. The further details, however, are important.

He began by saying that, unlike the other speakers who invited the citizens to vote *for* Drapeau, he thought it was appropriate, rather, to vote *against* La Flèche, regardless of who was running against him. "Because, in the present contest, to vote for La Flèche is to condone a perfidious political ploy." He would come around, later in his speech, to explaining why he used the word *perfidious*. But, first, he wrote down a sentence which contained an admission: "I have no intention, at the very beginning of a career that is possibly not about to end soon, of indulging in the traditional nasty duels." But he then crossed out the words *at the very beginning of a career that is possibly not about to end soon*. His first intention, it seems, was to reveal that he proposed to be active in politics for a good while. Then he reconsidered, and wrote only: "I have no intention of indulging in the traditional nasty duels."

Despite his protestations that he would not indulge in personal attacks, he quickly attacked La Flèche for campaigning in his military uniform. He then expanded his criticism: "The example has been given by highly-placed individuals, during this war, of people abusing their authority to let on that they are speaking in the name of the people, when in reality they are speaking merely as individuals. So it has been with the individual Godbout, the individual Cardin, the individual Sabourin, the individual Villeneuve." He was referring to the premier of Quebec, Adélard Godbout, the former federal minister from Quebec, Pierre Joseph-Arthur Cardin, to Father Sabourin and Cardinal Villeneuve. Three of these "individuals" who supposedly gave bad example had supported the position of the federal government. The exception was Cardin, who was no longer a "highly placed individual," having resigned on May 12 as Minister of Public Works and Minister of Transport in protest against his government's position on conscription. It was Trudeau's assumption that, when these people expressed themselves on such political issues as conscription, they had no right to speak other than in their own name. Otherwise, they committed an abuse of power. He included Church dignitaries in his criticism. Though a deeply committed Catholic, and though he recognized the authority of these two men of the cloth when they spoke on matters of faith and morals, he refused them any authority when they spoke out on politics. And he felt entitled to attack their presumption. "I feel especially justified in speaking my mind about these 'men of the church' inasmuch as they will be warmly supported by those atheistic papers you know all too well." What atheistic papers could he have been talking about, in the Quebec of 1942? Perhaps non-Catholic English language papers, such as the *Gazette*? Or the anti-clerical *Le jour*, whose editor Jean-Charles Harvey persistently defended liberal values and supported the allies? Or *Le Canada* or *Le Soleil*, which backed the position taken by the government and the cardinal? Surely, Trudeau was carried away by his own rhetorical passion.

He now came around to explain what he meant by the perfidious political ploy of the federal government. "They make a show of obtaining the consent of the French Canadians by extorting the consent of ministers who do not think like the people, who are French Canadians only in name, and who won election in those constituencies that are the least French Canadian in the whole province. . . . That is dishonest, and disgustingly dishonest." By this reasoning, if La Flèche, dispatched by the government, got elected in Quebec on a pro-conscription platform, Ottawa would claim that the people voted for conscription. But the truth, as enunciated with assumed authority by Trudeau, was that La Flèche and the other French-Canadian ministers in support of conscription did not think as the people did. So they were not "true" French Canadians. That almost suggested that they were traitors, and Trudeau would soon make that charge explicitly. Moreover, he went on, the only reason such people could get themselves elected was that they ran in ridings with a sparse French-Canadian population. This was Outremont, remember, where Trudeau lived, along with a substantial part of the French-Canadian elite. But that was also where a substantial community of English-speaking Jews was established. No doubt that was the reason for its being "disgustingly dishonest."

A few decades later, Trudeau's adversaries would serve him up, almost word for word, those same arguments to deny his right to speak as a legitimate representative of the Québécois "people." He was a Québécois only in name, it was charged, he did not think like the people, and, besides, he was elected from Mount Royal, a riding where most of the voters were not "true" Québécois. Same story, different actors. This might explain Trudeau's ironic smile and blunt reaction when he heard shouted at him the same arguments that he had used more than a quarter of a century earlier. This argument dies hard. As late as 1995, Jacques Parizeau would dismiss the victory of the No side in the referendum on secession as that of "money and the ethnic votes."

The young orator, in full flight that night, did not disdain to use vulgar language: "It has happened all too often that our people got screwed with that kind of tactics." In a democracy, he argued, it is the government who must execute the will of the people, and not vice-versa. And, if we are not in fact in a democracy, he warned, "just say so, and that will be it: we will immediately launch the revolution." Anyone who had no knowledge of the manifesto of the L.X. would naturally assume that Trudeau suggested a revolution in order to institute democracy. In fact, those who read it would know that neither Trudeau nor his companions-at-arms nor even the Church had a high regard for democracy. But he seized the opportunity to plant publicly the idea that a revolution was needed.

As he pressed his attack on the government, Trudeau got nasty: "Did you know that, as far as I'm concerned, the present government is made up of two species of big shots: the big shots who are traitors, and the big shots who are honest." In its report on the meeting, *Le Devoir*, it will be recalled, mentioned only the honest big shots. Trudeau's next words make clear why the reporter chose the path of discretion. "The traitors should be impaled alive: we'll say no more about it, but let's not forget." Unbelievable. And that was only the beginning. The orator went on to warn his audience and all and sundry that "if Outremont is so infamous that it elects La Flèche, and if because of Outremont conscription for overseas service comes into effect, . . . I beg of you to eviscerate all the damned bourgeois of Outremont who voted for La Flèche just to serve their own interests." Eviscerate! To explain why Trudeau reacted so violently toward these "damned bourgeois," it helps to remember that, at Brébeuf, his teachers shared the revulsion professed by the Church and by Carrel for the decadent materialism of the bourgeoisie, source of the decline in moral values.

While Trudeau proposed that revolution was justified, absent democracy, he himself did not recognize the right of the citizens of Outremont to vote democratically for the candidate of their choice, unless they agreed with his choice. He also denied that La Flèche could claim to be Outremont's legitimate representative since he would have been elected by those who were not "true" French Canadians. Drapeau, on the other hand, could claim to be Outremont's legitimate representative even if he were to be elected by the same "damned bourgeois" and other voters who weren't genuine French Canadians. In a word, Trudeau was claiming the right to decide which of the members of Parliament from Quebec were legitimate representatives of the Quebec people and which were not. The only ones to pass the test were those whose political commitment coincided with his own.

Ironically, when Trudeau would eventually achieve the patriation of the Constitution in 1982, with the support of seventy-four of Quebec's seventy-five MPs, the nationalists would turn on him exactly those same arguments – and they repeat them to this day. They declared the patriation to be a *coup de force* – an assault – and that it was *imposed* on the Québécois, thereby minimizing the significance of the almost unanimous support of the Quebec MPs who had been democratically elected. These nationalists held that they alone knew the will of the people and decreed that these MPs were not legitimate representatives of the Québécois.

Trudeau also injected another nationalist dogma in that speech: that the French-Canadian people must defend itself from being contaminated by association with another people in the same country: "For too long a time altogether, felonious and corrupt governments have been able to debauch our people, body and soul. A people is a being that, like a man, has its own intrinsic value, and no one has the right to debase it into a tool, like a slave in the service of another people, even if it be the immortal Anglo-Saxons." For Trudeau at that time, as a faithful disciple of Lionel Groulx, a people possessed *one* body and *one* soul, it had all the characteristics of a human being. This conception of a people as a living organism is incompatible with a liberal vision. It goes directly against the spirit of the Canadian Charter of Rights and Freedoms that would be Prime Minister Trudeau's most important legacy. According to the Charter, only the individual, having "inherent value," is endowed with rights and responsibilities. In fact, the understanding of "a people" that he professed in 1942 would have denied the primacy and the dignity of the person as created by God which Trudeau was taught in his religion classes at Brébeuf. But, back then, with him, as with the intellectual and clerical elite of the period, the siren song of nationalism made one forget some tenets of the faith.

Returning to the struggle against conscription, Trudeau insisted that "the French Canadian people understands the meaning of war. It has never for one single instant since its birth been free of a struggle, at first against the Iroquois, and since then against other savages." He spoke entirely in the ethnocentric and xenophobic spirit of Charles Maurras as he appealed to his fellow French Canadians: "Citizens of Quebec, the election of Jean Drapeau must mark the close of an era when the French Canadians were the suckers and the beginning of the era when the dishonest outsider [*métèque*] starts to take a tumble." We are a long way off from the future father of Canadian multiculturalism. He had a long road ahead of him. But, in 1942, to turn on the *"métèques"* – the outsiders, those who don't belong, the aliens in our midst – was commonplace, both in Trudeau's circle and in the writings of France's right and extreme right.

He was now reaching the end of his speech. Here were his final words: "For far too long, [governments] have gotten away with acting irresponsibly, merely by applying band-aids to what they called, patronizingly, our little bruises. Enough, now of that whole ridiculous comedy; enough of the tragedy; enough of the big shots, enough of the traitors. Enough of the arrow [La Flèche] of the conqueror, long live the flag [Drapeau] of freedom! We've had more than enough of band-aids [cataplasmes], now let's move on to the cataclysm."

His final words clearly took him far beyond the topic of the evening. Trudeau seemed to forget that he was there only to support Drapeau, the informal candidate of the Bloc populaire. He knew full well that electing Drapeau would not put an end to any ridiculous comedy, to traitors, to band-aids, nor to the debauching of the body and soul of the French-Canadian people. That would, in fact, require a cataclysm: a national revolution. Trudeau's final words gave meaning to his whole speech.

---

After that speech of November 25, 1942, Trudeau would take part in only a single debate before his departure for Harvard University in 1944. Gérard Pelletier would attend the event. Writing in 1983, Pelletier would recall that "this academic exercise ended on a huge practical joke when Trudeau suddenly pulled out a revolver that he had concealed under his gown and fired a few blanks in the air, badly shaking up the federal minister who presided over the meeting."[40] Pelletier could not recall the topic of the debate nor could he remember the date. François Lessard, on the other hand, was also there and he also remembered the revolver. François Hertel, in a 1977 interview, maintained that Trudeau "kept arms in his basement."[41] That he stored weapons there does not seem beyond the realm of possibility, but what is certain is that he never made use of them except to make a scene with a revolver loaded with blanks.

What the debate was about is revealed in Trudeau's personal papers.[42] The debating society of the University of Montreal organized a debate on January 8, 1943, the topic: "Today's gallantry or that of yesteryear?" The debate seems to have attracted a fair amount of publicity. Each of

Montreal's two major dailies ran stories on the oratorical contest. An announcement in a magazine described the protagonists. We are told that the gallantry of the past was upheld by Pierre Elliott Trudeau and Marguerite Joron, while contemporary gallantry was defended by Michel Mathieu and Colette Toupin. Strangely enough, in the announcement only the two males are further identified, in what could well have been a demonstration of sexism. Here is how Trudeau was described: "The knight of noble causes, Pierre comes off as a revolutionary of our times. Exuberantly enthusiastic, possessing a sophisticated culture backed up by a solid study of the law, he comes across as a blend of Don Quixote, Bayard and Hans Wittenstein zu Witt. His daring and his taste for adventure drove him to retrace the voyage of Radisson all the way to Hudson's Bay. He is an ardent defender of the truth (as is to be expected of a worthy lawyer), but he also sometimes emerges from the civil code to become involved in politics."

Though the author of this description was not identified, there is good reason to believe that it was written by Trudeau himself. It displays his style, alternating between the humorous and the serious, his erudition and his fascination with the world of fantasy. Along with the universally familiar Don Quixote, he saw traits in himself reminiscent of Bayard, celebrated as "the fearless and impeccable knight," as well as of Hans von Wittenstein zu Wittenstein, the very pedestrian knight errant in Jean Giraudoux's play of 1939, *Ondine*, in which what is fairy-like merges with classical tragedy. Interestingly, among his other attributes, Trudeau, in January 1943, publicly presented himself as a revolutionary, and a person involved in politics.

The description of Michel Mathieu pales in comparison: "Unwilling to restrict his activity to the field of medicine, he has made the public aware of his beautiful voice and his warm persuasiveness. In addition to having spoken many times on the radio, today he will drink for the third time from the carafe of Debates." And there was more in the same style.

Trudeau put great care into preparing for the debate, covering twenty-four pages with a draft that has so many words crossed out that it is difficult to read and to follow the line of the argument. Some passages were attempted four or five times, with words written and struck out over and over. Clearly the orator in him took this contest very seriously, or was it simply that he did his best to turn a rather trivial debate into a disguised plea for the revolutionary cause? He began work on the draft on December 23. To judge by all the rewriting, he must have spent the Christmas break working on it.

He opened with a far-fetched anecdote. A gentleman, under the impression that he was on the ground floor of a building when in fact he was on the 78th floor, walked out to get some fresh air and "soon found himself obliged to take far more than he had expected" because he plunged down and hit the pavement. When he was asked by a policeman what was going on, the gentleman replied, spitting out fragments of the sidewalk: "I have no idea. I just got here, myself." Trudeau then made the parallel: just like this misguided gentleman, "contemporary gallantry has reached new lows. . . . I won't tell you that the modern code of gallantry leaves something to be desired. No, I will prove to you that modern gallantry itself simply doesn't exist at all. Its codification constitutes the most inept and monumental case of plagiarism since our own civil code."

For example, Trudeau argued, the terms of politeness in use no longer have any meaning. And so, when an orator addresses his audience with "Ladies and Gentlemen," he is in fact using "words that are a legacy of the era of lords and serfs; but, today, those words have lost all meaning. Precisely. In our contemporary system of gallantry, words and gestures no longer have meaning. And the people themselves have lost their senses."

This explanation served to illuminate the words Trudeau had used when first addressing the audience: "To the citizens, to those who are half free and to the slaves, I salute you!" But while his address and his argument seemed totally fantastic, they in fact conveyed a serious social criticism which reflected his political views. "Oh, of course, all ages have known gallantry, more or less; ours, less. . . . It is splendid, don't you know? We have preserved everything except what is essential. Truly, there is only one period that could display such a level of judgment: our own. Just as there is only one – also our own – that could be taken in by that well-known cry of freedom: Nothing matters now but victory."

He built his speech around a fictitious character that he called Toots. "Toots, my dear straying lambs, means Toots," he proclaimed sententiously and redundantly. "Toots," it seems, was a phonetic distortion of "toutes" – *all*, in the feminine. Toots included all women. Trudeau held them responsible for the death of gallantry. But he went much further.

Echoing the position of Carrel and of the Church, he stated that their "liberation" meant the destruction of traditional family values: "Toots means giving up all your privileges as women. . . . Toots means that you prefer the mechanical work in a factory to the infinite imaginativeness of cooking. . . . Toots means that you are man's equal; you are now free to sully yourselves by dirty politics, free to vote for governments that are each more cynical than the previous one, free to applaud the imbeciles who depopulate the patrie of its men and women. Toots means that it is extremely difficult to launch or to maintain movements to rehabilitate the family and to condemn the fact that women are being wrenched out of their homes. Because, now you earn a salary, Toots, and it is against your interests to refuse to obey a government that imposes on you the freedom to disgrace yourselves." Women, at the time of this speech, had only been given the right to vote in provincial elections in 1940, less than three years earlier. And so they had now gained the power to support the old parties made up of "cynics" and "imbeciles."

But why would Trudeau say that *it is extremely difficult to launch or to maintain movements to rehabilitate the family and to condemn the fact that women are being wrenched out of their homes?* What movement could he have been talking about? It seems unlikely that he was referring to the Bloc populaire, which at the time had already become a political party and was doing well. Could it be that he was disappointed because he was finding it difficult to win recruits for his L.X. movement?

His draft was replete with notes that were rather like the scenic instructions for a play, as though he anticipated that actors would intervene at different moments during his speech. Words like "Interruption," or "fires a shot," or "It is time to put a little lead in your head." What were such notes doing in a defence of old-time gallantry? At first sight, one is at a loss to know what to make of it, or to guess who was expected to follow these cues. But Lessard's letter to Trudeau that he wrote on March 30, 1977, clarifies the mystery. Lessard reminded the then prime minister of that earlier debate: "In the audience were dispersed as many of your Frères Chasseurs as were needed to interrupt your speech at the right moments and to set you up for flights of rhetoric on new themes. You picked me for the climax. I stood up and I shouted: 'But, Mr. Trudeau, did you ever ask yourself how you would end up if you persist in saying such things?' First of all, you drew a revolver and fired at me.

Then, having disposed of the heckler, you gave an answer to my question. You spun around on your heel so your back was to the crowd, you stretched out your neck and, acting out the image of Riel that you like to evoke, you joined your hands so that they were like those of someone who was hanged, tied behind the back, level with your bum, and you shouted out: 'With a Union Jack, right there!' "[43] [pointing to his arse.] So the heckling was pre-planned, as was the pantomime with the revolver. The theatrics and the debate on a trivial topic were turned into a political statement in favour of an anti-English revolution.

Forty years later, Gérard Pelletier would remember the revolver shot, but he had forgotten everything else. He thus reinforced the image of the youthful Trudeau as apolitical, interested only in pulling stunts. In 1972, when Trudeau was in his fourth year as prime minister, André Potvin, Michel Letourneux and Robert Smith would recall the same incident in the foreword to their book, *L'anti-Trudeau*. Leaving out entirely the incident of the revolver, they expressed their puzzlement at trying to reconcile the Trudeau that was with his more recent manifestation: "That guy, the one of the Lodge of the [Frères] chasseurs, the one who talked down to the 'touts' (women, in Trudeau's younger vocabulary), that same one who wanted to die with a Union Jack in his arse, it is he now who flies over the Peace Tower in Ottawa."[44] The phenomenal distance which separated the political opinions of Trudeau in his youth from those of the later statesman seemed simply incomprehensible. And so they attempted, by bringing together a range of writings about him in their book, to "carry out the psychoanalysis of this lost son."[45]

In 1977, George Radwanski would also relate the same incident in his biography of Trudeau. Whoever was his source seems, like Pelletier, to have forgotten what Trudeau actually said, to retain only a variation on the story of the revolver. Disappointed at losing the debate, Radwanski wrote, Trudeau pulled out a pistol and fired a blank at the terrified judge, while uttering the words: "That will put some stuffing into your head." And Radwanski drew his own psychological conclusions. The incident, he declared, proved that Trudeau was an "obnoxious prankster." Moreover, "such pranks, performed not by a child but by a highly intelligent young man in his early twenties, reveal a streak of cruelty, a willingness to amuse himself by frightening others."[46]

Memory can play tricks and lead to every shade of psychological deductions. But what did the actual witnesses of the debate think of Trudeau's performance? Both *La Presse* and *Le Devoir* reported that the debate was won by the other side, the defenders of contemporary gallantry. But, interestingly, neither of the two reporters seemed impressed by the performance of the winners. *Le Devoir* merely summarized without comment the argument put forward by Mathieu and Toupin. But, when he came to Trudeau, he mentioned that his speech was "very picturesque" and that he had argued his side with "an accomplished art and a spectacular eloquence." The *La Presse* reporter actually stated that he totally disagreed with the decision of the jury. In his view, the true humorist was the profound philosopher. "There is no need always to assume an emphatic and professorial tone when one comes out with more than banalities." He had discerned the social and political criticism that was masked by the burlesque posture. To be a good judge, he wrote, one has to know "how to distinguish what is deliberately playful and what is not. And experience proves that all are not equally able to know the difference. . . . And it would take a very foolish person to change his personal opinions on the basis of such a verdict." He implied that the members of the jury were simply not up to their task. And so he reached his conclusion with obvious regret. Today's gallantry, he wrote "prevailed in the minds of the members of the jury, even though a democratic vote of the whole audience would doubtless have given the victory to the defenders of the gallantry of the past."

This spectacular performance marked the end of the effervescent agitation and the passionate public speeches of our young revolutionary. During the year 1943, the storms of the recent past would slowly abate. We shall follow him next in the relative calm of his life up to his departure for Harvard University.

# Chapter 11

## AFTER THE STORM

*Before the age of 30, a man is not intelligent.*
– Adage quoted by Pierre Trudeau in his request<br>for admission to Harvard University, October 13, 1944

**BETWEEN THAT DEBATE ON GALLANTRY,** held on January 8, 1943, and the month of March of the following year, Trudeau published only three articles, one of which was a commentary on someone else's writing. Quite a change from his frantic activities of 1942. Also different was his choosing to write on topics that had little connection to politics. The titles revealed his changed perspective: "A Penetrating Persian Dialogue," "Where does a Savage come from?" and "Massons Clément." What was going on?

Trudeau was nearing the end of his studies in law and, in the spring of 1943, he would have to pass the Bar exams. As the serious student that he was, even though his courses mostly left him cold, we can be sure that he spent most of his time in preparation. But that alone would hardly explain the slowed pace of activity of a young man who had so recently displayed such energy and so much passion for politics. Moreover, a greater concentration on his courses would not explain why the calm continued even when his exams were behind him.

Something had changed, but what was it? Referring to this period, the journalist Michel Vastel wrote in his Trudeau biography: "The Pierre Trudeau who was admitted to the Bar of the Province of Quebec in 1943 was frustrated, bitter, disgusted with life and despising his own people."[1] Indeed, Trudeau was passing through a phase of bitterness and frustration.

But did he really "despise his own people"? That was a charge that was levelled against him all his life, and so we propose to look into it.

On February 18, 1943, Trudeau wrote down the draft of a piece that he entitled "O honte!"[2] ("For Shame!") After filling three and a half pages, he stopped writing. Was this to be an article meant for publication that he gave up on? Or was he merely jotting down his thoughts as he might have done in a diary? We don't know. But what was unmistakable was the tone of bitterness, almost despair. "If the ordinary people truly realized what sort it was that they were relying on to ensure their salvation, and to what degeneracy they were themselves condemned, they would not wait another day before giving up altogether." He then explored his bleak vision further: "The people are never wrong, no more than the rock that breaks a glass or the mineral that lets itself be crushed. The mass of the people always takes the direction to which it is pointed by its leaders. And so it is the ruling class that makes for the greatness or the failure of a people. . . . And so one must never shout at the people, say 'damn you!' or say that it was born for slavery. On the contrary, it is capable of everything if it lets itself respond to powerful forces." Trudeau, true to the strongly elitist tradition in which he was raised, was convinced that the mass of people was lost unless it was led by an enlightened elite. That explains why he and his fellow plotters proposed to create a hierarchical social structure in their society of the future, and why they granted paramount importance to the leader. He had assumed that the university students would, like himself, make every effort as a preparation to join the elite of the future. He was disillusioned when he discovered that it was otherwise.

"I have a bone to pick with the students," he wrote. "They have been told repeatedly and they repeat to themselves that they are the elite. What is true is that they will some day be the ruling class of our people." He was making the distinction between a true elite – an aristocracy based on merit – and a ruling class which merely exerted power. From early childhood Trudeau had heard the vibrant appeals of Groulx, of Laurendeau, of the Church, of the Jesuits, all asserting that the misfortunes of the French-Canadian people derived from the absence of a true elite. Now Trudeau was furious at his fellow students and wrote down his contempt: "I have a bone to pick with this contemptible bunch of mollusks, viscous and vicious . . . that makes up the student tribe. And that is what tomorrow will lead the nation?" The harsh words reflect the depth of his disenchantment. It is unlikely that he intended such a cry from the heart to be published. But it does reveal his dark mood at this time of his life.

And what was it about the other students that made him so bitter? "I can't believe that their duplicity is simply the reflection of a dual personality, because they don't have a personality. The words that come to mind, rather, are that they are two-faced. Just take a look at what they are writing, listen to them as they fulminate against the traitors to our race, against the goddamn wretched politicians, against Jean-Charles Harvey, against the *maudits Anglais*, against conscription, against the damned communists. Come election time or come a plebiscite, you must admire how they yelp and how they plot. You will be edified, and maybe even dazzled, by such pure nationalism." It is their hypocrisy that Trudeau holds against them, the disconnect between their brave words and their cowardly deeds. Over his entire life he would despise those who lacked the courage of their convictions and the convictions to match their words. He himself had acted from a sense of duty when he committed himself to a revolutionary struggle. But he came to realize that those who joined him claiming that they shared his determination to bring about a radical transformation of society lost all enthusiasm when the time came to act. "The students at the Université de Montréal are no better than nasty tricksters, they even lack the wit to be jokers," he wrote. Contrary to Vastel's assertion, it was not his people that was the object of Trudeau's contempt, it was, rather, the failed elite.

What were the facts behind so much resentment? We simply do not know. Was he put off because he was unable to find recruits for his movement? In the debate on gallantry, he stated how difficult it was to launch and maintain a movement aimed at promoting family values. Did the students he approached turn him down, claiming that the mass of the people was too supine to support radical action? Or did he find the other members of the L.X. more anxious to fight over formulas defining their revolutionary objectives than to become involved in action? These are all possibilities, but they don't come close to explaining so radical an ideological and political shift, nor the new direction of his writings in 1943 and 1944. To resolve the mystery requires us once again to consider how the context of war changed after 1942.

Immediately after the defeat of France, the enthusiasm of French Canadians for Pétain and his Vichy regime reflected that of the French. "On the left, people had confidence in Pétain because he remained for them the man required when the situation turned desperate. . . . As for the right, people there were enthusiastic, deliriously happy," Marc Ferro wrote to describe the reception that the Marshal received on his arrival in Paris in May 1940.3 With naive faith, people believed that a "new order" was achievable and desirable even in a country that was defeated, with half its territory occupied. Convinced that England was doomed to soon having "its neck wrung like a chicken's," Pétain and his regime were preparing for the time when "France would become an associate of victorious Germany."4 In its early years, the National Revolution even had the massive support of the clergy, since it was taking up again with the Church, honouring the family and the peasant, while condemning modernity and the secularizing of the country. The Church was even comfortable with the anti-Semitic measures adopted in the first months. Marc Ferro maintains that many members of the clergy "commented favourably on the banning of Jews from some professions."5

But the popularity of the regime declined quickly as a result of factors that were both external and internal. On November 8, 1942, President Roosevelt wrote to Pétain to let him know that the United States, now at war with Germany, was organizing with Great Britain a landing in North Africa. The Marshal's answer left no doubt as to where he stood: "It is with astonishment and sorrow that I learned this night about the aggression of your armed forces against North Africa. . . . We are under attack. We shall defend ourselves."6 The very next day, Mackenzie King broke off diplomatic relations between Canada and the Vichy regime.

The victory on November 12, 1942, of the army of General Montgomery at El Alamein, in Egypt near Alexandria, marked a major turning point in the war. Later, after the victory of Stalingrad, on February 2, 1943, it became more and more obvious that Hitler would be vanquished. In September 1943, Italy capitulated, causing the disintegration of the fascist and corporatist regime that had earlier set so many French Canadians dreaming.

Within France, the Loi du Service du travail obligatoire (S.T.O.), passed by the Vichy regime on September 4, 1942, was applied to send

hundreds of thousands of French citizens to work in Germany as conscripted labour – in other words, slaves. It had the effect of swelling the
ranks of the Resistance. The increasingly demanding levies that
Germany extorted from France weighed heavily on the population as a
whole. With the taking of hostages, the executions, and the increasingly
severe German measures of repression, hatred for the invaders spread
and the Vichy regime was increasingly viewed as their accomplice. All
those who came under attack as a result of the National Revolution,
notably those who favoured a separation of Church and state, the teachers and the unions, began to organize against the regime.

The Church also distanced itself increasingly from the Vichy regime.
In the summer of 1942, reversing their early approval for the measures
enacted against the Jews, many bishops and archbishops began to intervene in their favour and to denounce the persecutions to which they were
subjected. For example, the archbishop of Toulouse, Mgr. Salièges,
issued a pastoral letter on August 21 in which he wrote: "The Jews are
men and they are women. Everything is not permissible against them, . . .
They are our brothers, just as are so many others. A Christian must never
forget that."7 The Church in Quebec also reconsidered its approval of
the Vichy regime.

It is noteworthy that neither in France nor in Quebec was Marshal
Pétain himself discredited. Others of his regime were blamed for the
collaboration with Nazi Germany. His minister, Pierre Laval, served as
his lightning-rod. People wanted to continue to believe in the greatness
of Pétain who "made a gift to France of his person" in its most desperate hours. In Quebec, the enthusiasm for Pétain lasted longer than
in France, but the nastiness of the Vichy regime was increasingly recognized. Then as the victory of the Allies loomed closer and the failure
of corporatism became more obvious, French Canadians were at a loss
over where to turn. The model of the National Revolution, which
Trudeau and Boulanger and their would-be brothers in arms had
espoused with such conviction, simply fell apart. That makes it easier
to understand what Boulanger wrote with acute awareness in the
*Brébeuf* of January 1943: "The peace will be made without us and
against us." It is also easier to understand why, from 1943 on, Trudeau
has shed his fervent militancy. He had lost his bearings and, as he put

it in 1944, he felt the need "to relearn how to think."[8] Meanwhile, he busied himself elsewhere.

———◈———

On March 19, 1943, the *Quartier Latin* published his piece "A Penetrating Persian Dialogue," which he signed with the word PITRE, meaning clown. It took the form of a fanciful play, not unlike what he wrote sometimes in the *Brébeuf*. It introduced fifteen characters, some with made-up names that were a play on words, others the names of real people or real places, such as First Tourist, Le Trifluvien [man from Trois-Rivières], Claudel, Le Parisien, Léon Bloy. The plot was simple: two tourists in Montreal ask someone to recommend a live entertainment. The answer: "There is only one performance worth seeing. As it happens, tonight they are putting on Aeschylus's play *The Persians*, in the Gesu hall [of Collège Sainte-Marie]." The tourist replied with a pun: "Oh, Gesu! Am I anxious to see that." But a bystander suggests that the tourist might feel a little lost there. To which another character replies: "Of course not. If it touched a human chord 25 centuries ago, why would it leave someone cold today? Is this an intelligent tourist that I'm dealing with, someone who can count up to five? Or is it some dope who prefers the marching band of a circus, and drum-beat ballets, and ham actors performing at a penny arcade, and scenery such as you find at the Monument National?" Trudeau was expressing his own preference for ancient Greek tragedy over contemporary popular forms of entertainment that only bring about "the intellectual and financial impoverishment of the vulgar populace and of a frivolous elite." Just as the Church did, he considered popular entertainment as debasing the entire society. Greek tragedy, on the other hand, is "sublime poetry." In the event, the tourist chose to see *The Persians* and, Trudeau wrote, counted henceforth "among the 1,347 citizens of the Western Hemisphere who are acquainted with beautiful theatre." The heavy humour suggested his disenchantment with his own society.

That piece was followed by a long silence. The year 1943 was a time when even his notes on his reading became scarce. Until July, it is likely that Trudeau was fully engrossed in his studies. But he found time to send out inquiries to various American universities about the graduate courses that they offered. In an undated letter to Harvard University, he said that he intended to register for the fall session: "I am interested in [the] Departments of History, Government, and Economics," and he asked for their yearly prospectus. Harvard replied on May 15 that the prospectus was not yet printed up.9 He sent a similar request to Columbia University and added political science as a discipline in which he was interested. Then, on June 19, he wrote to the Georgetown Graduate School of Foreign Service that he would like to register there for the fall. But it turned out that the Canadian authorities withheld permission for him to leave the country, despite the very complimentary letters that supported his request. In a letter dated October 27, he got his answer: "Permission is not granted to go to the United States to take courses that are already offered in Canadian universities."10 In spite of the two medals and the three prizes that he received for his brilliant results in the Bar exams, he was unable to go abroad to attend graduate school.

Stuck in Quebec, he joined the law firm of Hyde and Ahern, but he was not happy; the law was not for him. "I practised one year," he told George Radwanski, "and I found it just terrible. A client would come in, and I'd be tempted to say, 'Well, you know, I'm not really interested in your case.'"11 He felt that he was at a dead-end, both politically and intellectually.

Though no longer a student, Trudeau continued to read the *Quartier Latin*. On November 5, 1943, the University of Montreal's student newspaper published a letter to the editor under the heading, "*Le Quartier Latin* to the graveyard." Its author, Clément Masson, was critical of the new editorial approach taken by the publication. "Previously, it was a real students' paper, sparkling with vigour and with youthfulness, truly reflecting the student spirit, and reading it could make us smile, sometimes even break out into a laugh. Today, when we pick up the *Quartier Latin*, we again break out, but now into tears, as one might before the tomb of a dear one." The whole letter was composed around the theme of death, with sombre words like *funeral procession*, *mourning*, and *shroud*.

Trudeau, on the contrary, was happy that the paper had just recently taken a courageous stand, demanding more editorial freedom from the students' association. And so, two days after Masson's letter appeared, Trudeau composed the draft of a double reply. He wanted to encourage the editorial team to continue in their new posture, and to put down the student for his criticism. His two letters were both published in the *Quartier Latin* on November 12, the first as a letter to the editor with a pun on the student's name, "Massons Clément" [Let's smash Clément Masson], and the second as a letter to the student, "Mon cher Clément." He signed the first Pierre Elliott Trudeau, the second PITRE. In the first he asked the editor to forgive the student "who is not a bad guy, though slightly puerile, somewhat thoughtless. But that's how they all are in the Faculty of Law." Again making a pun, he continued: "Let us be clement, ourselves." He then praised the editor, saying "our *Quartier* was often trivial in past years," whereas this year the editorial team "is precisely witty enough, so far, to rid our paper of its syrupy women's column letters, of its blundering essays, its insipid stories." He concluded the letter by confiding to the editor that he envied those who were in a position to use their pens as "weapons for sending to hell all pontificators."

The other letter addressed the student directly, putting him down with sarcasms expressed in a colloquial style: "My dear Masson, you are absolutely, totally and unfailingly on the wrong track with your article." Trudeau parodied his pathetic evocations of a burial. "You are such a sensitive soul! Sensitive beyond compare! You burst into tears . . . when the paper isn't what you expected!" Trudeau's criticism was not aimed at Masson alone: "Don't imagine that my little temper tantrum had only you in mind; since I don't believe in purely personal grievances, I intend to scold all those who agreed to publish your article." He then broadened his criticism to include all of Masson's fellow students who were like-minded. "I mean, what is it you wanted to go back to? Is it a college paper that you're after? Or a paper that publishes ignoramuses and their stale jokes? . . . You're nuts, that's what!" Trudeau countered that to be alive meant to struggle. He insisted on "living dangerously! Long live careers made up of pistol shots and walks on the tightrope! Long live the bearers of a black eye!" This was Trudeau the revolutionary making a reappearance. And the changed orientation of the *Quartier Latin* gave him new hope. "As far back as I can remember, I have never seen *le Quartier* so pointed in the right direction." Then, addressing the students directly, he advised that, if they learnt to be constructive in their criticisms, they could become "the agents of Renewal. And then, if the

*Quartier Latin* becomes what the *Quartier Latin* promises to be, there will no longer be good reason to define the students of the Université de Montréal as 'nasty tricksters who lack the wit to be jokers.'" (That last phrase: Trudeau had written it down nine months earlier in his bitter commentary, "O honte!")

Why did Trudeau write, "if the *Quartier Latin* becomes what the *Quartier Latin* promises to be," repeating the name of the publication? In fact, on his own copy of this issue of the paper,[12] he crossed out the capitals of the first *Quartier Latin*, and wrote, "if the quartier latin [the latin quarter] becomes what the *Quartier Latin* promises to be . . ." thus referring in the first instance to the campus or even the entire neighbourhood surrounding the university. The paper's copy editor, missing the subtlety, determined to correct a mistake by putting the first "quartier latin" in the upper case.

In that same issue, Trudeau had another piece, titled "Where does a Savage come from?" At that time in Quebec, and for at least the three following decades, it was normal to refer to Indians unselfconsciously as "*les sauvages*"; but Trudeau used the word ironically.

Gérard Pelletier would select this article to be included in the book he edited, *Against the Current*. In the English version of the book, the title was changed to a politically correct "Where Are Indians From?"[13] It was a review of a book by Paul Rivet titled *Les origines de l'homme américain*. Despite the scientific subject, requiring a technical vocabulary, and Rivet's often impenetrable style, Trudeau did his best to summarize the main themes of each chapter, and did so in a prose that was sprightly and humorous. In his conclusion, he expressed particular appreciation for the fact that Rivet aimed to sensitize "old Europe as well as young America" to the debt that both owed to Indian civilization. Trudeau quoted the last lines of the book, which made an appeal to the sense of human brotherhood: "More than at any time in the past, the sentiment of great human solidarity needs to be exalted and strengthened. Every man must understand and know that under every latitude and under every longitude, other beings, his own brothers, have contributed to making his life sweeter and easier, whatever the colour of their skin or the shape of their hair."

Trudeau himself would develop into a great defender of human solidarity and an ardent promoter of multiculturalism. But, in 1943, when he was twenty-four years old, he could not resist the temptation to seize on this beautiful message to deliver a blow against repugnant capitalists, corrupt politicians, and the censorship imposed by the King government because of the war. "So it is that a single scientist, by his calm and honest efforts, contributes infinitely more to promote Christian charity among human beings than all the fetid politicians and all the putrefied financiers. And it surprises me that our ever-wakeful censorship could have allowed so much dignity to annihilate the contemptible efforts to which four years of deplorable propaganda testified." Oddly, this sarcastic criticism, which revealed so much about Trudeau's political ideas during that period of his life, was actually left out of the version published in *Against the Current*.

---

Meanwhile, the Bloc populaire took up the cause that the Ligue pour la défense du Canada had defended. It endeavoured to lock up nationalist support by coming across as a breath of fresh air in comparison to the older parties. Trudeau was active in Bloc circles. That was why he had been asked in 1942 to speak on behalf of Jean Drapeau when he was the Bloc's unofficial candidate. However, right from the start, the Bloc was undermined by serious internal divisions, as was demonstrated by the excellent studies carried out by Michael Behiels, professor of history at the University of Ottawa, and by Paul-André Comeau, journalist and professor at Quebec's École nationale d'administration publique. Behiels explained its decline largely by personality conflicts, struggles for power, and conflicting views with respect to how it should be organized and what should be its policy direction.[14] The Bloc attracted people with disparate nationalist ideologies, who had also often belonged to antagonistic political parties. As the new party was about to choose its first leader, three founding members of the movement, all three disciples of Lionel Groulx, organized a cabal against the candidacy of Maxime Raymond, an admirer of Henri Bourassa.

The threesome included René Chaloult, that member of the Quebec legislature whose acquittal in August 1942 on the charge of counselling against the draft had provided the Ligue pour la défense du Canada with the occasion for a triumphant banquet. Chaloult was elected at various times under the banner of the Union nationale, the Liberal Party, and as an independent. He would be the man who convinced Maurice Duplessis to adopt a distinctive Quebec flag, which was done on January 21, 1948.

The other two were Paul Gouin, the founder of the now defunct Action libérale nationale, and Dr. Philippe Hamel, the ardent promoter of the nationalization of the electric utilities.

After Raymond had won the leadership, dissension broke out over a number of issues, including whether or not to create a provincial wing in addition to the federal party. The three dissidents demanded that a vote of confidence be held on Raymond's leadership. He won the vote hands down on December 5, 1943, but the tensions between the two camps only increased when Raymond surprised everyone by naming André Laurendeau as leader of a new provincial wing of the Bloc populaire. Laurendeau, then secretary of the federal party, had no previous experience in active politics.

It was in these circumstances that Trudeau received an invitation to attend the Bloc populaire's convention of February 3 to 6, 1944, in the capacity of secretary to the Committee on Education and Policy. He accepted, attended, and did serve as the committee's secretary. At the time, the Bloc was still going strong, but the public was also aware of the internal power struggles. On February 7, the day after the close of the convention, the three rebels reacted to the nomination of Laurendeau by addressing a public warning to Maxime Raymond: "Our confidence in you has been seriously shaken." They protested, however, that having at heart the superior interests of the French-Canadian people, they were ready to consider any serious and honourable proposal "to repair the injustice that you committed against us and to redeem yourself in our eyes and in public opinion."[15] One after the other, the attempts at reconciliation failed. On each such occasion, the acrimonious conflicts were acted out in public and had the effect of reducing support for the Bloc. In the provincial elections of August 1944, the Bloc took only four seats, including that of Laurendeau. In the federal elections of June 11, 1945, disaster struck. The Bloc carried only two of Quebec's sixty-five seats and took only 13 per cent of the vote. On July 6, 1947, Laurendeau abandoned the sinking ship. Angered by his resignation, Raymond warned him that, should the Bloc die because of him, "you will be able to boast that you were the gravedigger of a nationalist movement and you will have earned the gratitude of the old parties."[16]

It seems that each time that Trudeau hit a wall politically, he turned elsewhere in search of a diversion. For example, it was a month after writing the disconsolate "O honte!" that he published "A Penetrating Persian Dialogue," celebrating ancient Greek theatre. Then, it was just a month after the disappointing convention of the Bloc that, on March 10, 1944, he published "Pritt Zoum Bing" in the *Quartier Latin*. It was an homage to the motorcycle, "that perfect instrument of escapism." Tongue-in-cheek, he expanded on his passion for motorcycling, a passion that he would indulge almost all his life. He spun a tale about how the ancient Chinese invented this contraption and he provided a deadpan explanation of the scientific principles behind the motorcycle's roar. "Those ingenious Chinese, combining the principle of combustion with that of the rocket, had conceived of a mechanism that would be driven by the essence of banana and the juice of baked beans." And, in case anyone didn't believe him, he countered the incredulous with this observation: "Historical proofs have always left a few skeptics." Marvelling at the perfection of this machine, he concluded with a straight face that "man was designed to meet the needs of motorcycling: his nostrils, which open downwards, and his ears which adhere to the head, allow an optimum acceleration without stirring up an excess of wind or dust. . . . To be perfectly frank: the bike is steered by its two handles; and that is why we have two hands."

Trudeau has often been depicted as a cold and solitary individual. He communicated a different impression when he expressed his appreciation for this "authentic brotherhood of motorcyclists who have only one law, that of coming to the rescue of each other, and whose most distinctive gesture is to wave. . . . What shared emotion serves as the bond between them? Only a motorcyclist can tell. . . . You who praise team sports . . . tell me, is there a sport where friendship is as satisfying?" He described his delight in the varied scenery, in the speed, in the random stops. The motorcycle's speed, he maintained, communicates a feeling of serenity, "a high, or, better still, a quietude of the soul." The motorcycle shared this with some other sports in that it "frees the spirit; the body, abandoned to its own resources, learns anew to think." His choice of words about freeing the spirit and relearning how to think, suggest a need in him to feed his spirit from new sources. Trudeau, it seemed, was no longer eager to accumulate more information, but rather wanted to

relearn how to think. He had reached a wall, an impasse, and he was suffering. He felt the need to explore a different dimension, even if he didn't
yet know how.

Along with the article, Trudeau provided an incongruous photograph
that had been taken by his friend Charles Lussier. There he was, riding
pillion on a motorcycle. Stretched out in front of the bike was his friend
Roger Rolland. Trudeau explained the photo as illustrating "a punishment that the Northern Chinese mete out to marauding mandarins. . . .
What you see is a professional assassin and an amateur executioner about
to crush the brain of a condemned, who will arise alive from the ordeal
on condition that he have no brain." He went on to wonder: "I can only
guess whether or not this Chinese torture would prove fatal to people I
have known . . ." He might have been thinking of university students and
leaders of the Bloc populaire. What is obvious is that he has turned away
from the driving political militancy that had possessed him so frantically.
He was pausing now, waiting to set off in a new direction.

Over the three months that followed "Pritt Zoum Bing," Trudeau compiled notes on seven books. Only two dealt with issues of economics or
politics. He seemed to be moving toward a greater appreciation of
authors writing in English. About Thomas Hardy's novel *Jude the
Obscure* he wrote that it carried descriptions of tragic situations rendered so powerfully that "these events are more anguishing and poignant
than anything I have ever encountered until now in books."[17] He was also
impressed with another classic, Nathaniel Hawthorne's novel *The Scarlet
Letter*. "It is such a novel as the English (and this American) were writing
in the last century. . . . I think that it is a great book."[18] He also read two
short stories for children published in 1944 by the young French-Canadian
author Andrée Maillet: *Le Marquiset têtu et le mulot réprobateur*, and *Les
aventures de la Princesse Claradore*. Andrée Maillet would later be the
recipient of several important prizes for her books. His comments on
Maillet's early stories indicate that his perspective on literature was beginning to change. Until now, he had seemed convinced of the superiority of
the French mind when it came to literature or analytical thought. But now
he wrote: "The style is easy, brilliant, witty," although he also noted,
"We are a long way from the power of *The Man Who Was Thursday* or

of the dazzling style of *Alice in Wonderland*."[19] Perhaps it was unfair for Trudeau to compare the work of Andrée Maillet, who was only twenty-three when she wrote these stories, to the giants of English literature. But it is interesting to note that he chose English authors rather than French to make his comparison.

In June 1944, Trudeau covered half a page with his notes on *La Grande peur dans la montagne* by the Swiss novelist Charles-Ferdinand Ramuz. Characteristically, he wrote on the reverse side of the very page where, two years earlier, in June 1942, he had described his reaction to another novel by the same author, *La Beauté sur la terre*. Of the earlier book he had commented: "I expect better from Ramuz." Now, he began his comments on *La Grande peur dans la montagne* with this observation: "Here, I believe, we have the human story that I was hoping for on the reverse side." Trudeau displayed a truly remarkable sense of organization and control over the constantly expanding world of his own written records.

In 1944, as well, Trudeau read two novels by Maurice Barrès, the nationalist, royalist, and anti-Semitic author who was so appreciated by his Jesuit teachers. In Chapter 3, we saw that Trudeau had made notes on this author while a student at Brébeuf. Now, in May, he read Barrès's *Les Déracinés*, the first volume of his trilogy, *Le roman de l'énergie nationale* (1897–1902), which urged fidelity to the native soil. Trudeau's notes on the book filled three pages: "A novel advancing a thesis to prove what social mischief was caused by the education system of the Third Republic. . . . The novel makes no attempt to hide the fact that it is a thesis." He found stylistic weaknesses: "The thought process, at first so French, soon goes on too long and detracts from the unity." Nevertheless, he was in admiration before "the superhuman dramatic power of Barrès." In October, Trudeau went on to read *Un jardin sur l'Oronte*, published in 1922. He only put down a few lines of comments, though they were appreciative: "A beautiful story of tragic love. . . . The style is entirely pure and ethereal." Trudeau admired Barrès's talent as a writer. But he made not a single comment about his extremist political views.

And so Trudeau continued to read right-wing authors in the tradition of Charles Maurras: not only Barrès, but also Jacques Bainville and Lucien Romier. There was a difference, though. He no longer expressed the same fulsome enthusiasm for their politics. It will be recalled, from

Chapter 8, how Trudeau marvelled in February 1942 when he read Jacques Bainville's *Les Conséquences politiques de la paix*, and declared it to be "a remarkable example of what wisdom, perspicacity and calculation can accomplish in the area of politics." But it was a different story when, in April 1944, Trudeau read Bainville's posthumous book, *L'Angleterre et l'Empire britannique*. It brought together collected articles that had appeared in newspapers or periodicals before the author's death in 1936. Trudeau was unimpressed with the formula, finding that many of the items stood up badly to the test of time. But his criticism went further: "The Bainville you find here is not the historian with a broad vision, but the right-wing journalist. And the political animus that permeates his patriotism often leads him into an unpleasant conservatism." That was quite a reversal of perspective in a period of twenty-six months.

In May 1944, he read *Problèmes économiques de l'heure présente*, the compilation of a series of lectures that Lucien Romier had delivered in 1932 as a visiting professor at the Hautes Études Commerciales, the business and management institution of the Université de Montréal. The author was an economist, historian, and journalist. Two years after his sojourn in Montreal, he took over as co-editor of the Paris daily *Le Figaro*, along with Pierre Brisson. Their paths were to diverge during the war. In the summer of 1940, Romier quit the newspaper to join Marshal Pétain, who appointed him a minister of state in the Vichy regime on August 11, 1941. When Romier died in January 1944, Pétain attended his funeral. The fact that he had been invited to lecture in Montreal was an indication of the often close links between the French-Canadian intellectual elite and the thinkers who would rally to the Vichy regime. Brisson, on the other hand, suspended publication of the *Figaro* rather than submit to German occupation censorship. The *Figaro* would only reappear after the liberation of Paris in 1944.

When Trudeau read *Problèmes économiques*, Romier had already died, after being one of Pétain's close collaborators. And yet, Trudeau made no comment on the author's later career when he wrote down his notes on the book, perhaps because the lectures were given well before the war. But now Trudeau was exposed to a treatise on the economy that was far more rigorous than what he had previously been used to. "It is a serious book, that discusses frankly and honestly the facts of the economic world. . . . It provides, above all, a method of study inspired by observation, clarity and simplicity." Trudeau was used to discussions on the economy that were dominated by religious and resentful nationalist considerations. He now had to reflect on ideas that were new to him. He noted the benefits of free trade, which had made of the nineteenth century "the century of rapid progress." Economic nationalism, by contrast, had ruinous consequences. He quoted the author: "The excess of protection results in the technical retardation of industry." And he went on to add, between parentheses: "(Our protection lies in our genius for invention.)" And, as was his practice, he made a link between what he read and his reading of the contemporary situation: "This chapter certainly applies to Quebec."

Years later, he would return to this thought and argue that Quebec did not need a crutch to fulfill itself. But, given his own background then, he was struck by the fact that Romier did not advocate the corporatist model, but rather "a capitalism that is more honest, less hypocritical, one which would rehabilitate true liberalism and free trade."

Trudeau's views were perceptibly changing. His convictions about the need for corporatism and revolution were shaken. He had not yet adopted an entirely opposite approach, but at least he was considering new directions.

---

In June of 1944, Trudeau published an article that was inspired by his great canoe adventure of the summer of 1941. It appeared in the *Journal des Jeunesses étudiantes* and was titled "Asceticism in a Canoe."[20] As we related in Chapter 7, Trudeau had written to François Hertel a bittersweet account after his return from Hudson Bay. But time softens the memory of hardships. Writing now, almost three years after the event, Trudeau makes light of the difficulties to remember only what a marvellous experience he had when he communed with nature. "Travel a thousand miles by train and you are a brute; pedal five hundred on a bicycle and you remain basically a bourgeois; paddle a hundred in a canoe and you are already a child of nature."[21] In his *Quartier Latin* article, "Pritt Zoum Bing," Trudeau maintained that the motorcycle freed the spirit and so taught one to "relearn how to think." In this later piece he pushes that idea further. He admires the purifying and liberating power of canoeing:

"What sets a canoeing expedition apart is that it purifies you more rapidly and inescapably than any other. . . . For it is a condition of such a trip that you entrust yourself, stripped of your worldly goods, to nature. . . . To remove all the useless material baggage from a man's heritage is, at the same time, to free his mind from petty preoccupations, calculations and memories."[22]

For Trudeau, thought must guide action. So, when he sat down to write this article, perhaps ground down by months of pointless discussions, he appreciated the communion between body and mind that was fostered by voyaging in a canoe: "You return not so much a man who reasons more, but a more reasonable man. For, throughout this time, your mind has learned to exercise itself in the working conditions which nature intended. Its primordial role has been to sustain the body in the struggle against a powerful universe. A good camper knows that it is more important to be ingenious than to be a genius. And conversely, the body, by demonstrating the true meaning of sensual pleasure, has been of service to the mind."[23]

Trudeau exhibited in this piece a passion and a warmth that ran counter to the stereotypical view of him as cold and distant: "How can you describe the feeling which wells up in the heart and stomach as the canoe finally rides up on the shore of the campsite? . . . The canoe is also a school of friendship. You learn that your best friend is not a rifle, but someone who shares a night's sleep with you. . . . You watch your friend stumbling over logs, sliding on rocks . . . yet never letting go of the rope. . . . When this same man has also fed you exactly half his catch, and has made a double portage because of your injury, you can boast of having a friend for life, and one who knows you well."[24]

In a canoe, he continued, "the mind conforms to that higher wisdom which we call natural philosophy; later, that healthy methodology and acquired humility will be useful in confronting mystical and spiritual questions."[25] He did not consider the asceticism required by a canoe trip to be primarily a source of suffering. In the end, he considered that it brings the canoeist to a state of "blessed torpor" similar to "what the mystics of the East are seeking." For once, as he unfolded his ode to nature and to friendship, Trudeau abstained from any hint of sarcasm or irony.

In the event, the serenity which pervaded "Asceticism in a Canoe" would prove short-lived. In that same month when the piece was published, Trudeau commented at length on a federal government document that he described simply as the *Senate Report on BNA Act (1939)*,[26] but which carries an official title that requires three lines.[27] Its author, William F. O'Connor, was a legal expert and parliamentary counsel to the Senate. He had been asked to examine the legal foundations of the British North America Act. We shall refer to his study as the O'Connor Report. This study was conducted at the same time as the Rowell-Sirois Royal Commission, announced in August 1937 by the King government, in the midst of the Depression. In the United States, Franklin Roosevelt's New Deal had drawn the U.S. government to intervene dramatically in the economy. The Rowell-Sirois Commission had a similar aim for Canada and the O'Connor study was meant to confirm its constitutional propriety.

After Rowell-Sirois submitted its report in 1940, its proposals were considered at a federal-provincial conference in January 1941. They would have transferred to the federal government jurisdiction over social assistance. All the provinces recognized the centralizing effect on the federation of such a transfer. But, while Manitoba, Saskatchewan, and the Maritime provinces were favourable, the other English-speaking provinces were strongly opposed. In Quebec, the Liberal government of Adélard Godbout, closely allied with the King government in opposition to Maurice Duplessis's anti-war Union Nationale, hesitated. In fact, responsibility for unemployment insurance was transferred to Ottawa in 1940 by an amendment to the BNA Act and the federal government launched other social programs in the following years, such as a national old-age pension plan. But then, and ever since then, Quebec's nationalist intelligentsia would condemn what they considered an intrusion on the autonomy and jurisdiction of the Quebec government.

Trudeau, characteristically, recorded his opposition to the centralizing implications of the O'Connor Report: "As was to be expected, the study tends to centralization." He wrote, "as was to be expected," because he was at one with Michel Chartrand in his speech backing Drapeau, and with every proper nationalist, yesterday and today, in considering that "Ottawa" translates as "centralizer." Trudeau read the O'Connor Report in this light, even though it merely provided an historical analysis of the distribution of powers under the BNA Act, without making recommendations. Trudeau's reading of the report might also have been influenced by the general consensus on the centralizing character of the Rowell-Sirois recommendations.

Still, even though his political vision at that time was entirely premised on nationalism, Trudeau was compelled to recognize the fine analytical quality of the report. He demonstrated his ambivalence by following every positive appreciation with a critical comment. And so the words, "a serious study," were immediately countered by adding: "which betrays a *desire* for impartiality." Presumably, the desired impartiality was never achieved, though Trudeau nowhere presented his evidence for that failure. He praised the "Arguments which are occasionally original," only to add: "which all support a determinedly centralizing position." Likewise, while granting that the plan of the report was "rather well thought through," still "there are many verbose passages and the logic often is anything but clear." The report itself covered only fourteen pages, but its five appendices ran to hundreds of pages and included numerous submissions, usually of a legal nature, from both individuals and institutions. So it was hardly surprising that verbose and repetitive passages were to be found and that some analyses fell short of clarity.

After his initial ambivalent comments, Trudeau set out in search of the proof that the BNA Act, Canada's founding statute, was itself "founded on a fraud." In this enterprise he again showed his ambivalence. Each time that he thought he had discovered a fraud, he also noted an argument that countered such a conclusion. By and large, whenever he found reason to condemn some decision taken by Great Britain with respect to the union of its North American provinces, he soon had to revise his judgment and concede that it had behaved properly. The net result was a sinuous critique that sometimes fell into contradictions. It suggested that his attitude was beginning to waver with respect to "truths" that he had taken until then as given. We shall observe the twists and turns of his thinking.

O'Connor recalled that, at the Quebec conference of October 1864, the delegates of the provinces had only the "authority to discuss, but without authority to conclude or arrange, a union of all the provinces of British North America."[28] And he continued: "No proposals of Union of those provinces were ever presented to them, and the so-called compact of confederation is non-existent."[29] His report argued that the provinces never did conclude a compact for the simple reason that they lacked the power to do so, and no proposal for a compact was ever on the table. Oddly, though, Trudeau understood that "the thesis of the book is that the provinces made a compact between them, but that compact was never ratified." How could he have made an interpretation so contrary to O'Connor's plain argument? Obviously Trudeau, as an unswerving nationalist, was so fully convinced that the BNA Act was the product of a compact among the provinces that he could not imagine a contrary viewpoint, even when it was clearly put forward before his eyes.

This interpretation was to prevail in Quebec's nationalist circles down to the present. Recently, the historian Stéphane Paquin, who declares himself to be a nationalist, nonetheless demonstrated convincingly that "the various forms of the compact theory (between provinces or between two founding peoples) constitute historical falsehoods."30 But the compact theory has proven to be a difficult nut to crack. Paquin lays out a few examples: "[Historian] André Champagne, in his preface to Jacques Lacoursière, *Histoire populaire du Québec, 1841 à 1896*, presents the compact theory as an unquestionable fact. . . . In 1995, Claude Ryan puts forward the compact theory between two founding peoples as obvious. . . . More recently, Professor Alain-G. Gagnon of McGill University justified his commitment to sovereignty by the fact that the compact had been violated."31 Paquin asserted that "these theories are not the product of a search for the truth. They were invented, wholly or in part, to invoke the authority of history in defence of a thesis invented for the purpose of political mobilization."32

The day would come when Trudeau would also denounce the myth of the "founding compact." In 1944, though, he would believe in it with such conviction that he was unable to read correctly what O'Connor wrote. And, under his assumption of an original compact, he considered any change to it without the consent of the people of Canada to be a "fraud." And that is exactly what took place, he asserted: "They changed it, they drafted a different wording which the Imperial Parliament then passed, without first submitting it to the Canadian people," and that, despite the fact that "all the parties to the contract [had indicated] their constant interest in the revising of the Confederation [bill] before it was passed into law." But he had no sooner written these lines than he added: "The Imperial Parliament was all-powerful [*sic*]; why pay attention to these colonials?" So his commitment to truth forced him to recognize that England was not at all obligated to submit the bill to the approval of its colonials. He had not yet succeeded in demonstrating the "fraud" of the BNA Act, but he did not give up.

Pressing on with his reading, he noticed that it was said in one of the appendices that Nova Scotia had humbly requested the Crown – "Our prayer to your Majesty" – not to make a change to the province's constitution without submitting it to the approval of the population. Once again, though, Trudeau was misinterpreting what he read. O'Connor made it clear that the request to the Crown did not come from the government of Nova Scotia, but from a minority of the parliamentarians. In fact, he asserted, "overwhelming majorities of both branches of the Legislature"[33] backed the position of the Nova Scotia government. Under the misapprehension that the request came from the province, Trudeau wrote: "But nothing happened. London decided to act in conjunction with emissaries sent by the provinces." In this case as well, he felt that he had to admit that "you can hardly blame them [the government of the U.K.] for choosing this expeditious solution. It was up to the Canadian politicians to be more insistent on a matter of such importance. But they preferred to fool the people by pretending that what was passed was pretty much the Quebec resolutions." Logically, he might have concluded that, since the questionable decision was taken by the politicians who were the legitimate representatives of the Canadian people, he was in no position to claim that the BNA Act was based on a fraud. But he was not ready to come to that conclusion.

After writing the above, Trudeau drew his own conclusions in a passage he entitled "Essay." He wrote: "Quebec wanted a compact. London changed its terms without consulting. Therefore the compact does not exist. There is nothing but a coercive law. Therefore the parties to the compact are not bound by the compact. Therefore they may act just as they choose (that means disobeying an imperial law, but is one bound to obey a law that is unjust?")

It is possible that, in this "essay," he was sketching out some thoughts to be pursued and developed at a later day, on whether an insurrection was morally justified in the case of a compact that has been violated. It brings to mind the questions raised by Groulx on the same issue in his history class. Despite the contrary arguments that Trudeau himself put forward,

Trudeau wanted to find a moral justification for the French Canadians to disobey, and even for revolution. He wanted to believe that, because the founding contract of Canada was unjust, it became null and void.

When Trudeau read Appendix 5 of the O'Connor Report, which dealt with the Statute of Westminster, a thought struck him for the first time: "As the Imperial Parliament conferred this statute on us, it could just as well confer another on us at will, where it would enact, for example: 'Notwithstanding anything in section 4 of the Statute of Westminster . . . ,' we will *impose* on Canada such and such a measure without its consent." And that was how he became conscious of Canada's political dependence on Great Britain, given the fact that the Statute of Westminster was just another law. He reasoned: "*In law*, the Empire has total power since the Parliament could rescind tomorrow a law passed yesterday: it does not have the power to bind itself." And he concluded: "It is because of Section 7 of the Statute of Westminster that Canada is unable on its own to amend its Constitution."

He was realizing, probably for the first time in his life, that until such time as Canada had total control over its Constitution, including a means of amending it, it would remain constitutionally a British colony. This recognition provoked in him a line of thought that could be considered prophetic: "It occurs to me that, some day, it would be an excellent thing to conclude a treaty in which England and Canada were the parties, and where the attitude of the second party made manifest that it was entering into the contract on the basis of equality."

That passing thought would become reality on April 17, 1982, and Trudeau would be its architect. With the patriation of the Constitution negotiated, as he had hoped, as between equals, Canada finally achieved its total independence from England.

The four pages of notes that he devoted to the O'Connor Report reveal a gradual change of attitude in Trudeau. While it cannot be said that he had abandoned his nationalist and revolutionary commitment, he clearly was beginning to take an interest in constitutional reforms with respect to Canada.

———◈———

Until now, Trudeau's reading and writing had mostly concentrated on Quebec. What could have induced him to take an interest in the federation? In June of 1944, he wrote out a draft that he titled "Notes for a speech on the country's administration"34 that provides an answer. He was preparing to deliver a speech on behalf of the Bloc populaire, which was preparing to run candidates in both federal and provincial elections, on a platform of defending the autonomy of Quebec, threatened in particular by the centralizing proposals of the Rowell-Sirois Commission. It was likely in preparation for this speech that Trudeau had decided to read the O'Connor Report, in order to have a better grasp of the Constitution and its distribution of jurisdictions between the federal government and the provinces.

When Trudeau had given a political speech previously, in support of the candidacy of Jean Drapeau in November 1942, he had been at the height of his revolutionary frenzy, proposing to "impale the traitors alive" and "eviscerate the damn bourgeois of Outremont." He had rejected "band-aids" in favour of "cataclysms." But now it was 1944. What would be his message about "the country's administration"?

He again attacked the King government but, this time, without the same fire. He still opposed the war, but this time with qualifications. "If we are able to help out other countries, so much the better. But not countries which are bigger and richer." It had been the argument of the Ligue pour la défense du Canada that Canada, a small country, had no need to come to the aid of big countries, like England and the United States. Until the very end of hostilities, the Bloc populaire would remain opposed to the war. Trudeau repeated that message, but without his earlier virulence: "You were blue [Conservative or Union Nationale], you were red [Liberal], but you didn't want the war. Show that you have a sense of honour, that you demand respect for the promises of peace."

He went after the King government for its misplaced priorities: "You complain that the government is not helping out the country and they reply that they are saving the world, democracy . . . Fine, but that was not why they were elected. What we ask of the government is that it govern. And to govern means to bestow well-being on the governed. To provide bread, housing, clothing, work. A family salary." His tone had changed, but he retained still a communitarian vision of the state as a good father whose duty it is to bring happiness to its people. He wrote in the margin beside his last sentence: "This is the sign of its morality."

As a good father toward its family, the government, Trudeau insisted, must "tighten its belt a little," put on "clothes that have been mended." Instead of lavishing money "on the war, on whiskey, on sumptuous roads, on the elected representatives, on senators and the advisers," it should use the money to "hand on an unencumbered country, without a mortgage, to the children." But, since the government is failing to fulfill its responsibilities, "it is now time to put the house back in order. To change the steward." Back in 1942, his solution for changing the steward was revolution and doing away with the traitors. Now, in 1944, the message has changed. "I am not calling for a revolution. I am not saying that we absolutely must do in the traitors. But you must at least have enough pride to act yourselves. Vote against the Bloc if you think that justice requires it. But how could that be the path of justice? You don't know them, while you have seen the traitors at work."

Now it was the path of democracy that Trudeau explored as he rec-ommended that people vote for the Bloc. He remained a nationalist and still called on French Canadians to unite. But the racist dimension of this call had begun to cause him qualms. "I am not appealing to racism. But the race must save itself." He still sees no way out of the dilemma. It will take several more years before he would discover a solution to the problems of Quebec and its minorities that was not based on "race" or ethnicity.

He has come a long way from the inflammatory speeches of the past. This measured discourse was given two months before the elections of August 1944 and seemed intended to support the Bloc generally, rather than designate a particular candidate. He was calling on the citizens to vote for change, and for a better quality of candidates to bring change about: "Vote for men who are up to it. If there are none, refuse to vote. Run as candidates yourselves. Go out in search of competent people. There are many worthy people who would accept. But get organized, protest, get moving."

We can't be certain whether he ever delivered this speech. If his objective was to rally the multitudes in support of the Bloc, it was hardly a barnburner. Nowhere in the speech did he offer a single concrete per-suasive argument in favour of the party. He was simply asking the voters to give the Bloc a chance. Unlike in 1942 when he spoke with passion for a cause, now he sounded more like someone reminding people to do their civic duty by attending to public affairs. It would seem that Trudeau's enthusiasm for the Bloc had cooled considerably.

———※———

About the time when Trudeau published "The Ascetic in a Canoe" and wrote out the text of a speech, elsewhere on planet Earth the war had reached a turning point: the Allies landed on the shores of Normandy on June 6, 1944. One would never have known it from the election campaign waged by the Bloc Populaire. In his book *La Crise de la conscription*, André Laurendeau quoted an article that appeared in the party's paper, *Le Bloc*, on May 27, 1944, which reported that a member of the Royal Canadian Mounted Police had shot dead a young deserter. Laurendeau explained that this event was exploited in the Bloc's propaganda; it presented itself "as the watchdog, as the instrument of the French Canadians' legitimate revenge against their unworthy masters." The conclusion of the article was an appeal to the people. "We will put an end to the nightmare of the old parties, to establish at last a regime that is national and social, that will treat men as men and will not track them down like beasts."[35] To the very end of the war, the Bloc would remain silent about the suffering of the millions of war victims, while finding beyond endurance the suffering of French Canadians. It is remarkable, as well, that as late as 1944, the Bloc still put side by side the words *national* and *social*, which evoked the national-socialism of Hitler.

Despite such insensitivity, the Bloc was enjoying considerable success. Laurendeau wrote that their election rallies drew enthusiastic crowds: "the masses that we encountered in these meetings which had become, once again, enthusiastic, shared our feelings, which our adversary characterized as criminal demagogy."[36] Even after D-Day, the Bloc candidates continued to denounce conscription in terms that some would stigmatize as pro-fascist. For example, Mason Wade, the author of a classic history of the French Canadians, declared that the Bloc's candidate in the riding of Maisonneuve, Jacques Sauriol, had delivered a speech at Saint-Eustache on July 2, 1944, in which he said: "Five years have now gone by in which we have been told repeatedly of the threat of Fascism and Nazism. Have you seen Mussolini in Canada? You have not. But you have seen King and Churchill."[37] Jacques Sauriol was then investigated by the ministry of justice.[38]

Paul-André Comeau confirms that the Bloc came under criticism as being pro-fascism. "Dostaler O'Leary, a Bloc candidate in the 1945 federal elections, went so far as to find excuses for fascism and even approve of it in his work on separatism. Another candidate, Jean Mercier, was accused of having been active within Adrien Arcand's [fascist] party. So that was enough for the accusations of fascism to be raised against the Bloc from the start."[39]

The leaders of the Bloc who accepted that Dostaler O'Leary should run as a candidate must have known of his Anglophobia and his anti-Semitism. He wrote in 1935 in his *L'Inferiority Complex*: "The Anglo-Saxon, whether he be from the United States or Britain, is the man of the big schemes. . . . He is also the man of the 'trusts,' of the super-capitalized businesses . . .; with the Jew, he can boast that he monopolizes the monopolies."[40] Faced with the inappropriate statements of some candidates, André Laurendeau was forced to counter-attack in order to ward off the association with extremism that attached to his party.[41]

That reputation was hurting the Bloc. As late as July 1944, the opinion polls projected a bright future for the party. But, in the provincial elections of August 8, it won only 16 per cent of the vote and four seats, which included that of Laurendeau. The election was won by Maurice Duplessis's Union Nationale even though it received only 29 per cent of the vote, while Godbout's Liberals took 40 per cent. The lopsided result was generally attributed to the fact that English-speakers were concentrated in only a few ridings. The poor performance of the Bloc was explained, according to some observers, by the verbal radicalism of some candidates, which frightened off the voters.[42] Others, notably Michael Behiels, blamed the defeat on the quarrels among the party leaders.[43] Lionel Groulx, bitterly disappointed, put the blame on his people, forever unable to unite even for a good cause. He had hoped that the "old parties" would be forever wiped out. "It was demonstrated once again that the Quebec people is the one that, in all of Canada, has the least political and national education. . . . The French Canadians are more divided than ever. They replaced one ham actor by another ham actor."[44] Whatever the explanation, the fact remains that the Bloc took a beating from which it would never recover.

Trudeau had witnessed the internal quarrels between the leaders even before the party was put to the electoral test for the first time. He

remained an active member, but with reservations. In fact, he was not in
Quebec to witness the Bloc's discomfiture. On April 6, 1944, he received
permission from the military authorities to absent himself for the
purpose of study. He was relieved of military training until September 15,
1944.⁴⁵ Then, on May 16, he was granted permission to be away from
Canada from June 12 until September 15.⁴⁶ He was part of a contingent
of one hundred students sponsored by the University of Montreal to
spend the summer in Mexico studying Spanish. The trip had been organized by an organization founded by the aforementioned Dostaler O'Leary,
the Union des Latins d'Amérique. O'Leary had been a long-time supporter
of an independent Laurentie and, as we have seen, was on the fringe of the
extreme right. His aim was to create closer links with the countries of
Latin America that were favourable to his ideology. According to Mason
Wade, the party publication, *Le Bloc*, would have been in favour of the
creation of a pan-American alliance that would enable the countries of
Latin America to unite against "Jewish-American finance."⁴⁷ So it happened that Trudeau was away in Mexico both for the Quebec elections of
August 8 and the liberation of Paris on August 25, 1944.

It is hardly surprising that, for the months of July and August, we found
reading notes on only two books, one of which deserves notice. Trudeau
would fill four pages with his comments on *Pouvoir: les génies invisibles
de la Cité*. The author, Guglielmo Ferrero, was an Italian historian and
philosopher who became known for his fierce opposition to fascism. In
1929, he was forced into exile and took up a teaching position at the
University of Geneva. He died in Switzerland in 1942. "This book tries
to establish the dynamics that underlie all political upheavals," Trudeau
wrote. "Trouble starts as soon as an illegitimate government takes power
in any country. In other words, peace can only be present when governments are legitimate. Here is his argument: a legitimate government is
one that has the sanction of time and of tradition. The illegitimate government does not enjoy such a sanction; it fears to be overthrown; it
takes defensive measures, it provokes reactions, revolutions, wars."

This must have come as a shock to Trudeau: Ferrero was pointing
out the problem of legitimacy that would accompany any revolution.
And so he wrote down several of the author's sentences: "The power that

was conquered by a coup d'État has the diabolical capacity to terrify the one who seized it before terrifying the others. . . . A legitimate government is a government that has freed itself of fear. . . . Totalitarianism is nothing more than the externalization of the fear that torments the revolutionary government." Now, these were perspectives likely to unsettle the young man and to further undermine his revolutionary fervour. Until then, he had not anticipated any particular problem in carrying out his corporatist revolution, because he was satisfied that its objective was as moral as could be, that is, the common Good. He had thought that once power had been seized, he and his brothers in arms would be in a position to do Good. He had not entertained the possibility of dissension and corruption within their own ranks, or that the people might choose not to recognize the legitimacy of their coup. It had never occurred to him that fear could drive them to a dictatorship.

This book cast doubt on his previous convictions. Though he found weaknesses here and there, he was obliged to recognize the cogency of Ferrero's argument. "And so this book *is clearly anti-revolutionary*, impartial, a little bizarre, rather wordy in its style and often off base. But the plan of the work is clear and *it contains great ideas* . . . I have to admit that Ferrero clarifies many historical problems, especially those dealing with revolutions." Trudeau was disturbed by his discovery. He was able to see, probably for the first time, the potentially disastrous consequences that could attend a revolution, even one that was approved by the Church. Another disillusion was added to the previous ones.

He must have had the feeling that all his political agitation had led him nowhere. When he sang the praises of the motorcycle,[48] he called it the "perfect escapist instrument" and expressed the need to "relearn to think." And that is what he now set about to do. On September 12, 1944, just as soon as he was back from Mexico, he made another attempt to register at Harvard University and, as a first step, he applied to the government for permission to leave the country:

I now propose to undertake advanced studies in economics and political science at Harvard University in Cambridge, Massachusetts. That is why I am asking that the Commission postpone my military training until December 22, 1944, and also asking permission to be absent from Canada until that date. . . .

I am without pretension, as also without humility. I make no special claims just because I scored first in the province at the Bar exams, and that I was also first of my graduating class when I finished my studies at Collège de Brébeuf, and the first among those who obtained a licentiate degree in Law at the Université de Montréal, having obtained these two pig parchments with great distinction.

But, at the same time, I see no reason for thinking that my request deserves less consideration than that of many others.

And that is the thought that encourages me to send you this request with confidence.

Yours obediently and attentively.[49]

On October 8, while he still awaited an answer, he wrote Harvard University for application forms.[50] On October 13, he filled out the forms and, in answer to question 13, wrote out an explanation for his choice. We shall come to his reply presently. Meanwhile, on October 18, 1944, he was granted permission to be absent from Canada from October 22, 1944 to January 22, 1945.[51] On that same day, he received permission to postpone his military training until April 18, 1945. In the meantime, on October 16, Harvard sent him his acceptance for the winter session, which was to begin on November 1.

———◦———

Early in October, Trudeau wrote down seven pages of notes on *An Inquiry Into the Nature and Causes of the Wealth of Nations* by the father of economic liberalism, Adam Smith.[52] The book was on his reading list for a course he intended to take at Harvard. On every page, Trudeau expressed his appreciation for what he read: "A beautiful example of creative thinking . . . It exudes productive thoughts and a kind of *inspiration*." It was as though he was discovering Smith for the first time. And yet, during his last year at Brébeuf he had received a mark of 97.6 per cent for a course on economics. He must, surely, have had

Adam Smith on the program. Then, at his fall session of 1941 in the law faculty at the Université de Montréal, he took a course in political economy from Professor Édouard Montpetit, who served as the secretary general of the university from 1920 to 1950. Montpetit (1881–1954), who was both a lawyer and an economist, had founded the university's l'École des sciences sociales économiques et politiques. A street, a subway stop, and a building of the Université de Montréal have all been named in his honour. On September 21, 1981, Canada Post issued a stamp commemorating his birth. So highly qualified a professor could hardly have ignored the inevitable Adam Smith.

Indeed, the course outline in Trudeau's archives[53] indicate that Smith was, in fact, on the program. Three traditions of economic theory were there laid out. The first, which included such liberal thinkers as Adam Smith, John Stuart Mill, and David Hume, was summarily dismissed as being entirely centred on the individual. The second tradition, which included socialism and communism, was quickly and categorically rejected on the grounds of going too far and being statist. Only the third tradition, that of the École sociale catholique inspired by Leo XIII and Pius XI, deserved to be approved. It was titled: "The remedy: the Catholic social doctrine." Professor Montpetit presented corporatism as the ideal and the middle way between the individualist and statist models. His approach raises a question: was he teaching the fundamentals of economics or preaching an ideology? How could he present "corporatism" as the superior economic tradition when its scientific assumptions were so primitive and it had been put in practice in none but fascist countries?

No wonder that Trudeau, from his first arrival at Harvard, began to recognize the enormous failings of the instruction he had received at the Université de Montréal. His own plan for a post-revolutionary society envisaged no other economic system than corporatism because all of those who were positioned as his intellectual mentors, whether Pope, Jesuit, or professor of political economy, preached with authority and conviction the unquestionable superiority of corporatism. So when he studied Adam Smith on his own, in 1944, it was a revelation.

His notes on Smith were written, as usual, in French, even though he was reading the book in English. He admired Smith's overall approach: "All told, this work offers principally a method for thinking from the point of view of economics, and that constitutes its value." He saw the model's power for extending the analysis to social problems: "Smith initiates us in how to analyze the problems of society, he shows us how to grasp the interdependence of phenomena, he fashions a framework for sorting out the complexity of institutions and grasping the central issue." For Smith, as is well known, "the invisible hand" ensures that the individual's pursuit of wealth and of the satisfaction of personal interests will lead paradoxically to the progress and the improvement of the nation.

Did Trudeau immediately become a convert to economic liberalism thanks to his encounter with the munificence of the "invisible hand"? That seems hardly likely: he was typically careful about adopting a new perspective. But reading Smith clearly undermined some of his unquestioned assumptions, such as the superiority of the French analytical tradition. "True, this is English-style thinking and has perhaps not the compressed appearance of French thinking, where the principles are hard diamonds. *But I have learnt that there is not only the French way of being condensed.*" He had been brought up with the conviction that, so to speak, outside French thought there was no salvation. He does not now shed his admiration for that French tradition, but he has discovered that "English-style thinking," namely the empirical method of Adam Smith, can also come up with diamonds.

He found that Smith would sometimes give a twist to phenomena to make them fit into his scheme. Still, he granted: "He does not practise this to the point of abuse, and he is never in bad faith. *The system came after the study of the facts, and did not drive it.* Moreover, Smith himself never claims to have attained the Absolute, and in his detailed study of the mechanisms, he never fails to observe that, in this or the other circumstance, liberalism is not practicable." Implicitly, and perhaps without fully realizing it, Trudeau was contrasting Smith's empiricism, which took as its starting point concrete facts to end with a theoretical system, with the scholastic method of the Jesuits, which took as its starting point a pre-established system postulated as True and Good because created by God, and with the facts made to fit in accordingly. At the age of twenty-five, he was delighted to discover the scientific method. He summarized Smith's principles, so different from everything he had been taught: "1. In man, the principle economic driving force is egotism. 2. The play of all the egotistical pursuits results in the common good. 3. Therefore, *laissez faire*: liberalism or non-interventionism." Trudeau was learning for the first time that egotism was not necessarily an evil. It could serve a social purpose in making the economy operate more efficiently.

For Smith, the state's responsibility is no longer to intervene in order to impose the common good, it is now to guarantee to each person freedom and security. Trudeau quoted Smith: "The natural effort of every individual to better his own condition, when suffered to exert itself with freedom and security, is so powerful a principle, that it is alone, and without any assistance, not only capable of carrying on the society to wealth and prosperity, but of surmounting a hundred impertinent obstructions with which the folly of human laws too often encumbers its operations." As he worked through Smith on his own, Trudeau did not choose for quotation the classic passage most cited to illustrate the beneficence of the invisible hand: "It is not from the benevolence of the butcher, the brewer, or the baker, that we expect our dinner, but from their regard to their own interest. We address ourselves, not to their humanity, but to their self-love, and never talk to them of our necessities but of their advantages."54 This passage illustrates how the individual pursues personal self-interest. The passage quoted by Trudeau brings out the need for government to intervene to create a framework of freedom and the security of the person, and the drag on social development when government regulates excessively.

According to Smith's model, each individual must be free to attend to his own interests. This thought caused Trudeau to discover a weakness of corporatism: "Danger of a corporatism that does not leave each individual free to choose his work." But then he qualified that: "Economic dangers, not political." Thereby he showed that he had not fully appreciated a concept that he had just admired, namely the interdependence of the various constituents of life in society. According to Smith, economic dangers will necessarily have political repercussions. While Trudeau was beginning to perceive, thanks to Smith, the threat to freedom that corporatism presents in the economic sphere, he continued to assume that the state would guarantee the freedom of the members of the corporations.

He was at the same time shaken by the devastating implications for corporatism, and delighted with the theory of supply and demand. "One begins to see how this marvelous instrument of equilibrium functions: the law of supply and demand, *which is so wisely developed throughout the book*." Now Trudeau could not have failed to recognize that "this marvelous instrument of equilibrium" needed no revolution in order to function. It did not require forming a new man or a new order. Then and there, the first section of the manifesto on which he had worked so hard had become redundant. Where was the need, now, for "The permanent struggle that the French Canadian will wage to ensure the triumph and then the maintenance of the Good in French Canadian society"? This formula represented a communitarian perspective according to which, since the Authority alone knew what was Good, it alone could ensure that it was achieved. *The Wealth of Nations* totally undercut what had been his postulate. Smith taught that the government can neither have the knowledge nor the capacity to achieve the common good. Its responsibility was much less ambitious but still essential, that is to ensure the freedom and security of its citizens. For everything else, the pursuit of self-interest and the invisible hand would be adequate.

And so it was that, as Trudeau reached the end of the period under consideration, he discovered a new way of thinking, the scientific method, and a new way of acting, through reform rather than revolution. The scientific method went against the approach that had hitherto been inculcated in him inasmuch as scientific discourse is never absolute, unlike the verities of the Church. But Trudeau advanced on this new path with caution. He wrote down the word *anti-Catholic*, without specifying to what he referred. For Adam Smith, liberalism implies separating the temporal from the spiritual, contrary to Catholic doctrine at that time. This could have been what Trudeau meant by "anti-Catholic."

The seed had been planted for the separation of Church and state. It would grow to maturity in time. Trudeau would never reject the universe of God and consequent absolutes, which he would approach through faith. But, when it came to temporal realities, he would apply empirical criteria and the scientific method.

---

On November 1, Trudeau would begin his studies at Harvard University. We shall follow his progress thereafter in Volume 2. But, before leaving him, we must consider the draft that he prepared in order to answer question 13 on his application forms. It required him to write an essay laying out his reasons for applying, and his personal qualifications. One notices immediately that Trudeau's writing in English cannot compare with the quality of his French. His essay includes awkward constructions, Gallicisms, and several mistakes in spelling; for instance, instead of marvellous, he wrote *marvaleous*. His draft shows that he started each sentence over several times. It is a fact that, throughout his life, Trudeau wrote more gracefully in French than in English.

He began by noting that he had taken courses in economics at both Brébeuf and the Université de Montréal, only to add: "But I dare say that more progress was made by personal studies of such political thinkers as Plato, Aristotle, Cicero, J.J. Rousseau, Adam Smith, Georges Sorel, Charles Maurras, Leon Trotsky, Aron-Dandieu, Maritain, Lucien Romier and many others. Montesquieu, J.S. Mill and Marx, I have already met, but thus far more superficially." He was telling the truth. We have seen his written observations on all of the authors he cited, with the exception of Cicero, who was translated extensively in all the classical colleges. Addressing the question of his motives, he replied that it would be more appropriate to ask a young man of twenty-five like him who always pursued instruction "with fondness and often with ardour," why he would not want to undertake graduate studies, especially when the opportunity presented itself to study with professors enjoying a great reputation.

He stated that his thirst for knowledge was unquenchable. "Such am I; to study pleases me, therefore I study." Sometimes, he acknowledged, to pursue one's pleasure was not the wisest course. But in his case, "pleasure would have suggested the very course I would have chosen out of mere duty. Verily, had I decided otherwise, I would have acted unwisely (though not without enjoyment). For in a young man the yearning for action is at times stronger than that for knowledge." There were times, he confessed, when his political activities, which he considered a duty, brought him more pleasure than his studies. Now, though, he has matured: "But the first to act is not always the wisest, and what is needlessly premature is useless. Besides there may be some truth in the aphorism: 'Avant 30 ans un homme n'est pas intelligent.' With such thoughts in mind, I easily refrain from accomplishing such little things as may be of more utility today in the hope that reflection and study may make my work fitter tomorrow." His words suggest that he has lost confidence in his revolutionary activities and his past political commitments. He now considers them premature and perhaps even harmful. Before again plunging into action, he wants to "relearn how to think."

Next, he is required to explain why he chose the study of "Political Economy and Government." He admits that what he is about to say could seem lacking in modesty, "for in a friend's ear alone can ambition enter along with modesty." But he will declare himself anyway: "I need not hide my conviction that Canada is decidedly lacking in statesmen. We French-Canadians in particular have too few political thinkers to lead us, and the sight of such splendid people going to ruin appalls me." This reaffirms his recent disenchantment with the political scene and the general absence of people with vision. He might have been recalling the hypocrisy of the university students, the failure to create a truly different political party, the petty internal quarrels of the leaders of the Bloc. And so he sees it as his duty to prepare himself for the future with a strong foundation in politics: "Let me assure you only this, that governments will still exist after the war. Therefore the work of all other men in a given nation – scientists, philosophers, artists, labourers, farmers – will profit to the nation or will go to waste, in direct ratio to the competency or the nullity of its politicians. At present, education and ardent will is producing men of sciences and of letters who will honour Canada in peace, even as her soldiers will have honoured her in war. But too few are training to serve the Res Publica directly. Should then the facilities of learning be refused even to these few?" He apparently believed that the education system in Canada, adequate in other respects, failed to produce politicians of the quality needed to fulfill their responsibilities.

A sentence in his essay was surprising. He spoke of "men of sciences and of letters who will honour Canada in peace, *even as her soldiers will have honoured her in war.*" Was this the same Trudeau who had raged against conscription and against any support for the war? It could be an indication that his perception of the war changed after the landing in Normandy and the liberation of Paris, and that he was becoming aware of the perverse dimensions of the "new order."

Trudeau concludes his essay with a truly remarkable avowal: "I shall make Statesmanship my profession and, if God permit, I shall know my profession well." *At the age of twenty-five, Trudeau knows that he is destined to be a statesman.* His prediction would be realized two decades later. And he would have kept his promise: he would have done his duty. He would prepare for his career meticulously, with immense determination and intelligence. He would go out and explore the many peoples of the planet. Always searching for the truth, he would learn and mature, broadening his vision as he grew.

*When the time came, he would be ready.*

# CONCLUSION

A LONG ESTABLISHED MYTH presents the image of a Pierre Trudeau who, even in his early years, was unable to submit to authority, who always rowed against the current, and who enjoyed irritating the other students and their teachers by his conspicuous anti-nationalism. Since such an attitude was so out of place, a range of explanations have been put forward, most of them from the field of psychology, to make sense of such an enigma. We hope this first volume of his biography will have laid to rest all such speculation by demonstrating that the enigma has always been nothing but a fiction. On the contrary, Pierre Trudeau, in his youth, was perfectly integrated into his social environment, he shared its most fundamental values, and he was the very exemplar of what a Jesuit education hoped to turn out.

Brilliant, earnest, taking to heart all the exhortations he received from his teachers, from his intellectual models, from the Church, he yearned for the establishment of a "new order" that would ensure the triumph of the common Good as defined by the Catholic Church. Always in harmony with the people around him, he rose to the defence of an ethnic and organic nationalism. That led him to commit himself, body and soul, to the planning for and preparation of a revolution to turn Quebec into an independent, Catholic, and French state. Trudeau was, unquestionably, a "son of Quebec" who was a credit to his teachers.

But resolving this enigma leaves us with another that is much more complicated: the Trudeau who is known to history is "the father of Canada," the father of a new understanding of Canadian identity, the father of multiculturalism, and of the Charter of Rights and Freedoms. That Trudeau is the passionate defender of liberal values who fought for the separation of Church and state, who vested in the law controversial measures that sometimes went against Catholic doctrine. The true mystery is how he travelled from a vision of the nation that was organic, ethnic, and communitarian, to the vision of a society that is based on citizenship, that is pluralist and liberal – a rare and difficult transition.

How was Trudeau able to go from that first perspective to its precise opposite, while still remaining deeply committed to his religion as a believing and practising Catholic, and without ever rejecting his identity as a French Canadian? What became of his early search for the True and the Good? Resolving this second mystery, no small undertaking, will be the subject of the second volume of our biography.

# ACKNOWLEDGEMENTS

We wish to thank all those who helped us carry to a conclusion an undertaking that, fascinating as it proved to be, still seemed at times beyond our strength. We give heartfelt thanks to Roy Heenan and Alexandre Trudeau, who placed their confidence in us by giving us access to the personal archives of Pierre Trudeau. We much appreciated the amiability, the competence, and the devotion of Christian Rioux, in charge of administering the Trudeau archive, of Michel Wyczynski and all the personnel dealing with national archives at Library and Archives Canada. Thanks to them, our work sessions there were both productive and pleasant.

Several people generously agreed to read the first draft of our book. Our thanks go to Pierre Billon, Bill Echard, Gwenda Echard, Marc Lalonde, Pierre Léon, and Monique Léon. Their judicious comments were very helpful for the final draft. Monique Perrin-d'Arloz generously translated many of our quotations, with the unfailing expertise for which she is recognized.

Our thanks to Suzette Rouleau (née Trudeau), to Thérèse Gouin, to Vianney Décarie, to Pierre Vadeboncœur, to Jean de Grandpré, and to Jacques Hébert. They had known Trudeau well when he was young, and were generous with their time as they shared with us their memories of him. We appreciated our interview with Jacques Monet, S.J., an expert on the educational system of the Jesuits. We extend our warmest thanks to Roger Rolland, who not only allowed himself to be interviewed several times, in person and by telephone, but who also made available personal letters that Trudeau had written to him. These letters, stretching over a great number of years, proved priceless.

We are grateful to the Éditions de l'homme for having undertaken to publish this book before they had seen the manuscript. We hope that they will have no reason to regret their gamble. We also thank Doug Gibson, publisher of Douglas Gibson Books at McClelland & Stewart, for his meticulous editing and for having made a heroic effort, with the aid of his colleagues, to publish the English version on an impossible timetable.

Our translator and friend, William Johnson, deserves special thanks. He not only turned out the English version while the French version was still a work in progress – with all the inevitable corrections, revisions, and frustrations – but he also generously put at our disposal the expertise that he has acquired during a long career as a writer and a journalist. He located for us useful documents, corrected errors, and suggested new lines of research. Thanks to him, too, we gained a better understanding of the education provided in its earlier years by Collège Jean-de-Brébeuf, which he began to attend in the year that Trudeau left. Also helpful was his familiarity with the Catholic Church of the past, which he acquired on the inside as a Jesuit studying for the priesthood. His outstanding commitment to our enterprise made a great contribution to the quality of our manuscript.

While we are very grateful to all those who helped us and put their trust in us, we accept full responsibility for any errors or omissions that sophisticated readers will doubtless discover.

Max and Monique Nemni

# NOTES

## Chapter 1: THE TRUDEAU ENIGMA

1 Quoted by Will Ferguson in *Bastards & Boneheads: Canada's Glorious Leaders Past and Present*, Douglas & McIntyre, 1999, p. 236.

2 André Potvin, Michel Letourneux and Robert Smith, *L'anti-Trudeau, Choix de textes*, Montreal, Éditions Parti Pris, 1972, p. 8.

3 *Le Devoir*, May 10, 1971, in *L'anti-Trudeau*, op. cit., p. 75.

4 *Le Devoir*, May 10, 1971, in *L'anti-Trudeau*, op. cit., p. 71.

5 Michel Vastel, *Trudeau le Québécois . . . mais la colombe avait des griffes de faucon*, Montreal, Les Éditions de l'Homme, 1989.

6 M. Vastel, *Trudeau*, op. cit., p. 59.

7 Michel Vastel, *The Outsider: The Life of Pierre Elliott Trudeau*, Toronto, Macmillan of Canada, 1990.

8 *Le Devoir*, May 10, 1971, in *L'anti-Trudeau*, p. 75.

9 *La Vigile du Québec*, "Octobre 1970: l'impasse?" Hurtubise HMH, Montreal, 1971, in *L'anti-Trudeau*, op. cit., p. 70.

10 Guy Laforest, *Trudeau et la fin d'un rêve canadien*, Québec, Les éditions du Septentrion, 1992, p. 15.

11 Léon Dion, *Québec 1945–2000*, tome II: *Les intellectuels et le temps de Duplessis*, Sainte-Foy, Les Presses de l'Université Laval, 1993, p. 200.

12 Kenneth McRoberts, *Quebec, Social Change and Political Crisis*, Oxford University Press, 1993 (3rd ed.), p. 338.

13 Graham Fraser, "As Quebec Premier, Charest Is a Man of Firsts," *Toronto Star*, Sunday, April 20, 2003.

14 Donald G. Lenihan, Gordon Robertson and Roger Tassé, *Reclaiming the Middle Ground*, Montreal, Institute for Research on Public Policy, 1994, p. v.

15 See, for example, *Reconfigurations, Canadian Citizenship and Constitutional Change*, Selected Essays by Alan Cairns, edited by Douglas E. Williams, Toronto, McClelland & Stewart Inc., 1995, p. 431.

16  Stephen Clarkson and Christina McCall, *Trudeau and Our Times, Volume I: The Magnificent Obsession*, Toronto, McClelland & Stewart, 1990, p. 9.

17  Will Ferguson, op. cit., p. 236.

18  Even when he was reduced to a minority government in 1972, Quebec still gave him 48 per cent of its vote. In the following elections his popularity kept increasing. In 1974, his Quebec vote was 54 per cent. In 1979, even as he went down to defeat, his vote in Quebec rose to 62 per cent. Then, for his last elections in 1980, just a few months before the referendum, his Quebec vote rose again to 68 per cent.

19  Richard Gwyn, *The Northern Magus*, McClelland & Stewart, 1980.

20  Michel Vastel, op. cit., *Trudeau le Québécois*, p. 26.

21  Interview with Suzette Rouleau, December 9, 2002.

22  Jacques Hébert, *J'accuse les assassins de Coffin*, Montreal, Les éditions du Jour, 1963.

23  Interview with Jacques Hébert, December 10, 2002.

24  Peter Gzowski, "Portrait of an Intellectual in Action," *Maclean's*, February 24, 1962, pp. 23, 29 and 30.

25  Alain Stanké, *Pierre Elliott Trudeau: Portrait intime*, Montreal, Télé-Métropole/Les Éditions internationales Alain Stanké Ltée, 1977, p. 19.

26  Ibid., p. 23.

27  Ibid., p. 31.

28  George Radwanski, *Trudeau*, Toronto, Macmillan Company of Canada, 1978, p. 50. Radwanski was the only biographer to have been granted eight hours interviewing Trudeau.

29  Interview with Suzette Rouleau, December 9, 2002.

30  Pierre Elliott Trudeau, *Memoirs*, Toronto, McClelland & Stewart, 1993, p. 17.

31  Ibid., pp. 17–18.

32  Lionel Groulx, *L'appel de la race*, with an introduction by Bruno Lafleur, Montreal and Paris, Fidès, 1956 (1st édition 1922) p. 130.

33  Ibid., p. 131.

34  Ibid., p. 89.

35  Stephen Clarkson and Christina McCall, op. cit., p. 38.

36  K. McRoberts, *Misconceiving Canada: The Struggle for National Unity*, Oxford University Press, 1997, p. 56.

37  K. McRoberts, *Misconceiving*, op. cit., p. 59.

38  *Portrait intime*, op. cit., p. 44.

39  *Memoirs*, op. cit., pp. 48–54.

40  Interview with Marc Lalonde, December 12, 2002.

41  Interview with Roger Rolland, May 22, 2001.

42  Jean-Louis Roux, *Nous sommes tous des acteurs*, Montreal, Éditions Lescop, 1998, p. 75.

43  Interview with Marc Lalonde, December 12, 2002.

44  *Portrait intime*, op. cit., p. 57.

45  *Memoirs*, op. cit., p. 28.

46  *Portrait intime*, op. cit., p. 57.

47  Jean Pellerin, *Le Phénomène Trudeau*, Paris, Seghers, 1972, p. 95.

48  Quoted by A. MacEachen, "Faith," in N. Southam, (ed.) *Pierre*, McClelland & Stewart, 2005, p. 2.

49  Interview with Roger Rolland, May 22, 2001.

50  Justin Trudeau, in *Trudeau: The Life, Times and Passing of Pierre Elliott Trudeau*, Toronto, Key Porter Books, 2000, p. 15.

51  Interview with Roy Heenan (who attended the dinner), September 9, 2002.

52  *Portrait intime*, op. cit., p. 16.

53  Letter to Roger Rolland written at Harvard University and dated January 23, 1945.

54  Letter to Roger Rolland, written at Harvard University, April 13, 1945.

55  Letter to Roger Rolland, written at Harvard University, December 9, 1945.

56  Quoted by Edith Iglauer, *The New Yorker*, July 5, 1969, p. 36.

57  Letter to Roger Rolland, written at Harvard University, April 13, 1945.

58  M. Vastel, *Trudeau le Québécois*, op. cit., p. 32.

59  J. Hébert, telephone conversation, July 2005.

60  Clarkson and McCall, *Trudeau*, op. cit., p. 46.

61  M. Vastel, *Trudeau*, op. cit., second edition, pp. 46–47.

62  Linda Griffith, "The Lover: Dancing with Trudeau," in Andrew Cohen and J. Granatstein, *Trudeau's Shadow: The Life and Legacy of Pierre Elliott Trudeau*, Random House of Canada, 1998, pp. 35–46.

63  *Portrait intime*, op. cit., p. 56.

64  Edited by John English, Richard Gwyn and P. Whitney Lackenbauer, *The Hidden Pierre Elliott Trudeau: The Faith Behind the Politics*, Ottawa: Saint Paul's University, 2004.

65  Interview with Thérèse Gouin and Vianney Décarie, September 24, 2001.

*Chapter 2:* OBEDIENCE: THE JESUITS' FIRST PRINCIPLE

1   *Portrait intime*, Montreal, op. cit., p. 31.

2   George Radwanski, *Trudeau*, op. cit., p. 36.

3   *Memoirs*, op. cit., p. 21.

4   Robert McKenzie and Lotta Dempsey, "Pierre Trudeau: 'I became accustomed very young to rowing against the current,'" *Toronto Star*, April 8, 1968.

5   Radwanski, op. cit., p. 37.

6   P.E. Trudeau, *Against the Current: Selected Writings 1939–1996*, edited by
    Gérard Pelletier, Toronto, McClelland & Stewart, 1996.

7   Interview with Pierre Vadeboncœur on September 27, 2001.

8   René Latourelle, S.J., *Quel avenir pour le christianisme?* Montreal,
    Guérin, 2000, pp. 16–17.

9   *Memoirs*, op. cit., p. 4.

10  Ibid., pp. 6–7.

11  See the excellent study by Catherine Pomeyrols, *Les intellectuels québé-
    cois: formation et engagements, 1919–1939*, Paris and Montreal,
    L'Harmattan, 1996.

12  Paul-André Linteau *et al.*, *Le Québec depuis 1930*, Montreal, Boréal,
    1986, p. 169, in Robert Lahaise, *Une histoire du Québec par sa littérature:
    1914–1939*, Montreal, Guérin, 1998, p. 214.

13  For an excellent study on the Jesuits, see Jean Lacouture, *Jésuites. Une
    multibiographie. 1. Les conquérants*, Paris, Éditions du Seuil, 1991.

14  Constitution of the Order of the Jesuits, in Lacouture, op. cit., p. 112.

15  Loyola, *Letter to the Portuguese Jesuits*, in Lacouture, op. cit., p. 111.

16  Quoted by Pomeyrols, *Les intellectuels québécois*, op. cit., p. 73.

17  Règlement du Collège Sainte-Marie, in C. Pomeyrols, op. cit., pp. 71–72.

18  Jacques Monet, S.J., "The Man's Formation in Faith," in *The Hidden
    Pierre Trudeau: The Faith Behind the Politics*, John English, Richard
    Gwyn and P. Whitney Lackenbauer, editors, Ottawa, Novalis, St. Paul
    University, 2004, pp. 87–88.

19  William Johnson, the well-known journalist, attended Brébeuf from 1940
    (the year when Trudeau left) until 1947. We are grateful for all the impor-
    tant information that he gave us on the daily life of the college.

20  *Memoirs*, op. cit., p. 14.

21  Ibid., p. 30.

22  Stephen Clarkson and Christina McCall, *Trudeau and our Times. Volume I:
    The Magnificent Obsession*, Toronto, McClelland & Stewart, 1990, p. 34.

23  André Burelle, *Pierre Elliott Trudeau, l'intellectuel et le politique*,
    Montreal, Fides, 2005, p. 69.

24  Clarkson and McCall, op. cit., p. 36.

25  Edith Iglauer, "Prime Minister/Premier ministre," in *The New Yorker*,
    July 5, 1969.

26  Stephen Clarkson, "An Explicit Destination?" in John English, Richard
    Gwyn and P. Whitney Lackenbauer, editors, op. cit., p. 33.

27  Clarkson and McCall, *The Magnificent Obsession*, op. cit., pp. 36–37.

28  Library and Archives Canada (LAC), MG 26 *The Right Honourable Pierre*

*Elliott Trudeau Papers*, Series 02, *Documents Prior to the Political Career*, volume 1, file 2. From now on referred to on the model: LAC, vol. 1, f 2.

29  *Memoirs*, p. 21.

30  LAC, vol. 1, f 34.

31  *Brébeuf*, May 11, 1938.

32  *Brébeuf*, December 3, 1938.

33  Ibid.

34  In students' newspapers, the authors make common use of capital letters. We replaced them by italics, less distracting to read.

35  *Brébeuf*, December 23, 1939.

36  Georges-Émile Lapalme, *Mémoires I: Le bruit des choses réveillées*, Montreal, Leméac, 1969, p. 110, quoted by Catherine Pomeyrols, op. cit., p. 97.

37  A. Tessier, *Souvenirs en vrac*, Montreal, Boréal, 1975. Quoted by Pomeyrols, op. cit., p. 97.

38  Pomeyrols, ibid. Jacques Hébert, an alumnus of Collège Sainte-Marie, recalls that *Le Devoir* was among the forbidden newspapers.

39  Gabriel Compayré, *Histoire critique des doctrines de l'éducation en France depuis le XVIe siècle*, Paris, Hachette et Cie, 1883, 3rd edition.

40  Linteau, quoted in Lahaise, op. cit., p. 214.

41  François Hertel, "La littérature canadienne-française." *L'Action nationale*, May 1935. Quoted by Catherine Pomeyrols, op. cit., p. 80.

42  *Memoirs*, p. 22.

43  Ibid.

44  Pomeyrols, op. cit., p. 82.

45  François Hertel, *L'enseignement des Belles-Lettres*, Montreal, L'Immaculée conception, October 1938. Quoted by Catherine Pomeyrols, op. cit., p. 81.

46  G. Compayré, *Histoire critique des doctrines de l'éducation*, op. cit.

47  LAC, vol. 2, f 8–9. The notebook is dated from October 1936. It would seem that his teacher for this course was Father Gariépi.

48  Stanké, *Portrait intime*, op. cit., p. 60.

49  LAC, vol. 5, f 8. As what we found was the draft of the letter, our account of it might not coincide entirely with the letter as sent.

50  LAC, vol. 5, f 8.

51  LAC, vol. 7, f 6.

52  Ibid.

## *Chapter 3:* BRÉBEUF AND THE MAKING OF A LEADER

1  Words within quotations that are in italics were so in the original text, unless otherwise indicated.

2   Edith Iglauer, "Prime Minister/Premier Ministre," op. cit., p. 39.

3   Ibid.

4   Ibid., pp. 39–40.

5   Max and Monique Nemni, "A Conversation with Pierre Elliott Trudeau," *Cité libre*, vol. 26, no. 1, February–March 1998, p. 112.

6   *Memoirs*, op. cit., pp. 25–26.

7   It will be recalled that, in the 1930s, *Canadiens* designated exclusively French Canadians.

8   Lionel Groulx, "Nos positions," in *Orientations*, Éditions du Zodiaque, 1935, pp. 240–274.

9   Ibid., pp. 240–241.

10  Ibid., p. 247.

11  Ibid., p. 250.

12  Ibid., p. 253.

13  Ibid., p. 257.

14  Ibid., pp. 266–267.

15  LAC, vol. 3, f 18.

16  LAC, ibid. The text is riddled with spelling mistakes that we corrected.

17  René Lévesque's article was republished in *Le Devoir* on December 7, 1976.

18  LAC, vol. 2, f 10. March 1938.

19  LAC, vol. 2, f 10.

20  Ibid., March 25, 1938.

21  Ibid., August 1938.

22  Ibid., July 1, 1938.

23  Clarkson and McCall, op. cit., p. 44.

24  Radwanski, op. cit., p. 35.

25  LAC, vol. 2, f 10.

26  Denis Lessard, "Un homme d'influence," *La Presse*, Tuesday, February 10, 2004.

27  LAC, vol. 2, f 10, October 5, 1937.

28  Robert Lahaise, op. cit., p. 16.

29  G. Bessette, L. Geslin and Ch. Parent, *Histoire de la littérature canadienne française*, Montreal, Centre éducatif et culturel, 1968, p. 414.

30  William Johnson, *Anglophobie Made in Quebec*, Montreal, Stanké, 1991, pp. 123–125.

31  J.-L. Roux, "Lettre à Félix-Antoine Savard," *Le Quartier Latin*, January 28, 1944.

32  A. Laurendeau, "Nos écoles enseignent-elles la haine de l'Anglais?" *L'Action nationale*, 1941, vol. XVIII, (October), pp. 104–123.

33  Paul Gérin-Lajoie, "Canadiens français d'abord!" *Le Brébeuf*, December 3, 1938.

34  LAC, vol. 2, f 10. The notebook starts on October 12, 1937.

35  François Hertel, *Le beau risque*, les éditions Bernard Valiquette et les éditions A.C.F., Montreal, 1939.

36  Jacques Monet in *The Hidden Pierre Elliott Trudeau*, op. cit.

37  Esther Delisle, *Essais*, op. cit., p. 38.

38  F. Hertel, *Le Beau risque*, op. cit., p. 75.

39  E. Delisle, *Essais*, op. cit.

40  François Hertel, *Leur inquiétude*, Montreal, Éditions Jeunesse ACJC/ Éditions Albert Lévesque, 1936.

41  Ibid., p. 134.

42  Ibid., p. 93.

43  "Canadiens français d'abord!" *Brébeuf*, December 3, 1938.

44  LAC, vol. 4, f 5.

45  Alexis Carrel, *L'Homme, cet inconnu*, Paris, Librairie Plon, 1935.

46  Ibid., p. 179.

47  Ibid., op. cit., p. 22.

48  Ibid., op. cit., p. 151.

49  Ibid., op. cit., p. 327.

50  Ibid., op. cit., p. 323.

51  Ibid., p. 385.

52  Ibid., p. 361.

53  Ibid., p. 328.

54  Ibid., p. 165.

55  Ibid., p. 316.

56  Ibid., p. 23.

57  Ibid., p. 334.

58  Ibid., p. 151.

59  Ibid., p. 174.

60  Ibid., p. 159.

61  Ibid., p. 358.

62  Ibid., p. 334.

63  Ibid., p. 355.

64  Ibid., p. 346.

65  Ibid., p. 359.

66  Ibid., p. 367.

67  Ibid., p. 367.

68  Ibid., p. 389.

69  Ibid., p. 366.

70  Ibid., p. 388.
71  Ibid., p. 276.
72  *Against the Current*, op. cit., p. ix.


Chapter 4: THE LEADER SHARPENS HIS PEN

1   For the complete list of Trudeau's articles in the *Brébeuf*, please refer to
    the Bibliography.
2   Jean Lacouture, *Jésuites*, op. cit., p. 326.
3   Ibid., p. 361.
4   Pascal, *Pensées*, edited and annotated by Jacques Chevalier with a preface
    by Jean Guitton. Paris, éditions Gallimard, 1962, p. 22. In the edition
    cited by Trudeau, this *pensée* is numbered 16. In the edition that we cite, it
    is numbered 17.
5   *Against the Current*, op. cit.
6   LAC, vol. 5, f 7, letter of January 8, 1940.
7   *Brébeuf*, November 11, 1939.
8   LAC, vol. 8, f 6.
9   In capital letters in the text. We substitute italics for readability.
10  "An Explicit Destination?" in *The Hidden Pierre Trudeau*, op. cit., p. 34.
11  *Brébeuf*, February 22, 1940.
12  David Somerville, *Trudeau Revealed by His Actions and Words*,
    Richmond Hill, Ontario, BMG Publishing Ltd., 1978.
13  E. Delisle, *Essais*, op. cit., 2002.
14  François Lessard, *Messages au "Frère" Trudeau*, Pointe-Fortune:
    Les éditions de ma Grand-mère, 1979.
15  *Brébeuf*, March 23, 1940.
16  Gérard Pelletier, 1983, *Les années d'impatience: 1950–1960*, Montreal,
    Stanké, p. 35.


Chapter 5: LAW SCHOOL – WHAT A BORE!

1   Letter dated October 14, 1944. LAC, vol. 8, f 3, "Complete record of
    grades at Brébeuf."
2   LAC, vol. 3, f 16, *Collège Jean-de-Brébeuf*, "A few words about the gradu-
    ates," 1940.
3   J. Hébert, *Bonjour le monde!* Montreal, Editions Robert Davies, 1996, p. 16.
4   *Memoirs*, op. cit., pp. 44–45.
5   G. Radwanski, *Trudeau*, op. cit., p. 58.
6   These notes are undated, but their place in Trudeau's archives suggest that
    they were written in his last year at Brébeuf.
7   *Memoirs*, op. cit., p. 37.

8   LAC, vol. 5, f 7, *Demande de bourse Rhodes.*

9   LAC, ibid.

10  S. Clarkson, "An Explicit Destination?" in *The Hidden Pierre Elliott Trudeau*, op. cit., p. 34.

11  LAC, vol. 6, f 5. The first page containing notes is dated November 10, 1941, with Trudeau's usual heading during his youth, A.M.D.G.

12  LAC, vol. 6, f 14. The first page containing notes is dated September 18, 1940, and is headed with A.M.D.G.

13  *Brébeuf*, December 3, 1938. See Chapter 2.

14  We believe that the reference is to Pierre Rouleau, her future husband.

15  François Lessard, *Messages au "Frère" Trudeau*, op. cit.

16  Esther Delisle, *Essais,* op. cit. Delisle has devoted several serious studies to demystifying extreme right-wing currents of thought in Quebec. In this regard, see also her *Mythes, mémoire et mensonges*, éd. Multimédia Robert Davies, 1998.

17  David Somerville, *Trudeau Revealed*, op. cit.

18  Louis-Bernard Robitaille, "François Hertel: "On ne peut pas effacer 40 ans de vie . . . on peut rompre,'" *La Presse*, July 9, 1977.

19  LAC, vol. 1, f 35.

20  *Memoirs*, op. cit., p. 34.

21  Ibid., pp. 31–32.

22  Ibid., pp. 32–34.

23  André Laurendeau has devoted an entire book to this question, *La crise de la conscription – 1942.*

24  *Memoirs*, op. cit., p. 34.

25  For more information, see the website of Veterans Affairs Canada, www.vac-acc.gc.ca, *The Battle of the Gulf of St. Lawrence 1942–1944.*

26  *Memoirs*, op. cit., p. 35. The words in parentheses, "although I know that one Canadian ferry, the *Caribou*, was torpedoed, with heavy loss of life," appeared in the English version of Trudeau's *Memoirs* but not in the French.

## Chapter 6: CORPORATISM, A BLESSING!

1   Rosaire Morin, "Les origines de L'Action nationale," *L'Action nationale*, April 2000.

2   G.-Raymond Laliberté, "Dix-huit ans de corporatisme militant. L'École sociale populaire de Montreal, 1933–1950," *Recherches sociographiques*, vol. XXI, nos. 1–2, January–August 1980, p. 56.

3   Joseph-Papin Archambault, S.J., *La Restauration de l'ordre social d'après les encycliques Rerum novarum et Quadragesimo anno*. Montreal,

éditions de L'École sociale populaire, 1932. The book is an expanded version of his 1931 conference.

4   Ibid., pp. 5–6.

5   Ibid., p. 6.

6   Ibid., p. 88.

7   Ibid., p. 95.

8   Ibid., p. 43.

9   Ibid., footnote 1, p. 94.

10  "Circulaire au Clergé," Évêché de Chicoutimi, November 16, 1931, in *Mandements Lettres Pastorales et Circulaires des Évêques de Chicoutimi*, Volume premier 1929–1933, Chicoutimi, 1934, p. 282.

11  *Mandements Lettres Pastorales Circulaires et autres documents publiés dans le diocèse de Montreal depuis son érection*, Volume 18, Montreal, Arbour & Dupont Imprimeurs-Éditeurs, 1940, p. 211.

12  Quoted in R. Arès, *Plans d'études sur la restauration sociale*, 3rd edition, 1941, p. 26.

13  *Mandements Lettres Pastorales Circulaires*, op. cit., p. 208.

14  *Mandements*, volume 14, op. cit.

15  Op. cit., volume 18, pp. 326–327.

16  Louise Bienvenue, *Quand la jeunesse entre en scène. L'Action catholique avant la Révolution tranquille*, Montreal, Boréal, 2003, 291.

17  *Mandemants*, volume 14, op. cit., pp. 37–48.

18  Ibid., p. 44.

19  Ibid., p. 42.

20  Georges-Henri Lévesque, o.p., "La 'Co-operative Commonwealth Federation'", in *Pour la Restauration sociale au Canada*, numbers 232–233, April–May 1933.

21  *Mandements*, volume 14, op. cit., pp. 195–202.

22  *Mandements*, volume 18, op. cit., p. 331.

23  Ibid., p. 357.

24  "Programme d'action sociale catholique, préparé par S.E. Monseigneur J.-M. Rodrigue Villeneuve, O.M.I., pour la séance de clôture des noces d'argent de l'*Action Sociale Catholique*," in *Mandements Lettres pastorales et circulaires des Évêques de Québec*, volume 14, 1932–1935, op. cit., pp. 138–139.

25  Ibid., pp. 136–137.

26  Ibid., pp. 137–138.

27  Ibid., p. 139.

28  L'École sociale populaire, *Pour la Restauration sociale au Canada*, Montreal, Numbers 232–233, April–May 1933, p. 38.

29  "Lettre pastorale collective de Son Éminence le Cardinal Archevêque de
    Québec et de leurs Excellences les Archevêques et Évêques de la province
    civile de Québec sur le problème rural au regard de la doctrine sociale de
    l'Église," in *Mandements. Lettres pastorales et circulaires des Évêques de
    Québec*, volume 15, 1936–1939, Québec, Chancellerie de l'Archevêché,
    1940, p. 257.

30  Ibid., p. 261.

31  Ibid., p. 294.

32  Archambault, op. cit., p. 97.

33  *Le Devoir*, February 28, 1935.

34  Lionel Groulx, "La bourgeoisie et le national," in Esdras Minville, Victor
    Barbeau and Lionel Groulx, *L'Avenir de notre bourgeoisie*, Montreal,
    Éditions Bernard Valiquette, 1939, p. 125.

35  For more on fascist regimes, see the fascinating study by E. Nolte, *Three
    Faces of Fascism: Action Française, Italian Fascism, National Socialism*,
    Holt, Rinehart & Winston, 1966.

36  Ibid., pp. 218–219.

37  Ibid., p. 219.

38  Quoted by André-J. Bélanger in his now classic study: *L'apolitisme des
    ideologies québécoises. Le grand tournant de 1934–1936*, Quebec City,
    Laval University Press, 1974, p. 248.

39  *Mandements, Lettres pastorales et circulaires des Évêques de Québec*,
    volume 16, 1940–1943, Québec, Chancellerie de l'Archevêché, 1944,
    pp. 185–186.

40  Ibid., p. 181.

41  Ibid., p. 171. We italicized.

42  Ibid., pp. 185-86.

43  Ibid., pp. 186-87.

44  *Mandements,* volume 16, p. 187.

45  J-L. Roux, *Nous sommes tous des acteurs*, op. cit., p. 68.

46  J-L. Roux, op. cit., p. 72.

47  Bourassa conference of May 20, 1941. Fr. Archambault quoted him in the
    preface to R. Arès, S.J.

48  Quoted in the introduction of Arès, op. cit.

49  R. Arès, op. cit., p. 6.

50  R. Arès, op. cit., p. 10.

51  Ibid., p. 12.

52  Two works that we found particularly useful both appeared after Cardinal
    Ratzinger – now Pope Benedict XVI – granted access in 1998 to the
    archives of the of the Sacred Congregation of the Holy Office, as it was

known before the name was changed in 1965 to Congregation for the Doctrine of the Faith (the former Inquisition). *Hitler's Pope: The Secret History of Pius XII*, by John Cornwell, became a best-seller. The author, a Catholic writer, had set out originally to exonerate Pope Pius XII. David I. Kertzer, author of *The Popes Against the Jews: The Vatican's Role in the Rise of Modern Anti-Semitism*, is the son of a rabbi on whom the Vatican conferred a bronze medal in recognition of his contribution to a better understanding between Jews and Catholics.

53  J. Ridley, *Mussolini*, 1997, p. 263, quoted by Cornwell, op. cit., p. 175.

54  Cornwell, op. cit., p. 115.

55  "The Vatican Concordat With Hitler's Reich," in *The National Catholic Weekly*, September 1, 2003, vol. 189, no.5.

56  J.S. Spong, *The Sins of Scripture, Exposing the Bible's Texts of Hate to Reveal the God of Love*, New York, HarperCollins, 2005, p. 187.

57  R. Arès, op. cit., p. 13.

58  Ibid., p. 17.

59  Ibid., p. 24.

60  Ibid., p. 40.

61  Ibid., p. 53. Fr. Arès refers to two writings by Gérard Filion: *Le syndicalisme agricole*, written in 1941, and *L'Union Catholique des Cultivateurs*, written in 1938.

62  R. Arès, op. cit., p. 49.

63  R. Arès, op. cit., p. 58.

64  R. Arès, op. cit., p. 55.

65  Julien Harvey, S.J. "Richard Arès," in *L'année politique au Québec 1988–1989* Montreal, Québec/Amérique, 1989.

66  R. Arès, op. cit., p. 60.

67  Ibid., p. 57.

68  *Le Devoir*, April 19, 1937.

69  R. Arès, op. cit., p. 60.

70  Ibid.

71  We owe this reference to the excellent article by Daniel Vignola in *Le québécois libre*, Montreal, December 20, 2003, number 135, which we found on the website http://www.quebecoislibre.org.

72  Cornwell, *Hitler's Pope*, op. cit., p. 288.

73  André Laurendeau, *La crise de la conscription – 1942*, Montreal, Éditions du Jour, 1962, p. 115.

74  J-L. Roux, op. cit., p. 68.

75  *La Crise*, op. cit., p. 115.

76 Ibid., p. 64.

77 Ibid., p. 114.

78 Éric Amyot, *Le Quebec entre Petain et de Gaulle, la France libre et les Canadiens français 1940–1945*, Montreal, Fides, 1999, p. 100. According to Amyot, this book, published in 1943, is a collection of speeches given by Pétain between the months of June 1940 and October 1941.

## Chapter 7: READ TO LEAD

1 LAC, vol. 5, f 16, September 1940.

2 Ibid., January 1941.

3 Ibid., September 27, 1940.

4 Ibid., October 1, 1940.

5 Ibid., Trudeau wrote 1940, without specifying the date.

6 "Une représentation indigène du métier politique à la fin de la troisième République. Le réquisitoire d'André Tardieu contre la profession parlementaire," in Y. Poirmeur and P. Mazet, (directeurs), *Le métier politique en représentation*, Paris, l'Harmattan, 1999.

7 Tardieu here is quoting Louis Blanc the nineteenth century utopian socialist who favoured workplaces controlled by the workers themselves.

8 LAC, vol. 5, f16, March 1941.

9 Only Trudeau's notes on Bergson carry a more precise date – March 1941. His notes on Pascal were located right next to those on Bergson, so they would be from the same time period.

10 All our references are to Henri Bergson, *Les deux sources de la morale et de la religion*, Paris, Quadrige/Presses universitaires de France, 7th édition, 1997. The first edition was published in 1932.

11 Ibid., p. 97.

12 Ibid., p. 77.

13 Ibid., p. 68.

14 Ibid., p. 73.

15 Ibid., p. 76.

16 Ibid., p. 78.

17 *Memoirs*, op. cit., p. 40.

18 Bergson, op. cit., p. 78.

19 Ibid., p. 97.

20 Ibid., p. 98.

21 Ibid., pp. 101–102.

22 LAC, vol. 5, f 16, September 1941.

23 Ibid. The title means *Adventure and Voyage in the Land of the Real.*

24  *Memoirs*, p. 20.

25  Born in France, Pierre-Esprit Radisson migrated to Trois-Rivières in 1651. In 1659, he and his sister's husband, Médard Chouart des Groseilliers, also born in France, undertook a secret voyage of discovery, searching for new sources for the fur trade. They returned with more than one hundred canoes loaded with furs. But, since they had not obtained before leaving the required permit, they were fined and their furs were confiscated. They then decided to work for the English. In 1665, they travelled to London to meet King Charles II, who agreed to back them in a new expedition. It turned out to be a success and, in 1670, the King granted a charter for the new Hudson's Bay Company.

26  *Journal JEC*, June 1944. The article was republished in P. Trudeau, *Against the Current*, op. cit., pp. 9–12.

27  Notebook with the following information on the first page: "89 McCulloch, Outremont, U de M, Droit II$^e$, sept., 1941." From now on this will be referred to as: Notebook, U of M, Law II$^{nd}$.

28  Trudeau himself underlined the word *my*. Whenever a word is underlined within a quotation, it was the author of the quotation who underlined.

29  Alexis Carrel, *L'homme cet inconnu*, Paris, Librairie Plon, 1935, p. 375.

30  Alain Grandbois, *Les Voyages de Marco Polo*, Montreal, Éditions Bernard Valiquette, 1941.

31  P. Trudeau, "Les voyages de Marco Polo," *Amérique française*, November 1941, pp. 45–46.

32  Ibid.

33  *Memoirs*, op. cit., p. 20.

34  Interview of September 27, 2001.

35  *Memoirs*, op. cit., p. 23.

36  Notebook, U of M, Law II$^{nd}$.

37  *Memoirs*, op. cit., p. 32.

38  Ibid.

## Chapter 8: 1942: LONG LIVE PÉTAIN!

1  André Laurendeau, *La crise de la conscription*, Éditions du jour, 1962, p. 7.

2  "Péril des latins," in *Le Quartier Latin*, January 29, 1943.

3  Boulanger would depart for Paris in 1948 for further studies in psychiatry, in psychology, and in neurology. On his return to Canada in 1957, he would join the Faculty of Medicine of the Université de Montreal and go on to be recognized as one of Canada's eminent psychiatrists.

4  Letter to Roger Rolland. From the personal files of Roger Rolland.

5   LAC, vol. 5, f 16. All his reading notes are kept in this file.

6   Pierre Elliott Trudeau, *Memoirs*, op. cit., p. 23–24. Trudeau's memory,
    though, had played a trick on him, as Boulanger was to point out, many
    years later. On August 3, 1994, he wrote Trudeau to point out that his
    "prix Vermeil" from the Académie was not, in fact, for his 1937 book on
    Napoleon but rather for a home-published newspaper, *Le Petit Jour*, that
    he began putting out in Edmonton in 1929, when he was just seven years
    old. He kept it up until he left for Brébeuf ten years later. From the per-
    sonal papers of Jean-Baptiste Boulanger. Quoted by E. Delisle, *Essais sur
    l'imprégnation fasciste au Québec*, Les éditions Varia, 2002, p. 68.

7   In E. Delisle, op. cit., p. 68.

8   In this and all chapters, all italicized words within a quotation were
    underlined or italicized by the author of the quotation.

9   Adolphe-Basile Routhier in Robert Lahaise, *Une histoire du Québec*,
    op. cit., p. 162.

10  F. Paradis, in Robert Lahaise, Ibid., p. 6.

11  Marcel de la Sablonnière, "Génie français," in *Le Quartier Latin*,
    December 19, 1941.

12  Ibid.

13  "Le paysan français" from a speech by Marshal Pétain, then Minister of
    War, at the 1935 dedication of a monument to the dead at Capoulet-Junac.

14  Éric Amyot, *Le Québec entre Pétain et de Gaulle: Vichy, la France libre et
    les Canadiens français 1940–1945*, Montreal, Fides, 1999, p. 108.

15  J-B. Boulanger, *Charles Maurras a-t-il trahi? De Maurras à Pétain*, Le mot
    d'ordre, 1945.

16  Ibid., p. 2.

17  Ibid., p. 7.

18  Ibid., p. 4.

19  Ibid., p. 4.

20  Ibid., p. 12.

21  Ibid., p. 12.

22  LAC, vol. 4, f 5, Brébeuf, cards numbered 39–46.

23  Max and Monique Nemni, "A Conversation with Pierre Elliott Trudeau,"
    *Cité libre*, vol. 26, number 1, February–March 1998, p. 99.

24  "$50 millions par terre," *Le Quartier Latin*, November 29, 1940.

25  "Au sujet de nos hôtes," *Le Quartier Latin*, October 18, 1940.

26  Drapeau was referring to rue Saint-Laurent, often still called "la Main,"
    which was then the site for a multitude of small ethnic shops, bakeries,
    and restaurants. In more recent years, however, its character has changed:
    it has become chic with its upscale restaurants, bars, and shops.

27  André Laurendeau, *Maîtres de l'heure: l'abbé Lionel Groulx*, Montreal, Éditions de l'A.C.F, 1938, p. 4.

28  Éric Amyot, *Le Québec*, op. cit., p. 73.

29  Ibid., p. 74.

30  André Laurendeau, *Ces choses qui nous arrivent: Chronique des années 1961–1966*, Montreal, HMH, 1970, pp. 118–119.

31  François Hertel, *Nous ferons l'avenir*, Montreal, Fides, 1945, p. 50. Although published in 1945, this book was written in 1944.

32  Ibid., pp. 50–51.

33  J. L. Roux, *Nous sommes tous des acteurs*, op. cit., pp. 77–78.

34  Pierre Boutang, *Maurras, la destinée et l'œuvre*, Paris, Plon, 1984, p. 708.

35  C. Maurras, *La seule France, chronique des jours d'épreuve*, H. Lardanchet, 1941, p. 136.

36  Ibid., p. 204.

37  Ibid., p. 206.

38  Ibid., p. 83.

39  Ibid., pp. 83–84.

40  Ibid., p. 199.

41  Marc Ferro, *Pétain*, Paris, Librairie Arthème Fayard, 1987, p. 241.

42  Maurras, *La seule France*, op. cit., p. 191.

43  Ibid., p. 191.

44  Ibid., pp. 192–193.

45  Ibid., p. 197.

46  Pierre Boutang, *Maurras*, op. cit., p. 283.

47  Ibid., p. 281.

48  *L'Invocation à Minerve*, 1931, quoted by Pierre Boutang, p. 582.

49  Charles Maurras, *Enquête sur la monarchie*, followed by *Une campagne royaliste au Figaro* and *Si le coup de force est possible*. Édition définitive avec un discours préliminaire. Paris, Nouvelle librairie nationale, 1925, pp. 137–138.

50  Trudeau here quotes *L'Enquête sur la monarchie*, p. lxxvii.

51  Ibid., p. 458.

52  Ibid., p. 452.

53  Ibid., p. 278.

54  That expression was to recur often in *La seule France*. Maurras, for example, was delighted that Pétain had grasped the reins of power. On page 29 he writes: "Let us concentrate our efforts where they can provide immediate results: politique d'abord – politics first."

55  Maurras, *Enquête sur la monarchie*, op. cit., p. 487.

56  Trudeau underlined Proudhon's words, quoted by Sorel.

57  Robert Aron and Arnaud Dandieu, *La révolution nécessaire*. Paris, Jean-Michel Place, 1993.

58  Eulogy delivered by Maurice Druon, director of l'Académie française, on the occasion of Robert Aron's death, at the session of April 24, 1975. Institut, 1975, No. 9, p. 41.

59  R. Aron, *Histoire de Vichy: 1940–1944*, Paris, Librairie Arthème Fayard, 1954.

60  *L'action française*, August 13, 1908, in Pierre Boutang, *Maurras*, op. cit., p. 436.

*Chapter 9*: LA RÉVOLUTION NATIONALE

1  LAC, vol. 5, f 21.

2  F. Lessard, *Messages au "Frère" Trudeau*, Les éditions de ma Grand-mère.

3  Notebook, U of M, Law II[nd], op. cit.

4  The words in italics were in English in Trudeau's text. They no doubt referred to their training on the shooting range as part of the Canadian Officers' Training Corps. Words underlined or in italics within a quotation, here as elsewhere, were underlined or italicized by the author cited.

5  The corpus of writings dealing with the proposed revolution comprise:
   **A draft of 20 handwritten pages** in a "notebook" which includes:
   • Three drafts of the manifesto, each under a different title.
   • A section with the heading, "Critique of the Principles proposed by JBB."
   • A section titled "Explanations" in which Trudeau gives a detailed commentary on each article of the manifesto.
   **A series of typewritten documents**, dealing with the manifesto, which include:
   • A half-page document titled "The principles" that is, we are convinced, the final version of the manifesto. It spells out the five principles of the revolution.
   • A text titled "Comments," which explains the five principles.
   • A five-page document, "destined for the leaders only." It includes preliminary notes, a section titled "Origins," and two sections titled "Mystique," the first dealing with the mystique of the Patrie, and the second with the mystique of the Revolution.
   **A single-page document** – probably intended for propaganda – titled "Why we exist," which offered the answer to two questions: Why a new model? Why another movement?
   **Four short documents** dealing with recruitment.

**Four handwritten pages** that deal with the organization of the revolutionary cell.
Unless otherwise indicated, everything that we analyze or quote is to be
found in these documents. In the interest of easier reading, we do not
identify in each case the version of the document under discussion or in
what section it is located, with a few exceptions when it seemed necessary.

6    Jean-Louis Roux, *Nous sommes tous des acteurs*, op. cit., p. 74.

7    F. Lessard, *Messages*, op. cit., p. 144.

8    Charles Maurras, *Enquête*, op. cit. p. 448.

9    Ibid., p. 51.

10   F. Lessard, *Messages*, op. cit., p. 146.

11   *Hansard*, p. 4638.

12   Robitaille, Louis-Bernard, "François Hertel," op. cit.

13   F. Lessard, *Messages*, op. cit., p. 144.

14   Ibid., p. 138.

15   Ibid., p. 151.

16   LAC, vol. 5, f 15.

17   See Chapter 7.

18   Alexis Carrel, *L'homme cet inconnu*, Paris, Plon, 1935, p. 179.

19   Jean-Jacques Rousseau, *Du contrat social*, Paris, Garnier-Flammarion,
     1966, p. 44.

20   Ibid., p. 67.

21   Ibid., p. 133. Rousseau developed this idea in Chapter 11, "De la mort du
     corps politique," and in Chapter 12, "Comment se maintient l'autorité
     souveraine," of Volume III.

22   Ibid., p. 129.

23   Jacques Maritain, *Humanisme intégral: Problèmes temporels et spirituels
     d'une nouvelle chrétienté*, Paris, Aubier, Éditions Montaigne, 1968, origi-
     nally published in 1936.

24   Jacques Maritain, *Le crépuscule de la civilisation*, Montreal, Éditions de
     l'Arbre, 1941, pp. 78–79.

25   Jacques Maritain, *À travers le désastre*, New York, Éditions de la Maison
     française, 1941, p. 26.

26   Jacques Maritain, *Les droits de l'homme*, with an introduction by
     René Mougel, Paris, Desclée de Brouwer, 1989.

27   Ibid., p. 20.

28   Maritain used the word "peregrinational" to indicate a transitory state, to
     convey that he considered that "the temporal civilization is no more than
     a pure means with respect to eternal life." He considered that the earthly

city is "a society, not of people settled into permanent abodes, but people on a voyage." *Humanisme intégral*, p. 143 (1968 edition).

29  *Le Crépuscule de la civilisation*, op. cit., p. 66.

30  *À travers le désastre*, op. cit., p. 82.

31  Ibid., p. 50.

32  *Le Crépuscule*, op. cit., p. 10.

33  *À travers le désastre*, op. cit., p. 70.

34  Ibid., p. 89.

35  *Le Crépuscule*, op. cit., p. 16.

36  A. Burelle, *Pierre Elliott Trudeau*, op. cit., p. 21.

37  *Humanisme*, op. cit., p. 170.

38  Ibid., p. 179.

39  Ibid., p. 172.

40  Ibid., p. 205.

## *Chapter 10:* NOTHING MATTERS NOW BUT VICTORY

1  Letter from Father Marie-Joseph d'Anjou to François Lessard, in E. Delisle, *Essais sur l'imprégnation fasciste*, op. cit., pp. 62–63.

2  Louis-Bernard Robitaille, op. cit.

3  André Laurendeau, *La crise de la conscription*, op. cit., p. 33.

4  Letter published in *L'Action nationale*, vol. XV, June 1940, p. 435, reprinted in Paul-André Comeau, *Le Bloc populaire: 1942–1948*, Montreal, Éditions Québec-Amérique, 1982, p. 61.

5  "Chroniques," *L'Action nationale*, ibid., p. 434, in Comeau, op. cit., p. 61.

6  André Laurendeau, *La cris*, op. cit., p. 36.

7  William Lyon Mackenzie King, *The Mackenzie King Diaries, 1932–1949*, entry for August 21, 1942, University of Toronto Press, 1980, p. 740.

8  Laurendeau, *La crise*, op. cit., p. 82.

9  Laurendeau, *La crise*, op. cit., p. 67.

10  Ann Charney, "Pierre Trudeau: The Myth and the Reality," in "Their Turn to Curtsy – Your Turn to Bow," edited by Peter Newman and Stan Fillmore, MacLean-Hunter Ltd., 1972.

11  Jean-Louis Roux, *Nous sommes tous des acteurs*, op. cit., pp. 70–72.

12  Laurendeau, op. cit., pp. 92–94.

13  Ibid., p. 94.

14  E. Delisle, *L'imprégnation fasciste*, op. cit., p. 61.

15  See our Chapter 7.

16  Laurendeau, *La crise*, op. cit., p. 116.

17  Ibid., p. 121.

18  Mason Wade, *The French Canadians: 1760–1967*, Vol. II, Macmillan of Canada, 1968, p. 953.

19  According to Mason Wade, this slogan was first coined by the Defence Minister, Colonel Layton Ralston. op. cit., pp. 125–127.

20  F. Lessard, *Messages*, op. cit., pp. 125-127.

21  For those who are interested, we recommend the detailed, objective, and judicious article on Dollard in the *Dictionary of Canadian Biography*, which is available online.

22  Lessard estimated the crowd at several thousands (p. 125). This seems unlikely.

23  É. Amyot, *Le Québec entre Pétain et de Gaulle*, op. cit., pp. 98–101.

24  Lessard, op. cit., p. 125.

25  Ibid., p. 127.

26  W. L. Mackenzie King, *Canada and the Fight for Freedom*, The Macmillan Company, 1944, pp. 210–220.

27  Ibid., p. 216.

28  LAC, vol. 5, f 23.

29  According to the Wikipedia encyclopedia, this anecdote is related in William Repka and Kathleen Repka, *Dangerous Patriots: Canada's Unknown Prisoners of War*, Vancouver, New Star Books, 1982.

30  Laurendeau, *La crise*, op. cit., p. 135.

31  Ibid., p. 135.

32  Michael Behiels, "The Bloc and the Origins of French-Canadian Neo-nationalism, 1942–8," *Canadian Historical Review* 63 (December 1982), pp. 489–491. In Behiels, *Prelude to Quebec's Quiet Revolution*, p. 29.

33  Mason Wade, op. cit., p. 955.

34  André Laurendeau, "Nos écoles enseignent-elles la haine des Anglais?", *L'Action nationale*, vol. 18, October 1941, p. 104.

35  Laurendeau, *La crise*, op. cit., p. 138.

36  Ibid., p. 137.

37  Comeau, op. cit., p. 303.

38  Laurendeau, *La crise*, op. cit., p. 138.

39  Notebook, U of M, Law II[nd].

40  Gérard Pelletier, *Les années d'impatience*, op. cit., p. 36.

41  Louis-Bernard Robitaille, "François Hertel," op. cit.

42  LAC, vol. 5, f 10. All the references and all the quotations dealing with the debate are drawn from this file.

43  F. Lessard, *Messages*, op. cit., p. 127. Lessard maintains in his book that he and Trudeau were both members of the "Frères Chasseurs." But we

found no mention of that name in Trudeau's papers. We conclude that the reference was likely to the members of the L.X.

44  A. Potvin, M. Letourneux and R. Smith, *L'anti-Trudeau*, op. cit., p. 8.

45  Ibid.

46  G. Radwanski, *Trudeau*, op. cit., p. 60.

## Chapter 11: AFTER THE STORM

1   Michel Vastel, *Trudeau le Québécois*, op. cit., p. 47.

2   Notebook, U of M, Law 11[nd].

3   M. Ferro, *Pétain*, op. cit., p. 29.

4   Ibid., p. 161.

5   Ibid., p. 219.

6   Ibid., p. 431.

7   Ibid., p. 415.

8   P. E. Trudeau, "Pritt, Zoum, Bing," *Le Quartier Latin*, March 10, 1944.

9   LAC, vol. 7, f 4.

10  LAC, vol. 7, f 5.

11  George Radwanski, *Trudeau*, op. cit., pp. 65.

12  LAC, vol. 5, f 2.

13  *Against the Current*, op. cit., pp. 6–8.

14  Michael Behiels, "The Bloc Populaire Canadien: Anatomy of a Failure, 1942–1947," *Journal of Canadian Studies, La Revue d'études canadiennes*, vol. 18, no. 4 (winter), 1983–84, pp. 45–74.

15  Letter of February 7, 1944, from Gouin, Chaloult, Hamel to Raymond and the leaders of the Bloc populaire canadien. Quoted by M. Behiels, op. cit., p. 62.

16  Quoted by M. Behiels, op. cit., p. 70.

17  LAC, vol. 5, f 16.

18  Ibid.

19  Ibid.

20  The article was republished in *Against the Current*, op. cit., pp. 9–12. Our references will be to this edition.

21  Ibid., p. 10.

22  Ibid., p. 10.

23  Ibid., p. 11.

24  Ibid., p. 11.

25  Ibid., p. 12.

26  LAC, vol. 4, f 5.

27  *Report pursuant to resolution of the Senate to the Honourable the Speaker by the Parliamentary Counsel, relating to the enactment of the*

*British North America Act, 1867, any lack of consonance between its*
*terms and judicial construction of them and cognate matters.* Report presented on March 17, 1939, by William F. O'Connor, legal expert and
parliamentary counsel to the Senate of Canada.

28  Ibid., p. 8.

29  Ibid., p. 8.

30  Stéphane Paquin, *L'invention d'un mythe: Le pacte entre deux peuples*
*fondateurs*, Montreal, VLB éditeur, 1999, p. 22.

31  Ibid., p. 20.

32  Ibid., p. 22.

33  *O'Connor Report*, op. cit., Annexe II, "Address to the Queen by members
of the Legislature, and minute of the Executive Council thereon," p. 47.

34  LAC, vol. 4, f 5.

35  A. Laurendeau, *La crise*, op. cit., p. 150.

36  Ibid., p. 150.

37  Mason Wade, *The French Canadians*, op. cit., p. 1012.

38  P.-A. Comeau, *Le Bloc*, op. cit., p. 346.

39  Ibid., p. 164.

40  In André-J. Bélanger, *L'apolitisme*, op. cit., p. 265.

41  P.-A. Comeau, *Le Bloc*, op. cit., p. 346.

42  Interpretation of M. Wade, op. cit., Vol. II, p. 1012.

43  Interpretation of Michael Behiels in "The Bloc populaire canadien," op. cit.

44  Quoted by P.-A. Comeau, op. cit., p. 365.

45  Letter from the Ministry of Labour, National Selective Service,
Mobilization Division. LAC, vol. 7, f 5.

46  LAC, vol. 7, f 5.

47  Mason Wade, op. cit., Vol. II, p. 1079.

48  "Pritt Zoum Bing," *Le Quartier Latin*, March 10, 1944.

49  LAC, vol. 7, f 5.

50  LAC, vol. 7, f 4.

51  LAC, vol. 7, f 5.

52  LAC, vol. 5, f 16.

53  LAC, vol. 6, f 13.

54  Adam Smith (1723–1790), *An Inquiry into the Nature and Causes of the*
*Wealth of Nations*, London, Methuen and Co., Ltd., Ed., Fifth edition
1904. First published 1776, Book I, Chapter II, p. 122.

# BIBLIOGRAPHY

Amyot, Éric. *Le Québec entre Pétain et de Gaulle. Vichy, la France libre et les Canadiens français 1940–1945*. Montreal: Fides, 1999.

Archambault, Joseph-Papin, S.J. *La Restauration de l'ordre social d'après les encycliques Rerum novarum et Quadragesimo anno*. Montreal: published by L'École sociale populaire, 1932.

Arès, Richard, S.J. *Plans d'étude sur la restauration sociale*, based on the pastoral letter of the episcopate of the Province of Quebec on the encyclicals *Rerum novarum* and *Quadragesimo anno*. Third Edition, Reviewed and Augmented, 1941.

Aron, Robert, and Arnaud Dandieu. *La révolution nécessaire*. Paris: Jean-Michel Place, 1993. (First Edition 1933.)

Aron, Robert. *Histoire de Vichy: 1940–1944*. Paris: Librairie Arthème Fayard, 1954.

*Battle of the Gulf of St. Lawrence, 1942–1944*. Veterans Affairs Canada, http://www.vac-acc.gc.ca/general/sub.cfm?source=history/ secondwar/ battlegulf.

Behiels, Michael, and Ramsay Cook. *The Essential Laurendeau*. Toronto: Copp Clark, 1976.

Behiels, Michael. "The Bloc and the Origins of French-Canadian Neo-nationalism, 1942–8." *Canadian Historical Review* 63, December 1982.

———. "The Bloc Populaire Canadien: Anatomy of Failure, 1942–1947." *Review of Canadian Studies*, Vol. 18, No. 4, Winter, 1983–84.

———. *Prelude to Quebec's Quiet Revolution: Liberalism versus Neo-nationalism, 1945–1960*. Montreal: McGill-Queen's University Press, 1986.

Bélanger, André-J. *L'apolitisme des idéologies québécoises. Le grand tournant de 1934–1936*. Quebec City: Laval University Press, 1974.

Bergson, Henri. *Les deux sources de la morale et de la religion*. Paris: Quadrige/Presses universitaires de France, 7th Edition, 1997. 1932.

Bessette, Gérard, Lucien Geslin, and Charles Parent. *Histoire de la littérature canadienne française*. Montreal: Centre Éducatif et culturel, 1968.

Boulanger, Jean-Baptiste. "Péril des latins." *Le Quartier Latin*, January 29, 1943.

———. *Charles Maurras a-t-il trahi? De Maurras à Pétain*. Le mot d'ordre. 1945.

Boutang, Pierre. *Maurras, la destinée et l'œuvre*. Paris: Plon, 1984.

Burelle, André. *Pierre Elliott Trudeau: l'intellectuel et le politique*. Montreal: Fides, 2005.

Buriot, Alain, and Arnaud Coignet. "Le raid du 19 août 1942," www.mairie-dieppe.fr/canada/19aout/raid.html.

Cairns, Alan. *Reconfigurations, Canadian Citizenship and Constitutional Change: Selected Essays*, edited by Douglas E. Williams. Toronto: McClelland & Stewart Ltd., 1995.

Carrel, Alexis. *L'homme, cet inconnu*. Paris: Plon, 1935.

Chartrand, Michel. "$50 millions par terre." *Le Quartier Latin*, November 29, 1940.

Clarkson, Stephen, and Christina McCall. *Trudeau and Our Times, Volume I: The Magnificent Obsession*. Toronto: McClelland & Stewart Ltd., 1990.

Cohen, Andrew, and J.L. Granatstein (eds.). *Trudeau's Shadow: The Life and Legacy of Pierre Elliott Trudeau*. Toronto: Random House of Canada, 1998.

Comeau, Paul André. *Le Bloc populaire: 1942–1948*. Montreal: Québec-Amérique, 1982.

Compayré, Gabriel. *Histoire critique des doctrines de l'éducation en France depuis le XVIe siècle*. Paris: Hachette et Cie, Vol. I, 1883. In *Encyclopédie de l'Agora*, http://www.agora.qc.ca/reftext.nsf/Documents/Jesuites.

Cornwell, John. *Hitler's Pope: The Secret History of Pius XII*. New York: Viking, 1999.

Cortes, Juan Donoso. *Œuvres*, Vol. I. Paris: Librairie d'Auguste Vaton, 1858.

Delisle, Esther. *Essais sur l'imprégnation fasciste au Québec*. Montreal: Les éditions Varia, 2002.

———. *Mythes, mensonges et mémoire – l'intelligentsia du Québec devant la tentation fasciste 1939–1960*. Montreal: Robert Davies Multimedia Editions, 1998.

Dion, Léon. *Québec 1945–2000, Vol. II: Les intellectuels et le temps de Duplessis*. Sainte-Foy: Laval University Press, 1993.

*Discours prononcé en séance privée à l'Académie française pour la réception de M. Robert Aron, le jeudi 17 avril 1975*. Institut de France: Académie française, 1975, No. 9.

*Discours prononcé par M. Maurice Druon*, directeur de l'Académie, à l'occasion de la mort de M. Robert Aron, séance du 24 avril 1975. Institut de France: Académie française, 1975, No. 9.

Drapeau, Jean. "Au sujet de nos hôtes." *Le Quartier Latin*, October 18, 1940.

English, John, Richard Gwyn, and P. Whitney Lackenbauer (eds.). *The Hidden Pierre Elliott Trudeau: The Faith Behind the Politics.* Ottawa: Novalis, Saint Paul University, 2004.

Ferguson, Will. *Bastards & Boneheads: Canada's Glorious Leaders Past and Present.* Vancouver/Toronto: Douglas & McIntyre, 1999.

Ferro, Marc. *Pétain.* Paris: Librairie Arthème Fayard, 1987.

Fraser, Graham. "As Quebec Premier, Charest Is a Man of Firsts." *Toronto Star*, April 20, 2003.

Fraser, Sylvia. "The Private Trudeau." *Star Weekly*, June 29, 1968.

Gérin-Lajoie, Paul. "Canadiens français d'abord!" *Brébeuf*, December 3, 1938.

Grandbois, Alain. *Les voyages de Marco Polo.* Montreal: Éditions Valiquette, 1941.

Groulx, Lionel. *L'Appel de la race*, Fifth Edition, 1956. With an introduction by Bruno Lafleur. Montreal and Paris: Fides, 1922. (First Edition written under the pseudonym Alonié de Lestres.)

———. "Nos positions." In *Orientations*, Éditions du Zodiaque, 1935.

Gwyn, Richard. *The Northern Magus.* Toronto: McClelland & Stewart Ltd., 1980.

Gzowski, Peter. "Portrait of an Intellectual in Action." *Maclean's*, February 24, 1962.

Harvey, Julien. "Richard Arès." In *L'année politique au Québec, 1988–1989.* Montreal: Québec/Amérique, 1989.

Hertel, François. *Leur inquiétude.* Montreal: Éditions Jeunesse ACJC/Éditions Albert Lévesque, 1936.

———. *Le Beau Risque.* Montreal: Les éditions Bernard Valiquette and les éditions A.C.F., 1939.

———. *L'enseignement des belles-lettres.* Montreal: Ateliers de l'entraide, 1939.

———. *Pour un ordre personnaliste.* Montreal: Les éditions de l'arbre, 1942.

———. *Nous ferons l'avenir.* Montreal: Fides, 1945.

Iglauer, Edith. "Prime Minister/Premier ministre." *The New Yorker*, July 5, 1969.

Johnson, William. *Anglophobie Made in Quebec.* Montreal: Stanké, 1991.

Kertzer, David I. *The Popes Against the Jews: The Vatican's Role in the Rise of Modern Anti-Semitism.* New York: Alfred A. Knopf, 2001.

King, W.L. Mackenzie. *Canada and the Fight for Freedom.* Toronto: The MacMillan Company of Canada, Ltd., 1944.

———. *The Mackenzie King Diaries, 1932–1949.* Toronto: University of Toronto Press, 1980.

Krieg, Robert. "The Vatican Concordat With Hitler's Reich." In *The National Catholic Weekly*, September 1, 2003, Vol. 189, No. 5.

Lacouture, Jean. *Jésuites: Une multibiographie*, Vol. 1. *Les conquérants*. Paris: Éditions du Seuil, 1991.

Laforest, Guy. *Trudeau et la fin d'un rêve canadien*. Quebec City: Les éditions du Septentrion, 1992.

Lahaise, Robert. *Une histoire du Québec par sa littérature: 1914–1939*. Montreal: Guérin, 1998.

Laliberté, G.-Raymond. "Dix-huit ans de corporatisme militant. L'École sociale populaire de Montreal, 1933–1935." *Recherches sociographiques*, Vol. XXI, Nos. 1–2, January–August 1980, p. 56–96.

Latouche, Daniel, and Diane Poliquin-Bourassa (eds.). *Le Manuel de la parole, manifestes québécois*, Volume 2, 1900-1959. Montreal: Les Éditions du Boréal Express, 1978. For the 1934 Manifesto of the Action libérale nationale (ALN) see pages 147-151.

Latourelle, René. *Quel avenir pour le christianisme?* Montreal: Guérin, 2000.

Laurendeau, André. *Maîtres de l'heure: l'abbé Lionel Groulx*. Montreal: Éditions de l'A.C.F., 1938.

———. "Nos écoles enseignent-elles la haine de l'Anglais?" *L'Action nationale*, Vol. XVIII, October 1941, p. 104–123.

———. *La crise de la conscription – 1942*. Montreal: Éditions du Jour, 1962.

———. *Ces choses qui nous arrivent: chronique des années 1961–1966*. Montreal: Éditions HMH Ltée, 1970.

*Le Devoir*, "Finie la flèche du conquérant, vive le drapeau de la liberté!" November 26, 1942.

Lenihan, Donald G., Gordon Robertson, and Roger Tassé. *Reclaiming the Middle Ground*. Montreal: Institute of Research in Public Policies, 1994.

Lessard, François. *Messages au "Frère" Trudeau*. Montreal: Les éditions de ma Grand-mère, 1979.

Lévesque, Georges-Henri, o.p. "La 'Co-operative Commonwealth Federation.'" In *Pour la Restauration sociale au Canada*, monthly publication of the École sociale populaire, Nos. 232–233, April–May 1933.

*Mandements. Lettres pastorales circulaires et autres documents publiés dans le diocèse de Montreal depuis son érection*. Vol. 18, Montreal: Arbour & Dupont Imprimeurs-Éditeurs, 1940.

*Mandements. Lettres pastorales et circulaires des Évêques de Chicoutimi*. Vol. 1, 1929–1933. Chicoutimi, 1934.

*Mandements. Lettres pastorales et circulaires des Évêques de Québec*. Vol. 14, 1932–1935. Quebec City: Chancellerie de l'Archevêché, 1936.

*Mandements. Lettres pastorales et circulaires des Évêques de Québec*. "Lettre pastorale collective de Son Éminence le Cardinal Archevêque de Québec et

de leurs Excellences les Archevêques et Évêques de la province civile de
Québec sur le problème rural au regard de la doctrine sociale de l'Église."
In Vol. 15, 1936–1939. Quebec City: Chancellerie de l'Archevêché, 1940.

Maritain, Jacques. [First Edition 1936] *Humanisme intégral: Problèmes temporels et spirituels d'une nouvelle chrétienté.* Paris, Aubier: éditions
Montaigne, 1968.

———. *Le Crépuscule de la civilisation.* Montreal: Éditions de l'arbre, 1941.

———. *À Travers le désastre.* New York: Éditions de la maison française,
1941.

———. *Les droits de l'homme.* Collection of articles presented by René
Mougel. Paris: Desclée de Brouwer, 1989. (First Edition 1942.)

Maurras, Charles. *La seule France, chronique des jours d'épreuve.* Lyon: H.
Lardanchet, 1941.

———. *Enquête sur la monarchie,* followed by *Une campagne royaliste au
Figaro,* and *Si le coup de force est possible,* final edition with a preliminary speech. Paris: Nouvelle librairie nationale, 1925.

McRoberts, Kenneth. *Quebec, Social Change and Political Crisis.* Toronto:
Oxford University Press, 1993. (Third Edition with a postscript.)

———. *Misconceiving Canada: The Struggle for National Unity.* Toronto:
Oxford University Press, 1997.

Minville, Esdras, Victor Barbeau, and Lionel Groulx. *L'Avenir de notre bour-
geoisie.* (Speeches delivered at the first congress of the Jeunesse
Indépendante Catholique, Montreal, February 25–27, 1939.) Montreal:
Éditions Bernard Valiquette, 1939.

Morin, Rosaire. "Les origines de L'Action nationale." In *L'Action nationale,*
April 2000.

Mounier, Emmanuel. *Manifeste au service du personnalisme.* Paris: F. Aubier,
Montaigne, 1936.

Nemni, Max and Monique. "A Conversation With Pierre Elliott Trudeau."
*Cité libre,* Vol. 26, No. 1, February–March 1998, pp. 90–112.

Newman, Peter, and Stan Fillmore (eds.). *Their Turn to Curtsy – Your Turn to
Bow.* Toronto: MacLean-Hunter Ltd., 1972.

Nolte, Ernst. *Three Faces of Fascism: Action Française, Italian Fascism,
National Socialism.* New York: Holt, Rinehart & Winston, 1966.

O'Connor, William F. *Report pursuant to resolution of the Senate to the
Honourable Speaker by the Parliamentary Counsel, relating to
the enactment of the British North America Act, 1867, any lack of consonance between its terms and judicial construction of them and cognate
matters.* Report presented March 17, 1939, by William F. O'Connor, Law
Clerk and Parliamentary Counsel to the Senate of Canada.

Paquin, Stéphane. *L'invention d'un mythe: Le pacte entre deux peuples fonda-teurs*. Montreal: VLB éditeur, 1999.

Pascal. *Pensées*. Presented and annotated by Jacques Chevalier, with a preface by Jean Guitton. Paris: Éditions Gallimard, 1962.

Pellerin, Jean. *Le Phénomène Trudeau*. Paris: Seghers, 1972.

Pelletier, Gérard. *Les années d'impatience: 1950–1960*. Montreal: Stanké, 1983.

Pétain, Philippe. "Le paysan français." *Le Quartier Latin*, December 20, 1940. Excerpt of a speech delivered at the inauguration of a monument to the deceased of Capoulet-Junac.

Poirmeur, Yves, and P. Mazet (eds.). *Le métier politique en représentation*. Paris, l'Harmattan, 1999.

Pomeyrols, Catherine. *Les intellectuels québécois: formation et engagements, 1919–1939*. Paris and Montreal: L'Harmattan, 1996.

Potvin, André, Michel Letourneux, and Robert Smith. *L'anti-Trudeau: Choix de textes*. Montreal: Éditions Parti-pris, 1972.

*Pour la Restauration sociale au Canada*. Montreal: École sociale populaire, Nos. 232–233, April–May 1933.

Radwanski, George. *Trudeau*. Toronto: The Macmillan Company of Canada Ltd., 1978.

Repka, William, and Kathleen Repka. *Dangerous Patriots: Canada's Unknown Prisoners of War*. Vancouver: New Star Books, 1982.

*Right (The) Honourable Pierre Elliott Trudeau Papers*. Library and Archives Canada (LAC), MG 26 Series 02, *Documents Prior to the Political Career*.

Robitaille, Louis-Bernard. "François Hertel: 'On ne peut pas effacer 40 ans de vie . . . On peut rompre,'" in *La Presse*, July 9, 1977.

Rousseau, Jean-Jacques. *Du contrat social*. Paris: Garnier-Flammarion, 1966.

Roux, Jean-Louis. *Nous sommes tous des acteurs*. Montreal: Éditions Lescop, 1998.

———. "Lettre à Félix-Antoine Savard." *Le Quartier Latin*, January 28, 1944.

Sablonnière (de la), Marcel. "Génie français." *Le Quartier Latin*, December 19, 1941.

Smith, Adam. *An Inquiry into the Nature and Causes of the Wealth of Nations*. London: Methuen and Co., Ltd., 1904.

Somerville, David. *Trudeau Revealed by His Actions and Words*. Richmond Hill: BMG Publishing Ltd., 1978.

Southam, Nancy, ed. *Pierre*. Toronto: McClelland & Stewart Ltd., 2005.

Spong, John Shelby. *The Sins of Scriptures: Exposing the Bible's Texts of Hate to Reveal the God of Love*. New York: HarperCollins, 2005.

Tremblay, Arthur (Chairperson). *Report of the Royal Commission on Constitutional Problems*. Commission created by the Quebec legislature on February 12, 1953. Four volumes, province of Quebec, 1956. Known as the *Tremblay Report.*

Trudeau, Pierre Elliott. Articles in the *Brébeuf*:

"Le ronfleur et . . . le nouveau pensionnaire," Vol. 5, Nos. 7–8–9, February 12, 1938.

"Brève louange à tous," Vol. 6, No. 2, November 5, 1938.

"Pour réhabiliter Pascal," Vol. 6, No. 5, February 24, 1939.

"Utopie relative," Vol. 6, No. 7, April 8, 1939.

"Vers la Haute mer," Vol. 6, No. 9, May 27, 1939.

"Entre autres, sur le don de parole," Vol. 7, No. 1, October 7, 1939.

"De cette autorité," Vol. 7, No. 2, November 11, 1939.

"Bonne et Heureuse Année à tous nos lecteurs," Vol. 7, No. 3–4, December 23, 1939.

"Mer! Noël!," Vol. 7, No. 3–4, December 23, 1939.

"Sur les pompiers," Vol. 7, No. 5, February 22, 1940.

"À propos de style," Vol. 7, No. 6, March 23, 1940.

"Ceci est l'éditorial," Vol. 7, Nos. 8–9, June 12, 1940.

———. Articles in *Le Quartier Latin*:

"Perçant dialogue persan," signed PITRE, March 19, 1943.

"Massons Clément," November 12, 1943.

"Mon cher Clément," November 12, 1943.

"Ça vient d'où un sauvage?," November 12, 1943. Reprinted in P. Trudeau, *Against the Current.*

"Pritt Zoum Bing," March 10, 1944.

———. "L'ascétisme en canot." In *Journal JEC*, June 1944. This article has been reprinted in P. Trudeau, *Against the Current.*

———. *Memoirs.* Toronto: McClelland & Stewart Ltd., 1993.

———. *Against the Current: Selected Writings, 1939–1996*, edited by Gérard Pelletier. Toronto: McClelland & Stewart Ltd., 1996.

*Pierre Elliott Trudeau: Portrait intime.* Montreal: Télé-Métropole/Les Éditions internationales Alain Stanké Ltée, 1977.

*Trudeau: The Life, Times and Passing of Pierre Elliott Trudeau.* Toronto: Key Porter Books, 2000.

Vastel, Michel. *The Outsider: The Life of Pierre Elliott Trudeau.* Toronto: Macmillan of Canada, 1990.

Vignola, Daniel. "Pie XI, le corporatisme et le fascisme." In *Le québécois libre*, No. 135 of December 20, 2003, website http://www.quebecoislibre.org.

Wade, Mason. *The French Canadians: 1760–1967*, Vol. II: *1911–1967.* Toronto: Macmillan of Canada (Revised Edition 1968).

To download the index for this book, please go to
www.mcclelland.com/youngtrudeau/index.pdf